Taunton's

THIRD EDITION

WIRING COMPLETE

INCLUDES THE LATEST IN WI-FI, SMART-HOUSE TECHNOLOGY

The Taunton Press

T The Taunton Press
Inspiration for hands-on living®

The Taunton Press, Inc.
63 South Main Street, PO Box 5506
Newtown, CT 06470-5506
e-mail: tp@taunton.com

Editors: Christina Glennon, Peter Chapman
Copy editor: Seth Reichgott
Indexer: Jay Kreider
Jacket/Cover design: Kimberly Adis
Interior design: Kimberly Adis
Layout: Cathy Cassidy, Barbara Cottingham, Lynne Phillips
Illustrator: Trevor Johnston except Christopher Mills pp. 8-9, 110, 256, 260
Photographer: Michael Litchfield, except where noted on p. 281

The following manufacturers/names appearing in *Wiring Complete* are trademarks: AeroVironment®, Amazon Echo®, Amazon Prime®, American Aldes®, Android®, Apple Music®, BernzOmatic®, Big Ass Fans®, Bosch®, Bose Soundtouch®, Broan®, Chevrolet Volt®, Chromecast™, Clipper Creek™, COPALUM®, Decora®, Defiant®, Delta®, DeWalt®, Diva®, DMF Lighting®, Easy Connect™, E-Cut®, Emerson®, Energy Star®, Fanimation®, Fantech®, Farmers Insurance®, Federal Pacific®, Fein®, Fluke®, Ford Focus®, GE®, Google®, Google Play™, GRAFIK Eye®, Greenlee®, Greenlee®, Grip-Lok®, Haiku®, Harbor Breeze®, Hubbell®, Illumatech®, iOS®, iPad®, iPhone®, Kevlar®, Kindle®, Kobe®, Legrand®, Leviton®, Luméa®, Lutron®, Maestro®, Maestro Wireless®, Makita®, Milwaukee®, Minka-Aire®, Muletape®, Nail Eater®, National Electrical Code®, Nest®, Nest Protect®, NFPA 70E®, Nissan Leaf®, Nutone®, Nuvo®, Panasonic®, Pandora®, Panduit®, Pass & Seymour®, Phillips®, Pico®, PlugTail®, Radio Powr Savr™, RadioRA®, Ring™, Romex®, Roto-Split®, Schneider Electric®, Sirius XM®, Sivoia®, Skylark®, Snap-Tite®, Sonos®, Speed Square®, Spotify®, Tech Lighting®, Tesla®, Toyota Prius®, UL®, Wago®, WD-40®, Wire-Nut®, Yamaha®, Zinsco®

Library of Congress Cataloging-in-Publication Data
  Names: McAlister, Michael, author. | Litchfield, Michael W., author.
  Title: Wiring complete : includes the latest in Wi-Fi, smart-house technology /
    Michael McAlister and Michael Litchfield.
  Other titles: Taunton's wiring complete
  Description: Third edition. | Newtown, CT : The Taunton Press, Inc, [2017] |
    Revision of: Taunton's wiring complete, ?2008. | Includes bibliographical
    references and index.
  Identifiers: LCCN 2017014083 | ISBN 9781631868382 (alk. paper)
  Subjects: LCSH: Electric wiring, Interior. | Dwellings--Electric equipment.
  Classification: LCC TK3285 .L54 2017 | DDC 621.319/24--dc23
  LC record available at https://lccn.loc.gov/2017014083
Printed in the United States of America
10 9 8 7 6 5 4 3 2 1

Wiring is inherently dangerous. Using hand or power tools improperly or ignoring safety practices can lead to permanent injury or even death. Don't try to perform operations you learn about here (or elsewhere) unless you're certain they are safe for you. If something about an operation doesn't feel right, don't do it. Look for another way. We want you to enjoy working on your home, so please keep safety foremost in your mind.

ACKNOWLEDGMENTS

In the nine years since the first edition of *Wiring Complete* was published, there have been many new product developments, especially in the domain of energy-saving lamps, such as light-emitting diodes (LEDs), and in the realms of multimedia and whole-house control systems. Many of these systems start as niche products and soon become mainstream.

Gathering information from electricians in the field also unearths new ways of doing things with tried-and-true methods and materials. Ingenuity springs from a problem to be solved, so it's not surprising that you find it so often in the field.

Dozens of people made this book possible. We are especially indebted to the electricians and builders who got us onto job sites and allowed us to photograph them at work. Many thanks to Fran Halperin and Eric Christ of Halperin & Christ, San Rafael, CA; Stephen Shoup of Building Lab, Oakland, CA; Taya Shoup; Gary Ireland; and Elizabeth Zarlengo.

In addition, we would like to extend our sincere appreciation to Legrand US for their generosity and time in helping us to utilize some updated products and to Eric Jones at Electrical Sales Unlimited for helping us to coordinate and acquire those products. We were also greatly assisted by Jonah Teeter-Balin and Aris Gharapetian of AeroVironment; Sarah Ray of the Fluke Corporation; Jamie Siminoff of Ring Video Doorbells; Christian Thompson of Hubbell Wiring Systems; Nest Labs; Gennet Paauwe and the California Plug-In Electric Vehicle Collaborative; and Lauren Greathouse of Haiku Home/Big Ass Solutions.

Finally, high-fives to the Taunton Press family and friends, especially Executive Editor Peter Chapman, whose keen attention to detail made this a much better book.

—Michael McAlister and Michael W. Litchfield

contents

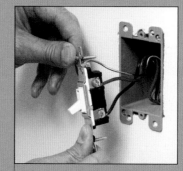

>> >> >> >>

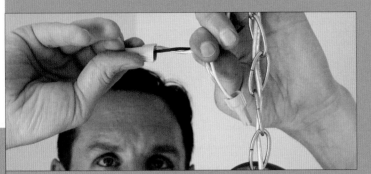
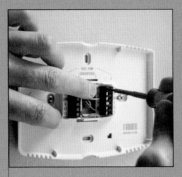
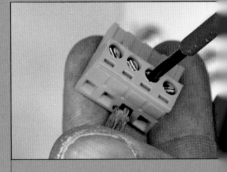

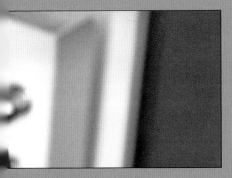
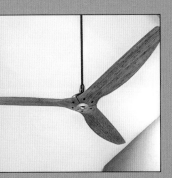

FANS
154

PLANNING
174

ROUGH-IN WIRING
194

≫ ≫ ≫ ≫

INTRODUCTION

In the last five years, wireless and Internet-connected devices have transformed home wiring. Thus, while this third edition of *Wiring Complete* continues to offer a solid overview of conventional wiring, it has been expanded to include products and technologies that will improve your home's comfort, safety, and security; conserve energy; save money; and allow you to adjust house settings from a smart phone. Moreover, wireless devices are especially well suited to remodeling because most can be installed with minimal mess and disruption. Best of all, today's video doorbells, smart thermostats, interconnected smoke alarms, and home media set-ups are quite affordable, replacing hard-wired systems that once cost a king's ransom.

Electrical wiring requires attention to detail, patience, and a little dexterity, but it's nothing the average homeowner can't tackle. Before you buckle on that tool belt, however, take a few moments to read the first section, which provides an overview of electrical systems and essential safety tips. Section Two walks you through tools and techniques you'll use again and again.

The remainder of the book takes you through every step of the wiring process —from replacing an old light fixture to installing an electric vehicle charger.

Before you gear up, however, check with local building code authorities. Although most local building codes do not forbid an owner's doing his or her own electrical work, most require a rough inspection—that is, before wires are connected to switches, receptacles and so on—and a final inspection when everything is wired, trimmed, and tested. Finally, check with your insurance agent to make sure that doing your own electrical work won't jeopardize your homeowner's insurance coverage.

WORKING WITH ELECTRICITY

BEFORE WORKING WITH ELECTRICITY, you should have a basic understanding of how it works. This chapter is designed to give you a quick overview of the electrical system in your home, including the major components. Since grounding is essential to keeping you safe, we cover that in detail. We'll also show you how to do a basic inspection of your home for wiring problems.

Respecting the power of electricity is essential to working safely. Always follow the instructions carefully, use appropriate safety equipment, and when in doubt consult a licensed electrician.

Before beginning work, check with local building authorities to make sure local regulations allow you to do your own work and that you are conforming to local code requirements.

BASICS

Understanding electricity, p. 6

Working safely, p. 7

Electricity in your home, p. 8

Service panels, p. 10

Grounding basics, p. 12

CUTTING POWER

Cutting power at the panel, p. 15

TESTING

Testing for voltage, p. 16

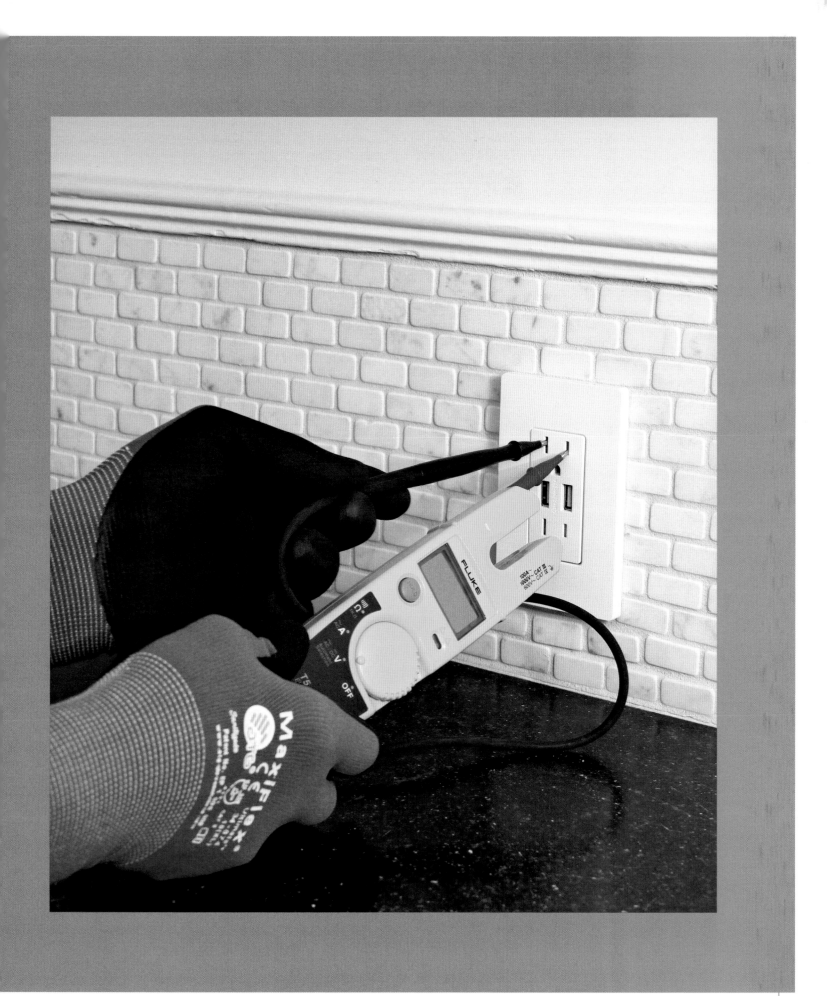

UNDERSTANDING ELECTRICITY

Electricity (flowing electrons called *current*) moves through a wire like water in a pipe. The flow of water is measured in gallons per minute; the flow of electrons is measured in amperes or *amps*. Water pressure is measured in pounds per square inch, and the force behind the electrons in a wire is measured in *volts*. The larger the pipe, the more water that can flow through it; likewise, larger wires allow a greater flow of electricity. A small-diameter pipe will limit the flow of water, compared to a larger pipe; similarly, wiring that is too small will resist the flow of current. If that resistance (measured in *ohms*) is too great, the wires will overheat and may cause a fire.

Think of an electrical system as a loop that runs from the generation point (or power source) through a *load* (something that uses electrical power, a lightbulb, for instance) and back to the generation point. In your home, the main loop, which is the service to your home, is split into smaller loops called *circuits*. Typically, a hot wire (usually black or red) carries current from the service panel to one of the various loads, and a neutral wire (typically white or light gray) carries current back to the service panel.

CIRCUIT BASICS

Electricity always flows in a circuit. The hot wire carries the current from the power source to the fixture and the neutral wire returns it to the power source.

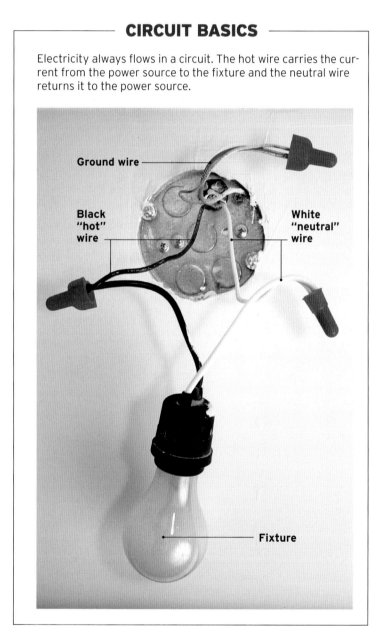

Ground wire

Black "hot" wire

White "neutral" wire

Fixture

Key Terms

Watts
A measure of power consumed. In residential systems, watts are virtually the same as volt-amps.

Voltage
The pressure of the electrons in a system. Voltage is measured in volts (v).

Amperes (amps)
The measure of the number of electrons flowing through a system (current).

Current
The flow of electrons in a system. Current is measured in amperes (amps). There are two types of current: DC (direct current) and AC (alternating current). AC power is supplied by utility companies to homes.

Effective power (volt-amps or VA)
The potential in the system to create motion (motors), heat (heaters), light (fixtures or lamps), etc. Volt-amps = available volts × available amps (VA).

Ohms
The measure of resistance to the flow of electrons (current) in an electrical system. The higher the resistance, the lower the flow of electrons.

WORKING SAFELY

To work safely with electricity, you must respect its power. If you understand its nature and heed the safety warnings in this book—especially shutting off the power and testing with a voltage tester to make sure power is off—you can work on electrical systems safely. The cardinal rule of home-improvement projects, which goes double for electrical work, is this: Know your limitations.

Unless you have previous experience doing electrical work and feel confident about your skills, you should leave certain projects to a pro. Working inside a service panel or even removing its cover can be especially dangerous. In most panels, there is an area around the main breaker that remains hot (energized) even after the breaker is set to the off position. Also, some older panels don't have a main breaker, and it takes experience to understand the layout of a panel.

Never attempt to remove the cover of, or work in, an energized service panel or an energized subpanel. Call a licensed electrician rather than risk harm.

The safety alerts and safe working practices explained in this chapter will go far to protect you, but the best protection is knowledge. We strongly recommend that readers visit the OSHA/NIOSH website on electrical safety (www.cdc.gov/niosh/docs/2009-113) as well.

Always wear appropriate safety gear, including rubber-soled shoes, sturdy gloves, safety glasses, and a respirator or dust mask when sawing or drilling overhead. Remember that 120 volts can kill or cause serious shock, so learn and use safe work practices; your life depends on it.

Turn off the power **to the circuit at the main service panel** before removing receptacle, switch, or fixture covers.

Test to make sure the power is off. Do this before **and** after removing the plate or cover on an electrical device. Never work on an energized circuit.

Wear gloves to protect your hands from the sharp edges of wires, cables, and metal boxes. These flexible gloves have rubberized palms for a good grip.

Wear safety glasses when sawing or drilling, especially when working overhead.

 SAFETY ALERT

Test the tester first and last. No matter what kind of tester you're using, test it first on a circuit that you know is hot to make sure the tester is working properly, and do the same after you've done the testing. Most testers run on batteries, and those batteries could die after your pre-test check and before the voltage test. The post-test check will catch that.

ELECTRICITY IN YOUR HOME

Power from the utility service is commonly delivered through three large wires, or conductors, which may enter the house overhead or underground. Overhead service wires are called a *service drop*. The drop runs to a *weatherhead* atop a length of rigid conduit. When fed underground, service conductors are installed in buried conduit or run as underground service-entrance (USE) cable. Whether it arrives overhead or underground, three-wire service delivers 120 volts to ground and 240 volts between the energized conductors.

Service conductors are attached to a meter base and then to the *service panel*. Straddling the two sets of terminals on its base, the meter measures the wattage of electricity as it is consumed. The service panel routes power to various circuits throughout the house.

The utility company will install the drop wires to the building and will install the meter. The homeowner is responsible for everything beyond that, including the meter base and breaker panel, which a licensed electrician should install.

Increasingly, wireless devices are an important part of a home's electrical capabilities, as battery-powered smoke alarms interlock automatically (p. 117), doorbells with integral cameras show who's at the door (p. 108), teachable thermostats save energy (p. 114), and smartphone apps allow you to manage it all even if you're a thousand miles from home.

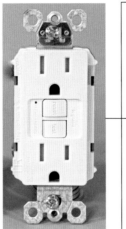

Ground-fault circuit interrupter (GFCI) receptacles detect minuscule current leaks and shut off power almost instantaneously. All bathrooms and kitchens must be GFCI protected, as well as outdoor outlets and garage outlets. Local codes may require additional GFCI protection.

Per the 2017–2020 NEC, AFCI protection is now required for the whole house, including all 15- and 20-amp branch circuits supplying outlets or devices in dwelling units.

Some appliances require dedicated circuits. This is a 30-amp 125/250v dryer receptacle; the breaker for this circuit must also be rated for 30 amps.

WIRING INSIDE OUT

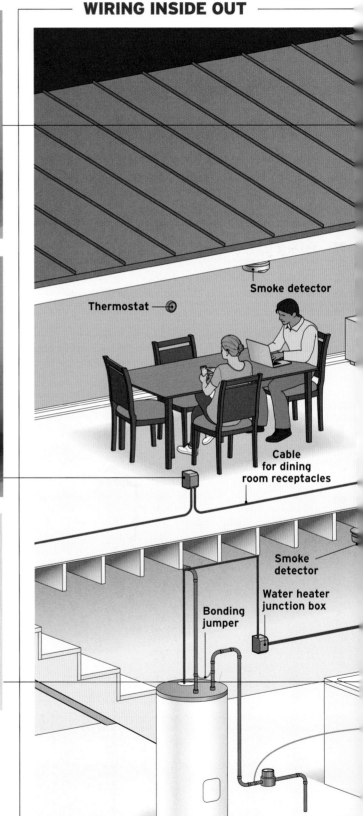

Thermostat

Smoke detector

Cable for dining room receptacles

Smoke detector

Water heater junction box

Bonding jumper

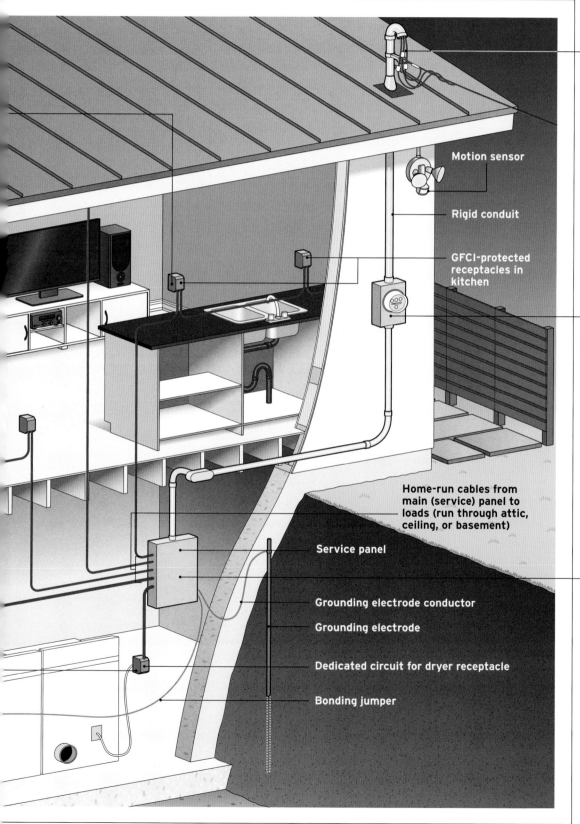

Motion sensor

Rigid conduit

GFCI-protected receptacles in kitchen

Home-run cables from main (service) panel to loads (run through attic, ceiling, or basement)

Service panel

Grounding electrode conductor

Grounding electrode

Dedicated circuit for dryer receptacle

Bonding jumper

A typical three-wire service assembly has two insulated hot conductors and a bare neutral. The bare neutral has an internal steel "messenger" to support the assembly.

The meter provides a measure of the electrical power consumed. Positioned outside the house, it allows the power company to monitor consumption.

The service panel distributes power to circuits throughout the house. Breakers interrupt power if the circuits become overloaded. Some service panels only house the main breaker.

SERVICE PANELS

At the service panel, the two hot cables from the meter base attach to lugs or terminals on the main breaker. The incoming neutral cable attaches to the main lug of the neutral/ground bus. In the main panel, neutral/ground buses must be connected together, usually by a wire or metal bar called the *main bonding jumper*. In subpanels and all other locations downstream from the main service panel, ground and neutral components must be electrically isolated from each other.

In a main fuse box, the hot conductors from the meter attach to the main power lugs and the neutral cable to the main neutral lug. Whether the panel has breakers or fuses, metal buses run from the main breaker/main fuse. Running down the middle of the panel, buses distribute power to the various branch circuits, either through fuses or through breakers. The neutral/ground buses are long aluminum bars containing many terminal screws, to which ground and neutral wires are attached.

Each fuse or breaker is rated at a specific number of amps (15-amp and 20-amp breakers or fuses take care of most household circuits). When a circuit becomes overloaded or a short circuit occurs, the breaker trips or a fuse strip melts, thereby cutting voltage to the hot wire. All current produces some heat, and as current increases, the heat generated increases. If there were no breakers or fuses, and if too much current continued to flow, the wires would overheat and could start a fire. Amperage ratings of breakers and fuses are matched to the size (cross-sectional area, measured as "gauge") of the circuit wires.

The main breaker

All electricity entering a house goes through the main breaker, which is usually located at the top of a main panel.

INSIDE A SERVICE PANEL

- Incoming ground
- Hot feeder lines (incoming power)
- Incoming neutral
- Main breaker
- Hot bus bar (behind breakers)
- Neutral bus bar
- Ground bus bar
- Individual circuits

Branch circuits

The service panel houses incoming cables from the meter as well as the breakers and wires that distribute electricity to individual circuits. At the service, neutral conductors (white wires), equipment-grounding conductors (bare copper or green insulated wires), the metal service panel, and the grounding electrode system (grounding rods) must be bonded together.

- Hot cables from meter attach to lug terminals
- Incoming ground
- Incoming neutral
- Neutral/ground cable attaches here.
- Main breaker
- Main bonding jumper
- Neutral buses
- Hot wire
- Neutral wire
- Ground wire
- Ground buses
- Hot buses
- Knockouts for circuit cables on all sides of panel
- Grounding electrode conductor

In an emergency, throw the main breaker to "off" to turn off all power to the house. The main breaker is also the primary overcurrent protection for the electrical system and is rated accordingly. (The rating is stamped on the breaker handle.) If the main breaker for a 200-amp panel senses current that exceeds its load rating, the breaker will automatically trip and shut off all power.

Meter-mains

Increasingly common are meter-mains, which house a meter base and a main breaker in a single box. Meter-mains allow a homeowner to put the main breaker outside the house, where it can be accessed in an emergency—if firefighters need to cut the power to the house before they go inside, for example. When meter-mains are used, electricians often locate a panel with the branch circuit breakers (called a subpanel) in the garage or another centralized location inside that is easy to access, such as a laundry room.

Fuse boxes

Many older homes still have fuse boxes. Fuses are the earliest overcurrent protection devices, and they come as either Edison-type (screw-in) fuses or cartridge (slide-in) fuses. Edison-style fuses are more common. They have little windows that let you see a filament. When the circuit has been overloaded and the fuse is blown, the filament will be separated. A blackened (from heat) interior could mean a short circuit—a potentially dangerous situation calling for the intervention of a licensed electrician. The less common cartridge fuses are used to control 240v circuits and are usually part of the main disconnect switch, or serve heavy-duty circuits for an electric range or a clothes dryer.

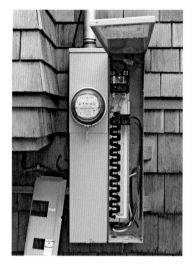
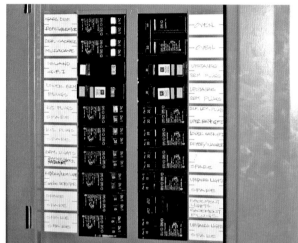

A meter-main combo, placed outside the house, provides easy access for service or emergencies.

Labeling breakers is required by code to identify the loads served.

Stay away from the area around the main breaker switch. The terminals above the breaker remain hot even when the main is off, presenting a serious hazard when the cover is off.

An older fuse box.

PLAY IT SAFE

Only a licensed electrician should work in a service panel—or even remove the cover. Even with the main fuse or breaker turned off, some of the parts inside a panel are always energized or *hot* (carrying voltage) and could electrocute you. Don't mess with electric meters, either. Call the utility company to remove or install meters or to upgrade their service drop wires.

To work safely on existing circuits, *always* turn off electrical power at the service panel, and use a voltage tester (see the photos on p. 16) at the outlet to verify the power is off.

GROUNDING BASICS

Because electricity moves in a circuit, it will return to its source unless the path is interrupted. The return path is through the white neutral wires that bring current back to the main panel. Ground wires provide an alternative low-resistance path should any of the electrical equipment or enclosures become inadvertently energized.

Why is having a grounding path important? Before equipment-grounding conductors (popularly called *ground wires*) were widespread, people could be electrocuted when they came in contact with voltage that, due to a fault like a loose wire, unintentionally energized the metal casing of a tool or an electrical appliance. Ground wires bond all electrical devices and potentially current-carrying metal surfaces. This bonding creates a path with such low impedance (resistance) that *fault currents* flow along it, quickly tripping breakers or fuses and interrupting power. Contrary to popular misconceptions, the human body usually has a relatively high impedance (compared with copper wire); if electricity is offered a path with very low resistance—the equipment grounding conductor—it will take the low-resistance path back to the panel, trip the breaker, and cut off the power.

→ See "Avoiding Electrical Shocks," below.

Ground wires (equipment grounding conductors) connect to every part of the electrical system that could possibly become energized—metal boxes, receptacles, switches, fixtures—and, through three-pronged plugs,

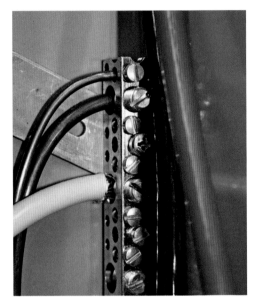

Inside this service panel, the smaller copper wire (top) and the insulated white wire feed a subpanel in the house; the thicker copper wire runs to a ground rod.

AVOIDING ELECTRICAL SHOCKS

GROUND FAULTS CAN KILL!

Current flowing unintentionally to ground ("earth") is called a *ground fault*. The ground wire is intended to be a low-impedance path to ground, to safely carry the current of a ground fault until the circuit breaker trips. You, however, can also be a path to ground should you come in contact with an energized conductor. In this case, you would become part of the circuit, with current flowing through you. So be careful: Only a little current flowing through your heart can kill you.

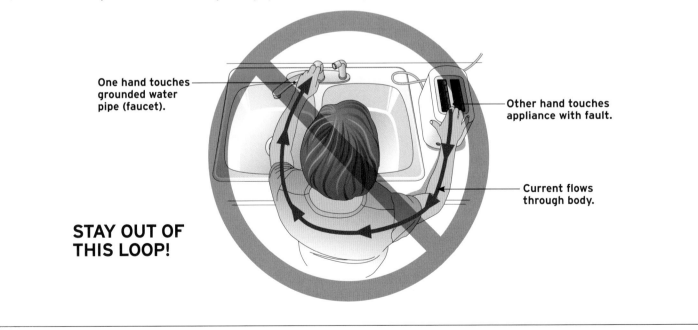

One hand touches grounded water pipe (faucet).

Other hand touches appliance with fault.

Current flows through body.

STAY OUT OF THIS LOOP!

Connections to cold-water pipes and gas lines prevent shocks should the pipes become inadvertently energized.

The main ground wire from the service panel clamps to an 8-ft. grounding electrode (or ground rod) driven into the earth. It diverts outside voltage, such as lightning strikes.

the metallic covers and frames of tools and appliances. The conductors, usually bare copper or green insulated wire, create an effective path back to the main service panel in case the equipment becomes energized. That allows fault current to flow, tripping the breaker.

The neutral/ground bus

In the service panel, the ground wires attach to a neutral/ground bus bar, which is bonded to the metal panel housing via a *main bonding jumper*. If there's a ground fault in the house, the main bonding jumper ensures the current can be safely directed to the ground—away from the house and the people inside. It is probably the single most important connection in the entire electrical system.

MAKING SENSE OF GROUNDING

Grounding confuses a lot of people, including some electricians. Part of the problem is that the word *ground* has been used imprecisely for more than a century to describe electrical activity or components. The term *ground wire*, for example, may refer to one of three different things:

■ The large, usually bare-copper wire clamped to a ground rod driven into the earth, or to rebar in a concrete footing. Because the rod or the rebar is technically a grounding electrode, this "ground wire" is correctly called a *grounding electrode conductor*.

■ Short conductors (wires) that connect two pieces of electrical equipment to eliminate the possibility of a difference in potential (impedance) between them. These short wires should be called "bonding conductors" or "bonding jumpers."

■ The bare copper or green insulated wires in all modern circuits, which ultimately connect electrical equipment, such as receptacles and fixtures, to the service panel neutral/ground bar. These connections create a low-impedance fault path back to the service panel. Why? In case the equipment becomes energized by a hot wire touching a metal cover or other part, this conductor allows high current to flow safely and trip the breaker. In this book, the term *ground wire* or *grounding conductor* refers to this conductor. These wires are properly called *equipment-grounding conductors*.

Also attached to the neutral/ground bus in the service panel is a large, usually bare, copper ground wire—the grounding electrode conductor (GEC)—that clamps to a grounding electrode, usually either a *ground rod* driven into the earth, or a "Ufer grounding electrode," a 20-ft. length of steel rebar or heavy copper wire placed in the building foundation prior to pouring. The grounding electrode's primary functions are to divert lightning and other outside high voltages to the earth before they can damage the building's electrical system, and to provide a

GROUNDING BASICS (CONTINUED)

MAJOR GROUNDING ELEMENTS

The equipment-grounding system acts as an expressway for stray current. By bonding conductors or potential conductors, the system provides a low-impedance path for fault currents. In a ground fault, the abnormally high amperage (current flow) that results trips a breaker or blows a fuse, disconnecting power to the circuit.

It's required by the NEC to ground metal water piping and metal gas piping in case it becomes energized. An underground metal water pipe can't serve as the only grounding electrode. Otherwise, someone could disconnect the pipe or install a section of non-conductive pipe such as PVC, thus interrupting the grounding continuity and jeopardizing your safety. In new installations, code requires that underground metal water piping be connected to the grounding electrode system and the system be supplemented with another electrode.

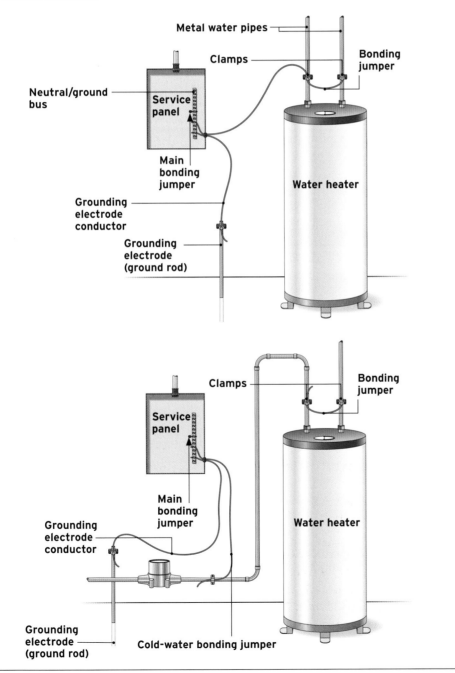

ground reference. Although the grounding electrode system (GES) is connected to the equipment grounding system at the service panel, the GES has virtually nothing to do with reducing hazards from problems in the wiring inside the house. That's the role of the equipment grounding conductors.

The National Electrical Code (NEC) requires grounding electrode conductor size to be based on the sizes and types of conductors in the service. Typically, residential GECs are size 6 American wire gauge (6AWG) copper. Ground rods are typically $1/2$-in. or $5/8$-in. copper-clad steel rods at least 8 ft. long. The Ufer or concrete-encased electrode is the preferred grounding electrode and must be used if new concrete footings are poured.

GFCIs

Ground-fault circuit interrupters (GFCIs) are sensitive devices that can detect very small current leaks and shut off power almost instantaneously. The NEC requires GFCI protection on all bathroom receptacles; all receptacles serving kitchen counters; dishwasher outlets; receptacles within 6 ft. of any sink, tub, or shower stall; laundry-area receptacles; all outdoor receptacles; all unfinished basement receptacles; receptacles in garages and accessory buildings; receptacles in crawlspaces or below grade level; and all receptacles near pools, hot tubs, whirlpools, and the like.

Further, recent code updates require that all new GFCIs have three important features. First, they must be self-diagnostic, with an LED indicator light that will flash or glow red to indicate device failure. Second, should the GFCI fail, it must be self-locking: Current will cease to flow, so that the device must be replaced. Third, GFCIs installed less than $5^{1}/2$ ft. above floor level must be tamper-proof, with plastic shutters that slide across terminal slots to prevent, say, a child from inserting something into a slot.

CUTTING POWER AT THE PANEL

A In a normal breaker box, simply flip the relevant breaker to the off position.

B If you're working on a fuse panel, unscrew and remove the fuse that protects the circuit you're working on.

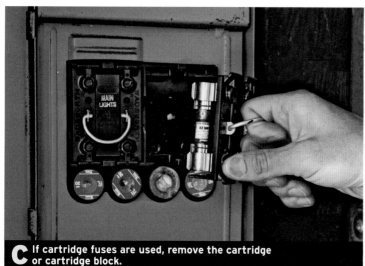

C If cartridge fuses are used, remove the cartridge or cartridge block.

D Once the power is off, lock the panel cover to prevent others from turning the power back on while you're still working on it.

Always shut off the power to an outlet before working on it—and then test with an electrical tester to be sure there's no voltage present. In rare instances, a circuit may be mistakenly fed by more than one breaker! Because individual devices such as receptacles, switches, and fixtures can give false readings if they are defective or incorrectly wired, the only safe way to shut off the electricity is by flipping a breaker in the service panel or subpanel.

Turning off the power at a breaker panel is usually straightforward. After identifying the breaker controlling the circuit, push the breaker's handle to the off position **A**. The breaker handle should click into position; if it doesn't, flip it again until you hear a click. (A breaker that won't snap into position may be worn out or defective and should be replaced by an electrician.)

If your home has a fuse panel instead, remove the fuse that controls the circuit **B**. Partially unscrewing a fuse is not a solution because the fuse body is still in contact with the socket and possibly could be jiggled or screwed in enough to reenergize the circuit.

Remove the fuse. Likewise, if circuits are controlled by cartridge fuses, pull the cartridge or cartridge block out of the panel **C**.

Once you've cut off the power, shut the panel cover and tape a sign to it, telling others to stay out. Better yet, lock them out **D**. Otherwise, someone not aware of the situation could flip the switch on or screw the fuse in, energizing the circuit you're working on.

TESTING FOR VOLTAGE

Before doing electrical work, always turn the power off to the circuit. There are several voltage testers you can use to verify that the power is off, but the most common are noncontact testers and probe testers. We recommend using both types.

A noncontact tester is an inexpensive battery-operated voltage tester that is generally reliable and small enough to fit in a shirt pocket. Its plastic tip glows (and it may beep, depending on the model) when the tip is brought close to or touched to a hot (energized) conductor. That is, it can "read" current through a wire's insulation or through a cover plate. Thus you can often detect electrical current at a switch, receptacle, or fixture without removing the outlet cover.

Each time you use a noncontact tester—or any voltage tester—test that it's functioning properly first on a receptacle that you know is hot ❶, and test it afterward as well. After shutting off power at the panel, insert the tester tip into the narrow (hot) slot of a receptacle ❷. If the tester tip does not glow, there is probably no voltage present.

Follow up with a probe tester. Although a noncontact tester is good for a quick initial reading, you should follow up with a probe tester, whose probes make direct contact with conductors. To test for voltage, touch probes to receptacle slots, screw terminals, or wire ends. Because probe testers do not rely on batteries, they are more accurate than noncontact testers.

The probe tester shown here, like many multimeters (p. 23), allows you to choose which electrical function to test. To see if power is present, turn the dial to **V** (voltage).

Insert the probe tester tips into the receptacle's neutral and hot slots ❸. Next insert the tips into a grounding slot and a hot slot ❹. This test should protect you in case the receptacle was incorrectly wired. The tester screen should indicate no voltage present.

1 Always test the voltage tester first, on an outlet that you know to be hot.

4 Next insert the tester tips into a grounding slot and a hot slot.

TRADE SECRET
It's possible to get shocked by touching the bare probes of probe testers. Whatever voltage tester you use, always hold it by its insulated shaft.

2 Turn off power to the circuit. To make sure power is off, test the hot slot first.

3 Follow up by testing with a probe tester. Insert the tester tips into the receptacle's neutral and hot slots.

5 Remove the cover and mounting screws. Without touching the sides of the receptacle, test both hot and neutral screw terminals.

If you need to remove the receptacle—say, to replace it—remove the cover plate *and test one more time.* Being careful not to touch the sides of the receptacle, unscrew the two mounting screws holding the receptacle to the outlet box. (If the box is metal, avoid touching it, too.) Grasp the mounting straps and gently pull the receptacle out of the box. Touch one tip of the tester to the brass screw terminal (hot), while touching the other tip to the silver screw terminal (neutral) ❺. If the tester screen does not indicate voltage, it's safe to handle the receptacle and the wires feeding it.

➡ **For more on testing switches and light fixtures, see Chapters 3 and 4.**

TOOLS & MATERIALS

YOU DON'T NEED A LOT OF EXPENSIVE tools to wire a house successfully. And there's little uniformity among the tools electricians prefer. Some pros carry a dozen different pliers and wire strippers in their tool belts, whereas others streamline their movements and save time by using the fewest tools possible. This chapter introduces the basic tools and materials you'll need and a few of the basic techniques you will perform repeatedly. All materials must be UL®- or NRTL-listed, which indicates that they meet the safety standards of the electrical industry.

The first test of any tool is to fit your hand comfortably; the second, that it feels solid and well made. Better tools tend to be a bit heftier and cost more.

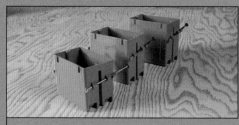

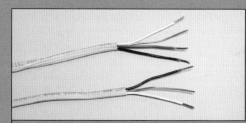

Fish tape

Lineman's pliers

Cordless screwdriver

Screwdriver set

Utility knife

CRAFTSMAN

CRAFTSMAN 3.6V

Xcelite

Needle-nose pliers

Diagonal cutters

Combination wire stripper/crimper

Cable ripper

KLEIN TOOLS

Wire stripper/cutter

Plug-in circuit analyzer

Noncontact tester

HAND TOOLS

A tool belt is especially helpful for wiring work. Assign each tool a specific place in the belt and you can easily retrieve it without searching.

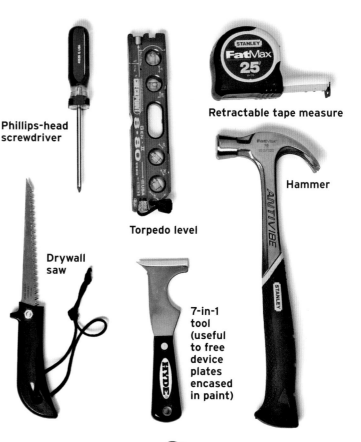

Phillips-head screwdriver

Retractable tape measure

Torpedo level

Hammer

Drywall saw

7-in-1 tool (useful to free device plates encased in paint)

A combination stripping tool not only cuts and strips wire but also crimps connectors, cuts small machine screws, and more.

A
ll hand tools should have cushioned handles and fit your hand comfortably. Manufacturers now make tools in various sizes, so choose the ones that are right for you. Don't scrimp on quality.

Pliers and strippers

Lineman's pliers are the workhorse of an electrician's toolbox. They can cut wire, hold wires fast as you splice them, and twist out box knockouts. *Needle-nose* (long-nose) pliers can grasp and pull wire in tight spaces. These pliers can loop wire to fit around receptacle and switch screws. A large pair can also loosen and remove knockouts in metal outlet boxes. *Diagonal-cutting* and *end-cutting* pliers can cut wires close in tight spaces; *end cutters* (sometimes called nippers) also pull out staples easily. A multipurpose or *combination stripping tool* is used to strip individual wires of insulation, cut wire, crimp connections, and quickly loop wire around screw terminals.

A *cable ripper* (see p. 32) strips the plastic sheathing from Romex® cable without harming the insulation on the individual wires inside. Many pros use a utility knife to strip sheathing, but that takes practice and a light touch to avoid nicking the insulation of individual wires. To strip armored cable, use a Roto-Split® cable stripper (p. 220); it's vastly superior to the old method of using a hacksaw and diagonal cutters.

Other useful tools

No two electrician's tool belts look the same, but most contain a tape measure, flashlight, small level, hammer, Speed Square®, and large felt-tipped marker. In the course of a wiring job, you may need several sizes of slot-head and Phillips-head screwdrivers or nut drivers. *Jab saws* (drywall saws) are also mighty handy in remodel wiring.

If you're wiring a whole house, rent a *wire reel* (p. 198), a rotating dispenser that enables you to pull cable easily to distant points. Reels hold 250 ft. of cable.

Adequate lighting is essential to both job safety and accuracy. If a site is too dark to see what color wires you're working with, your chances of making a wrong connection increase. LED headlamps are fantastic tools.

Sturdy stepladders are a must. In the electrical industry, only fiberglass stepladders are Occupational Safety and Health Administration (OSHA)-compliant because they're nonconductive. Wood ladders are usually nonconductive when dry, but if they get rained on, wood ladders can conduct electricity.

POWER TOOLS

Buy power tools that are appropriate to your strength and to the task at hand. More powerful tools tend to be heavier and harder to manage; and for wiring, they're often overkill. If possible, test-drive a friend's power tool before buying your own.

Drills

A ½-in. right-angle drill allows you to fit the drill head between studs or joists and drill perpendicular to the face of the lumber. The pros use drills with ½-in. chucks, such as the Milwaukee® Hole-Hawg, the DeWalt® stud and joist drill, and so on. They're very versatile tools. It's not necessary to get a drill with a clutch; such tools tend to be very heavy and expensive—overkill even for wiring a house. A right-angle, D-handle drill and a sharp bit are more than adequate.

To see a right-angle drill in action, see p. 195.

Drill bits

Spade bits cut quickly but tend to snap in harder wood. For this reason, most pros prefer auger bits. Self-feeding chipper bits drill doggedly through hard, old wood but won't last long if they hit nails. A ⁷/₈-in. Greenlee® Nail Eater® bit is a wise buy if your old lumber is nail infested; many companies offer similar nail-eater bits.

Reciprocating saw

A reciprocating saw with a demolition saw-blade (see p. 214) is indispensable for most remodeling jobs because it can handle the occasional nail without destroying the blade. You can use a recip saw to cut openings in plaster, but an oscillating tool with a Universal E-Cut® blade will cut plaster in a more controlled manner.

Oscillating multi-tools

Oscillating multi-tools, cordless or corded, are unequalled for cutting materials in place. Often called Fein® tools because that company has dominated the niche for decades, multi-tools have blades that vibrate rather than spin. Thanks to precise (3.2 degrees) oscillations per minute (OPM), they can make fine-kerf, controlled cuts where it would be hard or impossible for most cutting tools to fit.

Multi-tools are so good for creating box openings in finish surfaces that they have largely supplanted *rotary cutters*, long a favorite of drywaller installers. Typically, drywall installers hung sheets of drywall over installed outlet boxes, then used a rotary cutter to trim around the outside of a box. But it takes a seasoned hand, because rotary cutter bits tend to jump around and so can nick wire insulation. Oscillating multi-tools, in comparison, are easier to control.

Gone fishin'

Spring-steel fish tapes or fiberglass fish rods are used to run cable behind finish surfaces. A fish tape is invoked in almost every old wiring how-to book on the market. Today's pros, however, swear by a *pulling grip*, also called a *swivel kellum grip* (see p. 210).

In many cases, however, it's simplest to use a *flex bit* (flexible bit) to drill through the framing. When the bit emerges, a helper can attach the new cable to a small "fish hole" near the bit's point. Then, using a swivel kellum to keep the new cable from getting twisted, put the drill in reverse and pull the bit (and cable) back through the holes it drilled. No fish tape required.

A 48-in. drill extension will increase the effective drilling length of a flex bit. Use an insulated steering guide to keep the flex bit from bowing excessively.

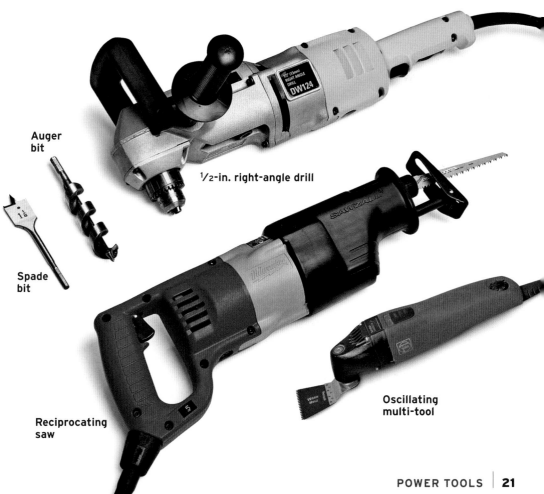

Auger bit

Spade bit

½-in. right-angle drill

Reciprocating saw

Oscillating multi-tool

CORDLESS TOOLS

Cordless tools are particularly well suited to electrical work, which often takes place in confined spaces where tool cords can get hung up. If there's no cord to accidentally cut through or extension cords to come apart, there's also less risk of shock. Many times cordless tools are the only practical choice when you need to turn off the power or you're working where outlets are scarce—or not yet energized. Today's cordless tools are brawny enough to handle almost any situation an electrician might encounter, so the pros just grab 'em and go.

Things to consider

Buy a tool that fits your project's scope, your skill level, and your budget. Research tools thoroughly online before you buy: You'll spend wisely and, more to the point, you'll learn about features you may not know existed. Pro tool reviews are especially helpful in this respect. Then hit the home centers and heft the tools. How long can you hold the tool aloft? Is the grip comfortable? Are there LED lights to help you see what you're drilling or cutting? Is it easy to change bits or blades? Does the tool feel well balanced or lopsided?

Voltage is a rough measure of how much power a tool can deliver; most professional-grade cordless tools are 18v to 20v systems, through a 12v or 14.4v drill/driver would be fine for incidental tasks such as screwing outlet boxes to framing, mounting receptacles to boxes, or screwing on face plates. However, if you're roughing in wiring and boring through studs, drilling into concrete, or doing an extensive rehab, go with 18v to 20v tools.

Amp-hours (Ah) indicate how much battery run-time the tool has: 2.0 Ah means that the battery can deliver 2 amps of current for 1 hour. If a tool draws 1 Ah from its 2.0 Ah battery pack, it can run for 2 hours

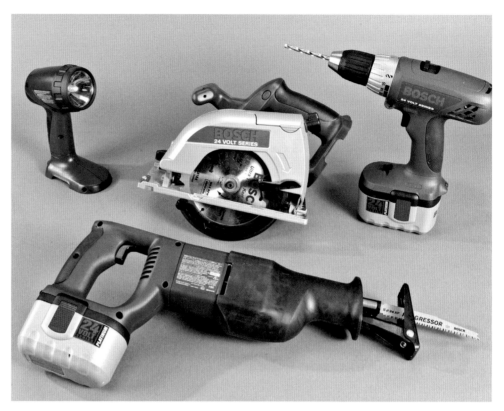

Buying tool kits **can be more economical than buying tools individually, and you can swap batteries between the tools in the kit.**

before you need to switch batteries. Battery packs up to 4.0 Ah are widely available, but, again, more is not necessarily better. Cordless tools use lithium-ion (Li-ion) batteries, but battery platforms are not interchangeable—you can't swap, say, a DeWalt battery into a Makita® drill. For this reason, most people stay with one brand as they add tools.

Brushless motors. Until recently most tool motors had an armature, a commutator, and carbon brushes. Brushed motors were cheap to assemble and didn't need electronics. As the brushes ride against the commutator, however, they wear down and eventually need to be replaced. These days,

better-quality cordless tools have brushless motors that are more efficient (less friction), have longer run times, are generally maintenance-free, and are typically more compact. They are definitely worth the money.

Combo kits. All cordless tool makers offer kits with some combination of a drill/driver, circular saw or reciprocating saw, two batteries, and a charger. Good-quality kits tend to offer considerable savings above buying tools individually, and you can swap batteries between the tools in the kit. Research tool kits carefully, however, because the quality of individual tools within a kit can vary greatly.

ELECTRICAL TESTERS

Testing to see if a circuit or device is energized is crucial to safety and correct wiring. Remember: Always test a tester first to be sure it's working correctly. The first three items below are voltage testers, and some perform multiple functions.

Noncontact testers

Noncontact testers provide a reading without directly touching a conductor. They often allow you to detect voltage without having to remove cover plates and expose receptacles or switches. Touch the tool's tip to an outlet, a fixture screw, or an electrical cord. If the tip glows red, it means there's voltage present. Noncontact testers rely on battery power and are not fail safe. They should not be used as the final test to determine whether or not a circuit is off and safe to work on. Instead, use a probe tester, such as the multimeter shown at right.

Plug-in circuit analyzers

Plug-in circuit analyzers or polarity testers can be used only with three-hole receptacles, but they quickly tell you if a circuit is correctly grounded and, if not, what the problem is. Different light combinations on the tester indicate various wiring problems, such as no ground and hot and neutral reversed. They're quite handy for quick home inspections.

Solenoid voltage testers

Solenoid voltage testers (often called *wiggies*) test polarity as well as AC voltage, and DC voltage from 100v to 600v. Most models vibrate and light a bulb when current is present. Solenoid testers don't use batteries, so readings can't be compromised by low battery power. However, because of their low impedance, solenoid testers will trip GFCIs.

In addition to voltage testers, get a *continuity tester* to test wire runs and connectors for short circuits or other wiring flaws prior to energizing the circuit.

Multimeters

Digital multimeters (DMMs) allow you to troubleshoot electrical problems by measuring several aspects of electrical energy, including volts, amps, and ohms. Most DMMs come with probe tips you touch to exposed conductors, though some also have forks or hooks that can measure current running through a cable without exposing the conductors within.

Unusually high voltage readings are a concern because surges can destroy computers, electronic devices, or appliances designed to operate at specific voltages. Conversely, low voltage can also cause damage and may indicate corrosion, loose connections, wiring too small for circuit loads, and so on.

High ohm readings may indicate excessive resistance, which can lead to overheated wires. The cause may be corrosion, faulty connections, cables bundled too closely, or a staple driven so deeply that it has damaged cable sheathing or the wires inside. DMM amp settings measure current flow through wires; amp readings that are too high may indicate a high resistance ground fault, an overloaded circuit, and the potential for overheating and insulation damage.

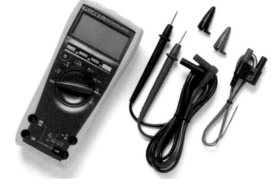

Digital multimeters provide precise readings of several electrical functions, including volts, amps, and ohms.

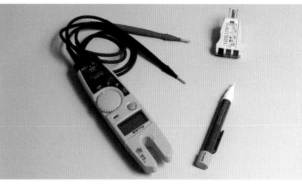

Popular electrical testers. Clockwise from left: Fluke® T-5 600 voltage and current tester; plug-in circuit analyzer; noncontact tester.

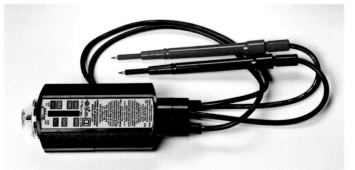

Solenoid voltage testers don't require batteries to give a reading.

CHOOSING ELECTRICAL BOXES

There is a huge selection of electrical boxes, varying by size, shape, mounting device, and composition. One of the first distinctions to note is that of *new work boxes* and *remodel* or *cut-in boxes*. New work boxes are designed to be attached to exposed framing, as is often the case in new construction and sometimes in renovations where walls and ceilings are gutted. Cut-in boxes are designed for attachment to existing finish surfaces–which frequently involves cutting into plaster or drywall.

But of all the variables to consider when choosing boxes, size (capacity) usually trumps the others. Correctly sized boxes are required by code and make your job easier because you don't have to struggle to fit wires and devices into a space that's too small.

Box capacity

The most common shape is a *single-gang box*. A single-gang box 3½ in. deep has a capacity of roughly 22½ cu. in., enough space for a single *device* (receptacle or switch), three 12-2 w/grd cables, and two wire connectors. *Double-gang boxes* hold two devices; *triple-gang boxes* hold three devices. Remember: Everything that takes up space in a box must fit without cramping–devices, cable wires, wire connectors, and cable clamps–so follow NEC recommendations for the maximum number of conductors per box.

You can get the capacity you need in a number of ways. Some pros install shallow *4-squares* (4 in. by 4 in. by 1½ in. deep) throughout a system because such boxes are versatile and roomy. If a location requires a single device, pros simply add a *mud-ring* cover. Because of their shallow depth, these boxes can also be installed back to back within a standard 2×4 wall. This allows you to keep even back-to-back switch boxes at the same height from one room to the next. Shallow *pancake boxes* (4 in. in diameter by ½ in. deep) are commonly used to flush-mount light fixtures.

Where you're installing GFCI receptacles or need more room for connectors and devices, use a 4S deep box. Finally, cover 4-square boxes with a mud-ring cover.

Metal vs. plastic boxes

Metal boxes are sturdy and are available in more sizes than are plastic boxes. Some metal boxes can be inter-

Single-gang plastic   **Double-gang plastic**   **Triple-gang plastic**

Single-gang adjustable with (orange) snap-on data ring   **Double-gang adjustable**   **Single-gang metal**

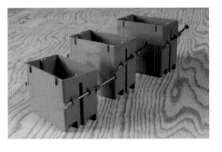

Single-gang boxes come in three sizes: 18 cu. in., 20.4 cu. in., and 22.5 cu. in. Bigger is better.

Throw a single- or double-gang mud-plaster ring on a 4-in. box and it's hard to overfill.

BOX-FILL WORKSHEET*

Item	Size (cu. in.)	Number	Total
#14 conductors exiting box	2.00		
#12 conductors exiting box	2.25		
#10 conductors exiting box	2.50		
#8 conductors exiting box	3.00		
#6 conductors exiting box	5.00		
Largest grounding conductor; count only one		1	
Devices; for each device, two times the largest connected conductor size			
Internal clamps; one for all clamps, based on largest wire present		1	
Fixture fittings; one for each type based on largest wire			

* Table based on NEC 2017 and adapted with permission from Redwood Kardon and Douglas Hansen, *Code Check: Electrical* (The Taunton Press, 2012).

locked for larger capacity. Also, metal boxes are usually favored for mounting ceiling fixtures because steel is stronger than plastic. If code requires steel conduit, armored cable (BX), or MC cable, you *must* use steel boxes. All metal boxes must be grounded.

For most other residential installations, plastic is king. (Plastic boxes may be polyvinyl chloride [PVC], fiberglass, or thermoset.) Electricians use far more plastic boxes because they are less expensive. Also, because they are nonconductive, they're quicker to install because they don't need to be grounded. However, even if a box doesn't need to be grounded, all electrical devices inside must be grounded by a ground wire that doesn't depend on a device for continuity.

Cut-in boxes

The renovator's mainstay is the *cut-in box (remodel box)* because it mounts directly to finish surfaces. These boxes are indispensable when you want to add a device but don't want to destroy a large section of a ceiling or wall to attach the box to the framing. Most cut-in boxes have metal or plastic flanges that keep them from falling into the wall cavity. Where they vary is with the tabs or mechanisms that hold them snugly to the back side of the wall: screw-adjustable ears, metal-spring ears, swivel ears, or bendable metal tabs also called "battleships" (Grip-Lok® is one brand).

➤ For information on installing remodel boxes, see p. 212.

SAFETY ALERT

All cut-in boxes, whether plastic or metal, must contain cable clamps inside that fasten cables securely. That is, it's impossible to staple cable to studs and joists when they are covered by finish surfaces, so you need clamps to keep the cables from getting tugged or chafed.

The screw on the side of an adjustable box enables you to raise or lower the face of the box to make it flush to the finish wall.

A remodel box (cut-in box) mounts to a wall surface such as drywall or plaster—rather than mounting to a stud. Typically, "ears" on the box flip out at the turn of a screw, and as they are tightened they draw the box tight to the wall.

CUT-IN REMODEL BOXES

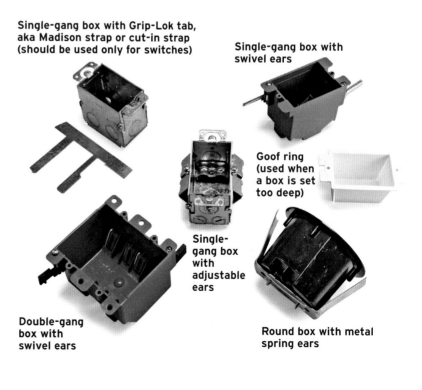

Single-gang box with Grip-Lok tab, aka Madison strap or cut-in strap (should be used only for switches)

Single-gang box with swivel ears

Goof ring (used when a box is set too deep)

Single-gang box with adjustable ears

Double-gang box with swivel ears

Round box with metal spring ears

INSTALLING NEW WORK BOXES

In residences, 18-cu.-in. single-gang PVC plastic boxes are by far the most common. They're large enough for a single outlet or a single switch and two cables.

Set each box to the correct height, as summarized on p. 202. Boxes for general-use receptacles are typically set 12 in. above the subfloor—which you can approximate by resting a box atop a hammer held on end ❶. As important, set the box depth so that its edge will be flush to the finish surface. If you use adjustable boxes, simply screw them to a stud ❷, then turn the depth-adjusting screw. Side-nailing boxes typically have scales (gradated depth gauges) on the side. If not, use a scrap of finish material (such as ½-in. drywall) as a depth gauge. Metal boxes frequently have brackets that mount the box flush to a stud edge; after the box is wired, add a mud ring (plaster ring) to bring the box flush to the finish surface.

Multiple-gang boxes mount to studs in essentially the same way, although they may require the additional support of blocking or brackets (p. 204).

1 For convenience, set boxes at hammer height.

2 Screw an adjustable box to the framing.

⚠ ACCORDING TO CODE

Before positioning outlet boxes, check to see if local building codes require them to be set at a certain height.

REMOVING KNOCKOUTS

Once you've mounted boxes, you'll need to remove the appropriate number of box knockouts and install cable connectors (clamps). Single-gang, new construction plastic boxes don't need clamps: Simply strike a screwdriver handle with the heel of your hand to drive out the knockout. To remove a metal-box knockout, jab it with the nose of a needle-nose pliers to loosen it ❹, then use the pliers' jaws to twist it free ❺.

Use a screwdriver to remove a plastic-box knockout.

A Strike a metal knockout to loosen it.

B Once the knockout is loose, remove it using pliers.

FIXTURE BOXES

Heavyweight bar for new work where there is access to framing.

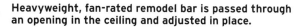

Heavyweight, fan-rated remodel bar is passed through an opening in the ceiling and adjusted in place.

Lightweight bars should be used only for a lightweight fixture such as a wall sconce.

The type of mounting bracket, bar, or tab you use depends on whether you're mounting a box to finish surfaces or structural members. When you're attaching a box to an exposed stud or joist, you're engaged in "new work," even if the house is old. New-work boxes are usually side-nailed or face-nailed through a bracket; nail-on boxes have integral nail holders.

The mounting bracket for adjustable boxes is particularly ingenious. Once attached to framing, the box depth can be screw-adjusted until it's flush to the finish surface.

Adjustable bar hangers enable you to mount boxes between joists and studs; typically, hangers adjust from 14 in. to 22 in. Boxes mount to hangers via threaded posts or, more simply, by being screwed to the hangers. Bar hangers vary in thickness and strength, with heavier strap types (rated for ceiling fans) required to support ceiling fans and heavier fixtures.

A mounting bar is screwed into the ceiling joists.

CABLE & CONDUIT

NONMETALLIC SHEATHED CABLE

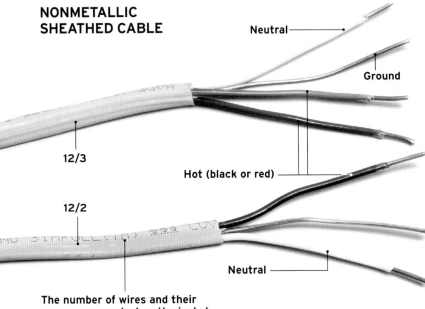

Neutral

Ground

12/3

Hot (black or red)

12/2

Neutral

The number of wires and their gauges are marked on the jacket.

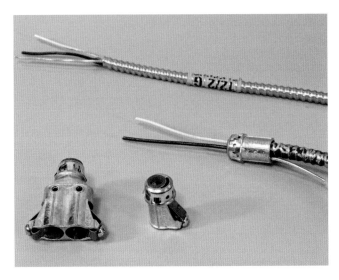

MCAP cable is faster to terminate than MC and so speeds installation. The double-barrel connector (at left) enables you to quickly feed two cables into a panel box.

Most modern house wiring is plastic-sheathed cable (Romex is one brand), but you may find any—or all—of the wiring types described here in older houses. Inside cables or conduits are individual wires, or conductors, that vary in thickness (gauge) according to the current (amps) they carry. More about that in a bit.

Nonmetallic sheathed cable

Nonmetallic sheathed cable (NM or Romex) is by far the most common type of cable. Covered with a flexible thermoplastic sheathing, Romex is easy to route, cut, and attach. Cable designations printed on the sheathing and the sheathing color indicate the gauge and the number of individual wires inside.

Typically, Romex cable has two insulated wires inside and a ground—which may be insulated or, more often, bare wire. Thus, the Romex used for a standard 15-amp lights-and-outlets circuit will be stamped *14/2 w/grd*. For a 20-amp circuit, *12/2 w/grd* is required. Three-way switches are wired with 14/3 or 12/3 cable, which has an additional insulated wire. Again, wire gauge is rated for the current it can carry, so although you

can wire 15-amp circuits with 12-gauge wire, you can't use 14-gauge wire anywhere in a 20-amp circuit.

Knob-and-tube

Knob-and-tube wiring is no longer installed, but there's still plenty of it in older houses. If its insulation is intact and not cracked, it may still be serviceable. You may even be able to extend it, but have an electrician do the work.

MC or AC cable

Metal-clad (MC) cable or armored cable (AC) is often specified where wiring is exposed and could be damaged. In AC cable, the metal covering of the cable acts as the ground; in MC cable, there is a separate insulated green wire that serves as a ground. To strip either type of metal cable, use a Roto-Split cable stripper; it's vastly superior to the old method of using a hacksaw and diagonal cutters.

MCAP or MCI cable

MCAP (or MCI) cable has been replacing MC cable in commercial production work because it's faster to terminate. You don't

have to bring the cable ground wire into the panel box to terminate it. Instead, the bare ground wire is pulled back around the aluminum jacket and the quick connectors just snap on. Snap the connector into a panel knockout and you're done. Quick connectors have spring-loaded clips that connect snugly to the panel, so there are no screws to tighten as there are with locknut clamps (p. 30). When knockouts are limited, using a double-barrel connector (see photo above) allows you to quickly put two cables into a panel box.

Conduit

Conduit may be specified to protect exposed wiring indoors or outdoors. It is commonly thin-wall steel (electrical metallic tubing, or EMT), or PVC plastic. Metal conduit serves as its own ground. Apart from service entrances, conduit is seldom used in home wiring. When connected with weathertight fittings, conduit can be installed outdoors—and PVC conduit even underground.

CABLE AND CONDUIT FOR SERVICE PANELS

Type-SER is used between panels and subpanels in dry, protected areas.

Flexible conduit is used in areas that are dry, but need hard-shell protection.

Schedule-40 PVC conduit is for damp crawlspaces or underground.

READING A CABLE

Cables provide a lot of information in the abbreviations stamped into the sheathing. For example, *NM* indicates nonmetallic sheathing, and *UF,* underground feeder which can be buried. The size and number of individual conductors inside a cable are also noted: *12/2 w/grd* or *12-2 W/G,* for example, indicates two insulated 12AWG wires plus a ground wire. Cable stamped *14/3 W/G* has three 14AWG wires plus a ground wire. (The higher the number, the smaller the wire diameter.) The maximum voltage, as in *600V,* may also be indicated.

Individual wires within cable have codes, too. *T* (thermoplastic) wire is intended for dry, indoor use, and *W* means wet; thus *TW* wire can be used in dry and wet locations. *H* stands for heat resistant. *N,* for nylon jacketed, indicates a tough wire that can be drawn through conduit without being damaged.

Finally, make sure the cable is marked *NM-B.* Cable without the final "-B" has an old-style insulation that is not as heat resistant as NM-B cable.

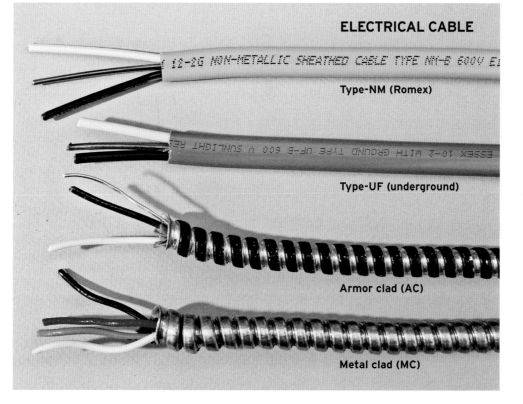

ELECTRICAL CABLE

12-2G NON-METALLIC SHEATHED CABLE TYPE NM-B 600V E...

Type-NM (Romex)

ESSEX 10-2 WITH GROUND TYPE UF-B 600 V SUNLIGHT RE...

Type-UF (underground)

Armor clad (AC)

Metal clad (MC)

The silver wire in the AC cable is a bonding wire, not a ground. In the MC cable, the green wire is ground, the white is neutral, and the red and black are hot.

CLAMPS

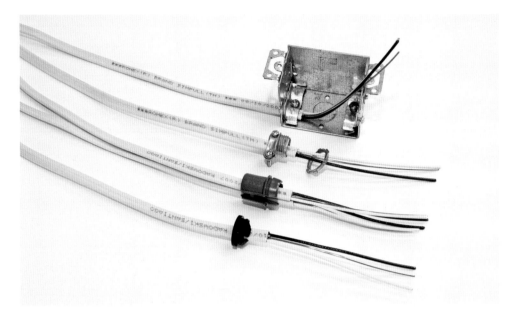

Romex cable connectors. From bottom to top: plastic push-in connector, two-cable hit-lock connector, ³/8-in. NM clamp with locknut, metal box with internal clamps. Cable connectors are set in box knockouts to prevent wires from wearing against sharp edges and to protect electrical connections in the box should a cable get yanked.

Every wiring system—whether nonmetallic, MC, or AC—has clamps (connectors) specific to that system. (MCAP connectors have integral clamps inside.) Clamps solidly secure cable to boxes to protect connections inside the box, so wire splices or connections to devices cannot get yanked apart or compromised. Cable clamps in metal boxes also keep wires from being nicked by burrs created when metal box knockouts are removed (see p. 26).

The exception to this rule is single-gang plastic boxes. If framing is exposed and cable can be stapled within 8 in. of the box, code doesn't require cable clamps in a single-gang plastic box. However, two-gang plastic boxes must have cable clamps—typically, a plastic tension clip that keeps cables from being pulled out. And, as noted earlier, all cut-in boxes must contain cable clamps.

Two-piece locknut connectors **A** are still the most common type of clamp, but professional electricians racing the clock swear by *plastic snap-in* cable connectors **B**, which seat instantly and grip NM cable tightly.

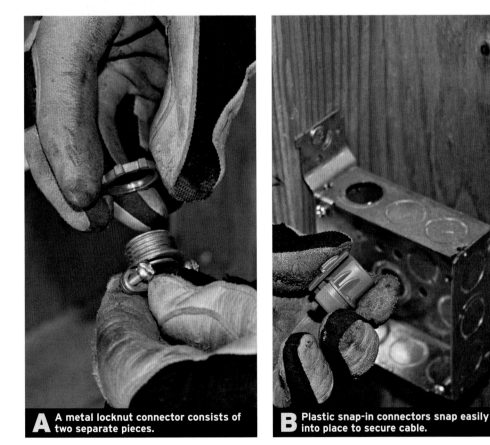

A A metal locknut connector consists of two separate pieces.

B Plastic snap-in connectors snap easily into place to secure cable.

> ⚠ **SAFETY ALERT**
> Cordless drills and screwdrivers reduce the tedium of screwing wires to terminals, attaching devices to boxes, putting on cover plates, and connecting myriad other items. But always tighten cable clamps by hand to avoid overtightening them and damaging the incoming wires.

SECURING CABLE TO FRAMING

Drilling and pulling cable between outlets is described on pp. 206-209; here we'll take a quick look at securing it to framing. The quickest way to secure cable is to staple it. The trick is to staple it correctly—staples should be snug but not too tight. Code requires staples at least every 54 in., within 12 in. of boxes, and within 8 in. of single-gang plastic boxes. Use particular care when stapling cable overhead ❶. Avoid making a sharp bend immediately after a staple.

Staple cable along stud centers to prevent nail or screw punctures. It's acceptable to stack two cables under one staple, but use standoffs ❷ to fasten three or more cables traveling along the same path. (Multi-gang boxes ❸ are fed by multiple cables, for example.) Standoffs and ties bundle cables loosely to prevent heat buildup. As you secure cable, install nail plates (p. 207) where needed.

ACCORDING TO CODE

Cables should be fastened to framing at least every 54 in. Cables must also be fastened within 12 in. of a box, or within 8 in. of a single-gang plastic box.

SAFETY ALERT

Cables should not be stacked tightly under single staples—it's called bundling—for a distance of more than 2 ft. Bundling may cause wires to overheat, thus reducing the amperage they can carry safely. Instead, use a cable standoff to hold cables loosely apart in the middle of the stud so they can't get pierced by drywall screws.

1 Staple snugly but not tightly enough to squeeze the sheathing.

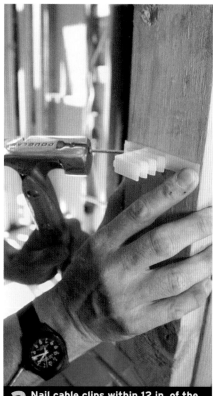

2 Nail cable clips within 12 in. of the box the cables will enter.

3 Neatly feed the cable into the clip.

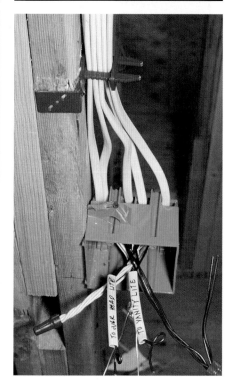

Another style of cable clip. It holds the cable near enough to the box but out of harm's way.

STRIPPING NM CABLE SHEATHING WITH A CABLE RIPPER

Most professional electricians favor utility knives for removing plastic sheathing. But DIYers should use a cable ripper to avoid nicking wire insulation. Because the ripper's tooth is intentionally dull (so it won't nick wire insulation), it usually takes several pulls to slit the sheathing completely ❶. Once that's done, pull back the sheathing and the kraft paper and snip off both, using diagonal cutters ❷.

Because cable clamps grip sheathing—not individual wires—there must be at least ¼ in. of sheathing still peeking out from under cable clamps when you're done. If you leave more than ½ in., you make working with the wires more difficult.

If there is only one cable entering a box, just cut the individual wires to length—typically, 8 in. If the box is metal, first bond the cable's ground wire to the box, using a grounding clip or a green grounding screw ❸. Once the wires are stripped and the box is grounded, fold the rest of the wires back into the box until you're ready to wire devices ❹ during the trim-out phase.

1 Pull a cable ripper along the length of the last few inches of cable.

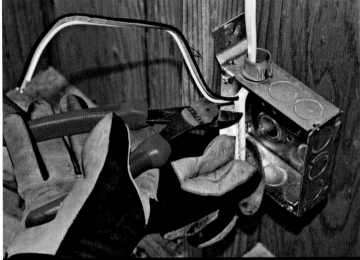

2 Snip both the sheathing and the paper.

3 Attach the ground wire to the metal box.

4 Tuck wires into the box until you're ready to wire the device.

STRIPPING CABLE WITH A UTILITY KNIFE

1 Lightly score the front and back of the sheathing. Be careful not to cut into the insulation of individual wires inside.

2 Slide the sheathing off of the cable.

3 Remove the kraft paper covering the ground wires, and you're ready to make connections.

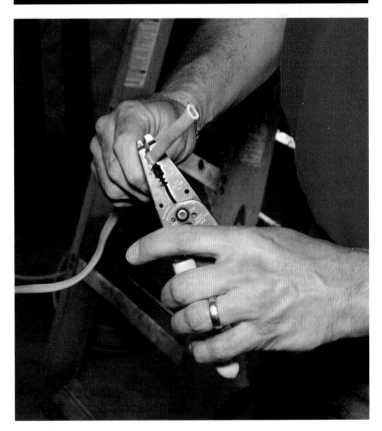

Cable strippers remove the wire's jacket without damaging the conductor insulation.

Many electricians use a utility knife to slit and remove NM cable sheathing, but it requires a light touch that takes a lot of practice. Using a cable ripper is a safer method for amateur electricians.

Typically, pros hold the blade at a low angle to the cable and lightly run the blade tip down the middle of the cable and over the bare ground wire inside. Alternatively, you can score the front and back face of the sheathing with diagonal slits **1** and then yank the sheathing and slide it off **2**.

Once the sheathing is off, cut off the kraft paper covering the bare ground wires **3**. You can also use cable strippers for the task; they are easy to use and reasonably priced.

CHOOSING WIRE

WIRES AND WIRE CONNECTORS

6-gauge stranded

60 amps: central air-conditioners and furnaces

10-gauge stranded

30 amps: ranges and central air-conditioners

12 gauge

20 amps: lights, 20-amp receptacles

14-gauge bare copper ground wire

14 gauge

15 amps: lights, average duty receptacles

Circuit components must be matched according to their load ratings. For example, a 20-amp receptacle must be fed by 12AWG cable, which is also rated at 20 amps, and protected by a 20-amp breaker or fuse. Thus, wire comes in several gauges meant for different loads. The higher the gauge number, the smaller the wire. Larger wires can carry greater amperage, just as a larger pipe can carry greater water volume. If you use too small a wire, the resistance (measured in ohms) is too great and the wire can melt, causing a house fire. That's why it's important to use the right gauge wire for the load. Calculating loads and sizing a system is described at length in "Planning" (p. 174).

Wire connectors

Wire connectors, sometimes called by the popular brand name Wire-Nut®, twist onto a group of like-colored wires to splice them together and ensure a solid mechanical connection. The importance of solid connections between spliced wires (or between wires and devices) can't be overstated. If wires work loose, electricity can arc (leap the gap) between them and cause a house fire. Wire connectors are sized according to the number of wires and/or wire gauge they can accommodate; each size is color coded.

Twist-on wire connectors are color coded to fit wires of different sizes. Green connectors, used to splice ground wires, have a hole in the cap that facilitates running a bare ground wire to a device or a metal box.

A divided pouch transforms a 5-gal. bucket into a portable hardware store of wire connectors, cable clamps, screws, staples, and other small items.

SPLICING WIRES

After removing sheathing from cables, rough-cut individual wires about 8 in. long, group like wires, and, to save time later, splice all wire groups. This step, called "making up a box" (p. 216) is the last step of rough wiring.

Typically, electricians start by splicing the ground wires, which are usually bare copper. (If they're green insulated wires, first strip 3/4 in. of insulation off the ends.) If you use standard wire connectors, trim the ground wires and butt their ends together, along with a 6-in. pigtail, which you'll connect later to the green ground screw of a receptacle.

However, many pros prefer to twist the ground wires together, leave one ground long, and thread it through the hole in the end of a special wire connector ❶. If the box is metal, first bond the ground wire to the box, using a grounding screw or clip.

Splicing hot wire groups and neutral wire groups is essentially the same. Trim wires to the same length ❷. Strip 3/4 in. of insulation off the cable wires ❸, and use lineman's pliers to twist the wires together ❹. Then twist on a wire connector ❺. If a box has more than one circuit in it, all the grounds must be spliced together, but the neutrals of the different circuits must be kept separate.

Once wire groups are spliced, gently accordion-fold the wires back into the box ❻ until you're ready to wire switches and receptacles.

1 Twist ground wires and splice with a connector.

2 Trim hot wires, leaving enough length to work around the device.

3 Strip wire ends using a wire stripper (approximately 3/4 in.).

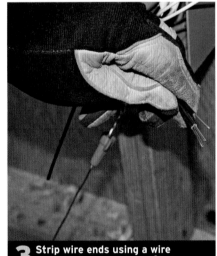

4 Twist the wires together with lineman's pliers.

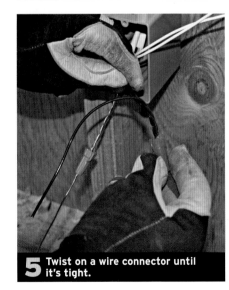

5 Twist on a wire connector until it's tight.

6 Carefully fold the wires into the box.

RECEPTACLES & SWITCHES

RECEPTACLES AND SWITCHES ARE the most-used electrical devices in a house. They're generally reliable and durable, but they are often replaced when they become outdated or cease to work. Replacing them is straightforward and safe if you first shut off the power to the circuits that feed them—and test with a voltage tester to be sure that power is off. *All work in this section must be done with the power off.*

Wiring an electrical device is considered part of finish wiring—also called the *trim-out stage*—when finish walls are in place and painted. At trim-out, everything should be ready so that the electrician needs only a pair of strippers and a screwdriver or screw gun.

CHOOSING RECEPTACLES & SWITCHES

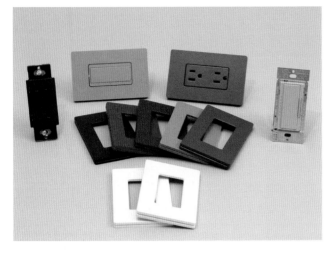

Receptacles and switches now come in a wide range of quality, functionality, and colors—with matching cover plates.

Better-quality receptacles and switches are usually heftier and more reliable. The quality receptacle on the right has a nylon face and its back is reinforced with a brass yoke.

Most of this chapter will focus on installing duplex receptacles and single-pole switches, the workhorses of household wiring. Next, we'll take a detailed look at GFCI and AFCI receptacles, which are increasingly required by code to protect you from electrical shocks and electrical fires. Then we'll move on to switches, dimmers, and vacancy sensors.

Quality tells

First, some advice that's true for all electrical devices: Buy quality. Receptacles and switches can differ greatly in capability, durability, and cost. Over the life of a device, the difference in price is trivial, but the difference in performance can be substantial. If, for example, you must call in an electrician to figure out why lights are flickering or outlets are dead, you'll quickly spend what you thought you had saved by buying cheap devices. Money aside, faulty electrical connections are not just a nuisance, they're not safe.

As you can see in the photo above right, cheap receptacles are pretty much all plastic, their thin metal mounting tabs will distort easily, and they tend to crack if subjected to heavy use. High-quality receptacles and switches tend to have heavier nylon faces and may have metal support yokes that reinforce the back of the device. Another indication of quality is how wires connect to a device, whether they are back-stabbed and held by a thin metal tension clamp or solidly secured by screws on the sides of the device or internal clamps. (These differences are explained at length on p. 42.)

Polarized receptacles
Receptacles, plugs, and fixtures are *polarized* so they can fit together only one way. A receptacle's brass screw terminal connects to hot wires and, internally, to the hot (narrow) prong of a polarized plug. The receptacle's silver screw terminal connects to neutral wires and, internally, to the neutral (wide) prong of a polarized plug. Finally, the green ground screw connects to the ground wire and the grounding prong of the plug.

POLARIZED RECEPTACLES

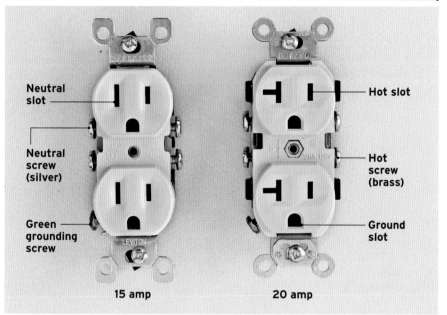

Neutral slot

Neutral screw (silver)

Green grounding screw

Hot slot

Hot screw (brass)

Ground slot

15 amp

20 amp

The 20-amp receptacle (at right) has a T-shaped neutral slot so it can receive a special 20-amp plug in addition to standard 15-amp plugs. But 15-amp receptacles cannot receive 20-amp plugs. Both receptacles are also polarized, so that only the large blade of a plug can fit into the large slot of the receptacle.

WHICH GFCI DEVICE BEST PROTECTS THE KITCHEN?

Should you use GFCI breakers or GFCI receptacles to protect kitchen outlets? A veteran electrician weighs in: "I would probably install GFCI receptacles to protect countertop outlets where small appliances are constantly in use. Often, if you plug in an appliance cord a bit crooked—so that one prong engages before the other—that can nuisance-trip a GFCI breaker, which means walking to the panel to reset the breaker. But if the outlet is protected by a GFCI receptacle, you can set things right by just pressing the reset button on the device."

If your budget allows, we recommend that you buy specification-grade (spec-grade) or commercial-grade devices from an electrical supply house. The quality of the residential-grade devices sold by home centers varies widely—some of it good, much of it so-so.

Household wiring

Planning your project, ordering electrical supplies, and room-by-room requirements are covered in "Planning" (p. 174), but here are a few rules of thumb to guide you. General-use and lighting circuits are typically served by 14-gauge (AWG) cable protected by 15-amp breakers, so standard duplex 15-amp receptacles will comprise the bulk of what you buy. However, the NEC requires 20-amp circuits (wired with 12AWG cable) protected by 20-amp breakers for bathroom receptacles; at least two 20-amp circuits for small-appliance receptacles on kitchen countertops; and 20-amp circuits for laundry, garages, workshops, and so on.

GFCI protection

To reduce the risk of electrical shock, the NEC requires ground-fault-circuit-interrupter (GFCI) protection on all 15-amp and

ACCORDING TO CODE

All new GFCI receptacles must have three important features. First, they must be self-diagnostic, with an LED indicator light that will flash or glow red to indicate device failure. Second, they must be self-locking. Should the GFCI fail, current will cease to flow through it; the device must be replaced. Third, GFCIs must be tamper-proof if installed less than 5½ ft. above the floor, with plastic shutters that slide across terminal slots to prevent, say, a curious child's inserting something into a slot. Shutters will slide open only if the two blades of a plug are inserted into both terminal slots simultaneously.

>> >> >>

CHOOSING RECEPTACLES & SWITCHES (CONTINUED)

20-amp receptacles located in bathrooms within 6 ft. of sinks, tubs, or shower stalls; in laundry areas; for all kitchen counter receptacles or any other receptacle located within 6 ft. of a sink; for dishwasher receptacles; and for receptacles that are outdoor, in garages, in accessory buildings, or in unfinished basements. GFCI protection may be achieved by installing a GFCI breaker or by installing GFCI receptacles (p. 46). (For more about grounding and ground faults, see pp. 12–14.)

AFCI protection

An arc fault is an explosive discharge of electrical current as it crosses a gap between two conductors, a serious condition because arcs can reach several thousand degrees Fahrenheit. Common causes of arcing in homes include corroded or loose electrical connections or a nail or screw driven through an electrical cable. To prevent house fires caused by arc faults, the NEC requires arc-fault-circuit-interrupter (AFCI) protection on all 15-amp and 20-amp receptacles in kitchens and laundry rooms, bedrooms, living rooms, rec rooms, parlors, libraries, dens, sunrooms, and hallways, and on switches serving any of those areas. AFCI protection may be achieved by installing an AFCI breaker, or by installing an AFCI receptacle at the beginning of a circuit and through-wiring (p. 46) the device to protect receptacles downstream.

Although they protect against different hazards, GFCI and AFCI breakers and GFCI and AFCI receptacles look quite similar. GFCI and AFCI receptacles are also wired similarly, so when installing either type of breaker or receptacle, check the label on the device carefully to be sure you are installing the right one. On house circuits that require both AFCI and GFCI protection, you can now buy a dual-function breaker.

AFCI receptacles (at left) reduce the risk of house fires, whereas GFCI receptacles (at right) protect people from electrical shocks. Although these two devices offer different protection, wiring them is essentially the same.

Tamper-resistant receptacles

Since 2011 the NEC has required that all receptacles (including GFCI and AFCI receptacles) be *tamper-resistant*, except for those more than 5½ ft. above the floor, those behind a not easily moved appliance, those that are part of a light fixture, and non-grounding receptacles used for replacements in non-grounding wiring.

Large appliances, dedicated circuits

Appliances that use a lot of energy, such as electric water heaters, electric ranges and ovens, clothes dryers, central heating and cooling systems, furnaces, whirlpools, and spas, are typically on a dedicated circuit. Cable wire serving such circuits must be matched to the load rating of the appliance, as must receptacles, plugs, and switches (if any).

Tamper-resistant (TR) receptacles have internal shutters (the milky plastic visible in the slots) held shut by tension springs. Shutters will not slide open unless both plug prongs are inserted at the same time and with the necessary pressure.

RECEPTACLES FOR DIFFERENT LOADS

Clockwise, from upper left: 30-amp dryer (125/250v), 50-amp range (125/250v), 20-amp duplex, 15-amp duplex, 15-amp tamper-resistant duplex, 15-amp GFCI.

Switches

There is a plethora of switches from which to choose. For decades, single-pole, three-way, and four-way switches were the only choice—until dimmers (rheostats) allowed homeowners to gradually lower or raise the current that flowed to a bulb, thus reducing or increasing the light that bulbs emitted. These days, switches may be dimmers, timers, occupancy or vacancy sensors, or multi-way convertibles. Switches may communicate via wires or radio frequency (RF), or with apps on your smartphone. Or you can combine a master dimmer with companion dimmers to dim a light from up to 10 locations.

Wireless switches are a boon to renovators because they can be installed without tearing up walls and ceilings (see "Installing a Wireless Switch" on p. 60). Perhaps the single most important thing to remember about today's switches is that they must be suitable to the load types they control, whether incandescent, halogen, compact fluorescent, or LEDs. LED fixtures with electronic components, for example, require electronic switches.

Matching load ratings

Circuit components must be matched according to their load ratings. That is, a 20-amp receptacle must be fed by 12AWG cable, which is also rated at 20 amps, and protected by a 20-amp breaker or fuse. A 15-amp receptacle or switch should be fed by 14AWG cable, which is rated for 15 amps, and protected by a 15-amp breaker or fuse. (Note that 15-amp receptacles on a multi-receptacle circuit may be installed on a 20-amp circuit as long as the receptacles are properly "pigtailed.")

There is no harm in using "oversize" components on a circuit, however, and there may be a benefit in some cases: for example, using 12AWG cable on a 15-amp circuit if the length of the cable from the breaker to the load is more than 75 ft. and if the expected load is close to the 15-amp rating of the circuit. In that situation, if 14AWG cable were used, there would be an unacceptable voltage drop due to the impedance of the wire. And using a larger-gauge cable (12AWG) reduces voltage drop.

NM cable manufacturers color-code the cable sheathing for the commonly used gauges to help correctly match wire size to breakers: White sheathing denotes 14 gauge; yellow sheathing, 12 gauge; and orange sheathing, 10 gauge.

ATTACHING WIRES TO DEVICES

There are several mechanisms for attaching wires to devices, which trade off time, ease of installation, and cost.

Screw terminals

A common and secure way to attach wires to receptacles or switches is to strip and loop wire ends and tighten them beneath screw terminals on the side of the device. This method takes a bit more time and technique but can be mastered quickly.

Most wire strippers have a small *looping hole* on the tool face. After stripping a wire end, simply insert it into the looping hole and twist your wrist 180 degrees to create a perfect loop, ready to slip onto a screw. Stripping and looping with one tool also saves time. If you bend the loop correctly—so its opening is just large enough to fit onto a screw shaft—you shouldn't need pliers to squeeze the loop smaller.

Three tips: As screws tighten clockwise, insert loops in that direction. Second, exert a slight pull on the wire you're attaching and it will be less likely to slip off as the screw head compresses it. Third, never cross a wire end over itself, which will create a high spot and prevent the screw head from making contact with the whole loop.

Backstab or push-in devices

Backstab devices, also called *spring backwire* devices, have holes in the back into which you insert stripped wire ends, which are held by a thin strip of metal inside that acts as a spring clamp. Backstabs are quicker to wire than screw terminals, but cheap backstab *receptacles* can be problematic. Each time you insert and remove plugs, the receptacles move slightly, which increases the likelihood of clamp failure, leading to loose wires, flickering lights, and arcing (pp. 40 and 70).

Back-wired *switches,* on the other hand, rarely fail because switches aren't subject to the stresses of inserting and removing plugs. Nonetheless, many pros don't like backstab switches either because their spring clamps can fatigue and loosen.

High-quality hybrids

Quality devices, such as the spec-grade GFCI receptacle shown at the bottom right, are reliable. The device is configured so that you can loop wires around its screw terminals or insert wires into holes on the back of the device. Here, back-stabbing is acceptable because instead of thin-metal spring clamps inside, the receptacle has strong internal clamps that are engaged as you tighten down screws on either side of the device to secure the wires. These solid mechanical connections are unlikely to loosen or fail.

Solid connections are the key to reliable wiring, and looped wire ends tightened beneath screw terminals are very solid. Screws tighten clockwise, so orient wire loops in the same direction.

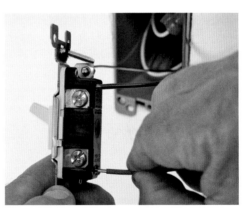

To speed the task of looping wires, insert stripped wire ends into the small hole on the face of the wire stripper. Flip your wrist 180 degrees and—voilà—a perfect loop.

Back-wired switches are usually dependable. After stripping the wire end, insert it into the push-wire slot until the wire bottoms out, then pull gently to make sure that the device's internal clamp has gripped the wire securely.

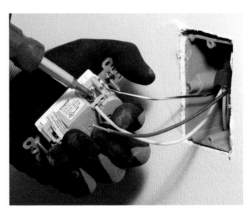

This spec-grade GFCI receptacle device allows you to attach wires to screw terminals on the side or to insert wire ends into holes on the back of the device. The wires are held securely by strong internal clamps. Such quality devices cost a bit more, but they're well worth it.

TESTING FOR POWER

To identify the circuit that serves a particular receptacle, insert the voltage tester prongs into the receptacle and have a helper at the service panel flip breakers until the tester indicates the power is off. To identify the circuit that serves a particular switch, turn on the fixture it controls and flip breakers until the light goes out.

If that test is inconclusive or you aren't sure if the receptacle or switch is operable, remove the cover plate and unscrew the device from the box. Being careful not to touch screw terminals or wires with your fingers, pull the receptacle out of the box. Touch the probe tester prongs to both screw terminals, as shown in "Testing for Voltage" on p. 16.

Once you've identified and turned off the breaker (or removed the fuse) controlling the switch, lock the breaker panel or fuse box until your repairs are complete.

Before touching an existing receptacle, switch, or fixture, use a noncontact tester to see if power is present. Then follow up with a probe tester.

SAFETY ALERT

In some old houses, the neutral wires—rather than the hot wires—may be attached (incorrectly) to switches, in violation of current code. So when testing existing receptacles, switches, or fixtures, test *all* wires for voltage.

WIRING A DUPLEX RECEPTACLE

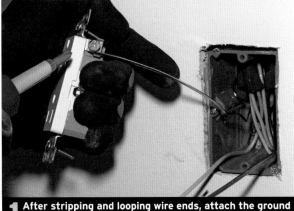

1 After stripping and looping wire ends, attach the ground wire to the green ground screw on the receptacle.

2 Next connect the neutral-wire pigtail to a silver screw terminal.

3 Finally, connect the hot-wire pigtail to a brass screw terminal.

4 Fold wires into the box so the face of the receptacle will be parallel to the wall, then secure the device to the box.

PRO TIP

Many electricians also tighten down the screw terminals that aren't attached to wires, to reduce radio-frequency interference and static. It's only a theory, but in an electronic world, it seems like a good practice.

The duplex receptacle is the workhorse of house wiring, because it enables you to plug in a variety of energy users at locations around the house. Receptacles are so indispensable to modern life that code dictates that no space along a wall in a habitable room should be more than 6 ft. from a receptacle and any wall at least 2 ft. wide must have a receptacle.

→ For detailed drawings of receptacle wiring, see pp. 188-189.

Wiring a duplex receptacle in mid-circuit

When a duplex receptacle is in the middle of a circuit, there will be two 14/2 or 12/2 cables entering the box—one from the power source and the other running downstream to the next outlet.

To ensure continuity downstream, all wire groups will have been spliced with wire connectors during the rough-in stage. A pigtail from each splice will need to be connected to a screw terminal on the receptacle. Unless the small tab between screw pairs has been removed, you need attach only one conductor to each side of the receptacle.

Loop and install the ground wire to the receptacle's green grounding screw first **1**. Place the loop clockwise on the screw shaft so that when the screw is tightened down the screw head will grip—rather than dislodge—the wire.

Next, loop and attach a neutral conductor to a silver screw terminal **2**. Then flip the receptacle over to access the brass screw terminals on the other side. If a looped wire end is too wide, use needle-nose pliers to close it.

Screw down the brass screw so that it grips the hot wire **3**. Pros frequently use screw guns for this operation, but weekend electricians should tighten the screw by hand to ensure a solid connection.

Push the wired receptacle into the box by hand, keeping the receptacle face parallel to the wall **4**. You can hand-screw the device to the box, but if you take it slow and use

>> >> >>

a fresh bit, a cordless drill/driver is much easier. Finally, install a cover plate to protect the electrical connections in the box and to prevent someone from inadvertently touching a bare wire end or the end of a screw terminal.

Wiring a duplex receptacle at circuit end

When a receptacle is at the end of a circuit—where only one cable feeds an outlet—there's no need for pigtails. Just attach incoming wires directly to the receptacle as shown in the photo at far right. As with pigtail wiring, connect the ground wire first, then the neutral, then the hot wire.

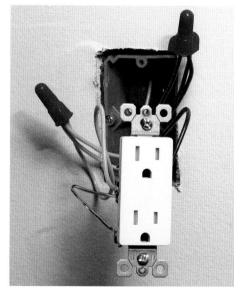

The preferred way to wire a mid-circuit receptacle.

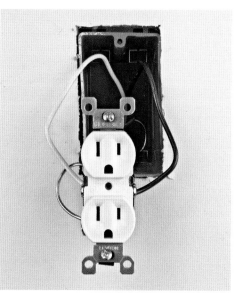

At the end of a circuit, wires from the cable attach directly to the receptacle.

Wiring in an orderly way

Any habit that increases your safety is worth adopting. When connecting wires to devices, most electricians connect the ground wire first, then the neutral wire, and then the hot wire. When disconnecting wires, they reverse the order: Disconnect the hot first, then the neutral, then the ground wire. Because the ground wire offers the lowest impedance path to ground, it makes sense to leave it connected as long as possible. Even if you're working on circuits that are disconnected, as veteran electricians say, "Treat every conductor as if it were live and you'll stay alive."

TWO-SLOT RECEPTACLES (NONGROUNDING)

Receptacles with only two slots are ungrounded. Because they are fed by 2-wire cable without a ground wire, they are inherently less safe than three-slot receptacles fed with a cable that has a ground wire. If existing cables and receptacles are correctly wired and in good condition, most codes allow you to keep using them. Should you add circuits, however, code requires that they be upgraded—that is, wired with grounded cable (12/2 w/grd or 14/2 w/grd) and three-slot receptacles.

Replacing a two-slot receptacle with a GFCI receptacle can be a cost-effective way to add protection to that outlet. There will still not be a ground wire on the circuit, but the GFCI will trip and cut the power if it detects a ground fault.

➤ **For more on wiring GFCI receptacles, see the next page.**

Note: If one slot of a two-slot receptacle is longer, the receptacle will be polarized. That is, a receptacle's brass screw terminal will connect to a hot wire and, internally, to the hot (narrow) prong of a polarized two-prong plug. The receptacle's silver screw terminal connects to neutral wires and, internally, to the neutral (wide) prong of a polarized plug.

➤ **For more about polarity, see p. 38.**

Receptacles with two slots (instead of three) are nongrounded types. If the two slots are the same height, the receptacle is also nonpolarized and should be replaced with a polarized nongrounding receptacle.

WIRING A GFCI OR AFCI RECEPTACLE

Ground-fault circuit interrupters (GFCIs) and arc-fault circuit interrupters (AFCIs) offer different but critical code-required protections, so if you are unfamiliar with either term, first review pp. 14 and 40. In brief, GFCIs protect you against electrical shocks, and AFCIs protect against arc faults and reduce house fires. You can achieve GFCI or AFCI protection on a circuit by installing a GFCI or AFCI breaker or, as described below, by installing a GFCI or AFCI receptacle at the beginning of a circuit to protect receptacles downstream.

Note that GFCI and AFCI receptacles look similar, and wiring either type is essentially the same. So before you start your installation, check the label on the device to be sure you are installing the correct one. (For circuits that require both GFCI and AFCI protection, you can buy dual-function circuit breakers.)

When wiring a GFCI or AFCI receptacle, it's important to connect incoming wires (from the power source) to the terminals marked "line" on the back of the receptacle. Attach outgoing wires (to outlets downstream) to terminals marked "load." To distinguish line and load wires during rough-in, write each term on small pieces of the cable sheathing and slip them over the appropriate wires before folding them into the box.

➤ **See p. 189 for drawings of GFCI or AFCI wiring.**

Protecting a single outlet

If the GFCI or AFCI is going to protect users at a single outlet ❶, attach wires to only one set of screw terminals. The yellow tape across one set of screws indicates that they are load terminals. If you are hooking up the device to protect only a single point of use, leave the tape in place and connect wires only to the screw terminals marked "line." After attaching the ground pigtail, screw down the silver screw to secure the neutral pigtail ❷.

Connect the hot pigtail to the brass screw last ❸ then push the device into the box carefully, hand-screw it to the box, and install a cover plate. *Note:* If you inserted wire ends into holes on the back of the receptacle, you must still tighten down the screw terminals on the sides of the device, which tightens internal clamps that hold the wires snug.   >> >> >>

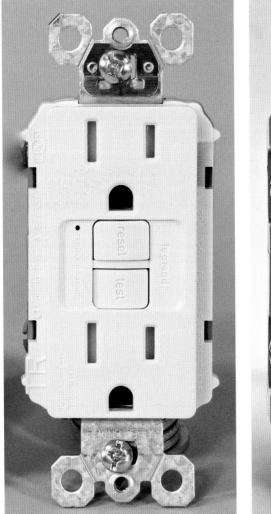

Quality GFCI and AFCI receptacles can be reliably wired by inserting stripped wire ends into terminal holes on the back of the device: Internal clamps grip the wire ends as screws are tightened down. Or you can loop and attach stripped wire ends directly to screw terminals on each side of the device. Note the "LOAD" and "LINE" descriptors; they are important.

1 By using pigtails from each wire group, you can wire a GFCI or AFCI to protect only its outlet and not outlets downstream.

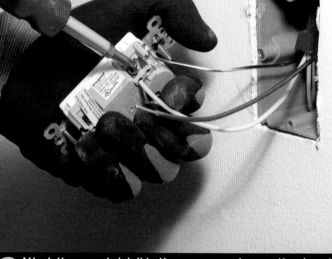

2 Attach the ground pigtail to the green ground screw, then insert the neutral pigtail into a neutral "LINE" terminal hole on the back of the device.

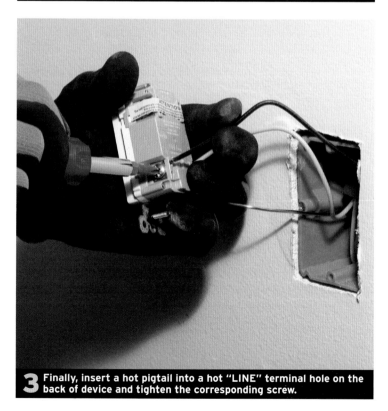

3 Finally, insert a hot pigtail into a hot "LINE" terminal hole on the back of device and tighten the corresponding screw.

A GFCI or AFCI receptacle protecting a single outlet has just three wires attached. Attach hot and neutral pigtails to "LINE" terminals.

WIRING A GFCI OR AFCI RECEPTACLE (CONTINUED)

Feeding the circuit through a GFCI or AFCI receptacle

If you want to use a single GFCI or AFCI receptacle to protect downstream outlets, feed them from the "load" terminals of the receptacle. That is, connect incoming and outgoing cable wires directly to the device, rather than using pigtails. (You should, however, splice ground wires to ensure continuity: Screw the ground pigtail to the receptacle's ground screw.) Again, it's important to connect incoming wires (from the power source) to the terminals marked "line" and outgoing wires to terminals marked "load." This is a code-approved way to offer protection downstream without using a breaker.

Attach the ground wire to the ground screw, neutral wires to silver screws, and hot wires to brass screws. If you instead inserted wire-ends into holes on the back of the receptacle, screw down all screws on the sides of the device, which tightens internal clamps holding the wires. Be patient as you push the receptacle into the box, folding wires as needed. Install the mounting screws and attach the cover plate.

A GFCI or AFCI receptacle protecting receptacles downstream does not use pigtails for hot and neutral wires. Incoming wires from the power source attach to terminals marked "LINE"; outgoing wires attach to terminals marked "LOAD."

ACCORDING TO CODE

A GFCI will operate properly and provide GFCI protection in a box without an equipment ground. If you install GFCI receptacles on an ungrounded circuit, however, the NEC requires that you label those receptacles as having "no equipment ground."

A GFCI protecting an ungrounded box must be labeled.

WIRING A SPLIT-TAB RECEPTACLE

Standard duplex receptacles have a small metal tab between the brass screw terminals. The tab conducts power to both terminals, even if you connect a hot wire to just one terminal. However, if you break off and remove the tab, you isolate the two terminals and create, in effect, two single receptacles—each of which requires a hot lead wire to supply power.

This technique, known as split-tab wiring, is often used to provide separate circuits from a single outlet, a configuration commonly used when connecting a disposal and a dishwasher. The disposal receptacle is almost always controlled by a switch, which allows you to turn off the disposal at another location. To supply two hot leads to a split-tab receptacle, electricians usually run a 12/3 or 14/3 cable.

To create a split-tab receptacle, use needle-nose pliers to twist off the small metal tab between the brass screws ❶. Next, connect the bare ground wire to the green grounding screw on the device and connect the white neutral wire to a silver screw. If you keep a slight tension on the wires as you tighten each screw, they'll be less likely to slip off ❷.

Flip the receptacle over to expose the brass screws on the other side, and connect a hot lead to each brass screw. If you're running 12/3 or 14/3 cable, one hot wire will typically be red and the other black ❸. Finally, push the receptacle into the box, install the mount-

1 Twist off the tab to convert a standard duplex receptacle into two single receptacles.

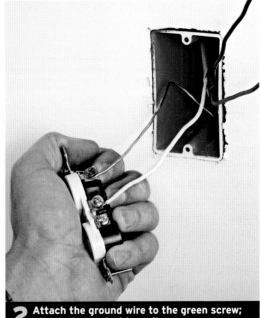

2 Attach the ground wire to the green screw; attach the neutral to a silver screw.

3 Attach the two hot wires last, to the two brass screws.

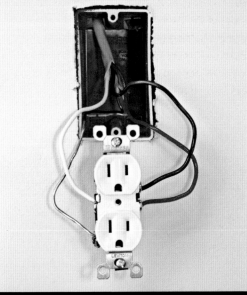

4 Correctly wired split-tab receptacle. One hot wire is typically controlled by a switch.

ing screws, and apply the cover plate ❹.

Although this 15-amp split-tab receptacle is fed with 12/3 cable (rated for 20 amps), there's no danger of the load exceeding the rating of the receptacle.

Because of the configuration of the slots, the receptacle can receive only a 15-amp plug.

MAKING RECEPTACLES FLUSH

Before starting this repair, turn off the power to the outlet and test to be sure it's off.

Outlet boxes installed below finish surfaces are a common problem in older homes. In some cases, box edges were installed flush but remodelers later drywalled over existing walls in bad shape. Code allows a maximum box setback of ¼ in. from noncombustible surfaces. If box edges are deeper than that, you must add a *goof ring* (box extender) to make box edges flush, as explained in the following section.

If an outlet box is only slightly below the surface, however (¼ in. or less), you should still bring the *device* flush to the drywall to mount it securely. If you're using adjustable boxes in new work, that's not a problem because you can turn a screw to raise the box until it's flush. But a nail-on box below a drywall or a plaster wall calls for a different solution: plastic spacers ❶.

Sometimes called *caterpillars*, plastic spacers build up the level of the receptacle or switch so its mounting tabs are flush to the drywall. These spacers take up the space between the mounting plate on the box and the device. Break off pieces from the strip; the style shown in the photos folds. Insert the spacer behind the screw tabs, tighten the mounting screws, and the box will be snug ❷.

Avoid the temptation to use the plastic cover plate to pull a device up to the surface. After a plug is inserted into the receptacle a few times, the receptacle moves and the cover plate cracks, which is both unsightly and unsafe. In time, wire connections to a device can loosen and the resultant arcing may cause a house fire.

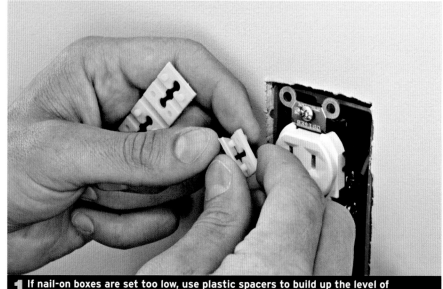

1 If nail-on boxes are set too low, use plastic spacers to build up the level of the receptacle or switch so its mounting tab is flush to the drywall.

2 After inserting the spacers between the device's mounting tab and the edge of the box, screw the device solidly to the box.

PRO TIP

If a box is recessed more than ¼ in. from a noncombustible surface, you must use a box extender, also known as a goof ring, to make it flush to the surface.

GETTING BOX EDGES FLUSH

1 If you suspect faulty wiring, check the circuit with a plug-in analyzer.

2 Cut the power, then test to be sure. This noncontact tester shows no voltage.

3 Unscrew and pull out the receptacle, then slide a goof ring over it.

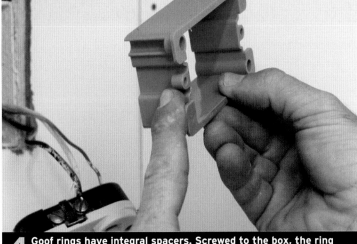

4 Goof rings have integral spacers. Screwed to the box, the ring should raise the device flush.

5 If needed, install additional spacers to raise the device flush to finish surfaces.

If an outlet box is more than 1/4 in. below a noncombustible surface, use an add-a-depth ring (aka a goof ring or a box extender) to make box edges flush. Plastic goof rings, being nonconductive, are best.

Before starting this repair, turn off the power to the outlet and test to be sure it's off. If this condition has existed for some time, it's also wise to plug in a circuit analyzer **1** to see if the circuit is correctly wired. Remove the plastic cover plate to expose

the conductors in the box and test again **2**. Once you've again verified that the power is off, unscrew the device and pull it out from the box.

Slide the plastic goof ring over the receptacle and fit both back into the outlet box **3**. As most goof rings have integral spacers **4**, you may not need to use plastic spacers to make the device flush. In the example shown, the cabinet back was not parallel to the wall (and to the outlet box behind it) so the elec-

trician added plastic spacers behind the top mounting tab of the receptacle **5**. When the cover plate was reinstalled, it now sat flush and the receptacle was solidly mounted.

Note: The cabinet back was particleboard, so the goof ring also corrected another code violation: Outlet boxes must be completely flush with combustible surfaces such as wood paneling or wood composites, with no gaps around the box.

WIRING SWITCHES

Before connecting or disconnecting wires to a switch, use a voltage tester to make sure that the power to the switch box is off. Test with the switch both on and off to be sure. And never assume an existing switch is correctly wired: Test all receptacle slots: hot, neutral, and ground. After removing the cover plate, test all conductors for power.

Be especially wary of outlets controlled by dimmers. Some dimmers that don't require neutral wires may be a type of "trickle device." If such a dimmer is attached to, say, an incandescent lamp, the dimmer allows a minuscule amount of current flow all the time to power the dimmer. This trickle of current flows through the switch and the switch leg (facing page); at the fixture, it makes its way to the neutral wire to ground. **Beware:** Trickle current can be enough to shock you if you work on the light fixture without first turning off the breaker (or fuse) that controls the circuit. Always test the dimmer and the fixture with a voltage tester and turn off the controlling breaker if you have any doubt.

Switch wiring can be quite complex, especially three-way and four-way switches and switches with electronic components. The electronic switch arrays shown on p. 66 are just the tip of the iceberg of what's available. So follow the manufacturer's instructions carefully.

Switches (from left): single-pole, three-way, four-way. Although these switches may be modest, even simple switches have a top and bottom, so wire them correctly.

BACKSTAB SWITCHES

Back-wired (backstab) switches are popular because not looping wire ends saves time. Use the stripping gauge on the back of the device to determine how much insulation to strip from wire ends. After stripping each wire end, insert it into the hole on the back of the switch, then pull gently to make sure that the device's internal clamp has gripped the wire securely. For good measure, tighten down the screw terminals on the side.

Back-wired switches are acceptable, but side-wired ones are better. Use the stripping gauge on the back of the device to determine how much insulation to strip from the wire end.

WIRING A SINGLE-POLE SWITCH

The most commonly installed switch, a single-pole, is straightforward to wire. Spliced together during the rough-in stage, the neutral wires stay tucked in the outlet box ❶. Pull ground and hot-wire groups out of the roughed-in box. Use the hole in the handle of your wire strippers or use needle-nose pliers to loop the conductor ends so they can be wrapped around the screw terminals.

First, attach the ground wire to the green grounding screw on the switch. Orient the wire loop in a clockwise direction—the same direction the screw tightens. When the loop faces the other way, it can be dislodged as the screw head is tightened.

Next, connect the hot wires to the switch terminals ❷, again orienting wire loops clockwise. One black wire is hot (power coming in), and the other is the *switch leg* (power going out to the fixture). With a single-pole switch, however, it doesn't matter which wire you attach to which screw. Generally, pros attach the hot wire last, much as they attach the hot wire on a receptacle last.

Once the ground and hot wires are connected, the switch can be tucked into the box ❸. Always

WIRING A SINGLE-POLE SWITCH

Ground

To fixture

Neutral

Incoming power

Hot

This switch controls a fixture at the end of a cable run. See p. 190 for the complete picture.

1 When wiring switches, leave neutral wires tucked in the box. Switches interrupt the current flowing through hot wires only.

2 Attach hot wires to terminals. One wire is hot (from the power source). The other is the switch leg running to the fixture.

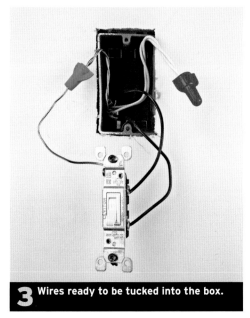

3 Wires ready to be tucked into the box.

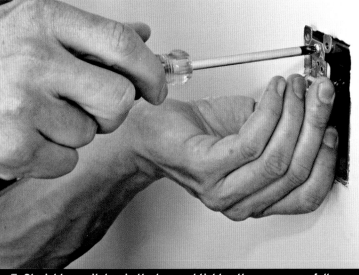

4 Straighten switches in the box, and tighten the screws carefully so you don't strip the box's threads. Using a drill-driver will speed the task.

push the device into the box by hand until it's flush to the wall **4**. Don't use screws to draw a device into a box because the device may not lie flat and it's easy to strip the screw holes in a plastic box. Using a cordless drill/driver is a lot faster than using a screwdriver, but use a light trigger finger or the torque clutch on the driver to avoid stripping the screw head or snapping off the screw.

 ACCORDING TO CODE

The NEC requires that there be a neutral wire in every switch box because many new electronic switches and devices require a neutral to function properly. If your switch doesn't need a neutral to operate, cap the neutral and tuck it into the box.

WIRING A SWITCH LOOP

HISTORICAL METHOD

1 In this historical method, tape the white wire black to show it is a hot wire.

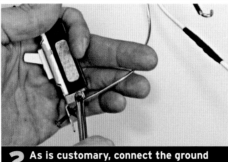

2 As is customary, connect the ground wire first.

3 Connect the switch leg (black wire).

4 Connect the hot lead wire to the fixture last.

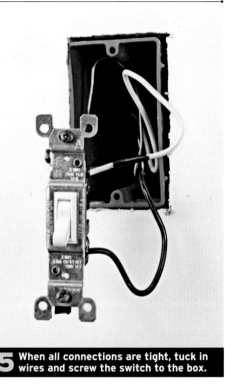

5 When all connections are tight, tuck in wires and screw the switch to the box.

This section shows two ways of wiring a switch when an outlet or fixture box is closer to the power source than to the switch box—commonly called a *switch loop*. The first way to wire a switch loop, shown in the drawing at right, can probably be found in 90 percent of homes but has been superseded by changes in the electrical code. The second way to wire a switch loop, shown in the drawing on the facing page, conforms to the NEC requirements and should be used for new installations.

The historical method

Before the code changed, it was common to run a single length of 12/2 or 14/2 cable as a switch loop. This means bringing the power down from the fixture to and through the switch and then back up to the fixture. As such, the white wire taped black in the 12/2 or 14/2 switch loop functions as the incoming hot wire, and the black wire acts as a switch leg to return the power to the fixture. Here, the white wire is actually a hot wire and is taped black to identify it as such.

Turn off the power and test to be sure. At the outlet or fixture box, splice all the grounds together. Attach the source neutral wire to the fixture neutral wire. Attach the source hot wire to the white wire (taped black) of the switch loop. Last, connect the switch loop black wire to the black fixture wire.

Note: Here, for convenience, we bend the rule of using a white wire only as a neutral wire and instead wind black tape on each end of the white wire to show that—in this case—the white wire is being used as a hot wire.

At the switch, start by stripping and looping the wire ends. Next, tape the white wire with black electrician's tape to indicate that it is serving as a hot wire to the back-fed switch **1**. The NEC dictates that the white wire in back-fed wiring is always the hot lead (power coming in). The black wire, on the other hand, is the switch leg that runs back to the fixture.

First, connect the ground wire to the green ground screw **2** on the back-fed

---

WIRING A SWITCH LOOP: THE HISTORICAL METHOD

In the "old school" way of wiring a switch loop, a single length of 2-wire cable serves as a switch loop. The white wire in the cable is taped black to show that it is being used as a hot wire. This method was a good solution because it conserved copper and was quick to wire, but it has been superseded by the method shown on the facing page.

A single length of 2-wire cable serves as a switch loop.

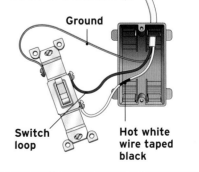

Ground

Switch loop

Hot white wire taped black

MODERN METHOD

1 With power off, strip sheathing from the 3-wire cable that runs from fixture box.

2 If the switch does not need a neutral wire, cap it and fold it into box.

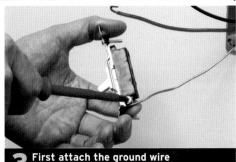

3 First attach the ground wire to the switch.

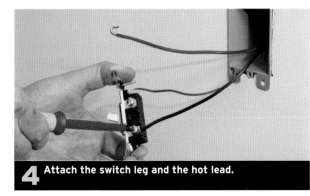

4 Attach the switch leg and the hot lead.

5 Fold the wired device into the box and secure it with mounting screws. Replace the cover plate.

switch. Next, connect the switch-leg wire (black) **3** (see the facing page), then the hot wire (white taped black) to the switch terminals **4** (see the facing page). To keep looped wire ends snug against the screw shaft as you tighten down the screw, pull gently on wires, as shown. Not fumbling with wire ends saves time.

Finally, tuck the wires into the box **5** (see the facing page), screw the switch to the box, and install the cover plate.

The modern method

This method of wiring a switch loop reflects recent code changes. Specifically, the NEC requires that there be a neutral in every switch box because some electronic timer switches and other energy-saving controls need a neutral. So if you want to use a switch-loop approach, you must use three-conductor (3-wire) cable. The neutral of the 3-wire cable must be connected to the neutral of the circuit, even if the neutral is not going to be used.

This installation sequence is done with the power off. From the power source at the fixture, run a length of three-wire cable to the switch box. Remove cable sheathing **1** and strip 3/4 in. of insulation from the ends of insulated wires. If the switch doesn't need a neutral wire, cap the neutral wire **2** and fold it into the switch box.

If you are attaching switch wires to screw terminals, loop the wire ends. Connect the ground wire to the green ground screw **3** on the switch. Next, connect the switch-leg wire (red), and the hot lead (black), which runs back to the fixture **4**. Keep looped wire ends snug against the screws as you tighten them down. When all wires are secured, gently fold them into the box **5**, screw the switch to the box, and install the cover plate.

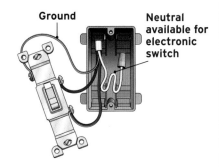

Ground

Neutral available for electronic switch

REMODEL WIRING: REPLACING A SINGLE-POLE SWITCH

The old saw in remodeling, "You never know what you'll find till you open the wall," is especially true to remodeled wiring. Be prepared for anything, form a plan based on what's there, and follow the code and common sense as you proceed.

Testing is the essential first in wiring

First test the tester (p. 16). If the switch is working, turn the light on and have a helper at the service panel flip breakers till you find the one controlling the switch's circuit. Turn that breaker off and lock the panel; if it's a fuse box, remove the fuse. If the switch isn't working, remove the cover plate and touch the tester to both wires attached to the switch ❶. Flip the switch toggle to off and on positions. Have your helper at the panel turn off power to the circuit, as above. Continue testing, however.

Being careful not to touch the sides of the switch, unscrew its mounting screws and gently pull it out from the box. Then test again, touching the tester to every wire–white, black, and ground–and to spliced wire groups inside the box. If your noncontact tester indicates no voltage, it's safe to handle the wires.

Disconnect switch wires and note their condition

If the wire insulation is intact (not brittle, cracked, or falling off), the wires are probably safe to attach to the replacement switch. But first scrutinize the inside of the box. In the sequence shown, we found several things that needed attention ❷ before we could wire a replacement switch: (a) the metal box was ungrounded, (b) though wire groups were twisted together and taped with electrical tape, they lacked a solid mechanical connector, (c) the white wire attached to the switch, though being used as a hot lead to the fixture, was not identified as a hot wire, and (d) the box was full of dust and debris.

Cover all connections

All electrical connections not ending at a switch, fixture, or receptacle must be housed inside a covered junction box so they can't be disturbed. All switches, fixtures, and receptacles must have a box in which the connections are made. Some kinds of fixtures (like can lights) have an integral junction box. Often, electricians will use an existing fixture box as a junction box in which to splice a cable feeding a new fixture. When there's not enough room in an existing box, use a separate junction box to house the splices.

Code requires all electrical connections to be housed in a junction box.

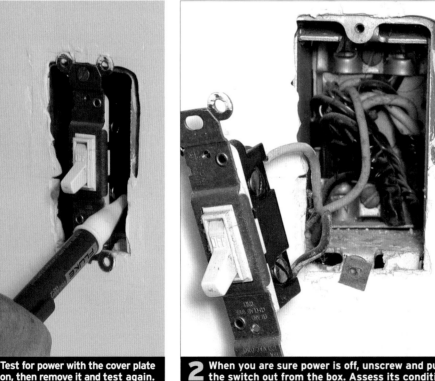

1 Test for power with the cover plate on, then remove it and test again.

2 When you are sure power is off, unscrew and pull the switch out from the box. Assess its condition.

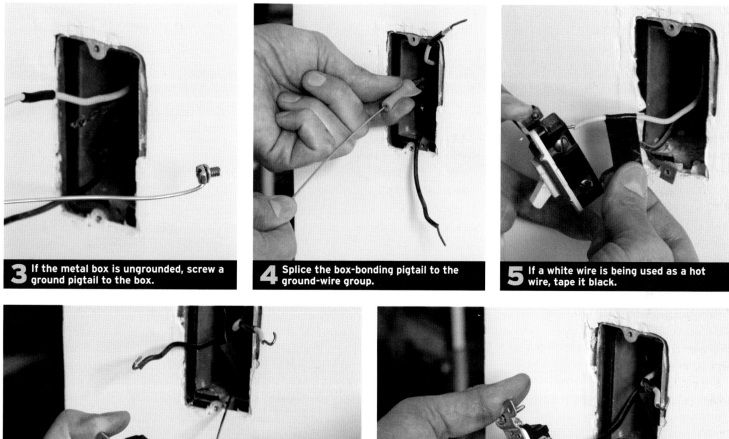

3 If the metal box is ungrounded, screw a ground pigtail to the box.

4 Splice the box-bonding pigtail to the ground-wire group.

5 If a white wire is being used as a hot wire, tape it black.

6 Attach the grounding wire to the new switch's ground screw.

7 Attach the switch leg (black wire), then the hot lead (white wire taped black) that runs to the fixture.

Attend to any code violations

We started by vacuuming the box, which also gave us a better view of its contents. After unwinding tape from each wire group, we looped a bare ground lead wire around a ground screw **3**, screwed it into a threaded hole in the back of the box, and spliced that new lead wire to the ground-wire group, using a special grounding connector **4**. This grounded the metal box. We next secured wire connectors to the other wire groups, using lineman's pliers. Then we taped the white wire **5** that had been attached to the switch to identify that it was a hot wire.

Connect the wires to the new switch

First attach the ground wire to the green ground screw on the switch **6**. If there's no ground wire feeding the box, code doesn't require grounding a switch. Connect the switch-leg wire (black) **7**, then the hot lead (white wire taped black), which runs to the fixture. Once the wires are connected to the replacement switch, fold them into the box, tighten the mounting screws that hold the switch to the box, and replace the cover plate.

WIRING A LINEAR SLIDE DIMMER

If you are replacing an existing dimmer, note: Dimmers that do not require neutral wires may be "trickle devices" that allow a minuscule amount of current flow all the time to power the dimmer. Trickle current can be enough to shock you if you work on a fixture without first turning off the breaker (or fuse) that controls the circuit. Always use a voltage tester to test the dimmer and the fixture to make sure no current is present.

All work in this section should be done with the power off.

Slide dimmers have a slide bar that allows you to set the light level and a separate on-off switch so you can turn the light on and off without changing a preset light level. Slide dimmers have largely replaced the old rotary type that combined both functions. Newer slide dimmers offer additional functions, so their wiring has become more complicated, and many sport wire leads rather than screw terminal connections.

For standard single-pole switches, it doesn't matter which screw terminals you connect a switch leg or hot wire to, but it may matter which wire you attach to dimmer leads, so always read the manufacturer's directions. The slide dimmer shown at right is a multi-way switch that is convertible: It can be wired as a single-pole or three-way switch, depending on which wires you connect ❶. It has a green insulated ground, red and black hot wires, and a red-and-white-striped wire that would be used as a signal wire to a companion dimmer.

Because the convertible device would be used as a single-pole dimmer, we didn't need the red-and-white-striped wire. So we capped it with a wire connector ❷. Because this dimmer does not require a neutral, we spliced the neutrals together to feed through to the fixture (without connecting them to the dimmer).

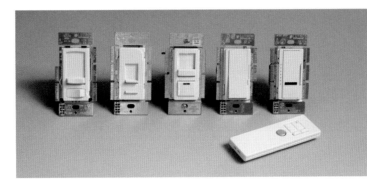

Slide dimmers. From left: Skylark® contour, Luméa®, Illumatech®, Diva®, Maestro® IR (infrared) with remote control. All have a slide bar to preset light levels and a separate on-off switch. The bare-metal flanges around the dimmers are heat sinks.

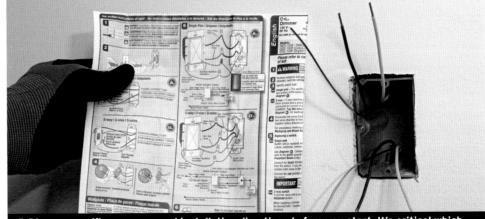

1 Dimmer specifics vary, so read installation directions before you start. It's critical which circuit wires you attach to dimmer lead wires.

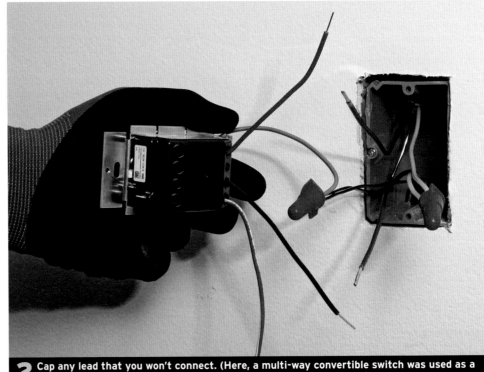

2 Cap any lead that you won't connect. (Here, a multi-way convertible switch was used as a single-pole switch.) Then attach the grounding pigtail to the ground screw.

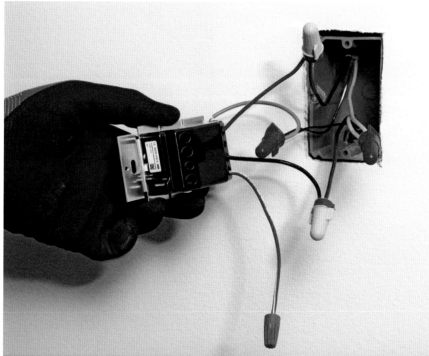

3 Connect the red lead to the switch leg—the wire that runs to the fixture—then the black lead to the incoming hot wire.

Splice the ground pigtail to the device's ground lead. Then splice the switch leg from the box to the red lead on the device. On devices with wire leads, typically a red lead attaches to the switch leg.

Finally, attach the incoming hot wire to the other hot lead (black) on the device ❸. Carefully fold the wires into the box ❹ and push the wired dimmer into the box. Screw the device to the box and install the cover plate.

Match the dimmer to the load A dimmer must match the type of fixture it controls, whether incandescent, halogen, fluorescent, or LED. Typically, the dimmer rating is stamped on its face.

4 Because dimmer bodies tend to be larger than the single-pole switches they may replace, make sure beforehand that the box is big enough.

INSTALLING A WIRELESS SWITCH

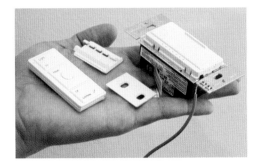

All you need to retrofit wireless switches. *From left*, a wireless controller, a visor clip, a wall-mounting plate for the controller, an electronic master switch.

Turn the power off, remove the cover plate of an existing switch, and test to be sure the power's off.

Electronic switches are expensive, so read installation directions carefully. Here, existing hot and switch-leg wires are attached to the electronic dimmer's terminals. The green switch lead is connected to a bare copper ground.

Tuck in wires, screw the electronic switch to the box, then install the cover plate. After testing the switch, program the wireless controller. The controller will *talk* to the dimmer, telling it to raise or lower the lights—in effect, it is a three-way switch.

Down the hall, a small mounting plate is screwed to or stuck on the wall. The controller slides into the plate. No cutting, drilling, or wire-fishing required! Cover plates will make it look like any other switch.

Traditionally, adding a light fixture that could be controlled from several locations meant retrofitting three-way or four-way switches—and fishing the wires that serve them behind finish walls—which can turn into a nightmare. Fortunately, today's electricians have another, almost effortless option—installing wireless switches.

Installing three-way wireless capability can be as simple as replacing a mechanical switch (a single-pole toggle, for example) with an electronic master switch and locating a wireless controller at some distant point. In the photo sequence at right, we installed a Lutron® Maestro Wireless® dimmer and a companion Pico® Wireless control.

Start by turning off power to the existing (mechanical) switch, and use a voltage tester to be sure it's off. Remove the switch cover plate. To be doubly sure the power is off, apply the voltage tester to the switch's terminals and wires. Unscrew the switch from the outlet box, then pull out the switch and disconnect its wires.

Electronic switches are sensitive (and expensive), so follow the manufacturer's installation instructions exactly. As most do, the Lutron electronic dimmer looks like a standard back-wired switch, with a green grounding lead coming off it. Attach the wires per instructions, screw the device to the box, install the cover plate, turn the

power back on to the switch, and program the Pico Wireless control via buttons on its face.

Mounting the wireless control—say, at the far end of a hall—is as simple as sticking an adhesive-backed mounting plate to a finish surface. If you want a more permanent mounting, use the screws provided (and expansion anchors if the wall is drywall). The wireless control slips into the mounting plate and is in turn covered by a snap-on plate. The controller needs no wires because it has a tiny battery that's typically good

for 10 years. It needs only enough power to "talk" to the master switch.

Even modest wireless devices have a lot of useful functionality. The Pico control also can be clipped to a car visor so that as you approach home you can turn on the porch light. Inside the house, you can program lights to turn off and on. In a baby's room, for example, you could program a light to dim slowly over a 10-minute period so the baby isn't startled by sudden darkness as he or she drifts off to sleep.

MAKING UP A THREE-WAY SWITCHBOX

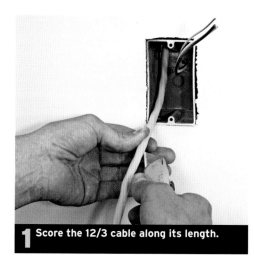

1 Score the 12/3 cable along its length.

2 Pull the sheathing free.

3 Twist the ground wires before splicing them.

Three-way switches allow you to operate a light from two locations. They're often used at the top and bottom of a set of stairs or at two entrances to a room. If you get confused about which wire goes where, refer to the wiring schematics on pp. 191–192 or make a drawing of your own.

In new wiring, wires are roughed in when the framing is still exposed. Here, 12/2 and 12/3 cables were fished in to feed a three-way switch that was added after the drywall was up.

> → **For more on fishing cables, see pp. 209–211.**

After stripping sheathing from the 12/2 cable, strip the 12/3 cable. Removing 12/3 sheathing is a little different: Start by lightly scoring the 12/3 cable along its length, up into the box ❶. Then, when you reach the end of the cable, cut through the sheathing. Because you'll soon be stripping the ends of individual wires, cutting through the sheathing end won't compromise wire insulation.

> → **For more on stripping cable, see p. 32–33.**

Starting at the cut-through sheathing at the end of cable, pull the sheathing free of the wires within ❷. The sheathing will separate easily along the scored line. At the cable's upper end in the box, carefully cut free the sheathing.

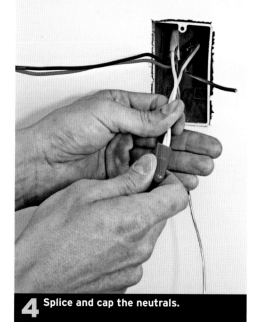

4 Splice and cap the neutrals.

Twist together the ground wires before splicing them with a wire connector ❸. To use a green wire connector, cut one of the leads shorter than the other so that it sticks out of the hole in the end of the wire connector. Then connect that ground lead to the switch's green ground screw. Next, strip wire insulation from the neutrals, splice them, cap them with a wire connector, and push them into the box ❹. (Neutrals don't connect to standard switches.)

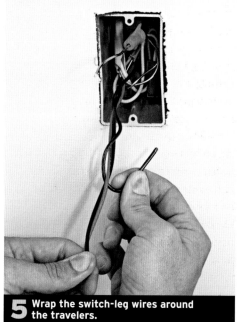

5 Wrap the switch-leg wires around the travelers.

After professional electricians strip cable sheathing, many wrap individual wires in a distinct fashion so any other electrician will know which wires are travelers and which are switch-leg wires. Group and twist traveler wires clockwise, then wrap the switch-leg wire counterclockwise about the travelers. This way there's no need to put tape or labels on the wires to identify them or to pull out all the cables and figure out which wire is what ❺.

WIRING A THREE-WAY SWITCH

To wire a three-way switch, pull the conductors out of the outlet box. Unwrap the switch-leg wire from around the travelers and separate the wires so the travelers are on one side and the switch leg on the other ❶. To strip wire ends, give the strippers a quick twist, use your thumb as a fulcrum to push the wire insulation off, and loop the wire ends ❷.

After attaching the bare ground wire to the green grounding screw on the device, attach the first traveler wire ❸. Loop wires clockwise around the screw shafts, and they'll be less likely to slip off when the screws are tightened. Flip the switch over and connect the second (red) traveler ❹. (Note: It doesn't matter which traveler wire goes where—you'll still be able to turn lights off and on. The only critical connection is the common terminal.)

If you connect traveler wires in the same position on two three-way switches—say, you attach the red traveler to the first terminal, as just described—the lights will be off when switch toggles are both up or both down. This is a fine point and most people needn't agonize about it: The three-way switches will still work as long as you attach traveler wires to traveler terminals.

After attaching the second traveler, connect the hot conductor (switch leg or hot wire) to the common screw terminal, which is color coded black ❺. Push the device into the box by hand, screw the device to the box, and install a cover plate.

Photo ❻ is a frontal view of the switch we just wired; it's typical for a three-way that's located between the power source and the light fixture it controls.

Traveler wires attach to brass screws

Common (COM) terminal

PRO TIP
When replacing a defective or outdated three- or four-way switch, use a felt-tipped marker to note which wires connect to which switch terminal before disconnecting the wires. Of course, turn off power to the switch before you begin.

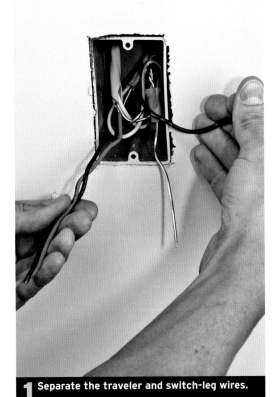

1 Separate the traveler and switch-leg wires.

4 Connect the second traveler.

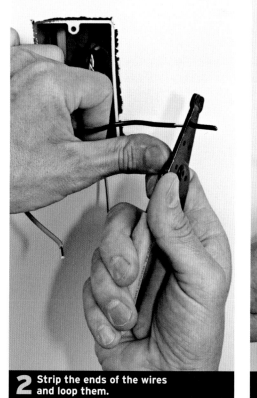

2 Strip the ends of the wires and loop them.

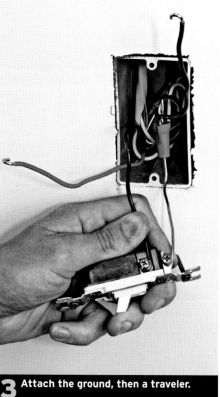

3 Attach the ground, then a traveler.

WIRING A THREE-WAY SWITCH LOOP

When an outlet or fixture box is closer to the power source than to the switch box, the wiring leg to the switch box is called a *switch loop*. When the switch is a three-way switch, a single 3-wire cable runs to it. In other words, the white wire taped black serves as a hot wire and runs from a splice in the fixture box, and the red and black wires are travelers. The white wire here is not a neutral; thus it is taped black to indicate that it is the hot conductor connected to the common terminal.

➡ **For more on wiring switch loops, see the drawings on pp. 54 and 55.**

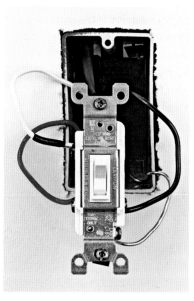

This is a typical **three-way switch with existing back-fed wiring.**

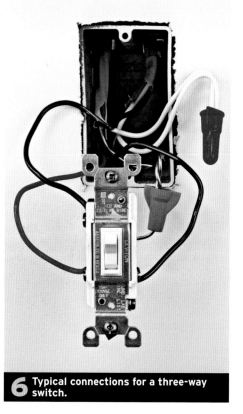

5 Connect the hot conductor last.

6 Typical connections for a three-way switch.

WIRING A FOUR-WAY SWITCH

Four-way switches have two travelers incoming (from the power source) and two travelers outgoing (to a second four-way switch) and they have a neutral in and a neutral out. Thus there will be two three-wire cables entering the box.

Twist and splice the neutral wires with a wire connector and push them out of the way, into the back of the box. Then strip and loop the ends of the ground wire and the hot conductors and twist them so they turn clockwise around the screw shaft. Next, connect the ground to the four-way switch, as you do for all devices ❶.

On each side of a four-way switch there is a black terminal and a brass terminal. The red and black travelers from one cable attach either to the brass terminals or to the black terminals ❷, and the red and black travelers from the second cable attach to the other (like colored) set of terminals ❸. Note how the electrician exerts a slight tension on the wires to keep them from slipping off as he tightens the screw terminals.

When you've got this many wires in a box, it's helpful if you partially accordion-fold the wires before you push them into the box. Screw the switch to the outlet box, then install the cover plate.

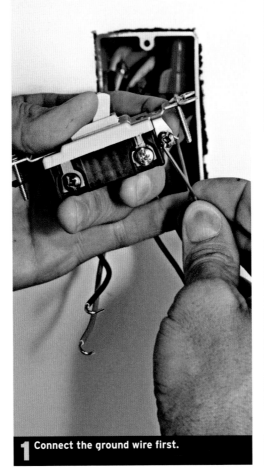

1 Connect the ground wire first.

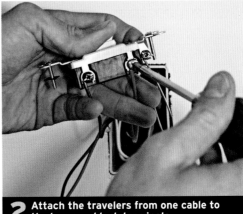

2 Attach the travelers from one cable to the brass or black terminals.

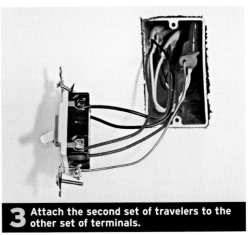

3 Attach the second set of travelers to the other set of terminals.

NEW DEVICES, OLD BOXES

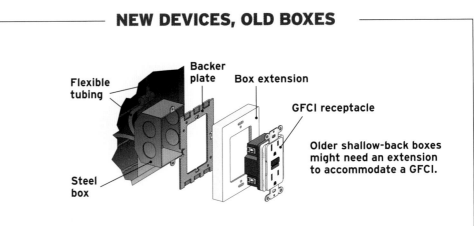

Flexible tubing

Backer plate

Box extension

GFCI receptacle

Steel box

Older shallow-back boxes might need an extension to accommodate a GFCI.

GFCIs, dimmers, and electronic switches are often larger than the older devices they replace and so they may be a tight fit in an old outlet box. Any upgrade must satisfy code requirements about box fill (see the chart on p. 24); there must be enough room so that device conductors do not come in contact with the box.

Some pros wrap electrical tape around the sides of switches or receptacles to prevent contact with steel box sides—not a bad idea—but correctly sizing the device is a better solution. You can buy "slim" versions of GFCIs and other devices, or you can add a wall box extender.

WIRING SPECIALTY SWITCHES

Push-in nuts

Splicing with twist-on wire nuts can be problematic in space-starved boxes or if an old box has very short leads. Wago® Wall-Nuts can ease the task: Strip wire ends about 1/2 in. and then push them into nut ports that hold the wires fast. The clear plastic housing also allows you to see if the wires are connected.

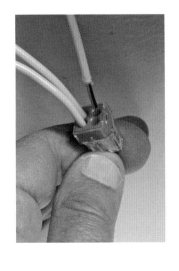

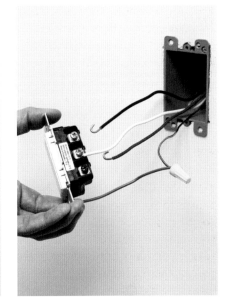

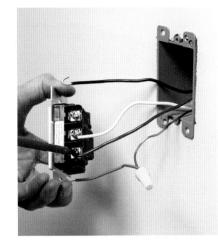

Top left: With the power off, first attach the ground wire to the green ground wire of this electronic switch.

Top right: If the electronic switch requires a neutral wire to operate, connect the neutral next.

Bottom: Attach the two hot wires, as specified in the manufacturer's installation instructions.

It's easy to be intimidated by the sophistication of electronic switches. So here are a few parting tips: **First**, always shut off the power and test to be sure it's off before installing or replacing a switch. **Second**, whatever bells and whistles a switch may have, its primary function is to interrupt the flow of current through hot wires: That's what switches do. **Third**, read manufacturers' instructions and follow them religiously to protect yourself and your equipment; many companies offer extensive support materials online, so use them. **Fourth**, be methodical: No matter how many wire leads a fancy switch may have, connect wires in the same order: ground, neutral (if any), and hot wires.

The switch above is a 3-wire version of the wireless switch shown on p. 60. Employing radio-frequency (RF) signals, it can speak to distant switches that require no hard-wiring. Yet you install the wires of this electronic master switch in the same order as the wires of simpler switches: ground, neutral (if any), switch leg, switch lead.

WIRING A VACANCY SENSOR

Vacancy sensors, occupancy sensors, and motion detectors are specialized switches that sense motion, typically by infrared or ultrasonic sensors. Their technology is similar, so each is distinguished more by where and how it's used. *Vacancy sensors* require an individual to turn the light on but will turn the light off automatically when motion is no longer detected. *Occupancy sensors* turn lights on automatically and off after an interval in which they sense no movement. *Motion detectors* turn lights on and off automatically like occupancy sensors, but motion detectors are typically installed outdoors and mounted in a light base. We'll use "vacancy sensor" as our default term.

Because manufacturing details vary widely, it's difficult to generalize about wiring vacancy sensors; the switch's location in the circuit—mid-circuit or switch loop—will also dictate the type of cables feeding it and how they're connected to switch leads. Many newer vacancy sensors combine functions (wireless, multi-location control, and dimming or timer functions), so they require neutral wires.

The vacancy sensor shown here also has a dimming function. So its energy-conserving vacancy sensor could make a bathroom code-compliant and its dimmer could create a nice ambience for a soak in the tub. Despite its dual functionality, it does not need a neutral wire (it uses a tiny amount of "trickle current" to operate the sensor). Thus it can be easily retrofit to replace a standard single-pole switch.

To wire it, cut power to the outlet and test to be sure. Cap the neutral wires because they aren't needed; likewise, cap the sensor's yellow lead if the device is being used as a single-pole switch. Connect the ground wire to the switch's ground screw and then attach the two hot wires to the switch's lead wires. Carefully push the switch into the box and secure it with mounting screws. The Legrand® vacancy sensor shown comes with an assortment of decorative cover plates.

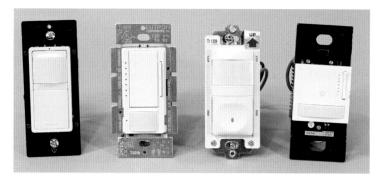

Vacancy and occupancy sensors frequently offer additional functions, including dimming, night lights, and multi-location infrared controls.

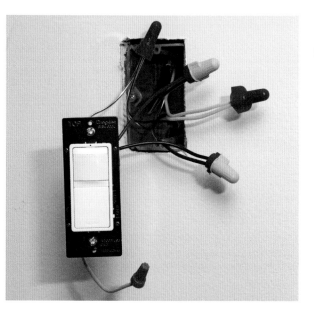

This vacancy sensor does not require a neutral wire to operate, so the incoming neutral wire was capped, as was the yellow lead from the sensor.

PRO TIP

When splicing stranded wire leads to solid conductors, place the tip of the stranded wire slightly beyond the solid conductors so that when you twist on the wire connector, its threads will fully engage the stranded wire and ensure a solid splice.

It's increasingly common to have a choice of decorative covers for specialty switches.

WIRING A TIMER SWITCH

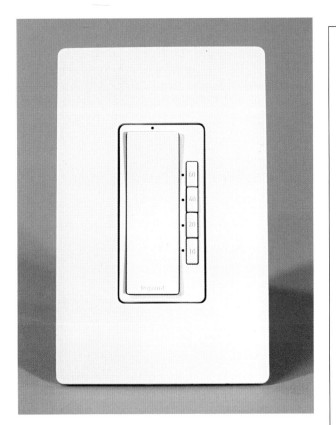

This timer switch allows you to select time in 10-minute increments, as displayed by tiny LEDs along the right side. When the time expires, the switch shuts off the fan or light.

Timer switches do a great job of saving energy, exhausting stale air, and removing excess moisture to forestall mildew and worse. Use it to control a bath fan or light, set it for 10 or 15 minutes, and . . . forget about it. It will shut off automatically. Timer switches are especially useful in out-of-the-way places such as attics, basements, closets, and garages, where a light might remain on a long time unnoticed.

As with other switch types, the more functions a timer switch combines, the more likely it is to be electronic, feature control screens and programming buttons, and require a neutral wire to operate. The countdown timer shown uses little LEDs to show how much time is left before the switch will turn off. Happily, this timer doesn't need a neutral and so is an easy retrofit for a standard single-pole switch.

THE FACE OF FUTURE CONNECTIONS

In their push to stay competitive, electrical contractors have long embraced products that simplify installation and cut costs on large commercial jobs. If products are innovative enough, eventually they start showing up in home centers—and homes. The PlugTail® components below speed rough-in considerably: strip wire ends, insert each into the appropriate Wago nut (ground, neutral, or hot), tuck everything into an outlet box, and you're ready for rough-in inspection. Trim-out is even faster. The component at right in the photo is the back of a PlugTail receptacle: Simply snap its three prongs into the three slots of the plug, screw the receptacle to the box, install the face plate, and you're done. And should electricians need to swap out a receptacle, they can do so without turning off the power—there are no exposed conductors. (**Caution:** Cut power to the outlet to be doubly safe!) There are also PlugTail switch components (available from Pass & Seymour®).

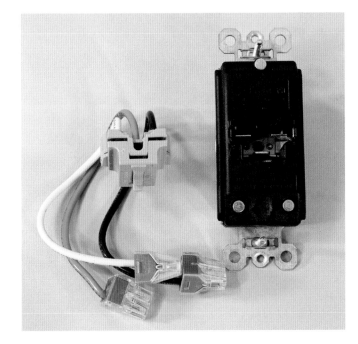

The PlugTail assembly speeds installation. Insert stripped wire ends into the orange Wago nuts, then snap the back of the receptacle (at right) into the three-slot plug.

LIGHTING

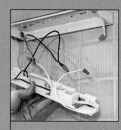

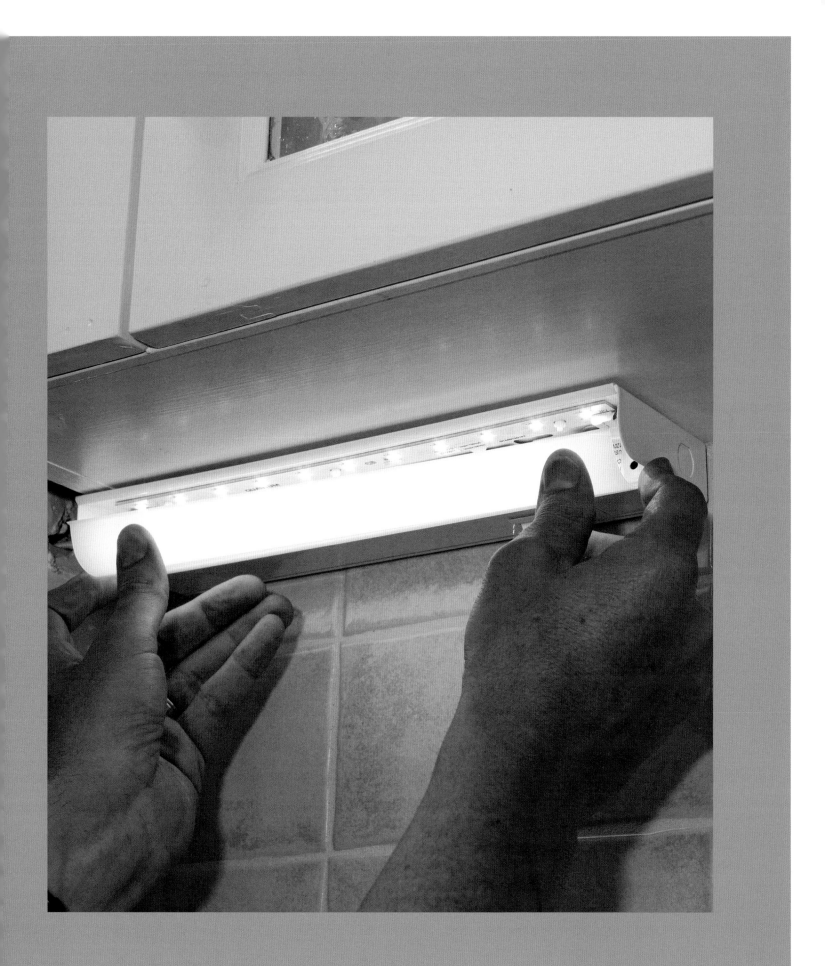

LIGHTING BASICS

The right lighting can transform a room and cut your energy bills big-time. In this chapter, you'll get a crash course in choosing bulbs and systems based on the quality of light you need for task, accent, and ambient lighting; different lighting systems, and the advantages of each; mounting options for securing fixtures to walls and ceilings; and a host of how-to sequences that show you how to install (or replace) fixtures such as wall sconces, chandeliers, recessed lighting, undercabinet lighting, and two types of stylish low-voltage lighting systems.

Take heed: Before disconnecting or installing a light fixture, always turn the power off—and test (p. 16) to be sure it's off. Connect fixture wires in this order: ground, neutral, hot. Disconnect them in the reverse order: hot, neutral, and then ground. In this manner, the grounding system stays connected as long as possible to protect you. Remember to ground metal boxes, mounting plates, and fixtures. Good working habits can help keep you safe. As the pros say, "Treat every wire as if it were live and you'll stay alive."

Wiring and Lighting Terms

CFL
Compact fluorescent

IC-Rated
Applied to recessed lighting fixtures whose housing can safely come in contact with insulation (IC = insulation contact) without danger of overheating or causing a fire.

Lamp
For most of us, a light fixture that sits on a table or floor. To an electrician, lamp is the preferred term for a light bulb: A standard incandescent bulb is thus a "type A lamp."

Leads
Wires preattached to a fixture. Leads are spliced to supply wires to energize the fixture. Typically, a fixture has ground, neutral, and hot leads. Fixture leads are often stranded wire.

LED
Light-emitting diode

Light Box
An outlet box that serves a light fixture.

Line Voltage
The standard current in most house circuits: 120v.

Lo Vo or LV
Low voltage. These systems are typically 12v but sometimes 24v.

Lumens
A measure of light on the surface of a bulb; the amount of light produced per watt.

Nipple
Short section of hollow threaded rod.

Primary Wires
In a lo-vo system, wires running from a 120v power source to the transformer.

Secondary Wires
Wires running from a transformer to lo-vo tracks, cables, or fixtures.

Source or Supply Wires
Wires from the power source, typically 120v.

Transformer
An electrical device that reduces line voltage to low voltage. All lo-vo lighting systems require a transformer.

THE EVOLUTION OF LIGHTING

The evolution of light bulbs. Left to right: incandescent A lamp, self-ballasted compact fluorescent (CFL), first-generation LED with heat sink, second-generation LED, modern A lamp with LED filaments.

Incandescent lighting has had a good run. For more than 100 years, the technology invented by Thomas Edison dominated household lighting around the world. Part of its appeal was its simplicity: A bulb screws into a threaded fixture socket and completes the circuit by making contact with an aluminum or brass shell (neutral) and a *contact tab* (hot) in the bottom of the socket. Typically, that socket is energized with house current (120v), which heats a tungsten filament in the bulb, which gives off heat and light. A *lot* more heat than light, however.

Although they produce a lovely light that approximates the hue of sunlight—the real key to their longevity—incandescent bulbs guzzle energy. Only 10% of the energy they consume becomes light; the other 90% is wasted as heat. So, as energy costs soared, environmental impact emerged, and energy codes reflected these changes, the lighting industry invested massively to find another technology that would be as pleasing to the eye and as popular as incandescent—and be energy efficient as well. The array of bulbs above nicely encapsulates that search.

Incandescents have a warm light that's similar to soft, golden, late-afternoon sunlight. (*Note* that incandescent lamps do not actually produce light that is equivalent to daylight.) However, they don't last long and guzzle a lot of energy for the amount of light they produce.

Compact fluorescents were the first energy-conserving alternative to incandescents, but their cool light was tough to warm to. In time, their color improved but because their light output is directly proportionate to the length of their tubes, their bulbs were always ugly.

First-generation LEDs didn't win any beauty contests either. Their light quality was decent and they saved an impressive amount of energy, but they did not dim well, the lumen output was limited, and they were expensive (upwards of $50 per lamp).

Second-generation LEDs had very good light quality, ran cooler, could be dimmed, and allowed light to emanate in all directions. But they still had that clunky parson's collar.

Today's LEDs have it all, including a dizzying array of lamp shapes and sizes. An LED-filament lamp, available in clear or golden hue globes, is incredibly energy-efficient. The lamp shown at right in the photo above uses 4W of energy and its life expectancy is 30,000 hours—virtually a lifetime bulb. And the quality of its light is phenomenal. Many newer LED bulbs can color-shift, so that as you dim them they can go from bright white to a golden hue, as incandescent bulbs once did. And their familiar A-lamp shape makes them look at home in fixtures of any vintage. In effect, we've made the transition from incandescents to energy-scrimping LEDs that look like incandescents.

LEDs (LIGHT-EMITTING DIODES)

LEDs are specialized semi-conductors (about 1 mm square) whose convex covers focus the light they emit. LEDs have been around for years, but initially they were colored (red, green, blue) and not practical for general lighting use. In time, however, LED makers figured out how to produce a warm white light and to create bulbs with enough output to satisfy almost any lighting requirement.

Individual LEDs are cool to the touch, but as manufacturers boosted LED output, they also increased heat. Consequently, first-generation white-light LED bulbs needed *heat sinks* near their bases to dissipate excess heat and prolong bulb life. Each suc-cessive generation of LED bulbs ran cooler and lasted longer. How long an LED bulb lasts depends on many factors—especially the quality of the bulb—but 25,000 to 50,000 hours is fairly common. (Based on average bulb use, that's 20 to 40 *years.)*

But the real story is LEDs' meager power consumption, which is a fraction of the power used by incandescent or even com-pact fluorescent (CFL) bulbs. A 4W LED pro-duces as much light (measured in lumens) as a 40W incandescent or a 9W to 12W CFL. An 18W LED produces as much light as a 100W incandescent or 25W to 30W CFL. And as LED bulbs' power consumption has plum-meted, so have their prices. At most home centers you can find LED bulbs ("100W incan-descent equivalent") for less than $5 each.

Equally intriguing, LEDs are revolutioniz-ing lighting design. LED diodes are so small that they can be incorporated into fixtures of almost any shape and size—or no fixture at all.

Throwing a highly focused beam, LEDs are superb for task and accent lighting. Recessed lighting (p. 84), which typically requires cans 5 in. to 6 in. deep, is a dino-saur; you can now buy LED fixtures that look recessed but which fit into a standard 4-in.-square box just 2 in. deep. Moreover, their light intensity, spread, and angle is the equal of any recessed can's beam.

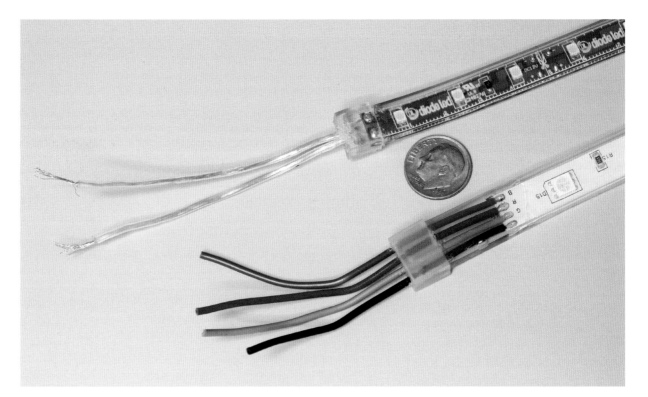

LED strips contain a series of light-emitting diodes 1 mm square. The upper strip yields white light; the lower strip has red, green, and blue LEDs and can be programmed to produce any color—including white.

LED LAMP TYPES

This array is a small sample of the LED lamps available. The descriptions list the size of each (such as A19 or Par 30), the wattage it consumes (W), the equivalent wattage (EQ) of the incandescent it replaces, and other pertinent information.

1. Par 38, 18.4W (120W EQ), dimmable flood lamp, titanium LED series

2. Par 30, 8W (65W EQ), small flood lamp

3. MRX16, 7.7W, 8W (75W EQ), bi-pin base, dimmable

4. Par 20, 7W (50W EQ), dimmable, titanium LED series

5. Antique G25, 4W (40W EQ), dimmable

6. Antique ST18, 4W (40W EQ), dimmable

7. Antique A19, 4W (40W EQ), dimmable

8. A19, 12.5 W (100W EQ), Philips® "warm white"

9. A19, 9W (60W EQ), dimmable, $1.08/year to operate, life expectancy 22.8 years

10. A21, 17W (100W EQ), dimmable, titanium LED series

11. G25, 8W (60W EQ), dimmable, titanium LED series

As you can see in the photo above, LEDs are now available as replacement bulbs for most common screw-in types. LED strips, which can be hidden almost anywhere, are naturals for undercabinet or under-deck-railing applications. LED lights are especially handy in fire-rated areas because as LED technology has matured, there's no driver, no heat buildup, and, in many cases, no fixture. Outdoor applications will also be big: Solid-state LEDs are impervious to cold, vibration, and, when properly encased, weather.

The evolution of candelabra lamps was similar to that of A lamps. Left to right: incandescent, self-ballasted CFL, first-generation LED with heat sink, energy-saving candelabra with LED filaments.

HALOGEN & COMPACT FLUORESCENT (CFL) BULBS

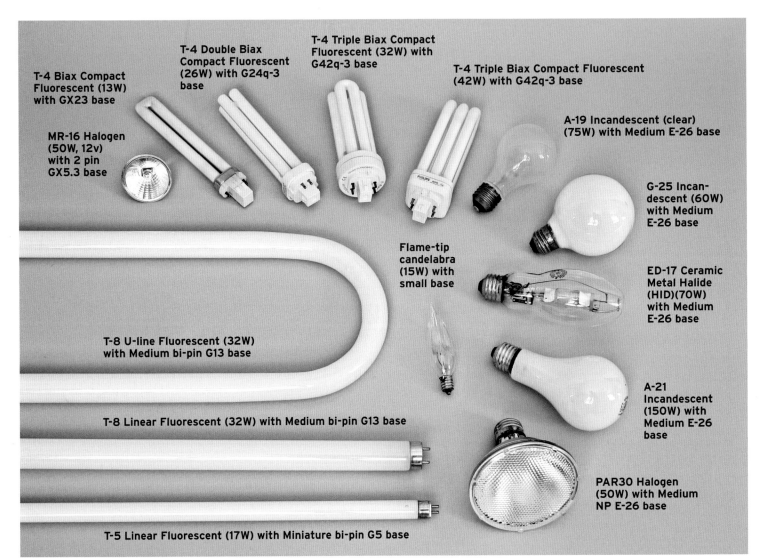

T-4 Biax Compact Fluorescent (13W) with GX23 base

T-4 Double Biax Compact Fluorescent (26W) with G24q-3 base

T-4 Triple Biax Compact Fluorescent (32W) with G42q-3 base

T-4 Triple Biax Compact Fluorescent (42W) with G42q-3 base

A-19 Incandescent (clear) (75W) with Medium E-26 base

MR-16 Halogen (50W, 12v) with 2 pin GX5.3 base

G-25 Incandescent (60W) with Medium E-26 base

Flame-tip candelabra (15W) with small base

ED-17 Ceramic Metal Halide (HID)(70W) with Medium E-26 base

T-8 U-line Fluorescent (32W) with Medium bi-pin G13 base

A-21 Incandescent (150W) with Medium E-26 base

T-8 Linear Fluorescent (32W) with Medium bi-pin G13 base

PAR30 Halogen (50W) with Medium NP E-26 base

T-5 Linear Fluorescent (17W) with Miniature bi-pin G5 base

Like incandescent bulbs, halogen bulbs produce light by heating a tungsten filament, but because halogen bulbs contain a different gas, they last longer (2,000 to 6,000 hours), burn hotter, and are roughly 20% more efficient than incandescent bulbs. Halogen lighting can be installed in both standard and low-voltage (lo-vo) systems. But even on reduced current, they burn bright—and hot. Thus, they must be installed with requisite clearances—typically 6 in. from combustible materials—and placed where bulbs can't be accidentally touched.

For a time, halogen bulbs were the rising star of lighting. They offered greater efficiency, and standard halogen bulbs (such as A-lamp shapes) were an easy swap with standard incandescents. Their real niche, however, was in directional-type lamps (MR, R, PAR) used as accent lighting in homes and retail environments. These shapes allow you to direct (aim) a lot of light with a good natural daylight color and a decent CRI (color-rendering index).

Installing halogen bulbs

Before inserting any bulb into a fixture socket, check its rating. If the halogen bulb pins don't fit the socket, don't force them—you may have the wrong bulb. Grip the protective plastic wrapping—not the bulb—as you insert the halogen bulb into the socket. As you remove the bulb from its packaging, gently pinch the end of the bulb—a little like squeezing a fast-food packet of ketchup—until its pins stick out through the plastic. Once you've pressed the bulb into the socket, slide the plastic off.

Lo-vo bulb pins are so tiny that if they become oxidized, carbon can build up in the socket, causing the bulb to flicker or not shine at all. To avoid replacing a socket, electricians typically apply an antioxidant paste to lo-vo pins before inserting them into a socket.

Touching a halogen bulb with bare fingers shortens the bulb's life. Instead, slit the plastic bag the bulb is shipped in and grip the bag as you insert the bulb.

The quality of light

White light is comprised of many colors; when the proportions of those colors change, so does the quality (hue) of light. Light's hue is assigned a correlated color temperature (CCT) measured in degrees Kelvin (K), which ranges from the 10,000°K of a blue sky to the 1,000°K of a fireplace ember. Humans tend to favor warm whites with the slightly amber hue of sunrise (2,700°K to 3,000°K), which tungsten-filament incandescent bulb-makers have successfully mimicked over the years.

The cooler white (4,100°K) of standard fluorescents is acceptable in workplaces, but it's not something that you'd want to illuminate a romantic dinner or a vanity mirror. Point being, pay attention to the CCT ratings of the halogen, CFL, or LED lamps you choose to replace incandescents. A 2,700°K to 3,000°K range will be most pleasing, and all lamp types now offer this range—but lamp quality varies greatly.

You may also see a CRI rating (color-rendering index), which refers to how "true" various colors look under a light source. CRI ratings range from 0 to 100, with ratings of 80 and above being most desirable.

Compact fluorescents (CFLs)

Fluorescent bulbs have been around for decades and have long been cooler and more energy efficient than incandescents—75% more efficient, on average. Compact fluorescents are available in a range of sizes and shapes, and many have onboard electronic ballasts. Screw-in bases allow CFLs to easily replace bulbs in many existing fixtures. (Other CFLs have the familiar bi-pin bases that fit fluorescent-only fixtures.)

CFLs can now approximate the warm daylight hues associated with incandescents. Producing lots of bright, diffuse light, CFLs are good for ambient and task lighting. Typically good for 10,000 hours, they last about ten times as long as incandescents. The knock on CFLs is that they contain 4 mg to 5 mg of mercury—very toxic—so you must be careful cleaning up a broken bulb and be diligent about recycling them. Though eclipsed by LEDs, CFLs will still be found in workshops, garages, and outbuildings for a while.

PRO TIP

If you want to dim halogen, CFL, or LED bulbs, read their specifications carefully. Some types are dimmable, but only with certain dimmers.

AN LED RETROFIT: CONVERTING AN INCANDESCENT FIXTURE

It probably takes more time to write about retrofitting an LED fixture than to do it. Turn off the power to the fixture, and use a voltage tester to be sure it's off. Remove the fixture's cover plate and unscrew the incandescent bulb. Screw the threaded adapter into the fixture socket. The other end of the adapter is an orange plastic quick-disconnect connector that snaps to a matching connector on the LED housing. Snap together the two cast-aluminum pieces of the housing and cover, then screw the cover to the recessed can with three screws.

Similar retrofit kits fit either 3-in. or 4-in. cans. Although all come with some means of dissipating excess heat, the model shown, from DMF Lighting®, features an integral heat sink. But the beauty is in the eyes of the beholder: The 650-lumen lamp is dimmable to 5%, and though of comparable brightness to a 50-watt incandescent, it consumes less than 12 watts.

This simple kit can convert an incandescent ceiling fixture into an energy-saving LED fixture. Clockwise from lower right: screw-in adapter, cast-aluminum trim plate, light source with heat sink.

After turning off the power to the fixture and testing to be sure, remove the trim plate and screw out the incandescent bulb. The recessed can stays put.

Snap the housing and trim plate together, screw in the adaptor, connect the (orange) quick-disconnect connector, and slide the assembly into the recessed can. Final mounting details will vary, but clips or universal mounting screws will hold the assembly to the can.

MOUNTING LIGHT FIXTURES

As shown on p. 27, there are many mounting options for boxes. The main choice is whether you nail or screw the box directly to a stud or ceiling joist or use an extendable mounting bar to which the box is attached. Either method works fine, but a box that slides along a mounting bar means you can more easily position the light fixture just where you want it.

Mounting fixtures to boxes

If mounting screws on all light fixtures were exactly the same diameter and spacing as the screw holes on all boxes, life would be simple and you'd screw the fixture directly to the box. But there are many different box sizes and configurations, and light fixtures vary considerably.

>> >> >>

CEILING FIXTURE ELEMENTS

In this basic setup, the ceiling box mounts to an adjustable bar, which is screwed to ceiling joists. The bracket is attached to the box and the fixture is screwed to the mounting bracket. All metal boxes and brackets must be grounded to be safe. Many electricians use grounding screws in both the box and the bracket, but one ground is sufficient. The metal mounting screws provide grounding continuity to box and bracket.

If the fixture has a ground wire, it must be attached to either the ground wire in the box or to the grounding screw on the mounting bracket. It's best to leave the ground wire in the box long enough to attach to the ground screw in the box, and extend out the box for attaching to the fixture ground wire.

Ceiling box · Supply cable · Adjustable bar · Grounding screw · Bare copper ground wire · Hot supply wire · Wire nut · Neutral supply wire · Mounting bracket · Bracket/Mounting screw · Grounding screw · Hot fixture lead · Neutral fixture lead · Fixture base · Globe-style bulb

MOUNTING BRACKETS

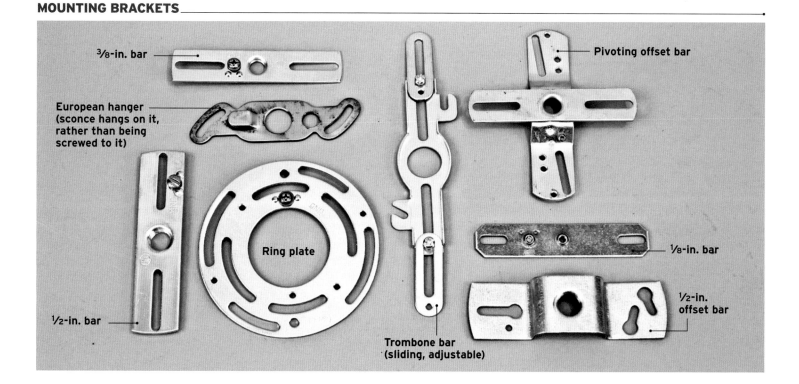

3/8-in. bar · Pivoting offset bar · European hanger (sconce hangs on it, rather than being screwed to it) · Ring plate · 1/8-in. bar · 1/2-in. bar · Trombone bar (sliding, adjustable) · 1/2-in. offset bar

MOUNTING LIGHT FIXTURES (CONTINUED)

Consequently, there are many mounting brackets to reconcile these differences.

Always examine existing outlet boxes before buying new fixtures and make sure that fixture hardware can be mounted. Otherwise, a routine installation could turn into a long, drawn-out affair with a lot of trips to the hardware store.

Here's an overview of how various fixtures mount to outlet boxes. All metal brackets, boxes, and lamp fixtures must be grounded to be safe. There are special grounding screws (10-32 machine screws, colored green) that ensure a positive connection to metal boxes or plates when installed in a threaded hole. Do not use a wood screw or the like to attach the ground wire to the box; it doesn't provide a good enough connection.

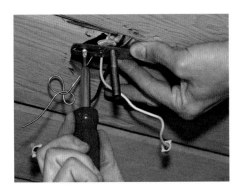
Screwing a mounting bracket with a threaded nipple to a ceiling box.

This wall sconce requires a special flanged ring bracket to mount it.

SAFETY ALERT

Most bar and box assemblies are rated for 50 lb.; if your light fixture weighs more than that, install a fan box instead.

➜ **For more on mounting ceiling boxes, see p. 81.**

An IC-rated incandescent fixture can be covered with insulation.

Flat-mounting brackets

Typically, a mounting bracket is screwed to a fixture box, and the fixture is attached to the bracket, either by machine screws or, as is more common for chandeliers, by a threaded post that screws into a threaded hole in the center of the mounting bracket. Brackets can be as simple as a flat bar with screw slots, but some adjust by sliding, whereas others are offset slightly to provide a little more room for electrical connections—and fingers. Ring brackets can be rotated so the slots line up perfectly with outlet-box and fixture screw holes.

No brackets

Some fixtures, such as the recessed lighting fixture shown on p. 85, don't require a mounting bracket. The fixture has its own junction box; once inserted into a hole cut in the ceiling, the fixture is supported by the ceiling. Integral clips and trim pieces pull the fixture tightly to the plaster or drywall ceiling. Recessed cans can be *IC-rated* (they may be covered with insulation) or may be *non-IC-rated* (cannot be covered with insulation).

Play it safe! Electrical codes require that all fixtures and devices—everything that gets installed—must be "listed" and must be recognized by the authority having jurisdiction (AHJ), usually the local inspector checking your installation. Typically, light fixtures will have an Underwriters Laboratories (UL) listing or an NRTL listing. If an inspector doesn't see a UL or NRTL sticker, he or she could ask you to remove the fixture.

Pay attention to a fixture's wattage rating, usually specified on a sticker on the fixture's base. Substituting a bulb with a higher wattage can overheat and damage the fixture and, in some cases, ignite nearby combustible surfaces.

REMOVING AN EXISTING WALL SCONCE

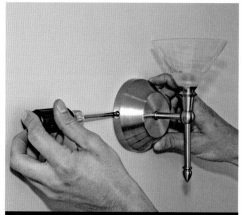

1 Test to make sure the power is off. Then remove the fixture's mounting screws.

2 As you pull the sconce away from the wall, support the glass shade if it's still attached.

3 Many low-voltage fixtures need a transformer—typically hidden under the fixture base—to operate.

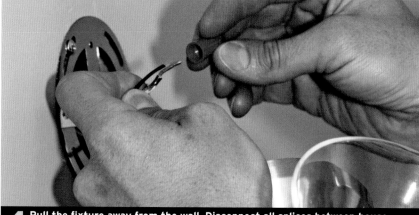

4 Pull the fixture away from the wall. Disconnect all splices between house wires and fixture wires and any wire attached to a ground screw.

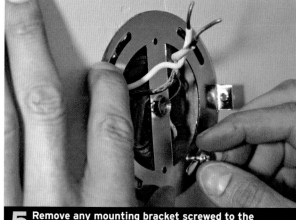

5 Remove any mounting bracket screwed to the outlet box.

When removing an existing sconce, save all the old screws and incidental hardware—you never know what you might need when you attach the new one. *Turn off power to the outlet*, then use a noncontact tester to make sure the power is off. Next use a probe tester to verify that the power is off.

Remove the fixture's mounting screws; in this case, they're on the side of the fixture base **1**. As you do so, always support the shade so it doesn't fall out and break **2**. Or you can remove the glass shade by unscrewing the small setscrews that hold it to the fixture.

Some low-voltage sconces, such as the one shown here, require a transformer, which fits under the fixture base **3**. Pull the fixture away from the wall to reveal its spliced wires. Remove the wire nuts splicing the supply wires to the fixture wires **4** and gently pull the wires apart. Then disconnect the ground wire that is attached to a green ground screw on the fixture or spliced to the fixture ground wire.

After disconnecting the wire splices, remove the mounting bracket because it won't be needed to mount the new fixture **5**. (Most likely, its holes won't line up with the new fixture's mounting screws.) Save this bracket in case you want to reinstall the old sconce elsewhere.

SAFETY ALERT

It's always best to turn off the circuit breaker or remove the fuse rather than relying on a light switch to disconnect power.

CONNECTING A NEW SCONCE

Once the old sconce has been removed, you're ready to connect the new one. Feed the incoming supply wires through the center of the new sconce's mounting bracket ❶ and then screw that bracket to the outlet box in the wall.

Screw the ground lead from the fixture (here, a yellow and green striped wire) to the ground screw on the mounting bracket ❷. Next splice the neutral supply wire to the fixture neutral, then splice the hot supply wire to the fixture hot wire ❸. Making sure that all wires are within the mounting bracket, screw the fixture base to the bracket ❹.

Attach the shade by tightening the small setscrews on the side of the shade holder ❺. Don't overtighten the set screws or the shade could crack when the bulb heats it up and it expands. Once in place, you should be able to rotate the shade slightly.

1 Feed existing supply wires through the new mounting bracket and screw it to the outlet box.

2 Attach the fixture ground wire to the ground screw on the bracket.

3 Use wire connectors to splice the supply neutral to the fixture neutral, and the supply hot wire to the fixture hot wire.

4 Gently push spliced wires under the fixture base and screw it to the mounting bracket.

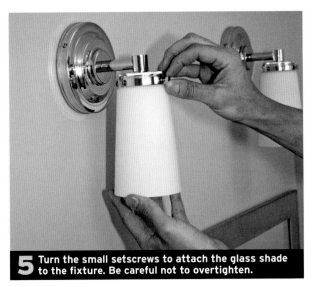

5 Turn the small setscrews to attach the glass shade to the fixture. Be careful not to overtighten.

PREPPING & MOUNTING A CEILING BOX

1 Remove the center knockout.

2 Insert the bar fitting into the knockout.

3 Screw the box bracket onto the bar fitting.

Standard ceiling box and bar assemblies are rated for 50 lb. If your light fixture weighs more than that, install a fan box instead.

➤ **For more on mounting fan boxes, see p. 158.**

Start by using a sturdy pair of needle-nose pliers or lineman's pliers to knock loose and twist out the center knockout in the box **1**. To attach the box to the bar, line up the threaded fitting on the bar to the knockout in the center of the box **2**.

Most bar or bar assemblies come with a center screw and washer designed to attach the box to the bar. Fasten the screw and washer to the threaded fitting on the bar **3**. Mounted together, the box and bar are rated to support a 50-lb. light fixture.

In new construction, this bar and box assembly would be installed before the ceilings are covered, from below. Thus the bar's tabs face down. In a retrofit, however, you'll often be screwing or nailing the tabs to joists from above (if there's access). So when retrofitting a ceiling box, bend up the tabs and they'll be easier to secure **4**.

4 Bend bar tabs upward for retrofit applications.

5 Extend the bars and screw them to joists.

Extend the bar until both ends are snug against the joists. Measure the thickness of the ceiling, adjust the height of the mounting bar so the box will be flush to the ceiling below, and screw the bar tabs to the joists **5**.

DISCONNECTING A CEILING FIXTURE

Turn off the power at the breaker panel or fuse box and test to be sure the power is off (p. 43) before disconnecting a ceiling fixture. *Warning:* Just turning off a wall switch is not safe, because there may be live wires in the ceiling box. Wear work gloves to protect against sharp metal edges, and safety glasses—many connections will be at eye level.

In the sequence shown here, the electrician swapped a modern fixture resembling a silver-plated manzanita bush ❶ with a more traditional chandelier with a fabric shade.

As quirky as the existing fixture looked, however, removing it was fairly straightforward. That is not always the case with older fixtures, which may have nonstandard mounting hardware and be attached to undersized ceiling boxes. A shallow "pancake box," for example, may not have enough room for electrical connections and would need to be replaced with a deeper 4×4 box. Or if the replacement fixture is especially heavy, you may need to install a mounting-bar assembly (p. 81) to support it. (Installation instructions typically specify mounting requirements.)

It's a good idea to have a helper support a ceiling fixture underneath while you unscrew its mounting screws. Otherwise, the fixture could come crashing down. So have a plan before you start, especially if you are working from a ladder. The fixture in our sequence wasn't terribly heavy, so the electrician's biggest challenge was snaking his forearm through the bush so he could unscrew the fixture canopy (base) from its bracket ❷.

As you lower the canopy, you will pull spliced wires out from the ceiling box ❸. If there's any question whether the power is off, avoid touching bare wire ends and test with a voltage tester. Once you're sure the power is off, twist off the wire connectors and separate the wires. Cap any bare wire ends sticking out of the box. Lower and remove the fixture. Then examine the mounting bracket screwed to the ceiling box. If it is identical to the bracket of the replacement fixture, you may be able to leave it in place and reuse it. More likely, you'll need to unscrew it ❹ and install the new mounting device.

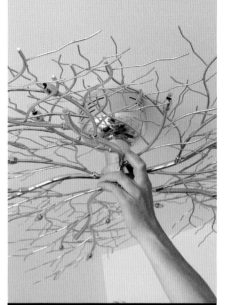

1 Turn off the power. Develop a plan for disconnecting the fixture safely.

2 Unscrew the canopy from the mounting bracket.

3 Gently lower the fixture to expose wires and connections. Unscrew wire connectors.

4 Unscrew and remove the existing mounting bracket from the ceiling box.

INSTALLING A CHANDELIER

This installation is done with the *power off*. Test to be sure. Wear work gloves to protect against sharp metal edges, and safety glasses—many connections will be at eye level.

Before you start: Review installation instructions, as each fixture is a little different. Check parts against the packing list and develop an installation plan. Often, you'll want to preassemble certain sections on the ground so you can hoist them into place and install them quickly. In our sequence, the electrician preassembled the threaded nipple to the mounting strip and then screwed that to the ceiling box.

He first attached the bare ground wire to the green grounding screw on the mounting strip ❶. On the ground, he assembled the fixture body, shortened the chain to put the fixture at the right height, slid the canopy over the chain, attached the collar loop to the last link, and wove the insulated fixture wire (and a separate bare ground) through the chain.

Holding the chain (and fixture) with one hand, he fed fixture wires through the threaded nipple ❷ attached to the ceiling box. Feed wires slowly so you don't crimp or nick their insulation. When the wires are fully through the nipple, screw the collar loop to the bottom of the threaded nipple ❸. (The collar loop is, in fact, a nut, with threads inside.) When the collar loop is snug, the fixture will be fully supported and you will have both hands free to make electrical connections.

Using wire connectors, the electrician spliced source and fixture ground wires, then neutral wires, then hot wires ❹. He carefully folded those spliced wires into the ceiling box, slid the canopy up to cover the spliced wires and the ceiling box, and then screwed on the nut that held the canopy in place ❺. A few minor tasks remained, including screwing the decorative finial onto the bottom of the fixture ❻, attaching socket sleeves, inserting bulbs, turning the power back on, and testing to see that everything worked.

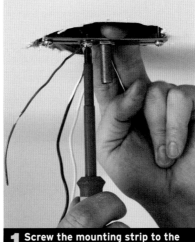

1 Screw the mounting strip to the box, then attach the ground wire.

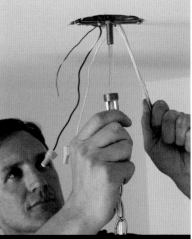

2 Carefully feed fixture wires through the threaded nipple.

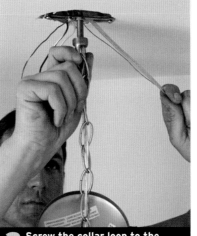

3 Screw the collar loop to the threaded nipple.

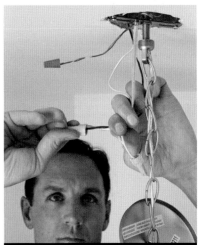

4 Use wire connectors to splice source wires to fixture leads.

5 Cover spliced wires in the box with the canopy.

6 Attach remaining parts, such as the final nut on the bottom.

INSTALLING RECESSED LIGHTING

As the name implies, recessed lighting fixtures fit into the space above the ceiling. Recessed fixtures produce a strong downward cone of light and are frequently used to provide general illumination, to illuminate work areas such as in kitchens, or to accent art, tables, or other features.

In new construction, recessed fixtures come with steel frames and bars that fasten directly to the ceiling framing. In remodel installations, as shown in the drawing at right, recessed fixtures are secured to the drywall or other wallboard via mounting clips. With the advent of LED light sources, recessed fixtures come in a wider variety of sizes and outputs and can fit in even the tightest of spaces.

RECESSED LIGHT FIXTURE

Recessed light fixtures vary. The low-voltage model in the photo sequence on the facing page has a transformer at the end of its assembly to reduce line voltage. This drawing shows a model that runs on line voltage (120v), so it has no transformer. If the unit is watertight, it will have additional trim or lens elements. Closely follow the installation instructions provided with your fixture.

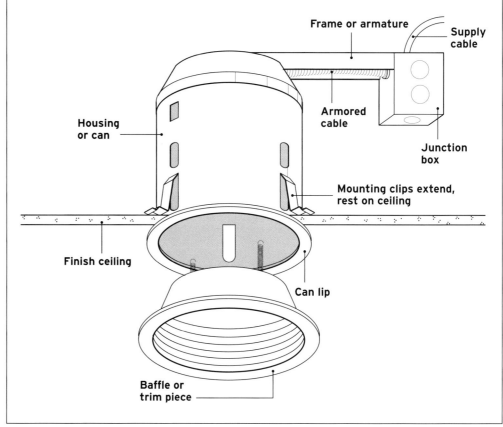

Frame or armature

Supply cable

Armored cable

Junction box

Housing or can

Mounting clips extend, rest on ceiling

Finish ceiling

Can lip

Baffle or trim piece

Retrofitting recessed lighting In retrofit installations, the supply cable to the recessed lighting unit typically comes from an existing ceiling box or nearby switch box. The supply cable feeds to an integral junction box on the fixture. Finding the nearest power source and fishing the wires often means thinking spatially: The nearest power source may be in another room or on another floor. If the recessed fixture is a low-voltage unit, such as the one shown on the facing page, it will come with a transformer, which reduces the 120v current of the supply cable.

CUTTING A CEILING HOLE FOR RECESSED LIGHTING

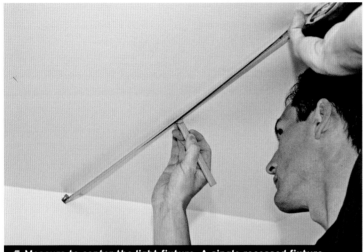

1 Measure to center the light fixture. A single recessed fixture centered in one direction or another usually looks good.

2 Drill a pilot hole.

3 Keep the drill bit aligned vertically.

4 If the can is too snug—or doesn't fit at all—enlarge the hole as needed.

5 Test-fit the fixture. Wires are housed in the (gray) junction box.

⚠ SAFETY ALERT

To minimize hitting pipes or cables when drilling into a ceiling, use a bit that's 1 in. long—just long enough to drill through the plaster or drywall. Use a cordless drill to further reduce the chances of shocks.

There's no absolute rule on where to place a recessed light, but in a small space, such as a shower alcove, a fixture centered in one direction or another will look best **1**. In addition, you may want to use a stud finder to avoid hitting ceiling joists above.

Drill a pilot hole to see what's above **2** and to make sure there's room for the can. Make the hole small because if there's an obstruction above it, you'll need to patch it. After drilling the hole, you can insert a 4-in.

piece of bent wire and rotate it to see if it hits a ceiling joist.

Also, use the small pilot hole to keep the point of a hole-saw blade from drifting. Keep the drill vertical, and the circle of the sawblade parallel to the ceiling **3**. There are special carbide hole saws for drilling through plaster. A bimetal hole saw will also cut through drywall, but plaster will quickly dull the blade. Wear goggles.

If the hole saw is the right size for the can, you won't need to enlarge it. But for

the light shown here, the saw was a shade too small, so the installer used a jab saw to enlarge the hole slightly **4**. In a pinch, you can also use just a jab saw to cut the hole.

Test-fit the unit **5**. Although you want the can to fit snugly, the unit's junction box and transformer also need to fit through. The black box about to enter the hole is the transformer.

WIRING A RECESSED FIXTURE

To wire a recessed fixture, remove a Romex knockout from the unit's integral junction box **①**. Inside the knockout, there is a spring-loaded strain-relief clamp that will grip the incoming cable, so you don't need to insert a Romex connector. Run a length of (unconnected) Romex cable from the nearest power source and feed it into the knockout just removed. Of course, the cable must *not* be energized when you are working on it. (To wire the box with AC or MC cable, remove one of the circular ½-in. knockouts and insert an appropriate connector.)

➡ **For more on connectors, see p. 30.**

Inside the fixture's junction box will be two sets of wires that were spliced at the factory. They connect the secondary wires that run from the transformer to the socket. (At the transformer, the current is reduced from 120v to 12v, so polarity is no longer an issue.) There are also three unconnected fixture leads in the box, to which you'll splice the supply wires **②**.

Using wire connectors, connect the incoming ground wire to the green fixture lead, the incoming neutral to the white lead, and the hot wire to the black fixture lead **③**.

Tuck the spliced wire groups into the fixture junction box **④**. At the right of the junction box is a piece of threaded rod that can be adjusted to support the transformer at the correct height. Snap the junction box cover **⑤** closed. As with other outlet boxes, code determines the number of wires you can splice in a fixture junction box, based on the cubic inches in the box.

1 Remove a knockout from the junction box.

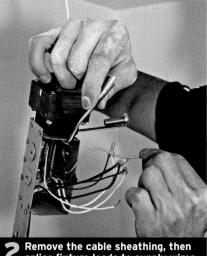
2 Remove the cable sheathing, then splice fixture leads to supply wires.

3 Always connect the ground wires first.

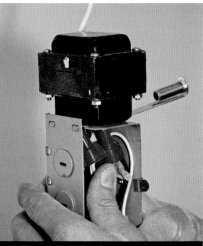
4 Tuck the spliced wires into the box.

5 Close the junction box cover, being careful not to pinch wires.

SECURING THE CAN

1 Feed the cable and the now-wired fixture into the hole.

2 If the fit is tight, use your fist to seat the lip of the fixture flush to the ceiling.

3 Use a screwdriver to engage the spring-loaded clips that secure the fixture.

4 Insert the bulb with steady pressure till all pins seat.

5 Install the trim assembly. The black ring is a moisture-proof gasket.

PRO TIP

If you have access to the space above a ceiling fixture, staple the Romex to a joist, leaving at least 12 in. of free cable so you can push the fixture components into the hole. A cable that's too short may prevent this.

Once the recessed lighting fixture has been wired, push the fixture into the hole, being careful not to bind the Romex cable as you do so **1**. If the fit is snug, use the side of your fist to seat the lip of the fixture flush to the ceiling **2**.

Use a screwdriver to push up the spring-loaded clips that pivot and press against the back face of the drywall to hold the fixture snugly in place **3**. To remove the fixture later, pop out the clips.

Insert the bulb (the fixture here uses an MR-16 bi-pin halogen bulb) into the fixture

socket **4**. Here, the installer is gripping the lamp's rim, to keep the sides of the lamp clean. Skin oils can cause hot spots on the very hot-running lamps, shortening the life of the bulb. The lamp pins should seat securely. Install the trim piece—this one has a gasket. Snap in the lamp and socket, and push the assembly up into the can. The three arms on the side of the assembly will grip the inside of the can **5**.

PRO TIP

The pros apply a tiny dab of anti-oxidant paste to the lamp pins before seating them in a fixture socket to prevent oxidation. A good practice, but not imperative.

UNDERCABINET LED FIXTURES

Light fixtures mounted to the underside of upper cabinets deliver focused light to kitchen countertops and other work areas. Because of their relatively slim profile, fluorescents were long the choice for under-cabinet lights—followed by halogens. But here again, LEDs are winning the day. LED fixtures are even easier to hide behind upper-cabinet valances, they sip energy and run cool, and they provide plenty of light.

In the sequence shown here, we replaced hot-burning halogens with LED under-cabinet lights. Thus we were able to connect our new LED fixtures to NM cable already in place. If any section of your wiring will be exposed, however, you must run metal-clad cable such as BX, MC, or MCAP. For more on metal-clad cable, see pp. 28 and 29.

Important: Undercabinet LED fixture sections come in varying lengths. Some come with separate junction boxes in which to splice wires, which then snap to prewired lighting sections, whereas other LED fixtures—such as the one we installed—house both wire connections and LED light strips. Always follow the installation instructions provided with the light fixture you purchase.

Identify the circuit breaker controlling the fixture you want to replace. Turn off the power to that fixture and use a voltage tester to make sure it's off. Remove the light lens cover from the existing fixture ❶, then unscrew or unsnap the heat diffuser ❷, if any. Unscrew the fixture housing from the underside of the upper cabinet, remove the cable clamp securing the incoming supply cable, and disconnect all wire connections ❸. Ideally, the supply wires will be 8 in. to 12 in. long.

Feed existing house wires through a knockout in the new fixture and tighten the cable clamp. Mount the housing for the new LED fixture to the underside of the cabinet ❹. (Note the LED strip along the front edge of the housing.) Connect supply wires to fixture leads sticking out of the wiring compartment: Connect the ground wire

first, then neutral, then hot ❺. To complete the circuit from the wiring compartment to the LED strip on the housing, snap together the quick-release plugs ❻. (To join additional sections, remove the knockout from the right end of the housing.)

Carefully fold the wires into the assembly and snap the wiring compartment to the housing ❼. Finally, swing the plastic light diffuser into place ❽.

1 Test to be sure the power is off, then remove the light lens cover.

2 Unscrew the heat diffuser (heat sink) from the halogen undercabinet fixture.

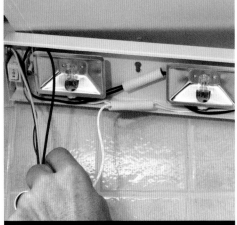

3 Unscrew the fixture housing, remove the cable clamp securing the incoming supply cable, and disconnect all wire connections.

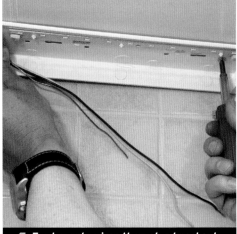

4 Feed supply wires through a knockout in the housing and mount the new fixture to the underside of the cabinet.

5 Using wire connectors, splice supply wires to lead wires sticking out of the wiring compartment.

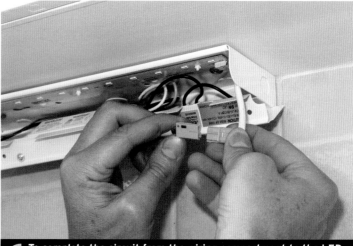

6 To complete the circuit from the wiring compartment to the LED strip on the housing, snap together the quick-release plugs.

7 Fold wires into the assembly and snap the wiring compartment to the housing.

8 Restore power and shut the light lens cover to protect the LEDs and diffuse the light more evenly.

Halogen hot spots?

Some electricians prefer not to use halogen strips under cabinets because the individual lamps are visible as "train tracks" when installed over a dark, shiny countertop. Plus halogen bulbs get hot. If you want more uniform illumination without such hot spots, go with LEDs.

LOW-VOLTAGE FIXTURES

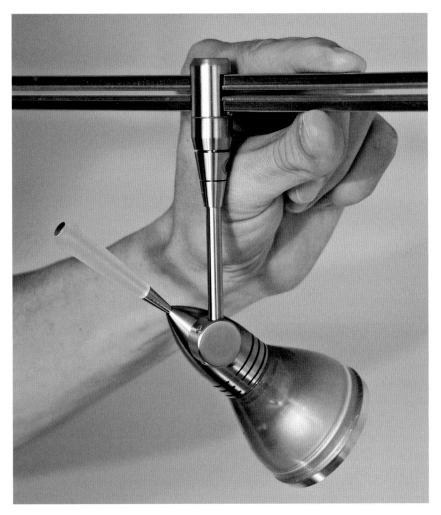

Low-voltage tracks are safe to touch, but you should shut off power to the circuit before working on them.

Safety and low-voltage systems

Experienced electricians often handle low-voltage tracks while those parts are energized—with 12v of current—downstream from the transformer. If you install your lo-vo system correctly, and are careful never to touch the supply wires that run to the transformer, you can touch energized lo-vo tracks and install light fixtures without getting shocked. But if you have any confusion about which wires are 120v and which are 12v, shut the power off before doing any work on your lo-vo system. Best to be too cautious . . . and stay safe.

Low-voltage lighting systems are installed inside and outside houses and typically operate on 12v current, so they require a transformer to reduce standard house voltage from 120v. Transformers vary—some are coil-wound magnets, whereas others are electronic—so follow the installation instructions provided with your unit.

➤ **For more on low-voltage systems, see p. 106.**

Lo-vo systems have become extremely popular because, with voltage roughly the same as a car battery, there is no risk of shock or electrocution. However, the large currents used in some instances can create a fire hazard if connections are poor. Systems can also be creatively constructed from a variety of different lighting materials. Lo-vo systems can generally be controlled by standard switches or dimmers, but you should check the literature that comes with your system.

Though it's safe to touch the tracks of a lo-vo system, you should turn off the power when working on the system. The upstream part of the system (between the transformer and the power source) has 120v power, which could deliver a fatal shock. On the low-voltage side, there is a potential to short the system and damage the transformer.

After installing all the parts and doing a preliminary check of the system, it's safe to energize the system. (*Note:* Because any high-intensity bulb can get very hot, do not install any cable fixtures within 4 in. of a combustible surface.) Track-lighting systems are inherently complex, so read the instructions carefully before you begin the installation.

INSTALLING LOW-VOLTAGE CABLE LIGHTING

Track lighting systems may have a remote transformer or a surface-mounted transformer. There is also a range of cable standoff supports, both rigid and adjustable, mounting to walls and ceilings; they must be mounted solidly to framing if they are to keep position when the cable is tensioned. Cables are typically spaced 4$\frac{1}{2}$ in. or 8 in. apart. The illustration has been adapted from installation instructions for a product from Alfa Lighting Systems; your instructions may vary.

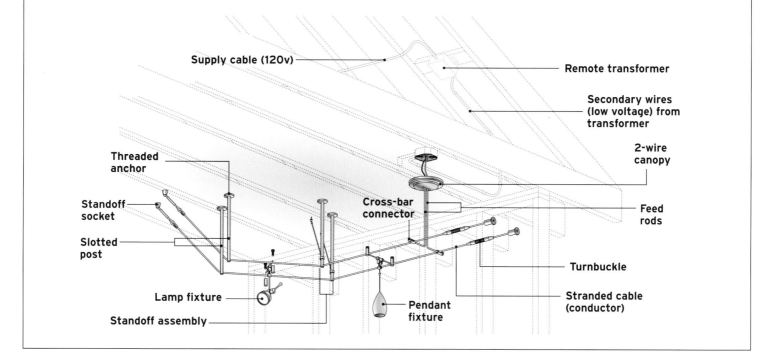

ANCHORING LOW-VOLTAGE STANDOFFS

The key to a good-looking, correctly functioning cable system is getting the cables taut and level. Thus your first task in installing a lo-vo system is finding solid locations in which to anchor the cables. In this installation, the principal anchors were standoffs in each corner so the cable could be stretched around the perimeter of the room. Alternatively, you can anchor standoffs in a ceiling to support cables and bulbs. Standoffs are also called *re-routers* because cables often change direction as they emerge.

Use a laser level to establish level anchoring points around the room. Predrill holes in the plaster for anchor screws ❶. Plaster is harder than drywall and there may be lath nails in the way, so wear goggles and have extra drill bits on hand.

Because cables will be stretched taut, standoff anchors must be screwed to wood framing—in this case, into doubled studs in the corner ❷. Use screws at least

>> >> >>

❶ Predrill all anchor holes.

❷ Sink the anchors into the framing.

ANCHORING LOW-VOLTAGE STANDOFFS (CONTINUED)

2 in. long to attach the anchors. After sliding a chrome base plate (washer) over the anchor, screw the standoff socket to the exterior threading of the anchor ❸. Insert the ball end of the fiberglass rod into the standoff socket ❹. This ball-and-socket assembly allows the standoff to swivel freely so you can fine-tune the cable positions. The cables will be spaced 4¹/₂ in. apart.

3 Screw on the standoff socket.

4 Insert the standoff into the socket.

RUNNING CABLE

The next step in installing this system is to run the cable. Note the standoff at the top of photo ❶. Because the walls in this room were only 12 ft. apart, both cables could be run through a single angled standoff with two slotted posts, located in each corner. If the walls are farther apart, you may need a cable support in the middle of the run.

Measure the cable length you need and cut it 3 in. to 4 in. longer than your measurement so you can insert the ends into turnbuckles without having to struggle. Once you tighten the turnbuckles and tension the cable you can snip off any excess cable. On the other hand, if you cut a cable too short, you'll have to discard it and start again with a new piece.

Place each cable into a slotted post, rather than pulling it through the slot, whose sharp edges can cut into stranded cable ❷. (This is a quirk of the particular system shown here; other standoff types allow you to pull cable more freely.)

After placing the cable into a slotted post, screw on the post cap to keep it from popping out when the cable is tensioned ❸. As you place the cable into the subsequent standoffs, loosely tension it to take up the slack ❹. With this system, the second cable will be about 4¹/₂ in. from the first.

1 Cut the cable a bit long.

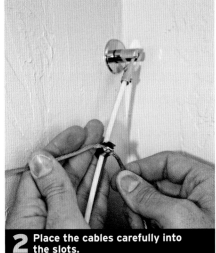

2 Place the cables carefully into the slots.

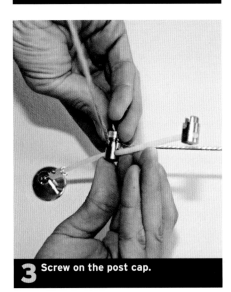

3 Screw on the post cap.

4 Tension the cable to take up the slack.

TENSIONING CABLES

Correctly installed, the cables of a low-voltage system should be more or less horizontal and equally spaced (parallel along their length). As with most systems, this installation uses turnbuckles to tighten the cables after they have been placed in the standoffs. The cables' Kevlar® core prevents stretching or sagging once the lightweight fixtures have been installed.

Once you've loosely run the cable, insert an end into a turnbuckle ❶. The cable end feeds in the end of the turnbuckle and exits in a slot in the middle. Tighten the setscrew(s) on the assembled turnbuckle to keep the cable from pulling out, then trim the excess cable sticking out ❷. Don't rush trimming the cable: Wait until you've made final adjustments to the whole layout before trimming.

A turnbuckle's center post has a thumbscrew with threads on both ends. As you turn the thumbscrew in one direction, it draws tight both ends of a cable; turn in the opposite direction to slacken cable tension ❸. With cable attached to both sides of a turnbuckle, the installer may struggle to draw the cable tight enough to join them ❹. This is a good reason not to trim the cable until the turnbuckle starts tightening both ends.

A certain amount of adjustment is necessary after both cables are taut. Here, the installer adjusts the cables so that the standoff comes out of the corner at a 45-degree angle, thus ensuring that the wires will be equidistant ❺.

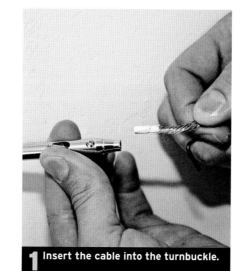

1 Insert the cable into the turnbuckle.

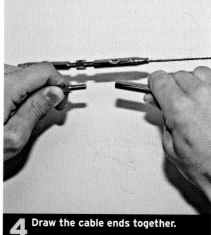

2 Trim and discard excess cable.

3 One section of the turnbuckle threads into the thumbscrew.

4 Draw the cable ends together.

5 Fine-tune cable angles and spacing.

PRO TIP

When working with stranded cable, tape the cable ends and then cut in the middle of the tape to keep the strands from unraveling.

LOCATING THE CANOPY

Once the tensioned cable has been installed, you'll need to locate the canopy. The canopy (also called a canopy feed) receives low-voltage current from the transformer and delivers it to the cables. The canopy mounts to a junction box on the ceiling or wall.

Before installing the canopy, make its holes—or those of its mounting bracket—line up to the holes of the junction box you'll be installing in the wall or ceiling ❶. The slotted mounting bar on the back of this 2-wire canopy can fit several box widths.

If the canopy will be ceiling mounted, drill a hole for it. To minimize the mess, use a hole-cutting tool with a dust cover ❷. *Note:* A screw gun with a ½-in. chuck will accept large-shank tools such as the one shown here. Set the hole-cutting tool's blade to the diameter of the junction box ❸. For large holes, this tool has a counterweight that attaches to the right side of the cutting bar to balance the torque of the blade.

Hold the cover of the tool snug against the ceiling so it can contain the dust ❹. Wait a few seconds for the dust to settle inside the cover before lowering the tool.

PRO TIP

Fixture canopies are often polished chrome, which is easy to cloud with fingerprints. Wearing lightweight plastic gloves solves the problem; nitrile plastic gloves are especially flexible.

1 Make sure the screw holes line up.

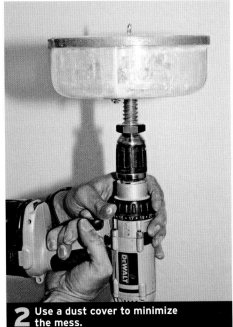

2 Use a dust cover to minimize the mess.

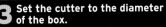

3 Set the cutter to the diameter of the box.

4 Hold the cover snug against the ceiling as you drill.

MOUNTING THE BOX & WIRING THE TRANSFORMER

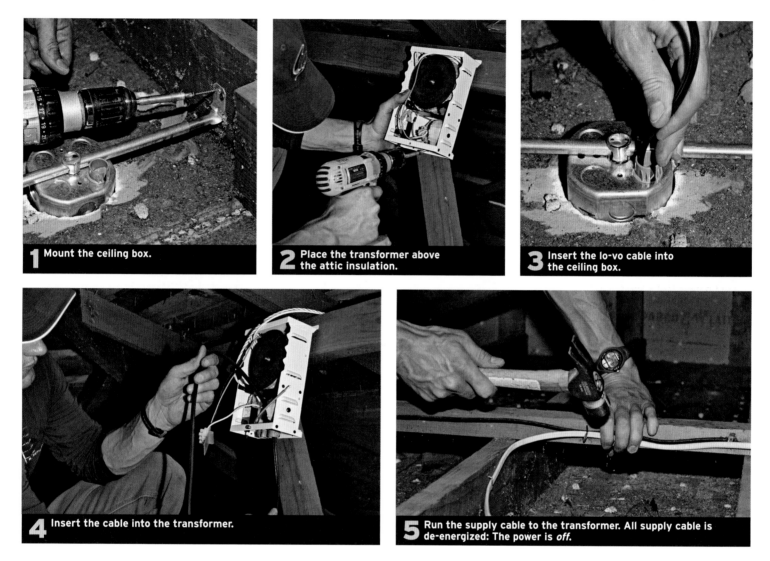

1 Mount the ceiling box.

2 Place the transformer above the attic insulation.

3 Insert the lo-vo cable into the ceiling box.

4 Insert the cable into the transformer.

5 Run the supply cable to the transformer. All supply cable is de-energized: The power is *off*.

After the canopy has been located, it's time to mount the box and wire the transformer. The transformer shown here permits 12v or 24v wiring. Your installation may vary, so follow the instructions provided. Note: All wiring is done with the power *off*.

When retrofitting a ceiling box, bend up the bar tabs to make them easier to nail or screw. Extend the support bar until its tabs are snug against joists, adjust the height of the bar so the box is flush to the ceiling, and then screw the tabs to joists **1**.

➡ **For more on installing ceiling boxes, see p. 81.**

Install the transformer above the insulation so that its vents work properly and the unit can be accessed easily **2**. Run the secondary (lo-vo) cable between the transformer and the ceiling box, stapling it within 12 in. of a box and every 4 ft. along its run **3**. Feed the other end of the lo-vo cable into the transformer **4**. The gray cable connectors are one-way clamps: easy to insert but difficult to pull out.

Run the supply cable (120v) from an existing switch to the transformer **5**. Protect the cable by stapling it to the side of a joist or to a runner added for the purpose.

>> >> >>

MOUNTING THE BOX & WIRING THE TRANSFORMER (CONTINUED)

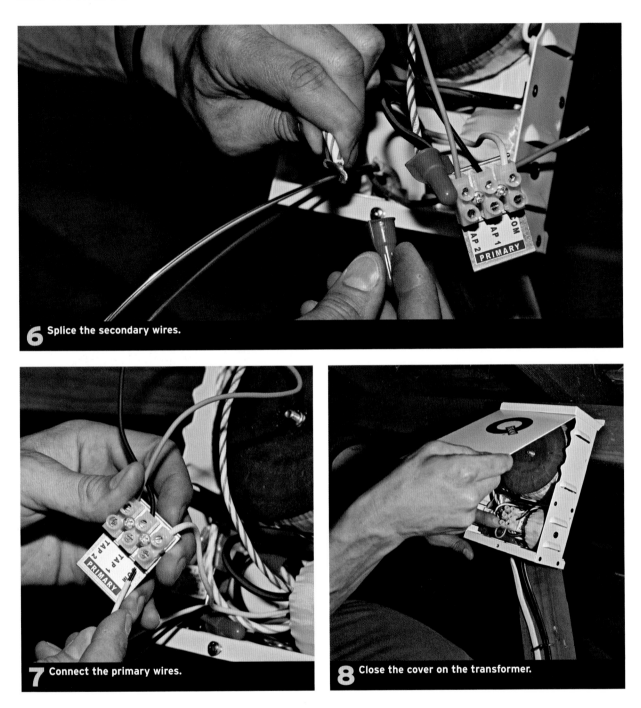

6 Splice the secondary wires.

7 Connect the primary wires.

8 Close the cover on the transformer.

After stripping ½ in. of insulation off the wire ends, use wire connectors to splice the secondary wires, which run from the transformer to the ceiling box **6**. Next, splice the primary ground wires, using a wire connector. Then connect the primary neutral to the common (neutral) terminal, as shown, and the primary hot wire to one of the tap terminals. Tighten the terminal screws to grip the wires **7**.

Close the transformer cover to protect the connections inside **8**.

INSTALLING THE CANOPY

The canopy is installed after the transformer has been wired. Install the mounting bracket to the new ceiling box; it will support the canopy that supplies lo-vo power to the cables ❶. The wire hanging from the box is the secondary (lo-vo) cable from the transformer.

Separate and strip the two wires in the lo-vo cable and solder their ends. Soldering fine-strand wire makes it solid and unlikely to smash flat as you tighten down the set screws on the canopy terminals. Soldered wire is also less likely to arc and overheat ❷. (Note the tiny Allen wrench inserted into the setscrew on the right of the photo.)

Use mounting screws that are long enough to extend beyond the canopy face ❸; they're faster to install than short screws because they give you room to maneuver.

Slide the canopy over the mounting screws and turn the canopy cap nuts onto the mounting screws ❹. When the nuts bottom out on the screws, continue turning the cap nuts, which will turn the extra-long screws back up into the box. This will make the canopy nice and snug.

1 Attach the mounting bracket to the ceiling box.

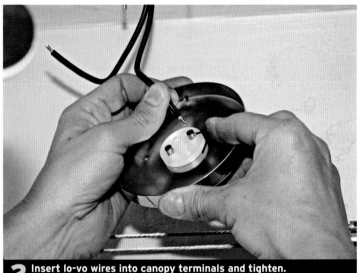

2 Insert lo-vo wires into canopy terminals and tighten.

3 Using extra-long mounting screws eases the installation.

4 Install the cap nuts on the mounting screws.

ATTACHING THE FEED RODS & FIXTURES

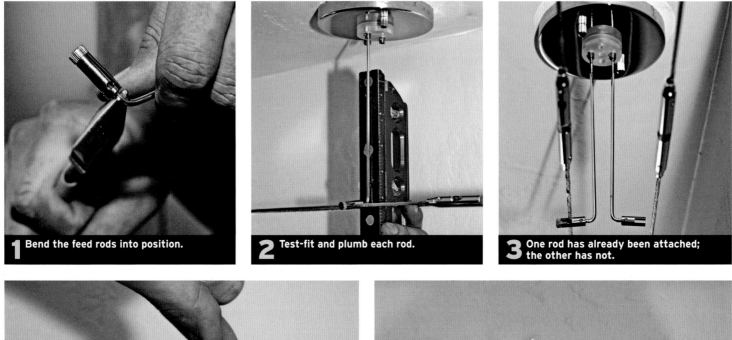

1 Bend the feed rods into position.

2 Test-fit and plumb each rod.

3 One rod has already been attached; the other has not.

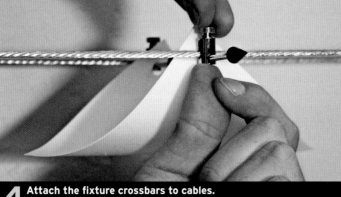

4 Attach the fixture crossbars to cables.

5 Once everything is installed, turn on the power.

The final task for installing a low-voltage system is adding the feed rods and fixtures. The feed rods transfer low-voltage current from the canopy terminals to the cables. Setscrews on the terminals secure the rods.

Because the canopy is centered over the two cables, you may need to bend the feed rods to bring them to the cables **1**. Secure the rods in a vise between two wood scraps (to minimize marring the finish) and bend them at the point equal to the distance from the canopy to the cables. Some systems will provide horizontal connectors for this purpose, eliminating the need for bending.

Bend the first rod and test-fit it, using a torpedo level to ensure that the rod is plumb and the cable is still level **2**. If the first rod fits well, use it as a template for the second. Repeat the process with the second feed rod. Note that rod ends are slotted like the standoff posts that anchor the cables in the corners of the room. A cap nut screws on to the slotted rod end to capture the cable **3**.

Insert the bulbs into the fixtures before you attach fixtures to the cables. If your system uses halogen bulbs, don't touch them with your bare hands because the oil in your skin will shorten the bulb life. In general, fixtures need to connect to both cables to become energized, so each fixture has a crossbar that spans the cables. Hand-tighten the fixture connectors so they're snug **4**. After you've installed all the fixtures and surveyed the system, turn on the power **5**.

INSTALLING LOW-VOLTAGE MONORAIL TRACK LIGHTING

Before installing lo-vo monorail track lighting, turn off the power at the breaker panel or fuse box. As with any low-voltage system, a transformer will reduce the 120v current to 12v or 24v. Because monorail track systems have a lot of small parts that are easily lost, don't open the packages until you're ready to use the parts.

In cross-section, the monorail track is two square pieces of chrome-plated copper conductor sandwiched together with a clear (insulating) plastic piece. Although the track is sturdy, it can be bent freehand or shaped against a curved piece of plywood.

LOW-VOLTAGE MONORAIL SYSTEM

In the installation shown, the transformer is surface-mounted in a circular housing. Although the transformer housing must be mounted to a ceiling box to be adequately supported, individual standoff supports can be anchored in drywall or plaster alone because the track and fixtures are lightweight. The illustrations have been adapted from installation instructions from a product by Tech Lighting®; your instructions may be different.

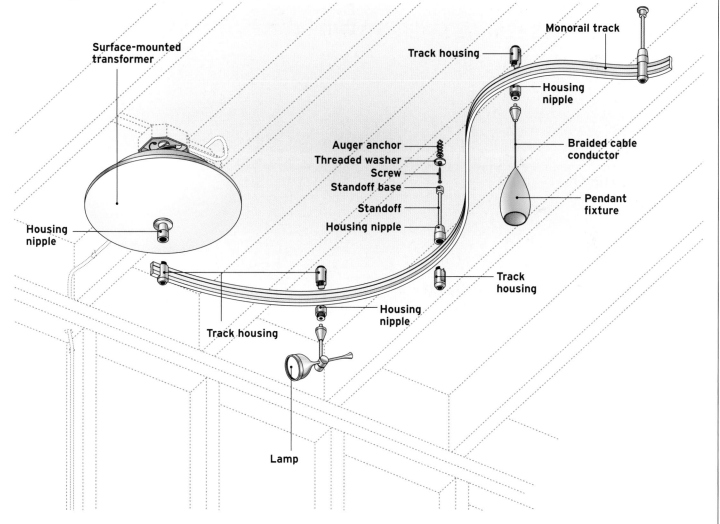

Surface-mounted transformer

Housing nipple

Track housing

Auger anchor
Threaded washer
Screw
Standoff base
Standoff
Housing nipple

Track housing

Housing nipple

Lamp

Track housing

Monorail track

Housing nipple

Braided cable conductor

Pendant fixture

Track housing

LOCATING THE TRACK & STANDOFFS

If possible, before working overhead shape the track sections of your monorail system and preassemble them on the floor, then use a plumb bob or laser level to plumb up to the ceiling. First determine where you'll place the transformer box for the system, then mark off the standoffs that will mount the track to the ceiling.

With a helper holding one end, hold sections of the track against the ceiling and mark off standoff points at the track ends, where sections meet, and at intervals suggested by the fixture maker—usually, every 3 ft. ❶. Standoffs have multiple parts, which anchor them to the ceiling and support the track (see "Standoff Parts" below).

Fortunately, because the track weighs little you can mount standoffs almost anywhere on a drywall or plaster ceiling, using auger anchors with wide threads. (That is, you don't need to mount standoffs to framing.) Sink the anchors flush, then screw a threaded washer to each anchor ❷. Then, using a setscrew, screw the standoff base to that threaded washer ❸.

Mount all the standoffs so that when you raise the monorail again you can attach it quickly to the standoffs and to the bottom of the transformer housing. If you need to reposition a standoff or two, it's easy to patch the small holes left by misplaced standoff anchors.

1 Mark out the standoff locations on the ceiling.

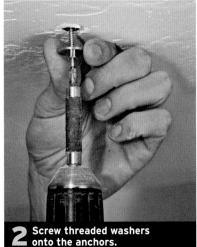

2 Screw threaded washers onto the anchors.

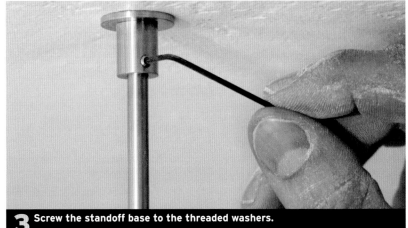

3 Screw the standoff base to the threaded washers.

STANDOFF PARTS

Standoff supports for monorail track systems consist of many small parts.

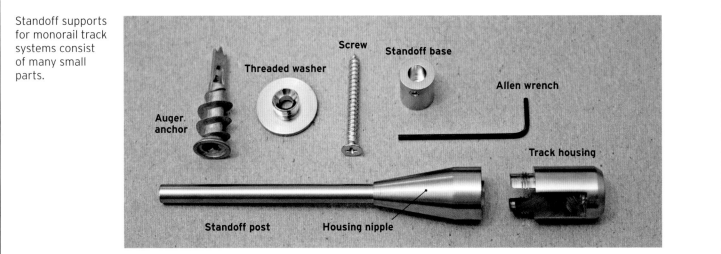

Auger anchor · Threaded washer · Screw · Standoff base · Allen wrench · Track housing · Standoff post · Housing nipple

MOUNTING & WIRING THE TRANSFORMER

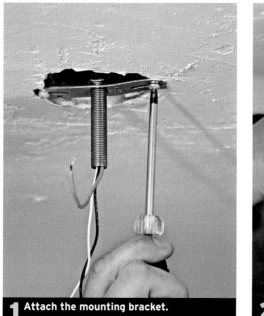

1 Attach the mounting bracket.

2 Feed the supply wires into the housing.

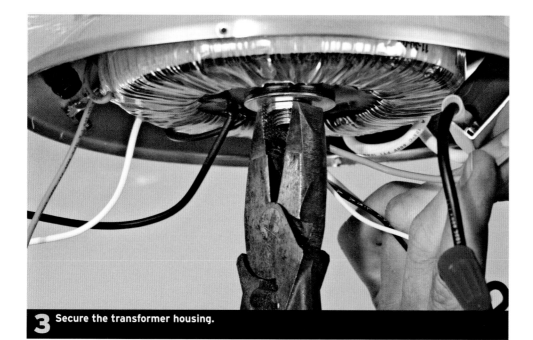

3 Secure the transformer housing.

Once the standoffs are installed, mount the ceiling box to a ceiling joist and attach the bracket that will support the transformer **1**. In this case, a nipple screws into the bracket and runs through the center of the transformer housing. The supply wires sticking out of the box will connect to the primary leads on the transformer.

➔ **For more on mounting boxes, see p. 81.**

Feed the supply wires into the center of the transformer housing **2**, push the top piece of the housing snug against the ceiling box, slip a washer over the end of the nipple, and then tighten the inside nut that secures the transformer housing **3**. The circular mass inside the housing is a magnetic transformer, which has a series of copper coils.

>> >> >>

MOUNTING & WIRING THE TRANSFORMER (CONTINUED)

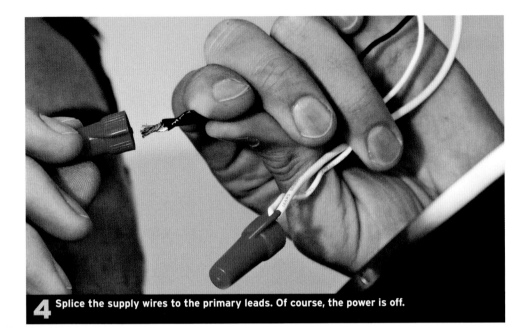

4 Splice the supply wires to the primary leads. Of course, the power is off.

5 Test the connections and then close the housing.

Many transformers come with secondary leads preattached, so that the installer need only splice supply wires to the primary fixture leads. Using the wire connectors provided, splice the ground wires first, then the neutral leads, and finally the hot wires **4**. When all the wire connections are snug—gently tug on the spliced wires to be sure—close the transformer housing by snapping the bottom to the top and installing the screws provided **5**. (By the way, the fat striped wires are secondary leads, which run from the transformer to the lo-vo power feed that energizes the track.)

HANGING THE TRACK

1 Place the track into the track housing.

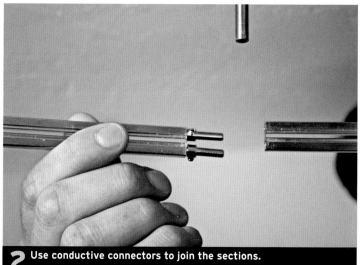

2 Use conductive connectors to join the sections.

3 Attach the track to the standoffs.

PRO TIP

If you can't find anyone to help you support the track, bend short lengths of coat hanger into Z-shaped hanger brackets. Drill a 1/4-in. hole into the ceiling and insert one end of the bracket; the other end supports the track. Once the track is up, remove the hangers and patch the holes with joint compound.

With the transformer secured and the standoffs installed in the ceiling, you're ready to hang the track. Get help supporting the track until you have two or three points secured. Place the track into the track housing—the lowest piece on that assembly—then screw on the housing nipple **1**. Once that's done, tighten the setscrew that holds the nipple to the standoff post.

Where track sections meet, join them with conductive connectors and support the junction with a standoff **2**. Once the track is supported at several points, loosely attach the track housing and nipple assemblies at several points, slide them beneath the support rails, and use an Allen wrench to tighten the setscrews that join the nipples to the standoff posts **3**. Make sure the connections are tight.

Because the housing on the bottom of the transformer has setscrews on the side and the bottom, you'll need two different sizes of Allen wrenches. Loosen the small screw on the side of the housing nipple so you can

>> >> >>

HANGING THE TRACK (CONTINUED)

4 The transformer support requires two wrenches.

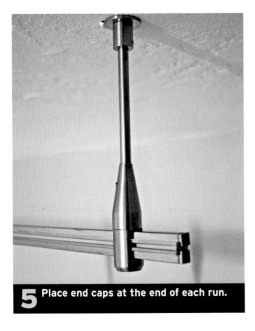

5 Place end caps at the end of each run.

turn it onto the threads of the housing. Once the nipple is tight on the housing, retighten that small screw. Then use a ³/₁₆-in. Allen wrench to tighten the setscrew on the bottom of the housing **4**. Finally, retighten all connections and place end caps on the ends of the track **5**.

INSTALLING THE LIGHT FIXTURES

1 To attach lights, invert the track housing and screw on the nipple.

2 Insert the shaft of the light fixture.

3 Support pendant lights with braided cable.

4 Pendant light supports screw into housing nipples.

5 Energize the system for 20 minutes, then make sure the connections aren't overheated.

Once the monorail tracks are installed, you can add the light fixtures. The fixtures require a two-part assembly that straddles the monorail track; note that in this case the housing and nipples are inverted. Insert the housing on top of the track and the nipple on the bottom **1**. Screw the pieces together, insert the shaft of the light fixture into the inverted nipple **2**, then screw the fixture nipple onto the threaded housing nipple and hand tighten it.

Attaching the pendant lights is similar, although the light pendants use braided cable rather than a solid shaft. Braided cable can be shortened if necessary, allowing you to install the pendant lights at the same or varying heights **3**. Once you've adjusted the pendant cables, tighten the fixture nipple to the housing nipple on the track **4**.

Most manufacturers recommend energizing the system and turning the lights on for 20 minutes or 30 minutes before checking the monorail connections to see if any are hot to the touch. Warm is normal, but hot connections should be retightened **5**. Do not, however, touch any halogen lights; they are certain to be hot enough to burn you (which is normal).

PRO TIP

After installing a complex assembly such as monorail track lighting, disconnect the power and retighten all connections after the first 10 to 20 hours of use.

DOORBELLS, THERMOSTATS & ALARMS

WIRELESS AND INTERNET-connected devices have transformed our homes. Once-lowly doorbells, thermostats, and smoke alarms have sprouted new capabilities and can now be accessed by smartphones. As such devices become more affordable, it makes sense to replace them when they don't work, rather than trying to repair them.

Replacing low-voltage controls such as doorbells and thermostats will be familiar turf if you've read the earlier chapters. Basically, doorbell buttons and thermostats are switches. Their high-tech replacements may be powered by low-voltage wiring and/or batteries. Or, as in the case of interconnected smoke and carbon monoxide (CO) alarms, they may be hard-wired to 120v house current or powered solely by long-lasting lithium batteries.

Generally, you can safely test or handle *low-voltage wires* without turning off the power. However, we prefer to err on the side of caution, primarily to prevent damage to equipment if the wires are inadvertently shorted. Turn off power to the circuit and test to be sure. Always **turn off the power and test** before replacing hard-wired smoke and CO alarms, or before removing the covers of line-voltage thermostats.

DOORBELLS

THERMOSTATS

SMOKE AND CO ALARMS

USEFUL VIDEO DOORBELL FEATURES

According to law-enforcement professionals, most burglars first ring the doorbell to see if anyone's at home. So installing a video doorbell seems like a smart way to upgrade your home's security—especially now that video doorbells are affordable (less than $200) and easy to install in 5 to 10 minutes.

Assessing and installing a video doorbell comprises most of this section, followed by brief sections on repairing and replacing conventional doorbells. In this section we'll look at the features and installation of the Ring™ Video Doorbell.

Basically, a quality video doorbell is an Internet-connected device that combines a wide-angle HD camera, a motion detector, and a microphone and speakers to enable two-way conversation. The motion sensors activate the camera and trigger instant alerts whenever they detect motion or when someone rings the doorbell. Thanks to infrared LEDs, the device has "night vision" so it can sense movement day or night.

The Ring Video Doorbell communicates wirelessly through your Wi-Fi system. Once you have downloaded and configured a free Ring app, alerts will be sent automatically to your smartphone or tablet. (Your mobile device's operating system must be at least iOS® 7.1+ or Android 4.0.) This will enable you to answer the door from wherever you are. You can speak with and see whoever is at the door and thus greet a friend, instruct a delivery person, or deter a burglar. (The customer videos at www.ring.com are great fun.)

In addition to sending alerts to your smartphone or tablet, a video doorbell can be connected wirelessly to a separate chime unit that will sound when the doorbell button is pressed.

An inexpensive extension of this security system, Cloud Video Recording, is a running log of all activity recorded by your video doorbell. For a modest monthly or annual fee, you can access and download any event recorded within the last six months. You can also install additional video cameras (see the sidebar on p. 243) to increase the area you monitor around your house.

Who goes there? A video doorbell controlled by your smartphone enables you to answer the door from wherever you are. Some of your visitors will be surprised to hear from you.

INSTALLING A BATTERY-POWERED VIDEO DOORBELL

A Ring Video Doorbell can run on its built-in rechargeable battery, which is good for 6 to 12 months of operation between charges. The device can also be hard-wired to existing low-voltage doorbell wires. We'll look at installing a battery-powered unit first.

First remove the existing doorbell button (see photo 1 on p. 111).

If you are attaching the device to wood or vinyl siding, all the tools and screws you need are included in Ring's installation kit. If you are attaching to stucco siding, concrete, or brick, however, you will need a carbide-tipped drill bit to predrill holes for masonry anchors.

Insert the small level into the mounting bracket and level the bracket against the siding. If you need to predrill holes, mark hole locations on the wall and set aside the bracket until you've drilled the holes and inserted masonry anchors. Otherwise, go ahead and screw the leveled bracket to the siding, using the self-tapped screws provided ❶. For best results, start both screws and keep checking the level before screwing either screw all the way down. When the mounting bracket is secure, remove the level.

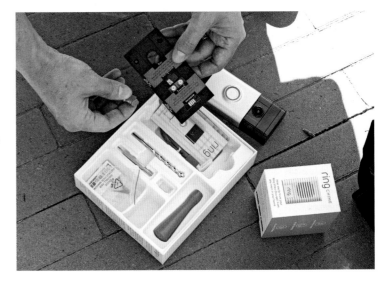

All the tools and hardware you need to install a video doorbell are included in Ring's kit.

1 Using the small level supplied with the kit, level and screw the mounting bracket to an exterior surface.

2 Place the video doorbell onto the mounting bracket.

3 Proprietary screws will prevent someone from removing the video doorbell.

4 Use a smartphone or tablet to download the free app, then set up the doorbell to communicate with other devices.

5 To power the companion chime for the video doorbell, simply plug it into an outlet. The devices will communicate wirelessly.

Place the video camera onto the bracket ❷ and secure it with the proprietary security screw to prevent theft ❸. (The company offers lifetime purchase protection for the Ring camera and will replace it for free if it is stolen.) Finally, attach the decorative face plate to the video camera.

You can download the Ring app and configure the video doorbell at any time ❹, but you will need to do so before it can communicate with your mobile devices or the optional Ring chime, which needs to be plugged into a receptacle to power it ❺.

CONNECTING TO LOW-VOLTAGE DOORBELL WIRING

I f you're powering off existing doorbell wiring, that wiring must be connected to a transformer and a mechanical doorbell with a voltage of 8VAC to 24VAC to ring your doorbell chime (see the wiring diagram below).

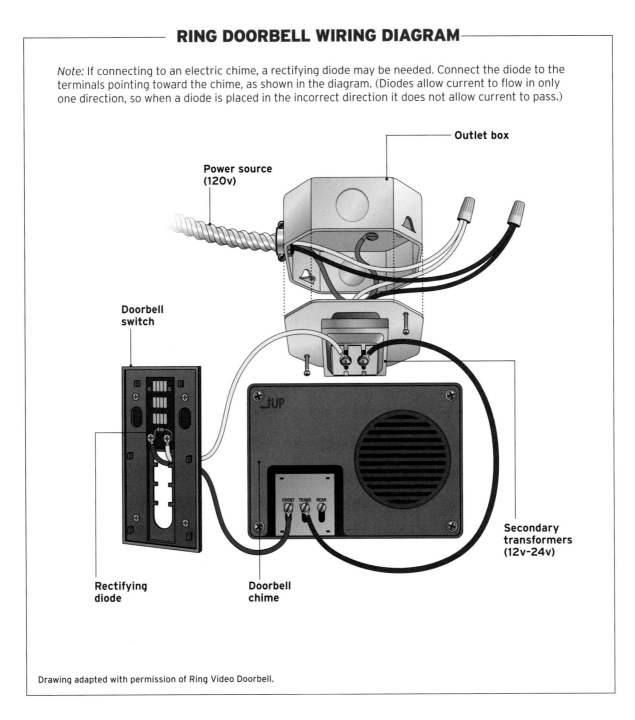

RING DOORBELL WIRING DIAGRAM

Note: If connecting to an electric chime, a rectifying diode may be needed. Connect the diode to the terminals pointing toward the chime, as shown in the diagram. (Diodes allow current to flow in only one direction, so when a diode is placed in the incorrect direction it does not allow current to pass.)

Outlet box

Power source
(120v)

Doorbell
switch

Secondary
transformers
(12v–24v)

Rectifying
diode

Doorbell
chime

Drawing adapted with permission of Ring Video Doorbell.

Note: As most conventional doorbells are attached to thin (18-ga.) low-voltage copper wires, there is little danger of electric shock when replacing doorbells. But if you are inexperienced or have any doubt, turn off the power to the doorbell before installation or–better yet– hire an electrician to install the video doorbell to existing wiring.

Unscrew the existing doorbell from the wall ❶ and detach its wires. Attach the thin copper wires to the screw terminals on the back of the Ring Video Doorbell ❷. Level the device, screw it to the wall ❸, and attach its decorative trim ❹. Then download the app and configure the device as described previously.

SAFETY ALERT

It's safe to handle the energized low-voltage wires that run from the transformer to the doorbell switch or from the chimes to the switch. However, because 120v current can harm you, turn off the power before testing a transformer or the wires upstream–that is, toward the power source–as shown in the drawing on the facing page.

1 Unscrew the old doorbell from the wall.

2 Attach the two thin copper wires to the screw terminals on the back of the doorbell camera.

3 After leveling the device (or plumbing a side), screw the device to the siding.

4 Attach the trim plate of your choice.

TROUBLESHOOTING AN OLD DOORBELL

Troubleshooting a doorbell system takes a little detective work. On older systems, the problem is usually the chime or bell unit—we'll use the term chimes to denote either. In many cases, the plunger springs on the chimes become compressed, resulting in chimes that no longer ring predictably—or at all. Corrosion or dust buildup can also silence chimes. Try the tests given here to determine whether the problem is the switch, the chimes, the transformer, or the wiring between the transformer and the switch.

Start by testing the doorbell switch. Unscrew it and gently pull it out from the wall to expose its connections on the back side. Disconnect one of the wires and, using a continuity tester, touch the tester clip to one switch terminal and the tester point to the other. Press the button: If the tester lights as you depress the button, the switch works. If not, the switch is faulty and should be replaced.

Alternatively, you can detach both wires from the switch and touch their bare ends together to perform several tests. If the chimes sound when you join the wires, the switch is defective. If the switch wires spark when you touch them but the chimes don't ring, test the chimes as shown in "Testing chimes," on the facing page.

If there's no spark when you touch the switch wires, the transformer may be defective and need replacement.

SINGLE DOORBELL WIRING

In a single doorbell system, the circuit runs from the transformer to the doorbell switch, from the switch to the chime unit, and then back to the transformer. By pressing the doorbell, you complete the circuit, and the chime unit rings.

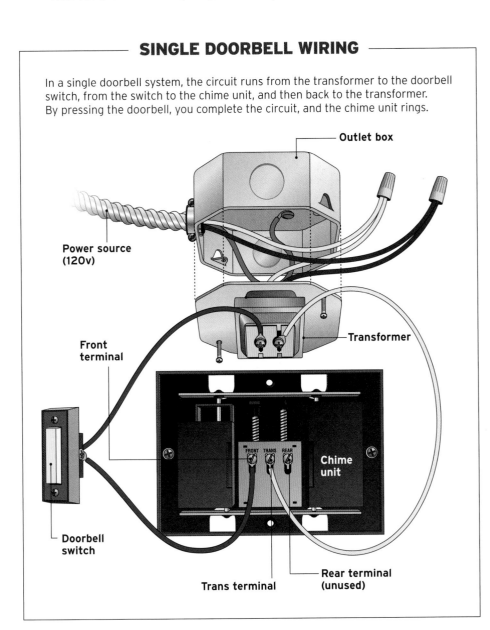

Outlet box

Power source (120v)

Front terminal

Transformer

Doorbell switch

FRONT TRANS REAR

Chime unit

Trans terminal

Rear terminal (unused)

Replacing a doorbell switch

Replace a doorbell switch if it sticks, it is damaged, or continuity no longer exists between the contacts when the switch is depressed. Unscrew the low-voltage wires and pull them out from the box for easy access. If they show corrosion, scrape or sand the wires lightly. Once the wires are clean and exposed, screw them to the terminals on the new doorbell switch. Then screw the new switch to the wall.

Screw the old wires to the terminals on the new switch.

DOUBLE DOORBELL WIRING

A double doorbell system has two circuits, each controlled by a doorbell switch, whose power comes from the transformer. Thus the chime unit for a double doorbell has three terminals. Typically, the chime unit has two different ring patterns (*ding* and *ding-dong*) so you can tell whether the visitor is at the front or rear door.

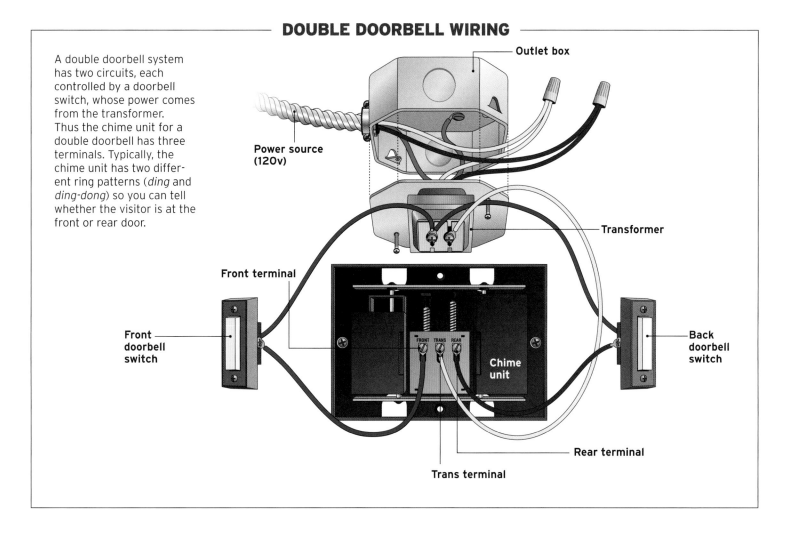

Outlet box

Power source (120v)

Transformer

Front terminal

Front doorbell switch

Back doorbell switch

Rear terminal

Trans terminal

Chime unit

Testing chimes If the chimes don't ring when you touch the doorbell switch wires together, remove the chime cover and vacuum out accumulated crud. If the chime plungers are rusty or corroded, spray them with WD-40® or a similar lubricant and move them by hand to get them sliding freely. Rubbing screw terminals with steel wool may improve electrical contacts, but chances are the old unit is worn out and needs to be replaced. To find out, dial a multimeter AC voltage setting that's close to the low-voltage rating on the chime unit, then touch the tester probes to the trans and front terminals and to the trans and rear terminals, as shown in the photo. If you get a reading close to the unit's rating but the chimes won't ring, the transformer is delivering power, but the chime unit is defective. Replace it.

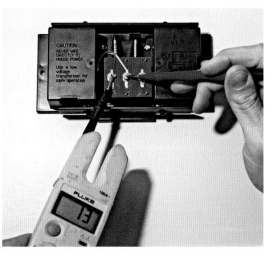

Test the chime terminals using a multimeter.

IS THE WIRING COMPATIBLE WITH YOUR NEW THERMOSTAT?

Most thermostats that control central heating and cooling systems are low voltage (24v), though there are three types in use: low voltage, line voltage (house current, typically 120v), and millivolt. Your first task will be to determine which type of thermostat is there now. (*Note:* The acronym HVAC stands for heating, ventilation, and air conditioning, the catch-all term to describe the complicated systems that control interior home environments.)

The easiest way to determine what type of thermostat you have is to unsnap or unscrew its plastic cover and look at the wires attached to the baseplate. Look, but don't touch the wires. Typically you can remove a cover with little danger of electric shock, but to be sure, *turn off the breaker* and then remove the cover.

Millivolt thermostats typically control in-floor gas furnaces or in-wall gas furnaces, which are no longer common. Unless you have such outmoded gas heaters, you probably don't have a millivolt thermostat. Millivolt wiring, usually two thin copper wires attached to the device, does not have enough power to run a low-voltage thermostat.

Low-voltage thermostats will be fed by 2 to 10 thin copper (18-gauge) wires with color-coded plastic sheathing. (In some cases, there may be more than 10 wires.) Again, this type of thermostat is the most common and can be used to control most modern HVAC systems. This type of low-voltage wiring will be compatible with today's smart/teachable thermostats.

Line-voltage thermostats (also called high-voltage) are used to directly control large energy users such as electric baseboard heaters, electric wall heaters, electric radiant floor heating, fan coil units in HVAC systems, circulator motors, and the like. Line-voltage thermostats typically have thick, stranded wire leads coming out of the back; those leads will be spliced (with wire nuts) to incoming 12-gauge or 14-gauge wires. In addition, the back of the device may have labels indicating power requirements such as 110VAC, 120VAC, or 240VAC.

CAUTION: *Never connect a low-voltage thermostat or millivolt thermostat to line-voltage wires.*

Installing the Nest® app will enable you to control your heating and cooling system from your smartphone.

 SAFETY ALERT

Old thermostats may contain mercury—which is very toxic—so don't throw them in the trash. To find a recycler who can dispose of one safely, please go to www.thermostat-recycle.org or call 888-266-0550.

PRO TIP

Photograph the wires! Before you replace the thermostat cover and restore power to the circuit, photograph the wiring. This is invaluable information when it's time to connect those wires to your new low-voltage thermostat. One company, Nest, will send you a personalized wiring guide for their thermostat if you first email them a photo of the old thermostat's wiring.

 SAFETY ALERT

Thermostats are specialized switches that open or close a circuit in response to temperature changes. Although most thermostats are low-voltage units that are safe to handle, your unit may be unsafe to handle if it mounts to an electrical box and is connected to house wiring (120v). Shut off the power, test to be sure it's off, disconnect the thermostat, and have a heating professional assess it.

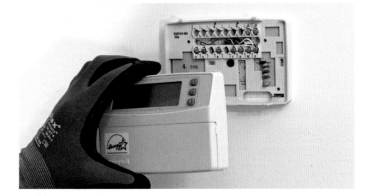

Low-voltage thermostats are energized by thin copper wires with color-coded plastic shells (sheathing). Photograph the wires before you remove them.

REMOVING THE OLD LOW-VOLTAGE THERMOSTAT

As noted above, the power should be turned off. If you have not already done so, remove the cover of the existing thermostat and photograph the wire connections to its baseplate.

Disconnect wires, either by unscrewing the terminal screws holding them, or by pressing a wire-release button at the back of each terminal. After you have disconnected all the wires, remove the mounting plate (or baseplate) from the wall. Wire ends should be straight. If any are twisted, trim their ends and restrip them so that each has $1/4$ in. to $3/8$ in. of bare wire.

Note: Any wires not connected to the old thermostat will not be attached to the new one.

If there are holes in the wall that the new thermostat or its trim plate won't cover, fill holes and paint patched areas.

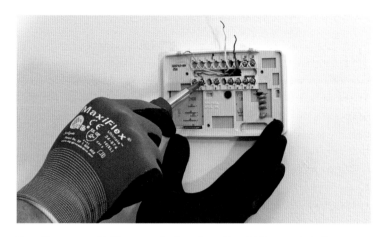

Turn the power off. Disconnect wires from the old thermostat, then unscrew the mounting plate from the wall.

INSTALLING A NEW LOW-VOLTAGE THERMOSTAT

Because we like its functionality, we will describe the installation of a Nest thermostat.

Feed the wires through the thermostat base. Start installing the top screw, but don't tighten it down all the way because you'll need to adjust the position of the base to level it. Chances are the self-tapping screws provided will be all you need to attach the device to drywall or plaster. But if you are attaching to a harder material, predrill screw holes with a $3/32$-in. bit. Use the built-in level to level the Nest base, then sink both mounting screws securely ❶.

Insert wires into the corresponding wiring terminals on the base (G for green wire, W for white wire, etc.) Press down the button for each wiring terminal and insert the wire. Buttons should stay down after wires have been inserted to ensure a solid connection. When you are done, press all wires into the base so they lie flush.

Then, holding the display so that the Nest logo is at the top, click it onto the base ❷.

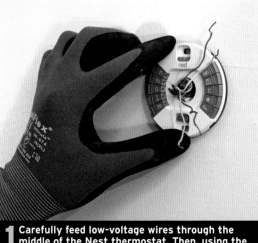

1 Carefully feed low-voltage wires through the middle of the Nest thermostat. Then, using the level in its baseplate, mount it to the wall.

2 After securing low-voltage wires to appropriate terminals, snap the thermostat display to the base.

SETTING UP YOUR INTERNET-CONNECTED THERMOSTAT

Turn the power back on. The Nest thermostat will turn on—its face will light up—and guide you through setup. Typically, a smart thermostat will first ask you to select a language and then connect the device to the Internet (assuming you have Wi-Fi, of course). Connecting to the Internet will enable the thermostat to download software updates periodically, and allow you to access and control your heating and cooling system from a smartphone.

During setup, the thermostat will check its wiring to be sure that you've connected wires correctly and that all connections are mechanically sound.

As setup proceeds, you'll be asked to verify your zip code; give an overview of your heating and cooling needs; identify the type of dwelling (single family, condo, etc.); and supply a few particulars about the heating and cooling system. Then you'll run a quick diagnostic test.

That done, you'll use your smartphone to download a free Nest app, which will enable you to create an account or to check into an existing Nest account. Once you've signed on to the app, you'll find a thermostat icon on your phone. Click on it. You will be walked through the settings available on your thermostat and how to control those settings from inside your home or from your smartphone. Nest also has an extensive video library on its website.

When you restore electricity to the circuit, the display will power up and guide you through setup.

 PRO TIP

If the thermostat works but its temperature settings are too high or low, it may need to be plumbed or leveled. Remove its cover and look for a pair of plumb or leveling marks on the base.

WHAT IF THE WI-FI GOES DOWN?

Wired and wireless CO and smoke alarms are roughly equivalent, as far as building codes are concerned. In remodels, wireless alarms are an obvious choice because you can install them without disturbing finish surfaces. Using the Internet to install and interconnect wireless alarms is also a big plus. But what if the Wi-Fi goes down? Do alarms stay interconnected?

In a word: yes. Once wireless alarms are configured, they use their own network protocols to talk to each other—not the house Wi-Fi network. For example, if your Wi-Fi fails, a Nest Protect alarm that detects smoke in a bedroom can still share that information with alarms throughout the house. Without Wi-Fi, obviously, your smartphone will not get alerts from house alarms, nor can you check the status of house alarms if you're not at home. But the alarms still work locally, so they are as safe as conventional alarms.

An important aside. Because there are no industry-standard interfaces or smoke-detection algorithms, different brands generally don't interconnect reliably. So if you want to add CO or smoke alarms to your system, stick with one brand.

SMOKE AND CARBON MONOXIDE (CO) ALARMS

Smoke and carbon monoxide (CO) alarms are now required in all new construction. Such devices must be installed in every sleeping room and in halls leading to them, and there must be at least one alarm on every floor, including attics, basements, and crawlspaces.

Smoke and CO alarms must be hard-wired into the house's electrical system and have battery backup to provide protection in the event of a power outage. Further, all smoke and CO alarms in a house must be *interconnected* so that if one alarm sounds, all will sound. Interconnection is crucial because it can alert inhabitants to fire or CO buildup that starts in another part of the house, giving them time to escape before they are overcome by smoke, flames, or toxic gas.

No one disputes that smoke and CO alarms save lives, but these requirements have not been universally adopted. Regulations are especially piecemeal when applied to existing homes and remodels. In new construction, when framing is exposed, hard-wiring smoke and CO alarms is straightforward; not so in remodels. In most renovations, adding hard-wired alarms often means tearing up finish surfaces to run wires—and thus is viewed as a hardship. So remodels are often exempted from smoke- and CO-detection code upgrades.

Fortunately, the evolution of building codes, the widespread acceptance of battery-powered backup systems, and the explosion of *wireless*, Internet-based home networks has delivered smoke- and CO-detection solutions that are highly reliable, affordable, and easily installed without destroying finish surfaces.

The Nest Protect® smoke and carbon monoxide alarm, which comes in battery-powered and hard-wired versions, is such a solution. So we looked at its features and installation.

Essential alarm features

Functionally, any modern smoke and CO alarm should do at least three essential things:

1. It should connect to your Wi-Fi network and alert your smartphone—wherever you are. You need to know of imminent danger, whether you are away from home or just busy in another room.
2. If the cause for a smoke alarm is relatively minor—say, the smoke of burned toast—the device should warn you what and where the problem is—before a loud alarm horn sounds. If you find that the problem is indeed minor, you should be able to silence the impending alarm easily by pressing a button on the device or by using a smartphone app.
3. Smoke and CO alarms should interconnect automatically. Nest Protect alarms, for example, are interconnected before the devices are installed. During setup, as you use your smartphone or tablet to choose where each device will be installed, the app establishes a Wi-Fi interconnection between them—whether they are hard-wired or battery-powered.

Setting up an Internet-based smoke and CO alarm

Nest Protect alarms come with a straightforward user guide, and the company's website includes a 3-minute video that walks you step-by-step through installation. You'll need a smartphone or a tablet that runs iOS or Android operating systems and, of course, Wi-Fi.

After downloading a free Nest app, follow the prompts on your smartphone or tablet to set up your account, scan in your device's QR code, choose the room where you'll place the alarm, and choose pathway settings for the night-light. After the Nest Protect alarm connects to the Internet and has made the necessary connections, its light will glow green and the app will ask if you have other Nest Protect products. If so, setup goes much faster for additional devices.

Note: To minimize nuisance alarms, place smoke detectors at least 10 ft. away from cooking appliances and at least 4 in. away from nearby walls.

COLORFUL PROTECTION

One of the most distinctive Nest Protect features—its color ring—is especially versatile. Each alarm has an RGB color ring with six LEDs, which enables the device to use different colors to denote different conditions:

Blue: The device is active, ready to be tested or configured.

Green: The device pulses green for five seconds after you turn off the lights at night to let you know that it is working correctly and all is well.

White: As you walk under a device at night, an integral motion detector inside the device turns on a short white light to guide your way.

Yellow: An advance warning, a yellow light comes on when the device senses a low level of smoke or carbon monoxide. In addition to telling you the location of the problem, a recorded voice tells you what to do, such as "Carbon monoxide detected in dining room. Go to fresh air." A yellow light may also shine when the device's batteries are low, the device has failed a test, or it is otherwise not functioning perfectly.

Red: Dangerous condition detected, accompanied by voice alerts and a loud emergency horn: 85 dB SPL (Sound Pressure Level) at 10 ft.

Note: Regulations also require that every *hard-wired* alarm must also have a small LED indicator light on its face to indicate that power (120v) is on. This small green dot is in addition to the ring colors described above. Battery-powered alarms lack this small LED.

INSTALLING A HARD-WIRED ALARM

1 Locate the new smoke alarm and run 120v house current to the new outlet box.

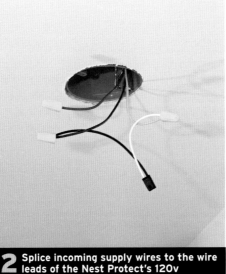

2 Splice incoming supply wires to the wire leads of the Nest Protect's 120v connector (lower right in the photo).

3 Carefully push spliced wires into the outlet box and screw the mounting plate (baseplate) to the box.

A hard-wired alarm will be attached to line voltage (120v), so first turn off the circuit breaker controlling the circuit you will be working on and lock the panel. Then test with a noncontact tester to be sure the power is off and verify power is off with a probe tester.

If you are replacing an existing hard-wired alarm, its green indicator light may remain lit for a few minutes after you turn off the power. To remove the old smoke alarm, twist or unscrew it from its mounting plate (baseplate). If the existing alarm has a 120v connector, unsnap it. Disconnect any wire splices, then unscrew the mounting plate from the outlet box.

If you are installing a Nest Protect hard-wired alarm where there was previously no alarm, you will need to mount an outlet box in the ceiling and run a 120V cable to it **❶**. Secure the incoming cable to the box and strip wire ends (p. 32). Screw the incoming ground wire to the ground screw inside the box.

Using wire nuts, splice the incoming supply wires to the wire leads of the Nest Protect's 120v connector **❷**, neutral to neutral, hot to hot. Nest smoke and CO alarms interconnect (communicate) wirelessly so if there is an interconnect wire in the outlet box, cap it. Then attach the new mounting plate to the box **❸**.

Plug the 120v connector into the back of the alarm **❹** till it clicks. Push the spliced wires up into the outlet box and twist the Nest Protect alarm clockwise to secure it to the mounting plate.

Restore power to the circuit: The small LED indicator light on the face of the device should glow green. The large color ring on the Nest Protect will glow blue, indicating that it is ready to be tested **❺**. Tap the button within the color ring twice. As Nest's website notes, "It will check its sensors, power, Wi-Fi connections, emergency horn, speaker, and lights."

Before the alarm's emergency horn sounds, however, a voice prompt will warn you to stand back. Reminiscent of Civil Defense alerts of years gone by, the voice will also note, "This is just a test." During this test, if you have installed more than one Nest Protect alarm, each should sound and light up to show that it is interconnected.

Hard-wired Nest Protect alarms also have backup power of three long-life AA lithium batteries, which are typically good for 10 years.

4 Plug the 120v connector into the back of the alarm, then twist the alarm clockwise to secure to the base.

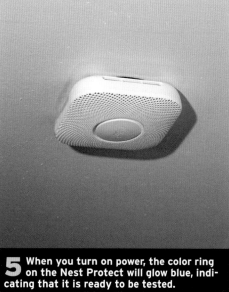

5 When you turn on power, the color ring on the Nest Protect will glow blue, indicating that it is ready to be tested.

Installing a battery-powered alarm

Follow the setup instructions described above before installing a battery-powered device. Installation, however, is much quicker because there are no wires to connect, nor is there a 120v connector. Nest Protect battery-powered alarms are powered by six long-life AA lithium batteries, good for 10 years.

Mount the mounting plate to a finished ceiling, using the special screws provided. There's no need to predrill holes. Turn the alarm clockwise to secure it to the mounting plate. The color ring should glow blue. Tap the button inside the ring twice to test the device.

This motion-activated video cam is one more smartphone-controlled device available from Nest, used to keep an eye on things whether you're at work or just in the next room.

HOME NETWORKING

HOME NETWORKING ENCOMPASSES various types of audio, video, telephone, and data signals. In addition to wired components, wireless transmission via smartphones is an increasingly important part of the mix.

The tools and methods used to install network cabling are similar to those used to install basic residential electrical circuits. Whether you're adding a phone jack or installing a home network center, you'll need only a few specialized tools. Multimedia connections are extremely precise, so follow installation instructions exactly to ensure strong signals throughout your audio, video, phone, and data cabling.

TOOLS & MATERIALS

Multimedia cable & connectors, p. 122

Stripping cable, p. 123

ADDING PHONE JACKS

Extending a phone line, p. 124

Mounting a new jack, p. 127

DISTRIBUTION PANELS

Installing a home network panel, p. 128

Running cable, p. 130

Installing panel modules, p. 131

Wiring panel modules, p. 132

INSTALLING A MULTIMEDIA OUTLET

Locating the multimedia outlet, p. 133

Installing cable connectors, p. 134

Connecting Panduit jacks, p. 135

Installing Leviton jacks, p. 136

Attaching jacks to an outlet plate, p. 137

HOME AUDIO SYSTEMS

Whole-house music systems, p. 139

Retrofitting a speaker, p. 141

USB CHARGER/ RECEPTACLE COMBOS

Retrofitting a USB charger/receptacle combo, p. 143

WALL-HUNG TELEVISIONS

Installing a wall-hung television, p. 145

WHOLE-HOUSE SYSTEMS

Whole-house control systems, p. 148

Integrating whole-house systems, p. 150

A typical installation, p. 152

Setting up the whole-house system, p. 153

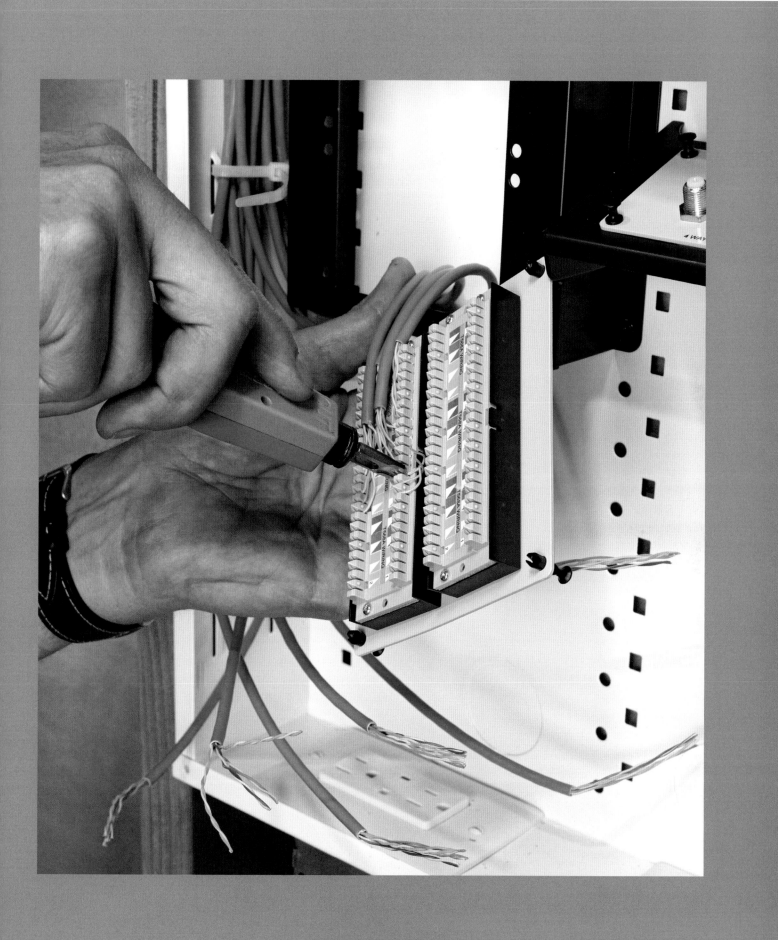

MULTIMEDIA CABLE & CONNECTORS

Here's an overview of the cable and connectors you'll need to wire your house for sound, video, data, and telephone service.

Coaxial cable is most often quad-shielded RG6, although double-shielded RG59 cable is still used. RG6 cable has a slightly thicker wire gauge than does RG59. Used for video distribution (cable TV), coaxial cable has been around for years. Video cable terminates in an F-connector, such as the watertight RG6 connector shown in the photo at right. To simplify life and forestall callbacks, many professional electricians install watertight F-connectors inside and out.

Data cable can carry data or phone signals; it is typically solid-wire unshielded twisted pair (UTP) cable. Category (Cat) 5e cable is the workhorse of data networking, but cable is constantly evolving: Cat 6 and Cat 6a are also specified. In general, higher cable numbers denote faster data-transmission capabilities. Data cable contains four pairs of wires, thus RJ-45 data jacks contain eight pins.

Data and telephone service. Cat 5e unshielded twisted pair (UTP) cable is typically used to distribute telephone and data. Cat 3 cable was previously used for distributing telephone, but given that it is a less robust cable type and there is no cost benefit to using it, few are using it for new installations.

Audio (speaker) cable is usually 18-gauge to 12-gauge finely stranded wire. Speaker-wire terminations vary from bare wires compressed between stacked washers to screw-on or crimped jacks that plug into speaker ports. Plug-in jacks are color striped to match speaker polarity: red-striped jacks for positive terminals and black-striped jacks for negative terminals.

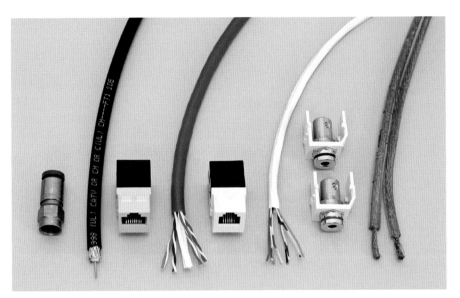

Each multimedia connector is to the left of the cable it terminates. From left: RG6 F-connector, dual-shielded RG6 coaxial cable; RJ-45 (eight-pin) jack, Cat 6 UTP data cable; RJ-11 (six-pin) jack, Cat 3 phone cable; two RCA audio jacks (sometimes called banana jacks), 14-gauge low-loss audio cable.

Signal strength: coming in loud and clear

Although solid connections are as important to multimedia as they are to all electrical wiring, signal strength—not voltage—is the objective when connecting data, audio, video, and phone components. In fact, most multimedia input is not impelled by AC, as is house wiring. Rather, video and phone signals are generated by cable or phone companies. Computers and routers amplify data signals, and stereo amplifiers boost sound signals; but although those devices run on house current, the signals themselves are not AC. Thus the cables that carry multimedia signals are dramatically different from, say, Romex cables, and require different connecting devices and a few specialized tools.

PRO TIP

Pros use watertight connectors on all coaxial cable connections, even those installed indoors. Watertight connectors such as the RG6 shown in the photo above don't cost much more and they always provide a solid connection.

STRIPPING CABLE

Electricians generally favor one type of stripper and use it to strip everything, thus reducing the number of tools in their belts.

Splicing scissors can trim tiny wires, but they can also score sheathing: Hold the cable in one hand, and, with the other, hold a scissors blade perpendicular to the cable and rotate it around the cable **Ⓐ**. It's not necessary to cut through the sheathing. Once scored, the sheathing will strip off when you pull on the scored sections **Ⓑ**. In fact, merely scoring the sheathing is less likely to damage individual wire insulation.

The cable scorer shown in photo **Ⓒ** is specifically designed for stripping cables, but pros who perform a lot of terminations save time by using scissors skillfully. Wire strippers are the most reliable way to strip insulation off individual wires because you can choose a stripper setting that matches the wire gauge **Ⓓ**. Finally, whether stripping wire, drilling holes, or doing any other wiring task, wear eye protection and sturdy gloves.

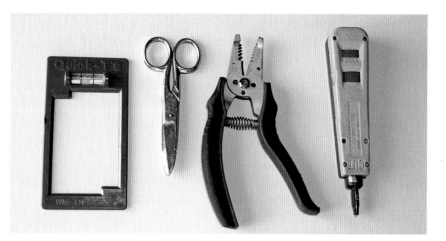

Multimedia installation tools. From left: low-voltage cut-in ring template, splicing scissors, wire strippers, and punch-down tool.

TWISTED WIRES

Remove the sheathing from Cat 5e or Cat 6 cable and you'll discover twisted wires within. Twisting wires reduces the occurrence of *cross-talk*, in which electromagnetic signals jump from wire to wire. Although it is necessary to straighten some data cable wires to attach them to some jacks, the twisting must be maintained to within ¼ in. of the termination on the jack.

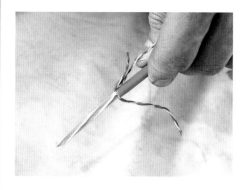

Cat 5e and 6 cables are examples of UTP cable, which is twisted to prevent signals from jumping between wires.

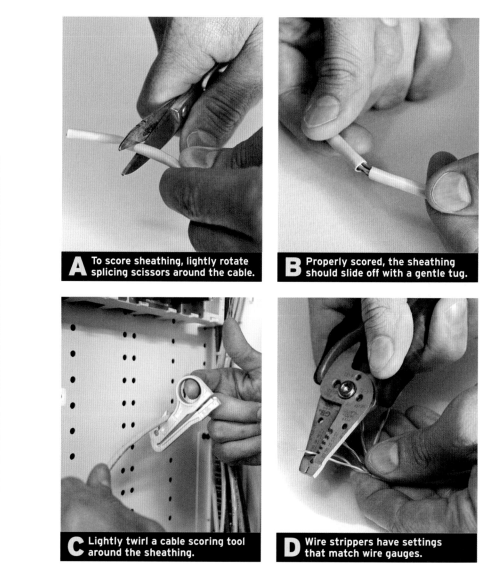

Ⓐ To score sheathing, lightly rotate splicing scissors around the cable.

Ⓑ Properly scored, the sheathing should slide off with a gentle tug.

Ⓒ Lightly twirl a cable scoring tool around the sheathing.

Ⓓ Wire strippers have settings that match wire gauges.

EXTENDING A PHONE LINE

Thanks to cell phones and remotes, we're no longer tied to the room where the phone line ends. But for clear, reliable service you can't beat a hard-wired phone plugged into a nearby jack. Happily, almost anyone can run an extension from an existing jack, thereby saving a hefty installation fee from the phone company.

The only tricky part of the job is running the cable to the new jack. You can tuck it under carpets, tack it atop baseboards, or run it around door jambs, but it won't look great. For the cleanest job, route that extension line into the attic or basement or—as shown here—drill through the wall and run it outside.

Before you start, disconnect the main incoming line at the interface. Then find the shortest route between the existing jack and the new one. Measure that route carefully and add enough extra cable for drip loops and at least 1 ft. extra on each end for the thickness of walls and for stripping and connecting to the jacks. Cat 5e cable, which contains four pairs of solid-core, 24-gauge wire, is generally used these days. If, however, you are extending an existing Cat 3 line, using Cat 3 is a reasonable approach. Because phone lines are low voltage, they're safe to handle. You can do the job with common tools.

Never work on a phone line during a storm: lightning striking an aerial phone cable could electrocute you.

Connecting to an existing jack

Start by unscrewing the cover on the jack and the mounting screws that hold the jack to the wall. Gently pull the jack out from the wall, being careful not to pull loose the wires attached to the jack terminals ❶.

If the jack is surface mounted, drill a hole for the extension cable that will be covered by the jack. If the jack is flush mounted, drill anywhere inside the ring, because the hole will be covered by the jack cover. Drill at a downward angle ❷ so that exterior water

1 Gently pull the jack out from the wall.

2 Drill downward to prevent water from traveling to the interior.

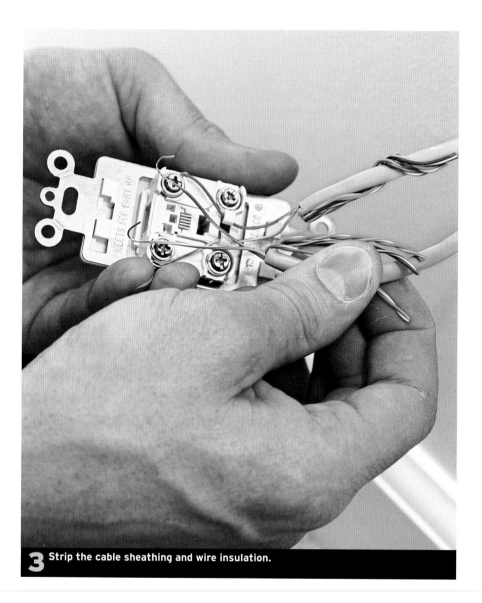

3 Strip the cable sheathing and wire insulation.

DATA AND PHONE FITTINGS

Cat 5e and Cat 6 cables have four pairs of color-coded copper wires, which require 8-pin plugs (RJ45). RJ45 fittings, wired in T568A or T568B configurations, can be used for data or phone cable. Cat 3 cable, used only for phone lines, requires 6-pin, RJ11 fittings.

T568A RJ45

1 2 3 4 5 6 7 8

T568B RJ45

1 2 3 4 5 6 7 8

RJ11 OSOC

1 2 3 4 5 6

will tend to run out of the hole. Look into the outlet opening before drilling to avoid electrical cables in the wall. Use a 1/4-in. extension bit in a cordless drill for the job.

After drilling through the wall, use duct tape to attach a piece of string to the bit and pull the bit back through the wall. Then tie the new Cat 3 or 5e phone cable to the string and pull it into the hole behind the jack. Once you've pulled the new cable to the existing jack, strip about 2 in. of the cable sheathing and separate the cable wires into pairs **3**. >> >> >>

EXTENDING A PHONE LINE (CONTINUED)

Using splicing scissors or a wire stripper, strip about ½ in. of insulation from a wire pair (for example, a blue and a blue-white wire), loop the bare wire ends clockwise, and attach one wire to each of the two jack terminals that are presently wired ④. Typically, terminals have stacked washers that hold several wires.

4 Attach the new wires to the existing jack's terminals.

Wiring techniques

When connecting to an existing phone line, avoid bending existing wires repeatedly because they can become weak and break off. Screw terminals come with multiple washers and are intended to have one wire under each washer. It is not recommended to twist wires together and install them under one washer. Finally, always wrap wires around screw terminals in a clockwise direction.

PRO TIP

Many electricians install Cat 5e cable for both data and phone lines to allow future expansion or modification. That is, Cat 3 is fine for phone service but inadequate for data, whereas Cat 5e can carry both signals.

Keep line and lo-vo cables apart! To avoid electromagnetic interference between lines, keep line-voltage (120v) and lo-vo cables separate. The NEC requires 2 in. of separation between line-voltage and low-voltage wiring. Do not secure them under the same staples nor run them through the same holes drilled in framing. If you must house both cable types in a two-gang box, use a snap-in plastic box divider to isolate their signals.

MOUNTING A NEW JACK

Before pushing the cables into the wall and remounting the existing jack, staple the new cable so it can't move and stress electrical connections. If the cable runs outside, loop it downward so water will drip off, and staple it with insulated cable staples ❶. Then fill the hole in the siding with siliconized latex caulk.

Locate the new jack and drill through the wall to bring cable to the location ❷. As described earlier, tape a string to the end of the drill bit before withdrawing it, then tie the new cable to the string. Once you've pulled the new cable into the room, remove its sheathing, strip insulation from a pair of wire ends, feed the cable through the new jack, and screw the jack to the wall ❸.

Loop the bare wire ends clockwise, insert them between the stacked washers on the jack, and screw them tight ❹. Finally, tug gently on the wires to be sure they're well attached, tuck the wires neatly out of the way, and snap on the jack cover ❺.

1 Form a drip loop, then staple the cable to the wall.

2 Drill a hole at the new jack location and pull in phone cable.

3 Mount the new jack in the opening.

4 Screw the stripped wire ends to the jack.

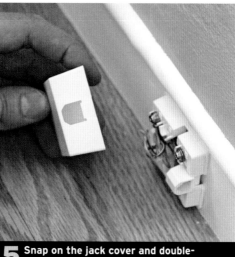

5 Snap on the jack cover and double-check to make sure it works.

PRO TIP

Low-voltage wire and multimedia cable are not stiff, so staple them at least every foot to prevent sagging, strains on connections, and an unsightly appearance.

PRO TIP

If you must drill through an exterior wall to bring lo-vo wiring or media cables into a room, drill downward to keep water from running into the walls. After inserting the wire or cable, fill the hole with siliconized latex caulk which, unlike pure silicone, is paintable.

INSTALLING A HOME NETWORK PANEL

A distribution panel is the heart of a home media network because it receives incoming signals and distributes them throughout a house. Today's panels generally address telephone, cable or satellite TV, and data (Internet connectivity) and are connected to the service providers through a variety of cabling types (fiber optic, unshielded twisted pair, and coaxial). These services are distributed throughout a house generally through unshielded twisted pair and coaxial cabling and may be further distributed via Wi-Fi.

The panel at right contains a mix of media technologies. However, for reasons we will explain in "Whole-House Music Systems" (p. 139), audio signals are distributed from another location. Many panel makers offer kits with prepackaged components or prewired modules, so you can configure a multimedia network today that can be easily changed tomorrow. As with other electrical installations, *connect the power last*, after wiring the panel and running cable to the outlets. Wear safety glasses at all times and work gloves to protect your hands and enable you to grip and pull cable more easily.

The big picture: A home network panel

Panel wiring can be confusing, so let's start with an overview of a finished panel. The callouts are keyed to the photo.

At the top of the panel, a coaxial cable ("the service cable") enters the left-hand side of a splitter ❶. The right-hand side of the splitter has two outputs. From one output, a coaxial cable emerges ❷ and travels to a cable modem ❸. In this case, the cable service provider is providing both cable television service and Internet service. The cable modem separates the data (Internet) signal and changes the medium to unshielded twisted pair (Cat 5e), which travels through a yellow cable ❹ down to a gigabit-enhanced router, ❺. Via two white patch cords ❻,

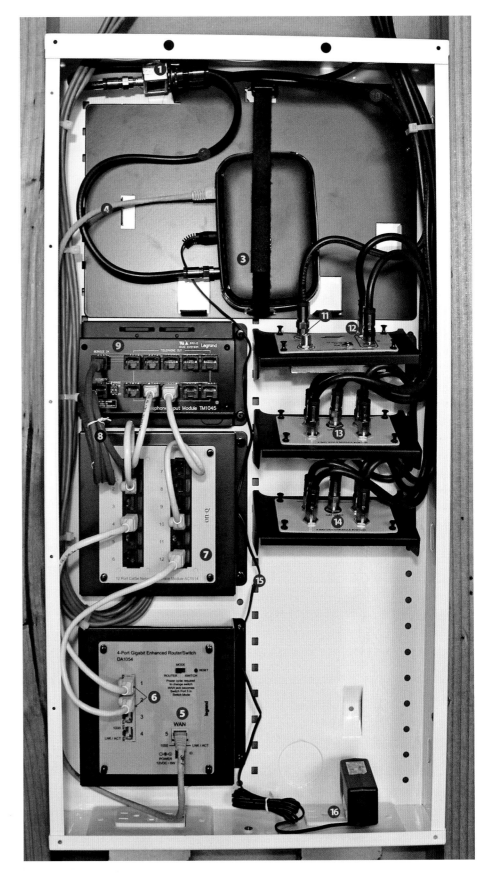

A home network panel receives **incoming signals from telephone, cable, or satellite TV and distributes them throughout a house.**

data runs from the router and is connected to the distributed cables throughout the home via the 12-port patch panel ❼.

The multiple blue cables entering the patch panel are Cat 5e cables that can distribute data or telephone. Each port on the patch panel connects to a jack location in your house that can be used for a phone, to connect to a computer, television, wireless router, printer, etc. The orange cable ❽ that runs from the patch panel delivers incoming phone service; it plugs into the "service in" jack on the telephone input module ❾.

The other coaxial cable that emerges from the splitter ❿ travels along the upper right corner of the panel and plugs into an input jack labeled, "CATV/ANT (Cable TV/Antenna)" on the amplifier module ⓫. The amplifier boosts the incoming signal. (We installed this amplifier because the house is large and we wanted to make sure that signals wouldn't be diminished by the time they arrive at the end of their runs.)

Below the amplifier are two splitters. Via coaxial cables plugged into two output jacks on the amplifier ⓬, one cable travels down to the input port on the first splitter below ⓭. There the signal is split four ways and sent to four different rooms in the house. The second cable coming off the amplifier runs to the second splitter ⓮, which also splits and sends the signal to four other rooms.

A few things we didn't mention: The power cord of the modem ⓯ plugs into a power outlet ⓰ in the bottom of the panel. Last, the cord colors are arbitrary: We used orange and yellow cords just so they would be more visible in the panel.

PRO TIP

When mounting panels, install screws loosely at the top to hold the panel in place. Set and secure the bottom, then reset the top screws as needed.

Mounting and prepping the panel

If you locate the distribution panel centrally, you'll have shorter cable runs. To minimize electrical interference, locate the multimedia panel away from the service entrance panel or a subpanel. Ideally, place the distribution panel on an interior wall to minimize temperature fluctuations—never locate it in an attic or unheated garage. You'll build in future flexibility if you run Cat 5e or Cat 6 cable for all data and telephone lines.

Install the panel box by screwing it to adjacent studs ❶. If you've already pulled most of the cables to feed the panel, as shown here, tack them to one side so they'll be out of the way. Slide the panel in or out so its edges will be flush with the drywall ❷ that will be installed later.

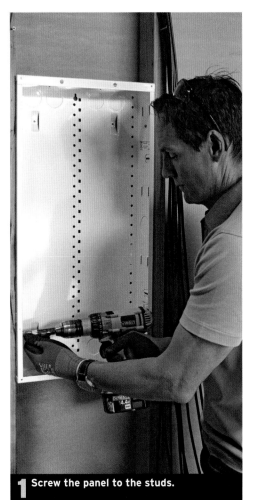

1 Screw the panel to the studs.

Remove the knockout(s) for the power supply outlet(s). If your panel will house only telephone and cable TV, you may not need a power supply, but routers and modems require line voltage (120v), so installing outlets will provide future flexibility. Fit the outlet box into the opening, screw it to the panel housing, run Romex cable to the box, and wire the receptacle ❸. Follow the sequence recommended throughout this book: Attach the ground wire first, then the neutral, then the hot wire.

Note: Do not energize the supply cable until the panel is fully wired and you have run cable to outlets throughout the house. To protect the sensitive electronic equipment in the panel box, we recommend that you install surge-protection receptacles.

2 Set the edges of the panel flush with the drywall.

3 Remove a power-supply knockout, screw an outlet box to the bottom of the panel, and wire the receptacle.

RUNNING CABLE

There's no one right way to run multi-media cable to a multimedia distribution panel. In new construction, electricians typically start from the distribution panel and pull cable outward. But remodel wiring is rarely predictable because you can't see obstructions hidden in walls and floors.

If panel openings have sharp edges after knockouts are removed, snap plastic bushings into the openings to protect cable sheathing before pulling cable into the box ❶. In our installation, panel edges were smooth, so we did not need bushings. As you pull cable into the panel, loop it gently so that you don't crimp it ❷. If you have a lot of cables entering a panel, roughly divide them between two or more knockouts so the box will look neater.

As you route cable through the panel, tie-wrap cable bundles to free up workspace and enable you to see connections easily ❸. Labeling both ends of every cable is also advisable, so you'll know which cable is which should you need to repair or modify the multimedia wiring later ❹. Finally, create a numbered house map to show the cable locations.

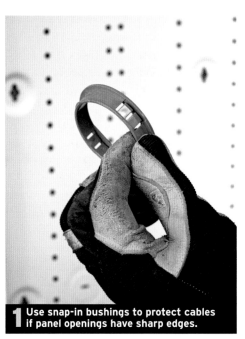

1 Use snap-in bushings to protect cables if panel openings have sharp edges.

2 Loop the cable to avoid crimping it.

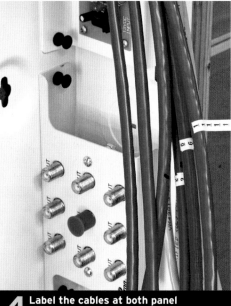

3 Bundle the cables to conserve space.

4 Label the cables at both panel and outlets.

INSTALLING PANEL MODULES

In general, when installing modules in a panel, place larger components first so they will be easier to wire. Minimize cable runs to create a neat, professional look, and, as noted earlier, bundle cables to conserve space. Because modules snap or screw into cutouts in the back of the panel, they can be removed easily to facilitate wiring or be rearranged to achieve a better configuration.

The panel's CATV service cable enters a splitter at the top of the panel, so we installed the cable-modem mount immediately below it ❶. We then installed a bi-directional amplifier to the right of the panel ❷ because the amplifier would receive a coaxial cable coming out of the right side of the splitter. Then, because two output cables from the amplifier would feed into them, two splitter modules were stacked under the amplifier. To the left of the stacked splitters we installed the telephone input module ❸.

Below that we installed the 12-port patch panel ❹, to which all the blue Cat 5e telephone/data cables would attach. Last, we installed the 4-port, gigabit-enhanced router/switch ❺. The router controls all the data transmission in the house—it's sort of a gateway to keep track of where signals are going. The router is the farthest device from the modem, but that's no problem because it's fed by flexible cables that can be routed easily.

Because the modem slides into its mount and is held in place by hook-and-loop straps ❻, you can install it at any time. We did so midway through wiring the modules.

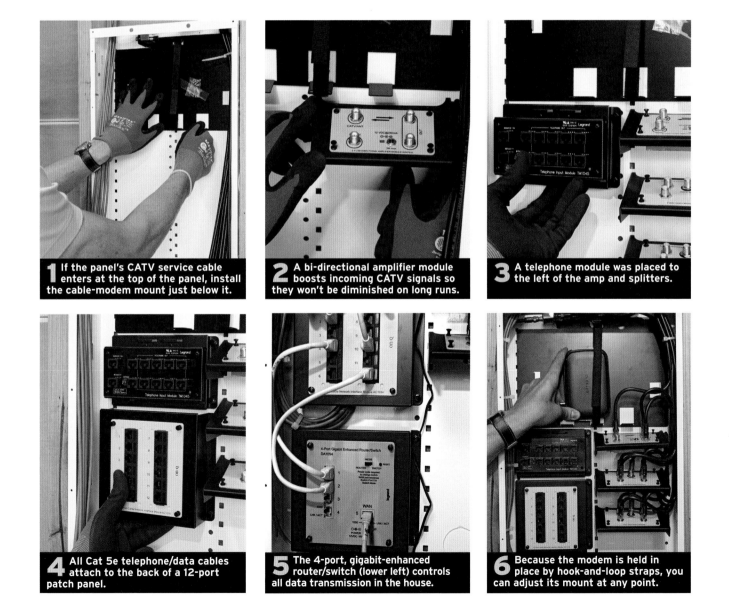

1 If the panel's CATV service cable enters at the top of the panel, install the cable-modem mount just below it.

2 A bi-directional amplifier module boosts incoming CATV signals so they won't be diminished on long runs.

3 A telephone module was placed to the left of the amp and splitters.

4 All Cat 5e telephone/data cables attach to the back of a 12-port patch panel.

5 The 4-port, gigabit-enhanced router/switch (lower left) controls all data transmission in the house.

6 Because the modem is held in place by hook-and-loop straps, you can adjust its mount at any point.

WIRING PANEL MODULES

Because different types of cable are used in a distribution panel, there are, naturally, different connectors used to attach each one. Installing connectors is discussed at length on p. 134, so we'll keep it short here.

Using a combination stripping and crimping tool, strip the end of a coaxial cable ❶ and crimp an F-connector onto its end ❷. The F-connector then screws onto threaded input or output jacks.

As noted on p. 129, one coaxial cable that emerges from the splitter at the top of the panel plugs into the input jack labeled "CATV/ANT (Cable TV/Antenna)" on the amplifier module ❸. Via coaxial cables plugged into two output jacks on the amplifier, one cable plugs into the input port on the first splitter below, where the signal is split four ways and sent into four different rooms in the house. The second coax cable plugs into the input port on the bottom splitter, where it is also split four ways ❹.

Coaxial cable is stiff—especially in short lengths. To make wiring a bit easier, you can temporarily remove splitter shelves (modules) from the panel back, screw the coax onto the jacks, gently ease the wired splitters back into place, and reattach them to the panel.

Fortunately, Cat 5e cable is much easier to work with. Strip 3 in. of sheathing from the ends of Cat 5e cable and separate the stranded wire pairs. Then, using a punchdown tool, press the individual wires onto the insulation displacement connector (IDC) prongs on the back of the 12-port punch panel ❺. As the metal prongs displace the insulation, they create a solid electrical connection to the bare pins inside. The punchdown tool also removes excess wire.

The remaining connections between modules are typically achieved by using patch cords—lengths of cable whose data-cable plugs come preattached. So you can just insert them into jacks on the patch panel, router, telephone module, or modem.

1 After stripping the end of a coaxial cable, slide on an F-connector and . . .

2 . . . use a combination tool to crimp the F-connector securely to the cable.

3 One coaxial cable from the splitter at the top of the panel plugs into the input jack labeled "CATV/ANT" on the amplifier.

4 Two output cables from the amplifier plug into the two splitters below; each splitter sends signals to four different rooms.

5 Use a punchdown tool to press individual Cat 5e cable wires onto prongs on the back of the 12-port punch panel.

LOCATING THE MULTIMEDIA OUTLET

1 Place the new outlet at the same height as nearby receptacles.

2 Level the cut-in ring.

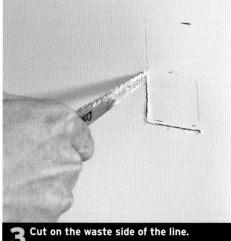

3 Cut on the waste side of the line.

4 Use a flexibit to drill access holes for the cables.

5 Hook the kellum to the bit and pull the cable to the outlet.

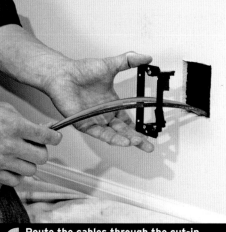

6 Route the cables through the cut-in ring and install it on the wall.

In general, electricians run one data, one phone, and one video cable to each outlet. In the example here, however, specs dictated two data lines (green and blue cables) and a coaxial cable for video.

When locating the cut-in ring for a new outlet set alongside an existing receptacle, always measure from the center of the existing box so the center screws on the cover plates will line up **1**. The two types of cover plates may be different sizes, so lining up their tops or bottoms won't look good. Level the cut-in ring and trace its outline on the wall. (The template shown in the top photo

on p. 123 is another option.) Don't try to eyeball level: If you're even slightly off, the outlet will look cockeyed **2**.

Use a jab saw (drywall saw) to cut out the opening. To start the cut accurately, strike the heel of your hand against the saw handle. To avoid cutting too large a hole, cut on the waste side of the outline **3**.

To bring cables from the distribution panel, drill holes into the wall plate using a flexibit **4**. Use a drilling guide to protect your hands while guiding the bit. Flexibits have a hole in the point. After the bit emerges through the wall plate, have someone tape

the cables together, slide a swivel kellum over the taped wires, and hook the kellum to the bit **5**. The kellum swivels, so the wires won't twist up as you reverse the drill and pull them back up through the hole. Install the cut-in ring to provide a mounting surface for the outlet plate **6**.

➡ **For more on running wires, see pp. 206–211.**

INSTALLING CABLE CONNECTORS

In the next few pages, we'll discuss the installation of several different types of cable connectors: F-connectors used on coaxial cable (video), as well as two popular systems (from Panduit® and Leviton®) that connect to Cat 3 cable (phone), Cat 5e, and Cat 6 cables (telephone or data). Each connector maker specifies tools and methods of assembly, so follow its installation instructions closely.

There are several types of F-connector styles, including twist, push-on, crimp, and (shown in the photo sequence at right) compression fittings. Each type has its merits, but in our opinion, compression fittings are the most reliable and the least

likely to damage coax cable. Whatever style you choose, be sure it's compatible with the cable being installed.

Use a combination stripper-crimper to strip insulation off the end of the coaxial cable. Stick the cable in the end of the tool, spin it, and peel off both types of insulation from the outer sheathing ❶. The tool leaves about ½ in. of bare copper and ¼ in. of white insulation with the shielding on it. Slide an F-connector over the stripped end of the coaxial ❷. Place an F-connector in the crimping bay, insert the stripped cable, and squeeze the tool to crimp the connector tight to the cable ❸. (*Note:* The F-connector shown here is a watertight variety.)

1 Spin the stripper-crimper on the coaxial cable.

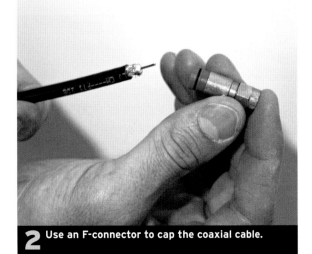

2 Use an F-connector to cap the coaxial cable.

PRO TIP

It's not necessary to house lo-vo multimedia connections in covered junction boxes (required for high-voltage splices). Install flush-mounted cut-in rings (data rings) to provide a secure device to which you can attach outlet plates and insert jacks. A brush faceplate (p. 137) is an inexpensive way to finish the data ring. Whether you're mounting doorbell chimes or a multimedia wall outlet, take the time to level and plumb the device and, if there's another outlet nearby, to align the height of the new outlet.

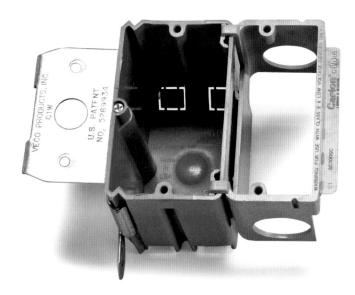

3 Crimp the F-connector to the cable.

CONNECTING PANDUIT JACKS

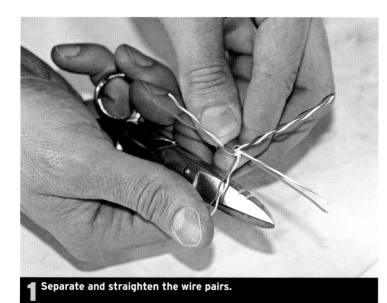

1 Separate and straighten the wire pairs.

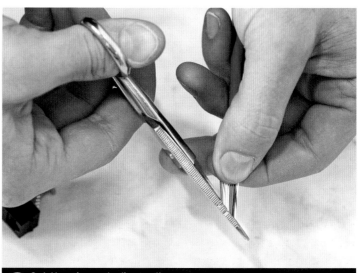

2 Cut the wire ends diagonally.

3 Push the wires in all the way.

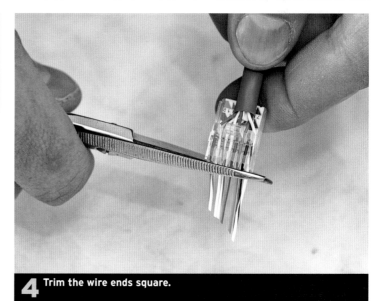

4 Trim the wire ends square.

Connecting phone or data cable jacks to a multimedia outlet requires a few steps. Start by reviewing Stripping Cable (see p. 123). Cat 5e and Cat 6 cable are UTP cable, so after stripping about 3 in. of sheathing, separate the wire pairs before attaching them to a jack. If you use Panduit jacks (often referred to as Pan jacks), you'll also need to unwind (untwist) the wires.

Use stripping scissors to unwind the individual cable wires before attaching them to a Pan jack **❶**. Using light pressure, pull the wires across a scissor blade to straighten them. Next, slide the wires into a plastic cap, which is color coded to indicate where the wires go. Flatten the wires and cut their ends diagonally so they'll slide easily into the cap **❷**. Push the wires all the way into

>> >> >>

CONNECTING PANDUIT JACKS (CONTINUED)

5 Pair a Panduit jack housing with a wired cap.

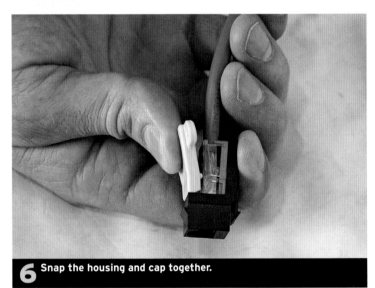

6 Snap the housing and cap together.

the cap **❸**, then trim the wire ends straight across **❹**.

The wired cap snaps into a jack housing, forcing the wires into V-shaped IDC prongs that slice the wire insulation to make the electrical contact **❺**. Place the wired cap onto the jack housing and use the small plastic lever provided to snap the assembly together **❻**. Panduit jacks are reliable because they make secure connections.

INSTALLING LEVITON JACKS

The Leviton jack system uses the 110 punchdown tool required to punch down wires in the distribution panel (see photo 5 on p. 132). But the system takes practice to avoid loose wires, so amateur electricians might get more predictable results using Panduit jacks.

In the Leviton system, there's no need to untwist wires. Separate the wire pairs and punch them directly into the IDC prongs built into the jack. Use the plastic disc provided to back the jack as you punch down **❶**. The punchdown tool comes with 110 and 66 blade sizes; each blade has a side that punches the wire down and a side that cuts off excess wire. For best results, work from back to front to avoid disturbing wires that are already down. Once you've connected the wires, snap on the jack's trim cap, which keeps wires in place and relieves strain on the connection **❷**.

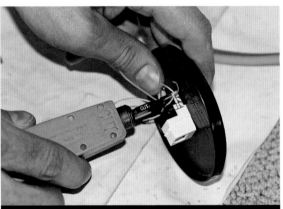

1 Punch down the wires to the Leviton jacks.

2 Snap the trim cap into place.

ATTACHING JACKS TO AN OUTLET PLATE

In the project shown here, we're installing both Leviton and the Panduit jacks to show that despite variations in jack wiring, both snap into the most common type of faceplate, the keystone style.

To install coaxial terminals, snap the threaded coupling into the faceplate ❶. The coaxial cable's F-connector screws to the coupling, creating a clean termination instead of having cable hanging out of the wall ❷. Snap a RJ-45 (eight-pin) Leviton jack into the faceplate ❸ (see p. 138). Note the color coding on the side of the jack to indicate the order of wires you punched down earlier. Finally, snap a RJ-45 Panduit jack into the remaining port in the keystone plate ❹ (see p. 138).

Carefully feed the cable into the wall, hold the faceplate flush to the wall, and screw it to the cut-in ring ❺ (see p. 138). The outlet shown uses phone and data jacks that are different colors so that users can quickly differentiate which jack is which. This differentiation is not an issue in residences, but it's imperative in business installations.

>> >> >>

(see p. 138)

FACEPLATE OPTIONS

There are many types of faceplates on the market for mounting telephone, data, coaxial, and specialty jacks. They come designed to match the adjacent electrical outlet (for example, duplex or Decora® style) and in various colors.

There are also faceplates and adapters for specific applications such as video (HDMI, S-video, component video, VGA), sound, and fiber optics. One favorite is infinitely flexible: A brush faceplate accepts up to four cables—just feed them through and its brushes fill the space between cables to give a finished look.

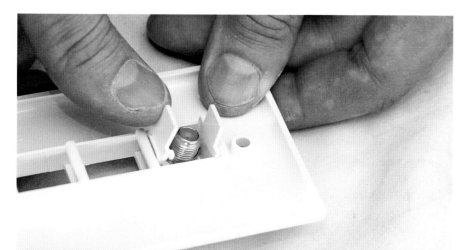

1 Snap on the screw-in coupling for coaxial cable.

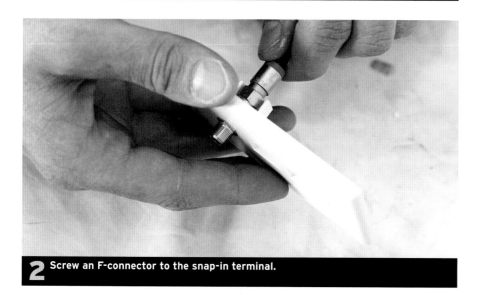

2 Screw an F-connector to the snap-in terminal.

ATTACHING JACKS TO AN OUTLET PLATE (CONTINUED)

3 Snap in the Leviton data jack.

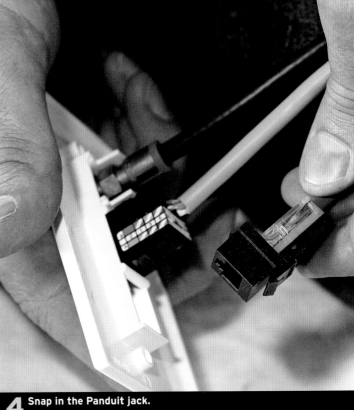

4 Snap in the Panduit jack.

5 Screw the faceplate into place.

WHOLE-HOUSE MUSIC SYSTEMS

Not long ago, whole-house audio systems required cabling to key-pads and cabling to input devices (CD players, tuners, etc.). With the rise of wireless transmission and smartphone control, however, much of that has changed. To be sure, speakers will still be physically connected to something, either a wireless receiver and power supply or directly to a player. But these days keypad controls have been replaced by the convenience of smartphones and tablets, whereas input sources like CD players have been replaced with digital audio files.

In addition, expensive music servers have been supplanted by high-capacity solid-state storage in smartphones, tablets, and USB storage devices. A smartphone or tablet has enough memory to store hundreds of songs, as does a USB drive plugged into the back of a multi-zone amplifier, such as the one shown on p. 140. In addition, there's the enormous capacity of streaming music services, such as Pandora®, Spotify®, Google Play™, Sirius XM®, Apple Music®, Amazon Prime®, and many more, which you can effortlessly access with a smartphone.

Let's take a look.

Music in the air: smartphone apps and streaming audio

Wi-Fi home audio systems are available from some of the giants of Internet and sound equipment technology, including Chromecast™ Audio (Google®), Bose SoundTouch®, Amazon Echo®, Yamaha®, Nuvo®, and Sonos®.

In this section, we consider the Nuvo audio system because its parent company, Legrand, has made high-end electrical products for years and the Nuvo app is highly intuitive and its audio hardware is easy to integrate.

Like most smartphone apps, Nuvo is free. After you download it, it walks you through setting up your system. You assign zones to different rooms—kitchen, dining room, master bedroom, kid's room, living room, den, etc. Then you access your music.

There are several ways to bring up music. If you are in the Nuvo app, it will find music that is in the Nuvo system, music that is on your phone, or music that you have downloaded into the Nuvo app specifically. If you go to a different application, Nuvo will populate that app with your zones, so you can control them from there.

If you can't directly access a music source—say, Spotify—from the Nuvo app, you can go to the Spotify app and select a song. As the music plays, "Devices Available" comes up on the bottom of the screen. If you click that, all your zones will come up. So you can tell it what music to play in each room.

In that manner, you can put different music in every room and control the volume of each from your smartphone. If you are streaming Pandora or Spotify and turn your phone off, the music will continue to stream. Of course, anyone who's on your network can also control the music from their phone.

Wireless vs. wired audio systems

When speaking of "wired" vs. "wireless" in regard to distributed audio, we are speaking of the wiring to the speakers and not the "control" of the system. The industry has shifted and wireless control is commonplace. However, speakers still require significant amounts of power and still need some physical connection to a power supply.

On a "wired" system like the NV-P3100, speaker cabling is run all the way back to the player, which has onboard amplifiers to drive

>> >> >>

The Nuvo smartphone app can direct music from various sources into rooms throughout the house.

Like most smartphone music apps, Nuvo enables you to add and control music sources, listening zones, and audio devices.

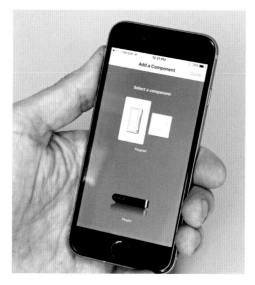

You can also add auxiliary control devices, such as wall keypads and players.

WHOLE-HOUSE MUSIC SYSTEMS (CONTINUED)

(power) them. A "wireless" system by contrast has a wireless receiver with a built-in amplifier that has to be powered separately. The speakers are then connected directly to the receiver/amplifier.

The choice between wired and wireless systems really comes down to cost benefit and the end goal of the installation. Generally speaking, wired systems are the most cost-effective solution where speaker cabling can be routed and concealed, where speakers are recessed in ceilings, in walls, or in landscaping, or where three or more zones are to be installed.

Wireless systems, by contrast, are better solutions where wiring cannot be concealed, where bookshelf or free-standing speakers are to be used, where a limited number of zones are desired, or in conjunction with a wired system—but in an area (zone) where cabling is not possible or a zone is added after the fact.

One sound system's specifics

Start by developing a house plan to show where speakers will be. In the home system shown here, three rooms were already wired and three more would be added. So six locations—zones—in all. Because most of the homeowner's sound came from online sources, it made little sense to put audio components in the home network distribution panel in the garage. Instead, the sound technician installed a new sound distribution system—the fancy name for black boxes with lights on them—on racks centrally located in the basement.

Based on the six zones in the house, the tech recommended two three-zone Nuvo NV-P3100 player-amplifiers. Each player has three sets of jacks for speaker cable, a USB port into which you can plug in a thumb drive full of music, and an analog input and output for each channel so you can connect the player to an existing audio source, such as a CD player.

The audio cables were 14AWG stranded copper. When evaluating speaker cabling, focus on low resistance, which comes down to conductor size relative to the load carried and the distance. Based on the speaker wattage served (in this case, 40w) and the distance (less than 75 ft.), increased wattage or distance would dictate a larger cable (12 AWG or 10 AWG).

Later on, the homeowner wanted to add speakers where there was no wiring, so he chose a compact, wireless player—the Nuvo P100 audio player, which can communicate to other parts of the whole-house system wirelessly (or wired). The P100 receives audio signals either wirelessly or via ethernet, and, because each is also an amplifier (the unit must be plugged into a 120v outlet), it can drive (power) a pair of speakers nearby. So there was no need to drill or cut holes in the walls. Once the new device was added to the network, it could speak to all other devices and could be controlled from a smartphone or tablet.

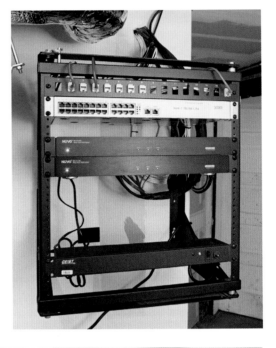

The brains of one family's whole-house audio system are the two Nuvo NV-P3100 multi-zone player-amplifiers in the middle of the rack.

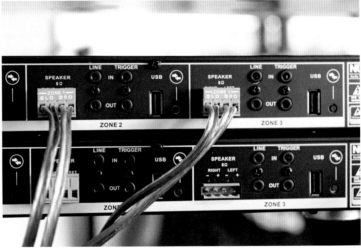

Speaker cables are connected to terminal blocks by zone.

The Nuvo P100 is used where running speaker cabling is not practical.

RETROFITTING A SPEAKER

Adding a speaker is largely a matter of running wire between two points and making solid electrical connections at both ends. You may also need to drill holes in framing to run wire and cut a hole in a wall or ceiling to inset the speaker.

To size speaker wire correctly, read the manufacturer's specs to find the *maximum output ratings* for the audio equipment you are connecting. Then determine the distance from the amplifier or sound-system controller to the speaker. For runs up to 80 ft., use 16-ga. wire; for runs 80 ft. to 200 ft., 14-ga. wire; longer than 200 ft., 12-ga. wire.

To minimize repairs, try to run speaker wire through unfinished attic or basement spaces. If you must fish wire (p. 209), use a long flexible drill bit and a swivel kellum grip to simplify the task. To locate speakers in finish surfaces, drill a small exploratory hole and insert a piece of coat hanger bent at a right angle to help locate studs or ceiling joists: That is, move speakers (as needed) to avoid cutting into framing. Most in-wall speakers are held in place by spring clips or swivel ears.

Typically, left and right speaker wires are identical and are not color-coded. But serious audiophiles with complex sound separation or surround-sound systems should identify L and R speaker wires with colored tape before fishing them through walls and connect them to appropriate terminals on both ends. Follow your system's set-up diagrams.

Most in-wall speakers have spring clips or *spring-loaded binding posts* that receive bare wire ends ❶. Use wire strippers to remove ³⁄₈ in. to ¹⁄₂ in. of insulation from the end of the stranded wires. Place the speaker into the wall or ceiling hole ❷, being careful not to pinch the speaker wires. Next tighten

>> >> >>

1 Close-up of speaker wire connections. Thin spring clips hold the speaker in place temporarily until you tighten the swivel ears on the side of the housing.

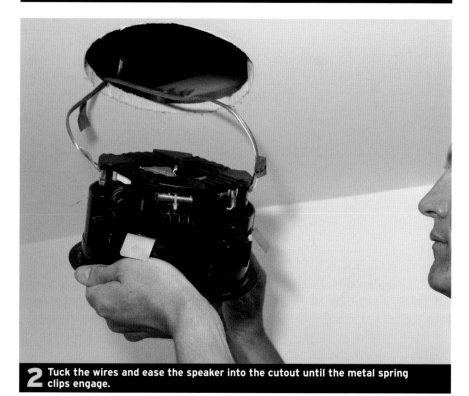

2 Tuck the wires and ease the speaker into the cutout until the metal spring clips engage.

RETROFITTING A SPEAKER (CONTINUED)

the mounting screws, which will extend swivel ears out from the speaker body and pull the unit's lip tight to the finish surface ❸. Attach the speaker face ❹, which is usually held on with magnets.

If your speakers are free-standing (not inset), choose fittings that will look good. The RCA audio jacks shown in the photo on p. 122 are popular and easy to install. The jacks fit into an audio wall plate and receive a gold-plated banana plug. (Fittings are gold-plated, by the way, to improve conductivity.)

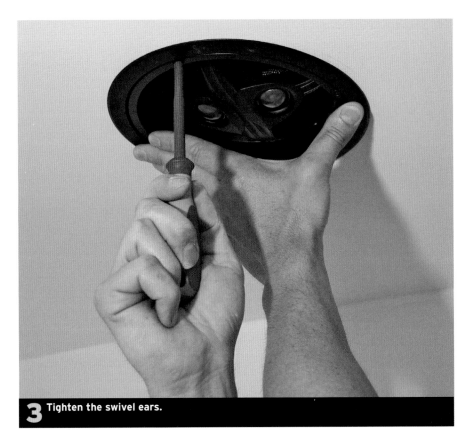

3 Tighten the swivel ears.

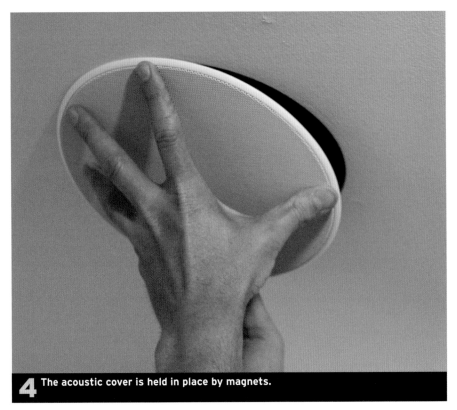

4 The acoustic cover is held in place by magnets.

RETROFITTING A USB CHARGER/RECEPTACLE COMBO

1 Cut power to the outlet and use a noncontact tester to be sure the power is off. Test all three slots in the receptacle.

2 Remove the snap-on cover (if any), then unscrew the mounting plate.

Mobile electronic devices go everywhere, yet, being battery-powered, they must stop from time to time to get recharged. In this section we will show how to replace a standard duplex receptacle with an ingenious USB charger/receptacle combo that speeds recharging and gets more use out of a one-gang outlet. As a bonus, the receptacle portion of the combo is tamper-resistant (TR). For more about TR receptacles, see p. 40.

Though the upper portion of this combo device has two USB ports, these ports do *not* enable you to transfer data. The USB ports exist solely to recharge mobile devices. Because the combo has a built-in transformer, you no longer need the cube-like adaptor into which an iPad®, iPhone®, Kindle®, etc., USB cord inserts.

The combo shown in the photo sequence above has a TR outlet rated 15A, 125v; its USB ports are rated 2.1A (DC), 5v (DC).

Installation

Turn off the power to an existing outlet and use a noncontact voltage tester ❶ to be sure the outlet is de-energized. Lock the breaker panel or remove the fuse controlling the outlet to be sure that no one inadvertently re-energizes the circuit while you are working on it.

Remove the cover plate ❷, unscrew the mounting screws holding the existing receptacle to the outlet box, and gently pull

>> >> >>

Hubbell's® USB Charger Duplex Receptacles provide both USB and electrical power in a standard single-gang opening. Hubbell also offers 4-port chargers.

RETROFITTING A USB CHARGER/RECEPTACLE COMBO (CONTINUED)

3 Without touching the sides of the receptacle, unscrew the mounting screws.

4 Remove wires from the old receptacle; attach them to the new device.

5 Clamps next to screw terminals receive the stripped wire ends.

the device out from the wall. Disconnect its wires in this order: hot (black), neutral (white), ground (green or bare copper) **3**.

Reconnect wires to the new USB combo in the reverse order: First connect the ground wire to the green grounding screw **4**, then connect the neutral wire, then the hot wire. As shown here, the installer reused the existing loop to attach the ground wire, but he elected to back-wire the neutral and hot wires. He used needle-nose pliers to straighten their loops, then snipped them so the stripped portion of each wire was $\frac{1}{2}$ in. long. He then inserted each straightened wire end into a clamp next to a terminal screw. The neutral (white) wire attached to the clamp next to the silver screw; the hot (black) wire attached to the clamp next to the brass screw **5**. Tighten terminal screws to grip wires firmly in the clamps.

Carefully fold the combo receptacle into the box, tighten mounting screws, and install the cover plate. Re-energize the circuit and you are ready to charge your mobile devices.

This USB charger/ TR receptacle combo charges more quickly than a standard USB adaptor; you can also charge two mobile devices on the top of the combo.

INSTALLING A WALL-HUNG TELEVISION

Securing the wall-hung TV bracket **is the key to all that follows: locating the outlet box, running cables to the box, and, of course, mounting the TV. Get help; wall-hung TVs are heavy.**

The principal challenge to installing a wall-hung TV is structural, not electrical, because flat-panel displays are heavy. Only once you have secured the TV's mounting bracket to the framing can you decide exactly where to place the outlet box that will supply power (120v) and low-voltage A/V cables. Correctly located, those cables won't be seen, even though the TV will be the most visible object in the room.

Note: All electrical work in this section must be done with the power off. Before you begin, test to be sure cables are de-energized (p. 43).

Install the bracket

Read bracket-mounting instructions carefully and make small exploratory holes to determine exactly where the stud centers are located. Lag screws used to mount brackets are hefty ($5/16$ in. to $3/16$ in. by 3 in.), and you want to be sure that they sink into the middle of studs; otherwise, you risk splitting them. Drill pilot holes. In most cases, you can install flat-panel TV brackets without having to open the wall and add blocking.

Locate the outlet box

The outlet box should be located so that cables won't interfere with the bracket's movement. As a

---

CHOOSING A WALL-HUNG TV BRACKET

TV brackets usually come with the television, rated for the weight of the unit. This bracket will likely be a standard, nontilting type that allows no adjustments once the screen is mounted. Consequently, many people buy a separate bracket that tilts, or tilts and pivots on an articulating arm.

If the screen is more or less at eye level, you can get by with a fixed bracket. But if the TV is mounted up high on the wall, at least get a tilting bracket so that you can tilt the screen to achieve an optimal viewing angle—roughly 10 to 20 degrees from your line of sight (when seated) to the top of the screen. If you like having friends over for movie night or

sports events, consider an articulating bracket that enables you to pull the screen out from the wall and tilt and pivot it till there's not a bad seat in the house.

Not surprisingly, durable, multi-directional brackets are pricey—$500 is not unheard of. If you watch a lot of TV, spend the money: Replacing a bracket later on may be a major pain, because it could require moving the outlet box, too. *Important:* When shopping for brackets, take the TV's technical literature to ensure that the new bracket can support the weight and that bracket holes will align with mounting hardware on the back of the set.

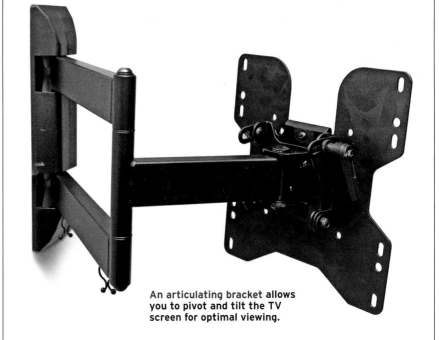

An articulating bracket allows you to pivot and tilt the TV screen for optimal viewing.

---

rule of thumb, putting the box over the bracket will keep cables from getting pinched when the top of the screen tilts forward. Expensive brackets often have cut-outs in the frame to accommodate a one-gang or two-gang box, and places in the articulating arm through which to run cable. So when the arm is pulled out, the cable(s) are hardly visible. These cut-outs typically line up with input jacks in the back of the TV. »» »» »»

INSTALLING A WALL-HUNG TELEVISION (CONTINUED)

Run power to the outlet box

After locating the new outlet but before cutting into finish surfaces, find the nearest existing outlet to tap into. (It must be on a circuit with unused capacity.) Think 3D: A power source might be on the other side of a wall, in a built-in cabinet, or on the floor above or below. If possible, run power down from an attic or up from a basement because drilling through wall plates to reach a stud bay will minimize patching finish surfaces later. (Drilling and fishing cable are discussed on pp. 209–211.)

The new box will contain both a line voltage cable (120v) and low-voltage cable(s)—most commonly, *high-definition multimedia interface* (HDMI) cable. (Keep line and lo-vo cables isolated from each other, as explained on the facing page.) To house both types of cables you will need either a two-gang box with a snap-in divider or a one-gang box paired with a data ring. We like the second option because the side of the one-gang box isolates the Romex cable from the lo-vo, and the data ring has 1-in. knockouts that receive 1-in. ENT conduit, which we'll explain next.

Wire for the future

High-tech equipment changes so often that it's impossible to know what data lines or A/V cable you will need five or ten years from now. However, if you run electrical nonmetallic tubing (ENT) to the outlet box and feed A/V cables through the ENT, future upgrades will be easy. ENT is a corrugated plastic conduit that offers little friction so it's easy to snake new wires through it. It has the secondary benefit of isolating lo-vo lines, too. ENT connects to outlet boxes and data rings via a screw-on connector that fits into a 1-in. knockout. Use PVC straps to secure ENT to the sides of studs, but remember to locate the ENT at least 1¼ in. back from stud edges so the ENT can't get perforated by drywall screws or nails.

Making connections

Trace the outlet box onto the wall. Use a jab saw to cut an opening into drywall or an oscillating multi-tool if the wall is plaster. Pull the cables (and the ENT) through the opening and feed them through knockouts in the cut-in box, tighten cable connec-

Locate the outlet box **only after the bracket is secured to the wall. This installer is tracing the outline of a two-gang box; you can also use a data ring clipped onto a one-gang box.**

Running low-voltage cables **through flexible ENT conduit will make replacing cables someday much easier.**

PRO TIP

A pro notes: "Until the TV bracket is mounted, don't install the outlet box: It will *always* be in the wrong place. If we're roughing out a room that will have a wall-hung, we run cable into the stud bay and tape it off, so that after the homeowner chooses the bracket, an electrician can cut a hole into the wall in the correct place, reach in and retrieve the cable, and mount the box where he *knows* it won't interfere with the bracket."

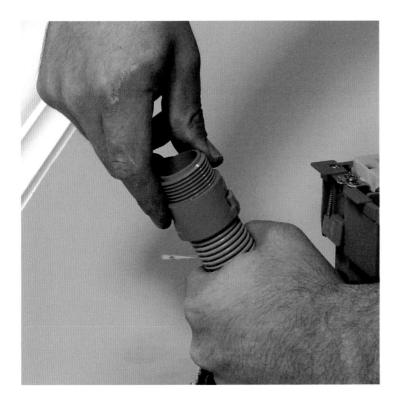

1-in. diameter ENT connectors will fit into most box or data-ring knock-outs. In retrofits, attach the connector to the box (or data ring) before securing the box to the wall.

Don't Mix Signals Keep line-voltage (120v) and low-voltage cables isolated from each other to avoid electromagnetic interference between lines. To achieve isolation,

1. Keep cables at least 2 in. to 6 in. apart when they run parallel.
2. Don't run cables through the same holes or under the same staples.
3. Where cables must cross, do it at a right angle to minimize contact.
4. If cables share a two-gang box, isolate them by inserting a plastic divider in the middle of the box. Alternately, you can feed the line voltage into a one-gang box and run A/V cables into a data ring next to it.

tors (if any), and then secure the box to the wall. Remove Romex cable sheathing, strip insulation from individual wires, and attach them to the screw terminals of a duplex receptacle.

Because the receptacle will be hidden by the TV screen, spend a bit extra to get a *transient-voltage surge-suppressor* (TVSS) receptacle with an audible alarm. Should outlet protection or function fail, the receptacle will sound a warning. TVSS receptacles are about the size of a GFCI receptacle, so you may need to remove the receptacle's mounting ears to allow the cover plate to sit flush. To finish off the data ring, we suggest using the brush faceplate shown on p. 137. It cleanly finishes the opening and accommodates a number of lo-vo cables.

Before energizing the new outlet, use a multimeter to test the new circuit for dead shorts.

Showtime

Once the electrical connections are complete, get several helpers to mount the wall-hung television onto its bracket and plug cables into the receptacle and inputs on the back of the set. This takes at least three people.

This TVSS receptacle will sound an audible alarm should the outlet protection fail. Audible alarms are especially appropriate if the receptacle is hidden by the TV screen.

WHOLE-HOUSE CONTROL SYSTEMS

Whole-house systems have been around for a while, mostly to control lighting and distribute music in high-end homes where entertaining was common, there were multiple lighting types in each room, and there were more rooms than one person could reasonably monitor. The solution to this privileged problem was automation, but it was complicated, typically installed during new construction and major remodels, and best left to professionals. And it cost the moon: $30K or $40K installations were nothing unusual.

Technology has changed all that. Solid-state devices now pack processing power in switches and other devices that were previously very basic. As important, wireless communication—specifically low-frequency radio waves that can penetrate walls and other solid barriers—has spawned a host of options for controlling lighting, shades, HVAC systems, and appliances such as televisions, computers, satellite dishes, and sound systems. New control systems are increasingly affordable, scalable, suitable for existing homes or retrofits, and (except for a few tasks) something do-it-yourselfers can take on.

Today, whole-house systems are installed mostly for convenience and comfort, though energy conservation is an increasingly important reason to do so, as federal and state agencies mandate conservation measures such as replacing incandescent bulbs with CFLs and LEDs and utilities incorporate smart-grid technologies.

Security is another big growth area. To cite one example, some control systems offer one-button "Away" settings that simulate the cycles of a busy household even when no one is at home. Lights come on at dusk and wink on and off in different rooms till bedtime when they all go out; shades go up and down; music plays in different rooms. A businessperson suddenly called out of town will have one less thing to worry about. And if you're away from home when a bad storm is approaching, you can change thermostat settings from your iPad.

Smart grids In many areas, electrical grids operate at close to maximum output and adding capacity isn't economically feasible. One way to optimize existing capacity is to reduce electrical demand during peak hours—by charging more for peak-hour electricity and charging less for off-peak usage. The key to monitoring this usage is a *smart grid,* in which there is an ongoing, two-way conversation between each energy user and energy suppliers (utility companies). In such a grid, each household has a *smart meter* that notes both use and time of use and bills customers accordingly.

Whole-house control systems would, in turn, interface with smart meters, inform homeowners about usage patterns, and suggest ways to save money by automatically cutting back on energy use during peak hours. But while smart-grid goals are generally lauded, smart meters are often lambasted as an invasion of privacy, an injury to health, and worse. Will the smarties prevail? Stay tuned.

INSTALLING REPEATERS

Repeaters are the brains of a whole-house control system. Lutron recommends installing repeaters in out-of-sight locations that will not be disturbed, such as closets and cabinets. All wireless devices must be located within 30 ft. (9 m.) of a repeater, so large homes may require auxiliary repeaters.

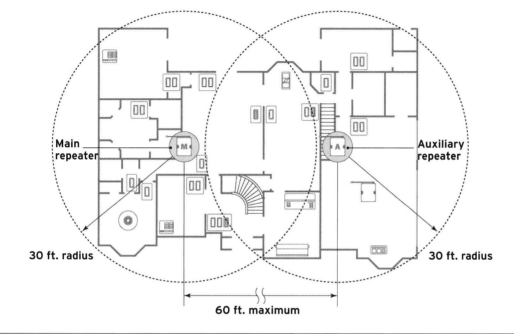

INSTALLING DEVICES

Repeaters communicate with multiple wireless devices, such as dimmer/switches, shade/ drapery controls, zone controls, occupancy/vacancy sensors, auto transmitters, and so on.

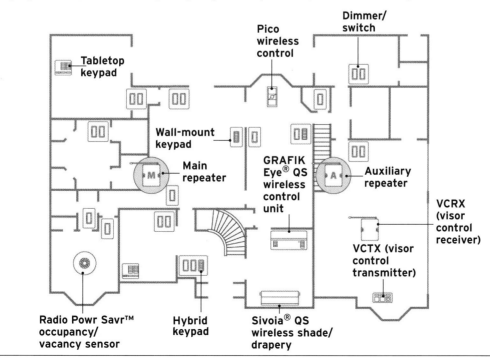

Drawings adapted from Lutron RadioRA® 2 "Manual Setup Guide," with permission of Lutron Electronics Co., Inc.

INTEGRATING WHOLE-HOUSE SYSTEMS

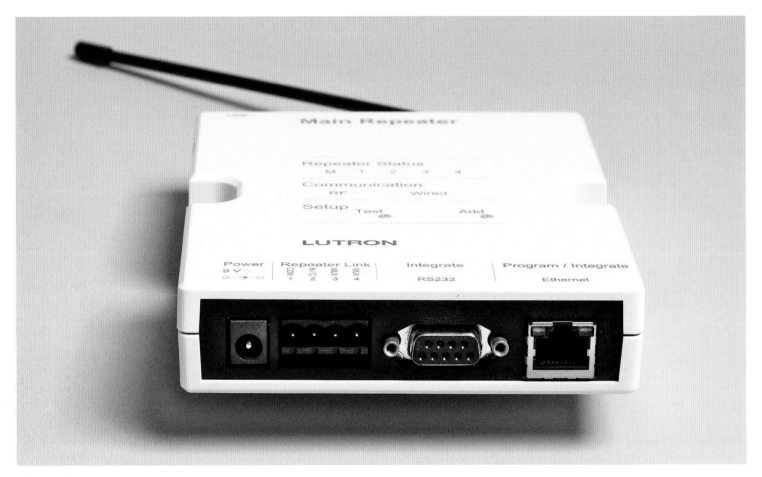

Multiple cables feed into the bottom of a main repeater. From left: power input; links to auxiliary repeaters (to extend signal); RS232 port (integrates different systems); Ethernet RJ45 port to connect to LAN, program and integrate devices into the system, etc.

Integrating whole-house control systems is complex. One logical set of systems to integrate are those impacting energy consumption—namely, lighting controls, raising and lowering shades (for solar gain and heat retention), and HVAC.

Lutron's RadioRA 2 product (along with their shade line) is an interesting solution because it's relatively affordable, integrates several functions, can be retrofit using existing wiring, and, with a little help setting it up, can be largely installed by a homeowner. (Ballpark estimate for a DIY installation: $2,000 to $2,500 for equipment, plus electrician fees to set up and activate the system.) The bulk of the installation is replacing existing devices with smart devices that communicate wirelessly, or adding in devices that do not require wiring at all. Reduced to bullets, it looks like this:

■ Replace existing switches with smart switches or hybrid keypads (keypads that don't just act as control points but also switch and dim light sources).

■ Install stand-alone keypads or controls.
■ Install dimming modules and switching modules at lamps and media-type appliances. (It's worth noting that when you switch off TV or computer screens, those appliances are on standby mode, drawing "phantom power." A keypad that controls the whole room turns appliances completely off, saving a considerable amount of energy.)
■ Install motorized wireless shades.
■ Replace conventional HVAC controls with smart thermostats and sensors.

All of these devices communicate with a central (programmable) *repeater* that creates a wireless network of communication and control that, once programmed, can perform multiple functions with a single button, monitor and conserve energy, and communicate two-way with utility company smart grids.

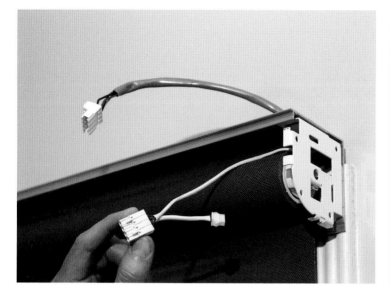

This motorized shade requires 24v, which the cable at top supplies. The clip in hand connects to the shade motor; the clip attached to the pigtail connects to a wireless dongle.

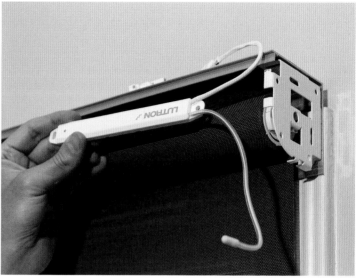

This Lutron wireless dongle communicates to a wireless controller via the RadioRA 2 system. The capped wire hanging down is the antenna lead.

Living-area shades are typically filtered; blackout shades are often spec'd for bedrooms. Tucked behind the shade, power and wireless dongle cables are invisible.

Basic wireless controls
Basic wireless controls communicate with other devices on a limited basis— as distinguished from wireless controls that oversee whole-house functions. The Maestro wireless switch and Pico controller shown on p. 60 are examples of basic wireless controls. Typically, such controls are programmed directly by pressing switch and/or program buttons.

Other types of basic wireless controls include the following:

- Wireless motion sensors that talk to a local wireless switch, used in a storage room, porch, or other space where occupancy sensing would be useful.

- Keypads that control a lamp, installed next to an existing light switch in a living room, dining room, or bedroom.

- Wireless switches retrofitted to replace inconveniently located manual ones.

A TYPICAL INSTALLATION

This wireless keypad communicates with the main repeater and so—via the repeater—this keypad can be programmed to control wireless switches and shades anywhere in the house. Though communicating wirelessly, the keypad is powered by line voltage (120v).

If your house is already wired for sound, you can plug ethernet cables into these keypad room controllers and select music without involving your smartphone.

Just as there is no average family, there are no typical installations, but yours might include these tasks: (1) swap out switches in major rooms and bedrooms with hybrid keypads; (2) where there are groups of switches in a room, replace one switch with a hybrid keypad and change out the others to wireless switches; (3) plug in dimming modules between wall outlets and the floor and table lamps; (4) for appliances with phantom loads, plug in switching units between the equipment and the receptacle serving them; (5) install wireless shades (light-filtering shades in family rooms, living rooms, and kitchens; perhaps blackout shades in bedrooms); (6) upgrade HVAC controls (such as thermostats) and add stand-alone controls by bedside tables.

With this system, entire rooms (lights, lamps, shades, or any other appliance that has a cord connection) can be controlled from a single location or via remote control; lights, shades, and HVAC can be programmed to operate automatically; a single button can gently turn up all of the lights in your home, drop the shades for privacy, and turn the heater on; and, if you like, you can monitor and control the system via your smartphone or tablet.

SETTING UP THE WHOLE-HOUSE SYSTEM

Setting up whole-house control systems such as RadioRA 2 is largely menu-driven and fairly intuitive once you get the hang of it. But the menu is complex and thus daunting to many people. More to the point, most homeowners won't know what the system can do or what their options are. So hire a pro to help set up the system—typically, a licensed electrician company-trained in the system he or she is installing.

An installer will start by sitting down with the homeowners to get a sense of their needs and to tell them what the system can do. From that input, the installer pieces together a system room by room. A basic floor plan emerges locating the repeater (main controller), keypad controllers, and all the devices you'll need to swap out. From a floor plan you can ballpark the costs of different options and estimate how complex programming will be.

If the homeowner wants to save money by installing most of the components (based upon the floor plan), the electrician will work up a list of equipment to buy. In general, installing devices is no more difficult than, say, replacing a switch. Once the new devices are in, the electrician will upload the software program and commission (activate) the system.

There are typically many steps to activate and fine-tune the system—it's not hard but you must go through the software and respond to many prompts that enable the controller to recognize installed components. After homeowners use the system for a month, they often have the installer return to tweak the system—make this button do this, turn on the furnace a little earlier, make the shades lower more slowly. The electrician makes and uploads those changes. Finally, when functions are all settled and everything works well, the manufacturer will engrave the names of functions onto keypad keys for free. Turn off the power, snap the engraved keys onto the proper locations, turn the power on, and you're done.

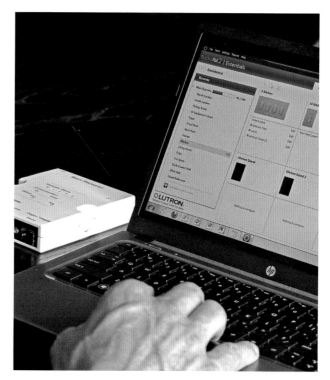

Menu-driven design/programming by manufacturer-trained professionals expands the options available and reduces the time required to set up and commission the system, solves compatibility issues as you go, develops complete parts lists, facilitates changes, allows for back-up, and, if properly networked, allows changes to be made remotely.

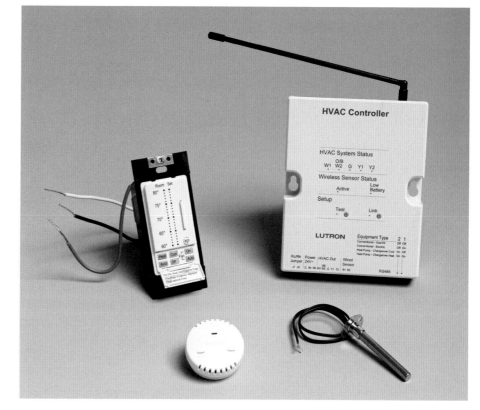

Clockwise, from upper right: HVAC controller mounts on and is wired to HVAC unit; duct sensor reads temperature of return air; wireless temperature sensor can be placed throughout the house; temperature control can be manually set, talks to HVAC controller.

FANS

RESIDENTIAL FANS CAN BE DIVIDED into two groups. The first group, primarily ceiling fans, circulate still, summer air and thus increase comfort by evaporating moisture on your skin. In cold climates, these fans push warm air down from the ceiling where it collects, so it can once again warm the bodies below. Whole-house fans, installed in attics in warm regions, also circulate hot air, but because they typically push it out roof or gable-end vents, whole-house fans are more like exhaust fans without ducts.

The second group might be better called exhaust or vent fans, because their primary function is to remove moist or odor-laden air from living spaces, route it through ducts, and expel it outside. Commonly installed bath fans and range hoods both fall into this category. By removing excessive interior moisture, these fans help forestall mold and other unhealthy conditions.

CEILING FANS

BATHROOM VENT FANS

RANGE HOODS

CHOOSING A CEILING FAN

There are a dizzying number of fan features and competing claims to sort out, so let's start with a few facts. The primary function of a ceiling fan is to move air efficiently. Ceiling fans don't cool the air in a room, they cool the *people* in a room by increasing the evaporation of moisture (sweat) on their skin. As obvious as this may seem, it's central to understanding energy efficiency because if there's no one in a room to cool, the fan shouldn't be running.

In addition to cooling a room's inhabitants, ceiling fans can also warm them by pushing heated air downward, thus increasing the efficiency of a home heating system.

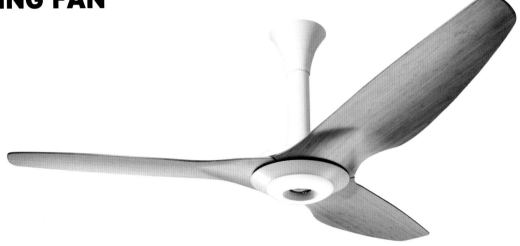

The integral LED light ring of this Haiku® Home fan fits within its sleek silhouette.

Where to start

To promote energy conservation, the EPA's Energy Star® program rates the efficiency of various products, including ceiling fans. So its website www.energystar.gov is a good place to start your search. It rates ceiling fans in a number of categories, including air-flow efficiency by speed, energy efficiency, fan motor warranty, and, for fans with light kits, light output, color quality, and light-source life. The site also offers helpful suggestions about sizing a fan and selecting a mounting system.

Choosing the right size

The spans of ceiling fans intended for home use typically range from 29 in. to 54 in. across, although one company, appropriately named Big Ass Fans®, offers home fans with spans of 54 in. to 84 in. Energy Star offers this chart:

FAN SIZES	
Floor area (in sq. ft.)	Suggested fan size (diameter)
Up to 75	29 in. to 36 in.
76-144	36 in. to 42 in.
145-225	44 in.
226-400	50 in. to 54 in.

Output may also be expressed in cfm (cubic feet per minute). For example, a good-quality fan with a 36-in. span will move 2,500 cfm to 4,000 cfm.

The number of fan blades (airfoils) will vary from two to nine, with three to five being the most common configuration. Generally speaking, more blades don't move more air. More important is the blade pitch (angle): the steeper the pitch, the more air it will move. The blades of less-expensive fans will have a 10-degree pitch and spin faster; better-quality fans typically have blades pitched 12 degrees to 16 degrees.

Choosing a mounting system

For optimal airflow, a fan should be installed in the middle of the ceiling, 8 ft. to 9 ft. above the floor, and at least 18 in. from walls. Some authorities, including Energy Star, suggest that ceiling fans may be mounted as low as 7 ft. above the floor, although we are not comfortable with that recommendation because someone 6 ft. tall could easily lift a hand into the orbit of a spinning fan blade. Where ceilings are low, it seems wiser to use another device to cool the room, such as a floor fan or an air conditioner.

Most fan makers offer several mounting options:

Standard mounts have a 3-in. to 6-in. metal *downrod* that runs from the ceiling bracket to the top of the fan motor housing. A downrod is typically a tube $1/2$ in. to $3/4$ in. in diameter that, being hollow, doubles as a conduit for the wiring from the outlet box to the fan motor.

Extended mounts employ downrods of different lengths (6 in. to 120 in.) to achieve an optimal fan height approximately $8^1/2$ ft. above the floor. Thus, for a 10-ft. ceiling, one would use an 18-in. downrod. The fan maker will recommend the downrod length.

Flush mounts anchor the motor housing directly to the ceiling, where its height is less than 8 ft. or where fan components would hang down too low. Flush mounts are often paired with (or part of) low-profile ceiling fans, also called "huggers." *Note:* Because low-profile fan blades are so close to the ceiling, they will move less air than the blades of a standard fan would.

Sloped mounts are used for angled or vaulted ceilings. There are also universal mounting brackets that can be used on flat or sloped ceilings, although in the latter usage the bracket opening must face the upslope side.

PRO TIP
Some localities require that fans be installed by a licensed electrician. So check local building codes before buying a fan.

Selecting fan controls

Not long ago, ceiling fans were operated by a pull chain hanging down from the fan body; if the fan also had a light, there were two chains. Although this simple mechanism lives on in economy-grade fans, convenience and energy conservation have driven controls to become more sophisticated. Today, ceiling fans may be controlled by some combination of onboard sensors, wall controls, handheld remote controls, and smartphone apps.

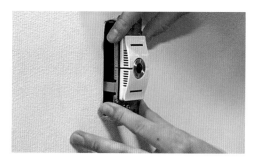

Wi-Fi modules housed in the body of the Haiku Home fan can communicate with this wall control, with a handheld remote control, or with a smartphone.

Among the more efficient fans listed on the Energy Star site, most generally have six forward and six reverse speeds (for winter use). Fan makers have gotten creative: Several offer an automated mode whose speed varies to simulate a natural breeze. Changing speed, however, is just the beginning of what fan controls can do.

Haiku Home fans, for example, have integrated sensors that enable them to detect motion, monitor temperature and humidity in the room, and predict future settings based upon past behavior. They also boast whole-house Wi-Fi modules that can communicate with a wall control, a smartphone, and devices such as the Nest learning thermostat (p. 116). In addition, all Haiku fan models easily accept an integral light unit whose 144 high-efficiency LEDs can also be programmed using a remote or from a mobile phone. Automating a fan's operation

---

CEILING FAN LIGHTS

Many rooms are designed with a single light outlet in the middle of the ceiling. So if homeowners want both a fan and a ceiling light in a given room, installing a ceiling fan light can be a straightforward and cost-effective solution. Thus many fan makers offer light kits, or fans with integral fan units. Until recently, this all-in-one solution resembled a man wearing two hats because the light looked glued to the fan, but that's changing. With a bit of digging online, you can find fans whose lights fit within or effortlessly extend aerodynamic fan lines.

The integral light unit of Haiku fans contains 144 high-efficiency LEDs.

is the key to saving energy and increasing your comfort. Haiku bills itself as "the world's first smart ceiling fan" and, given the fan's many functions, that seems a fair statement.

Looking for lasting beauty

The drive for energy efficiency has produced an interesting side effect: Ceiling fans are becoming beautiful. Not all of them, of course, but the few fan makers—Aeratron, Fanimation®, Harbor Breeze®, Minka-Aire®, TroposAir, Emerson®, Haiku Home—that top Energy Star efficiency lists are also creating artful pieces that will grace any ceiling.

There has never been a wider range of finishes to choose from, including polished aluminum, rubbed bronze, burnished copper, antique brass, brushed nickel—as well as a limitless palette of painted colors to match or accent a room's decor. Fan blades offer

---

almost as much variety, with natural wood, woven palm, and laminated bamboo blades being traditional favorites.

Look for durability in the details. Are finishes evenly and expertly applied? Are there nicks or blemishes along blade edges or ends? Examine mounting hardware—do blades attach snugly to holders and holders to the motor housing? Is quality hardware used? If possible, operate a floor model of the fan you're considering. Does it run quietly? Does it wobble or look imbalanced? How long is the fan motor warranty? Most fan makers at the top of Energy Star efficiency lists offer lifetime warranties.

Online videos can be a great source of information. At www.bigassfans.com (the parent company of Haiku Home fans), one video describes the protracted process of balancing fan blades, while another demonstrates the tensile strength of its bamboo blades by having a worker whack them repeatedly with a sledgehammer.

If you are thinking of installing the fan yourself, scour the company website to see if its installation guides and videos are clear and complete. Call phone support to see how accessible and knowledgeable its people are. (Asking for help choosing a fan model is a good place to start.) As ceiling fans have become more high tech, the smartest manufacturers have embraced a high-touch philosophy of supporting customers every step of the way.

MOUNTING A CEILING FAN BOX

All fans must be securely mounted to framing, but this is especially true of ceiling fans, which are weighty and subject to vibration and wobbling. All fans must be installed in a ceiling box rated for fan use—that is, capable of supporting 50 lb. or more. Check your fan's installation specs. If your fan is particularly heavy or complex, it may require a box with a higher weight rating or additional bracing.

If ceiling joists are exposed, you have several options. You can install a piece of 2x4 or 2x6 blocking to the ceiling joists (or rafters), then mount a 2-in.-deep octagonal metal box to the blocking. Mark the location of the blocking so the box will be flush to the finished ceiling surface. Then drive three 3-in. toenailed wood screws through each end of the blocking and into the joists, keeping the blocking on your marks.

If you must hang a fan from a ceiling joist's edge, screw a ½-in.-deep metal pancake box directly to the joist. Before doing so, however, be sure there is enough room inside the fan's canopy to hide electrical connections—because there's no room for them in the pancake box! If not, move the fan or modify your plans.

An alternative is to mount an adjustable hanger to the framing. Bar hangers are strong, easier than nailing up blocking, and easily positioned by sliding the box along its support bar. Remodel bar hangers are also available.

➡ **For more on bar hangers, see p. 27.**

If joists are not exposed, install a remodel bar (a braced box) if there's a finish ceiling. Locate the fan, cut a 4-in.-diameter hole in the ceiling, insert the bar into the hole ❶, and maneuver it until its feet stand on top of the drywall. Then hand-turn the bar to expand it. When the bar touches a joist on both ends, turn the bar with a wrench to drive the bar points into the joists ❷. Finally, bolt the ceiling box to the remodel bar using the hardware provided ❸.

⚠ SAFETY ALERT

If there's an existing fan box, turn off the power to it and test before proceeding. If the box is plastic, check the screw holes that the fan mounting bracket attaches to. If the screw holes are at all stripped, if the box is cracked or deformed, or if you have any doubts that it can support the new fan, replace the box.

1 Insert a remodel bar through the ceiling cutout.

2 Expand the remodel bar by hand. Then force the pointed ends into the joists by turning the bar with a wrench.

3 Attach the fan box to the remodel bar.

INSTALLING A CEILING FAN

The photos in this section show the installation of a Haiku L Series ceiling fan, which we chose because it's well made and utilizes devices such as prewired harnesses and snap connectors to simplify and speed installation. Also, its ceiling bracket is a sturdy type used by many fan makers. To give you a concise overview we condensed a 34-page installation guide, so, of necessity, some steps were omitted. *Note:* Every fan is a bit different, so the guide that came with your fan is the final authority on its installation. Follow it closely.

PRO TIP

If you get confused while installing your fan, take a digital photo of the assembly point that's baffling you. Then call tech support. If they can't quickly solve the problem, email the photo to help them better understand. In general, sending a photo is a faster way to find a solution than trying to describe a welter of unfamiliar fan parts. If you are still unsure how to proceed, hiring a licensed electrician may be money well spent.

Mounting the ceiling bracket

As noted on the facing page, a ceiling fan must be mounted to an outlet box rated for fan use—typically, capable of supporting 50 lb.—which is securely mounted to a ceiling joist or beam. Before beginning, *disconnect power to the outlet box* by turning off the circuit breaker or removing the fuse that controls it. Then use a voltage tester to make sure the power is off.

Using wire nuts, attach the supply wires in the outlet box to the fan wire harness: ground to ground, neutral to neutral, hot to hot. Tuck the supply wires and wire nuts into the outlet box, then install the mounting bracket to the outlet box using the machine screws that came with the box. If the mounting bracket itself has a grounding wire, as the Haiku bracket does, attach it now to the supply ground and the ground of the wire harness ❶.

Important: If you are mounting a similar bracket on a sloping ceiling, install it so that its open side faces upslope.

Connecting airfoils and the downrod

In the factory, quality fan makers carefully balance airfoils (fan blades) to the motor unit to ensure that the fan will run efficiently and smoothly. The process is a little like fine-tuning the balance of a tire, with incrementally smaller adjustments made until the balance is perfect in all directions. Before removing the airfoils for shipping, the manufacturer will often color-code each to an attachment point (hub) on the motor unit.

When attaching the airfoils to the fan's motor unit, it is thus important to match the colored sticker on each airfoil to the corresponding color on a motor hub ❷.

Press each airfoil firmly to a hub and screw it securely to the motor, using the screws or bolts provided. Use the washers provided to ensure that airfoils do not work loose during operation.

The fan's downrod (support rod) is a hollow tube that runs from the ceiling bracket to the top of the motor unit and doubles as a conduit for the wiring that powers the fan and its light (if any). On older or economy-style fans, you may need to feed wires through the downrod, but our model's downrod comes prewired, with its lower wires terminating in wiring harnesses that will snap into receptacles on the motor unit ❸.

To attach the downrod, lower it onto the motor shaft so that the alignment marks on the downrod (here, arrows) line up to those on the shaft. This will align the bolt holes in the downrod and shaft. To join the two parts, insert the bolt provided ❹ (see p. 160) and secure it with a washer and locknut.

Next make electrical connections. Follow your installation guide, but typically an

>> >> >>

1 If the mounting bracket has a grounding wire, attach it to the supply ground and the ground of the wire harness.

2 Bolt or screw airfoils (fan blades) securely to the fan's motor unit.

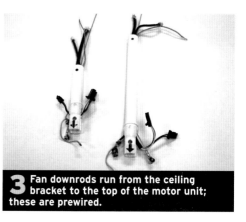
3 Fan downrods run from the ceiling bracket to the top of the motor unit; these are prewired.

INSTALLING A CEILING FAN (CONTINUED)

4 Align the downrod marks to those on the shaft, then join parts with the bolt provided.

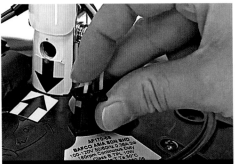

5 Here, a female ground connector attaches to a male connector on the motor.

6 Once all ground wires and wire harnesses are connected, slide the cover down and secure it to the motor unit.

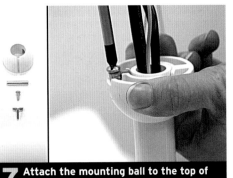

7 Attach the mounting ball to the top of the downrod.

8 Insert the mounting ball in the bracket, aligning the slot in the ball to the rib in the bracket.

9 If the fan has a safety cable, attach it now to keep the mounting ball securely in the bracket.

10 Slide the fan's Wi-Fi module into the fan control box on the mounting bracket.

electrician will first connect the ground wire emerging from the downrod to a captive ground screw on the motor shaft **5**. Then plug the wire harnesses into the receptacles on the motor. Finally, to remove slack, gently pull up on the wires coming out of the top of the downrod.

Cover connections on the motor unit

Once you have connected the ground wire and all wire harnesses, slide the cover down the downrod and secure it to the motor unit **6**. If the cover has two pieces, first lower the larger ring and rotate it till it seats snugly atop the motor unit. Then lower the (upper) trim piece onto the cover ring. Secure the covers with the screws provided.

Note: After you install the cover(s) there may be a gap between the lower ring and the airfoils. This is a common detail on many fans that allows heat from the motor to dissipate. Check your installation guide to be sure.

Mounting the fan

Before hanging your fan from the mounting bracket in the ceiling, it will be necessary to slide the upper wiring cover and the mounting ball onto the downrod—in that order. More advanced fans, such as the Haiku L Series, may also have an LED diffuser ring. If so, slide the diffuser ring onto the downrod first—but do not seat the ring in the wiring cover yet.

Now attach the mounting ball to the top of the downrod. Here again, details will vary. In our sequence, first slide a short steel pin through holes at the top of the downrod, then slide the mounting ball up till the ends of the pin seat in the inner slots of the ball. Insert the provided steel wedge into the mounting ball slot and tighten the screw to secure the parts and hold the mounting ball in place ❼.

Now you're ready to hang the fan in the mounting bracket. Align the slot in the mounting ball to the rib in the bracket, insert the mounting ball, and let it hang freely ❽. Gently twist the downrod to make sure the mounting ball is fully seated.

Thread the ground wire sticking out of the downrod through the mounting bracket and secure it to the captive screw on the outside of the bracket. If your fan also has a safety cable to prevent a fan's disengaging from the mounting bracket, install it now ❾. Note that some local building codes require that the safety cable be attached to a ceiling joist or to a metal brace mounted to two ceiling joists.

If your fan will be controlled by a wall unit, as the Haiku L Series fan is, insert its Wi-Fi module into the fan control box and slide it into the mounting bracket now ❿. Be careful not to pinch the wires between the mounting bracket and the control box.

Snap the LED indicator into the gap in the mounting bracket. Then connect the wiring harnesses from the control box to the harnesses from the power supply in the outlet box. Last, connect the wire harnesses emerging from the top of the downrod to the corresponding receptacles on the control box.   >> >> >>

WIRING A FAN-LIGHT COMBINATION

Fans are frequently configured with both fans and lights. Running a 3-wire cable (12/3 with ground or 14/3 with ground) enables you to operate the fan and light separately. When a ceiling fan's junction box is closer to the power source than to the switch box, as shown in the drawing below right, the switch is called a "back-fed switch." *Note:* Because of code changes, back-fed switches are not suitable for *new* construction.

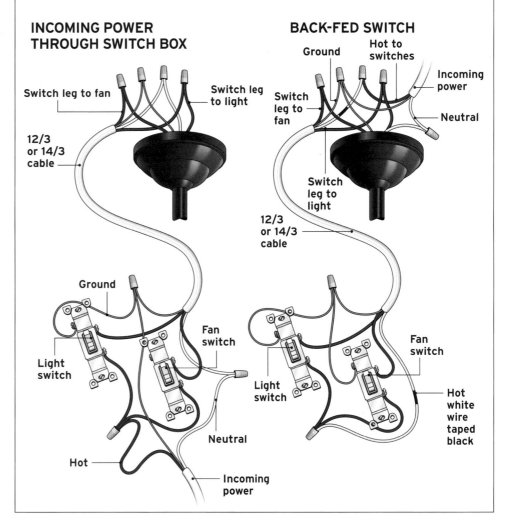

SAFETY ALERT

Although there are plastic ceiling boxes rated for fans, many installers won't touch them. Spooked by the possibility of stripped screw holes and crashing fans, they insist on using a metal fan box.

DAMP OR DRY?

Most ceiling fans are intended for dry indoor rooms. If you will be installing the fan in a humid indoor location, buy a UL-listed fan marked "Suitable for damp locations." If the fan will be installed outdoors, such as in a porch or a gazebo, select a UL-listed fan marked "Suitable for wet locations." Wet-rated fans will have sealed motors, rust-resistant housings and hardware, and all-weather blades.

INSTALLING A CEILING FAN (CONTINUED)

11 Slide the cover up until it sits flush with the mounting bracket.

12 After making sure all wiring is safely tucked inside the cover, screw it to the bracket.

Photo sequence courtesy of Haiku Home/Big Ass Solutions

Installing the wiring cover

Aligning the arrows on the mounting bracket to those on the wiring cover, slide the cover up until it sits flush with the mounting bracket **11**. After making sure all wiring is safely tucked inside the cover, screw it to the bracket **12**. If your fan model has an LED diffuser ring, slide it up and plug it into the LED indicator receptacle, accessible through an opening in the underside of the cover. Snap the diffuser ring securely into place.

Restore power to the fan outlet box. Use the remote control to turn on the fan and test its various functions. If you also purchased a wall control, follow its instruction guide to set it up.

—— CEILING FAN ELEMENTS ——

Mounting details and fan assemblies vary (shown here is an old-style fan, still common in many homes): Follow the installation instructions that come with your unit. Add downrod extensions as needed to locate the fan blades 8 ft. to 10 ft. above the floor.

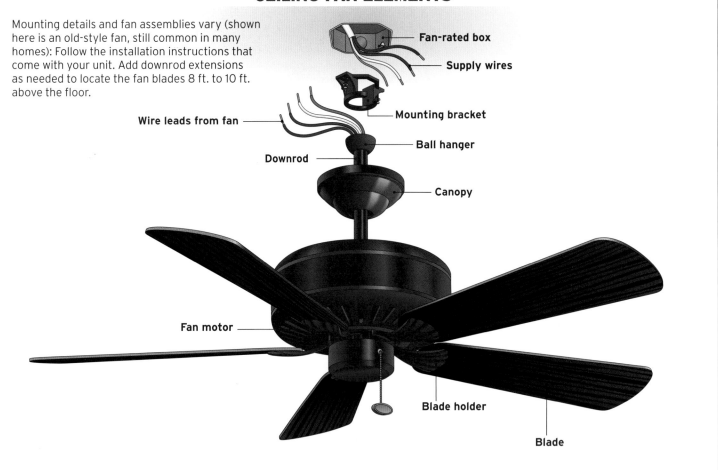

Fan-rated box

Supply wires

Wire leads from fan

Mounting bracket

Ball hanger

Downrod

Canopy

Fan motor

Blade holder

Blade

CHOOSING A BATHROOM VENT FAN

Bathroom fans are increasingly powerful, quiet, and available with numerous bells and whistles. When considering all the extra features, however, remember that the primary function of a bathroom fan is to remove moisture. Energy efficiency is a close second, thus Panasonic®, Delta®, Broan®, Nutone®, and other major fan makers offer a wide range of energy-conserving models.

SAFETY ALERT

When installing or replacing a fan of any type, always turn off the electrical power to that location. Then test with a voltage tester to be sure the power is off.

Before you begin

There are two important tips to note before wiring any type of fan. First, check out the wiring schematic that comes with the unit **A**. In most cases, the schematic is affixed either to the fan housing or to the backside of a cover. Or it may be included in the installation instructions. You'll also find essential information such as the fan's rating, expressed in amperes.

Second, most units have an integral junction box **B**. The junction box contains wire leads that you'll splice to the incoming house wiring. All metal boxes—including fan housings—must be grounded. >> >> >>

PRO TIP

Never assume that all the parts you need for assembly and installation are in the box. Check the contents before you start by comparing the parts in the box to the inventory list included in the owner's manual. Smaller parts, such as screws, are typically packaged in clear plastic so you can count them without having to open the packet—a good idea because they're easy to lose.

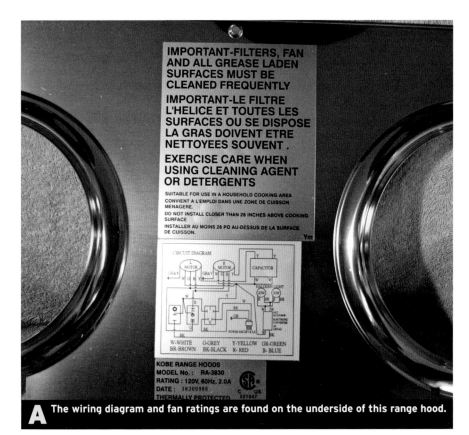

A The wiring diagram and fan ratings are found on the underside of this range hood.

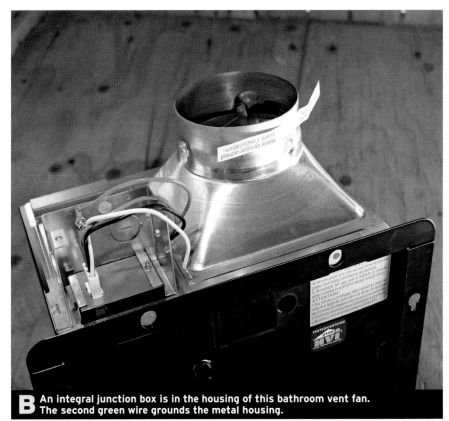

B An integral junction box is in the housing of this bathroom vent fan. The second green wire grounds the metal housing.

CHOOSING A BATHROOM VENT FAN (CONTINUED)

Choosing a bathroom fan

There are complex formulas for sizing bath fans, but a good rule of thumb is 1 cfm (cubic foot per minute) per square foot for bathrooms 100 sq. ft. or smaller. For bathrooms larger than 100 sq. ft., allot 50 cfm for each fixture (toilet, lavatory, shower) and 100 cfm for hot tubs.

Also, get a quiet fan. Whereas cheaper bath fans are rated at 3 sones to 4 sones, some energy-efficient models run at less than 0.3 sone. Two sones is tolerable, and 1 sone is very quiet. (By comparison, refrigerators average about 1 sone.) And remote inline fans, typically installed in attics some distance above bathrooms, are quieter still. Consequently, you can install a larger fan inline and still have a quiet bathroom.

Next, consider switches. Fans usually need to continue venting after you leave the shower or use the toilet, so get an electronic switch with an integral timer so that the fan continues running after the light is turned off. You can also connect the fan to a humidistat, which is a moisture sensor that turns the fan off once a preset moisture level is attained.

SAFETY ALERT

Never install a rheostat—commonly called a dimmer switch—to control an exhaust fan. Fan motors are designed to run on a fixed voltage, and if you reduce the voltage by using a rheostat, you may burn out the fan motor.

FAN COVERS

Most exhaust fans come with plastic covers, but they can be replaced with metal plates. Here, an antique wall register was plated to match the other fixtures in the room.

REMOTE INLINE FANS

Even a well-made bathroom fan will be relatively noisy if the motor is 2 ft. from your head in the bathroom ceiling. But if you install the fan some distance from the bathroom, you'll reduce the noise considerably. That remote location may mean that you have longer duct and wiring runs, but routing them is rarely a problem. In fact, with a large-enough fan motor and a duct Y-connector, you can vent two bathrooms with one fan. Because longer duct runs can mean greater air resistance, consider installing rigid-metal or polyvinyl chloride (PVC) ducts, whose smooth surfaces offer less resistance, rather than flexible metal ducts. Alternatively, you could oversize the fan slightly. Better fan makers, such as Fantech® and American Aldes®, offer acoustically insulated cases to deaden sound further.

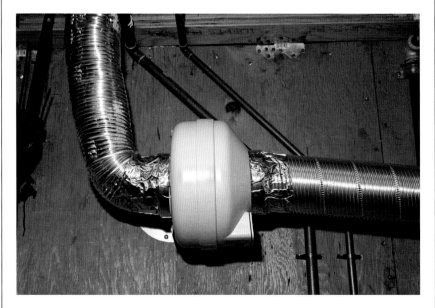

Remote inline fans require longer ducting, but they're quieter because they're located farther away from the bathroom.

LOCATING A BATHROOM FAN

There are three primary considerations when locating a bath fan. First, place the fan where it can expel moisture effectively–ideally, near the shower, where most of the moisture is generated.

Second, locate the fan so that its duct run is as short as possible and minimizes cutouts in the blocking or framing members–especially rafters. Vent the ductwork from the fan out the roof or through a gable-end wall. Avoid sidewall vents because moist air expelled by them could be drawn up into the attic by soffit vents in roof overhangs.

Third, locate roof vents away from problem areas such as skylight and valley flashing. Water usually dams up on the uphill side of a skylight, creating a leak-prone area that must be carefully flashed. Typically, skylight flashing consists of two pieces: a base flashing and a counterflashing that goes over it. Locate a roof vent near skylight flashing and you're inviting trouble. Valley flashing, on the other hand, may consist of a single broad piece of metal or elastomeric material folded up the middle. But because this flashing is located where roof planes converge, it channels an enormous amount of water during rainy seasons. So keep things simple: Locate roof vents away from obstructions in the roof or concentrations of water. Don't put a roof vent near an operable window, either.

A BATHROOM FAN

To keep moisture from leaking into the attic, apply silicone caulk between the fan box flanges and the ceiling drywall. Use metal foil tape to ensure airtight joints where ducting attaches to fan and vent takeoffs.

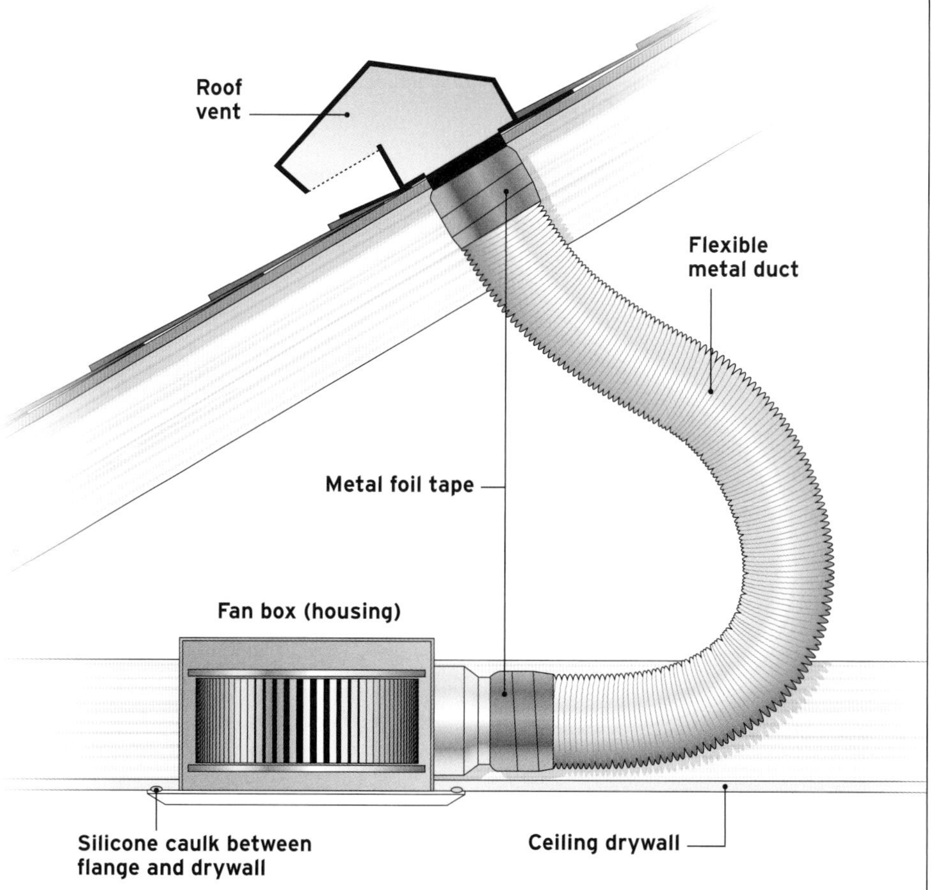

Roof vent

Flexible metal duct

Metal foil tape

Fan box (housing)

Silicone caulk between flange and drywall

Ceiling drywall

PRO TIP

Before you cut a hole in the ceiling, be sure there are no obstructions along the way. Tentatively locate the fan and use a $1/4$-in. extension bit to drill along the proposed duct path. You'll also want to drill an exploratory hole up through the roofing.

INSTALLING A ROOF VENT

1 Lift up on the shingle to remove the roofing nails.

2 Remove the shingles over the entire section.

3 With the vent in place, trim the shingles to fit the upper arc of the vent.

4 Use a utility knife to cut the shape of the vent hole through the roofing paper.

In the installation shown here, there was enough clearance around the exploratory hole and there happened to be a roofer on site, so the crew decided to install the roof vent first. (Roof vents vary; the model shown has a round stack and a weather-proof cap.)

Go onto the roof and find the 1/4-in. exploratory hole drilled while locating the fan. The hole represents the center of the vent hole you'll need to cut.

Most ducting and roof-vent takeoffs are 4 in. diameter, so sketch that circle onto the roof. If the circle would cut into the tabs of any shingle—roughly the bottom half of a shingle strip—use a shingle ripper or a cat's paw to remove the nails holding those shingles in place before cutting the vent hole ❶. Be gentle when removing shingles so you can reuse them ❷.

Slide the upper flange of the roof vent under the shingle courses above and use a utility knife to trim its arc onto the shingles above ❸, then cut out the vent's circle into any remaining shingles and the roofing paper ❹. Next, use a reciprocating saw to cut through the sheathing ❺.

5 Cut the roof sheathing to allow for the vent.

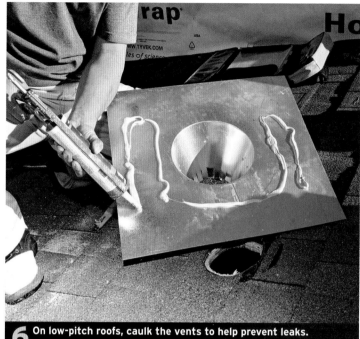

6 On low-pitch roofs, caulk the vents to help prevent leaks.

If the roof pitch is 4:12 or greater, it usually isn't necessary to caulk the vent edges. Here, a 2:12 pitch required caulking to forestall leaks **6**. Carefully lift the shingle course above the vent and nail the two corners of the vent's upper flange into place **7**. Do not nail the lower corners of the vent: those nails would be exposed to weather and could leak. Cut and replace removed shingles and renail them.

7 Nail only the top corners of the vent—shingles cover these nails.

PRO TIP

Keeping fan-expelled moisture out of attics and wall cavities is crucial, and the only way to do so is to create airtight connections: Caulk the fan housing to the ceiling and seal each duct joint with aluminum foil tape, not fabric duct tape.

MOUNTING A FAN BOX

1 If needed, add blocking between the framing members.

2 When positioning the fan, a scrap of drywall acts as a stand-in for the finished ceiling.

3 Slide on the flex duct and tape it in place.

If bathroom framing is exposed, mounting the fan is pretty straight-forward. If you remove the fan assembly from the fan box, the box will be lighter and easier to hold in place one-handed while you use your other hand to screw the unit to the ceiling joists. Most fans have expandable brackets which extend between joists spaced 16 in. on-center (o.c.). But you should always screw at least one side of the fan box to a joist, to ensure that it's anchored securely. For ceiling joist (or rafter) spacing greater than 16 in. o.c., it's a good idea to add blocking **1**.

If the fan-box flange mounts flush to the underside of the ceiling, use a piece of drywall scrap to gauge the depth of the unit relative to the finished ceiling **2**. Regardless of whether the box flange sits above or below the ceiling drywall, caulk the flange with polyurethane sealant to create an airtight seal between the two materials. If you removed the fan assembly earlier, reinstall it now.

Keep duct runs as short as possible to reduce air resistance. Slide the lower end of the flexible duct to the fan's exhaust port **3** and seal the joint with metal duct tape, then attach the other end to the roof vent takeoff. Or, if you haven't yet cut the hole in the roof, hold the free end of the duct to the underside of the roof sheathing and trace its outline onto the surface.

RETROFITTING A BATHROOM FAN

If you are remodeling or installing a bath fan and the finished ceiling is already in place, begin by creating a cardboard template of the fan housing. Mark the approximate position of the fan by driving a screw or nail through the ceiling and then go up into the space above the bathroom and find the marker. If there is an insulated attic above, take along a dustpan to shovel loose insulation out of the way and be sure to wear a dust mask and gloves. After you've located the marker, place the fan template next to the nearest joist and trace around it. Most fan boxes mount to ceiling joists. If the fan box has an adjustable mounting bar, you have more latitude in placing the fan. Use a jab saw or reciprocating saw to cut out the opening. To keep the drywall cutout from falling to the floor below, take a piece of scrap wood slightly longer than the cutout and screw it to the drywall.

Before placing the fan box on top of the ceiling drywall, caulk around the perimeter of the opening to create an airtight bond to the box flange ❶. Once the box is wired and the ceiling has been painted, install the trim piece to cover any gaps around the fan opening ❷.

1 Apply a bead of caulk under the flanges before you set the fan box in place.

2 Install the trim piece to cover the gaps between the fan and the ceiling cutout.

PRO TIP

If there's an existing ceiling light in the bathroom, a fan-and-light combination unit may simplify your remodel. If you want the fan and light to operate at the same time, you can reuse the 2-wire cable that's presently controlling the light switch. Another option is to install a fan/light with a built-in occupancy sensor (p. 66). The light is controlled by the switch on the existing 2-wire cable, and the fan turns on or off automatically when someone comes into the room.

WIRING A BATHROOM FAN

1 Staple cable no more than 1 ft. from the fan box.

2 Strip the sheathing off the wires.

3 Splice like-wire groups, starting with the ground wires, then neutrals, then hot wires. (At this stage the wires are not energized.)

4 Fold the spliced wires into the junction box and install the cover.

Before making any connections in the fan's junction box, make sure the power is off. Follow the wiring diagrams provided by the fan manufacturer. In general, it's easier if the incoming power runs through a switch box first; then you don't have to try to splice the switch legs in the fan junction box—junction boxes inside fan housings tend to be cramped and may not be rated for the additional wires. Bathroom fans should also have GFCI protection if installed in a shower whose ceilings are 8 ft. or less above the finish floor.

If the duct space is tight, it's usually best to wire the fan box before installing the duct. When running cable to the fan box, allow a generous loop of cable, just in case. As with light fixtures and receptacles, staple the cable within 1 ft. of the

fan box **❶**. Insert a cable connector into a junction box knockout, feed the cable through it, and strip the cable sheathing **❷**.

Using wire connectors, first splice the incoming ground wire to the fixture ground **❸**. (If the fixture lead wires are stranded, extend them slightly beyond the solid wire so that the wire connector will engage them first.) Splice the neutral wires and then the hot wires. If the light and fan are wired separately, there will be two sets of hot wires.

Tug each wire group gently to be sure the splices are secure. When all groups are spliced, carefully fold the wires into the fan junction box and cover the box **❹**.

Range hoods can be handsome additions to kitchen decor. This one is a European-style wall-mounted hood from Kobe®.

The height of the fan and the fact that it is not against a wall mean that the hood needs to draw more air to be effective. This stylish design is set higher than a typical range hood to provide sight lines across the room.

Choosing a Range Hood

All cooktops and stoves should be vented by a range hood. In addition to sucking up the smoke of a charred steak, range hoods exhaust airborne grease that might otherwise migrate to a cool corner and feed mold or adhere to woodwork and discolor its finish. Range hoods come in many configurations, but basically there's a *hood* to collect smells and smoke, a *fan* to expel them, *ducts* to carry exhaust out, and *shrouds* and other trim pieces. Range hoods vary from low-powered and inexpensive (less than $50) to custom-designed units (which cost thousands).

Range hoods are most often *wall-mounted* directly over a range. Alternatively, there are *downdraft* and *side-draft* vents that pop up from a counter area to suck away fumes. Over island and peninsula ranges, you can install *chimney-type* vents. In general, install the type of vent that will carry exhaust gases outdoors with the shortest and straightest duct run possible. Because heated air rises, wall-mounted and chimney types are inherently efficient, whereas downdraft and side-draft vents pull heated gases in directions they wouldn't go naturally and can even pull burner flames sideways.

Ideally, a range hood should be slightly wider than the range, say, 3 in. wider on each end, and mounted 30 in. above the range, but follow the hood maker's suggested mounting height. More powerful hoods can be installed higher. Finally, buy a unit with a good-quality filter that can withstand regular washing with soap and water. Most filters are aluminum mesh, better ones are stainless steel; many can be popped into the dishwasher. In general, be skeptical of range hoods that recirculate air through a series of filters rather than venting it outside.

SIZING THE HOOD

A 100-cfm wall-mounted hood should be adequate to vent the average four-burner, 30-in.-wide range. But if that same range is located on a kitchen island, its range vent should draw 125 cfm to 150 cfm. More is not better when sizing range hoods. For one thing, larger hoods are noisier. Midsize range hoods average 3 sones to 3.5 sones, which is too noisy to have a conversation nearby; monster hoods can reach 8 sones. (In comparison, refrigerators register 1 sone.) Oversize hoods can also expel so much air that they create *back-drafting,* in which negative in-house air pressure draws furnace or fireplace exhaust gases back down the chimney.

MOUNTING & DUCTING A RANGE HOOD

1 Slide the duct into the thimble.

2 Level, center, and mount the hood.

3 Bolt at least one side of the hood to a stud.

4 Lower the duct over the hood takeoff and seal the joint with metal tape.

PRO TIP

A well-sized hood should extend about 3 in. beyond the range on both ends.

Range hoods are typically screwed to the underside of a cabinet or mounted directly to a wall. A hood should be mounted about 30 in. above the range, and the ducting that vents it should exit the house as directly as possible. As you plan your duct route, use a stud finder to locate studs in the wall behind the stove or through ceiling joists above. The duct run should exit through the siding or the roofing. To locate the hole for the duct work, level the hood and center it over the range.

Cut a hole in the wall or ceiling and insert a thimble–a specialized fitting that creates an opening through a wall or ceiling into which the duct fits. If there already is a thimble in place, insert the duct from the range hood up into the thimble 3 in. to 4 in. above its final position **1**. Friction should hold the duct in place.

Level the hood, center it over the range, and bolt it to the wall **2**. Mount the hood in at least two points: If the studs behind the

hood are 16 in. o.c., you may have to bolt one side of the hood to a stud **3** and secure the other side of the hood with a toggle bolt. After the hood is mounted, slide the duct down over the takeoff atop the hood **4**. Tape all of the joints with self-adhering metal tape.

WIRING A RANGE HOOD

Many range hoods have discrete electrical junction boxes with knockouts into which you insert cable clamps and cables. In the example shown here, the shroud that encloses the duct doubles as a junction box. The lead wires from the fan and light emerge through a bushing on the top of the hood and attach to wires in a Romex supply cable, which emerges from the wall cavity.

Strip and splice like wire pairs using wire connectors. Splice the ground wires first—be sure there's a grounding pigtail to the hood itself—then neutral wires, and then hot wires ❶.

To minimize weight and avoid marring shiny trim pieces, many pros install the fan filters, trim, and other trappings after the hood shell is mounted. Most of the parts simply snap into place—just follow the instructions provided ❷. Then, if your hood has a bottom casing, screw it into place ❸. Finally, fit the shroud over the ducting and the wire connection—they're usually held in place with one pair of screws at the top and another pair at the bottom ❹.

SAFETY ALERT

Most hoods aren't heavy but they're unwieldy, so get help installing one.

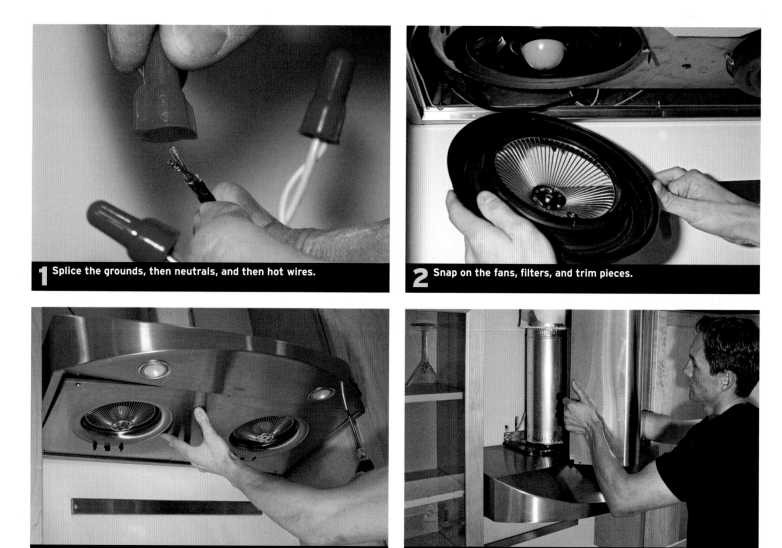

1 Splice the grounds, then neutrals, and then hot wires.

2 Snap on the fans, filters, and trim pieces.

3 Attach the bottom casing onto the hood.

4 Use screws to secure the shroud in place.

PLANNING

BEING DETAIL ORIENTED IS AS important to planning as it is to installation. When you plan a wiring project, be methodical: Assess the existing system, calculate electrical loads, check local codes, and draw a wiring floor plan.

If you are only replacing existing devices—changing a light fixture, replacing a faulty switch, or upgrading a receptacle, for example—you seldom need a permit from the local building department. However, if you extend or add any circuit, you must pull (or file) a permit.

Most local electrical codes are based on the NEC. When it's necessary to pull a permit, local code authorities will want to approve your plans and later inspect the wiring to be sure it's correct. Don't shortcut this process: Codes and inspections protect you and your home.

Whatever the scope of your project, if you work on existing circuits, first turn off the power and test to be sure it's off, and tag or lock the panel.

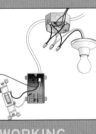

BEFORE YOU BEGIN

Inspecting the fuse box or breaker panel, p. 176

Assessing the condition of wiring, p. 178

Is the system adequately sized? p. 179

ACCORDING TO CODE

General wiring guidelines, p. 181

General-use circuit requirements, p. 182

Requirements room by room, p. 183

WORKING DRAWINGS

Developing a floor plan, p. 184

Electrical notation, p. 186

Wiring schematics, p. 188

INSPECTING THE FUSE BOX OR BREAKER PANEL

A This 30-amp main switch and fuses comprised the panel for the whole house. Even if it were safe, it would be dramatically undersize.

B Replace older panel brands that have had widespread failures. This panel cover is missing knockouts—very dangerous.

By looking at the outside of the service panel and wiring that's exposed in the basement and attic, you can get a basic overview of the system's condition. If the panel has unused breaker spaces and the wiring insulation is in decent shape, you can probably continue using it and safely add an outlet or two if there is sufficient capacity. However, if the system seems unsafe or inadequate, hire a licensed electrician to open the panel and do a more thorough examination.

Here's what to look for.

Start your investigation at the fuse box or breaker panel. You can learn a lot about the condition of the system by examining the outside of the service box. Examining the inside of a panel or fuse box is best left to a licensed electrician, however.

Rust and corrosion on the outside of a service box or on the armored cable or conduit feeding it can indicate corroded connections inside **A**. Such connections can lead to arcing and house fires, so have a licensed electrician replace the fuse box or panel. Likewise, if you see scorch marks on breakers or a panel—or near a receptacle cover—have a pro examine it.

Melted wire insulation is a sign either of an overheated circuit—usually caused by too many appliances in use at the same time—or of a poor wire connection in which arcing has occurred. In the first case, a homeowner typically installs an oversize fuse or breaker to keep an overloaded circuit from blowing so often; but this "remedy" exceeds the current-carrying capacity of the wire. The wire overheats and melts its insulation, which can lead to arcing, house fires, or—if someone touches that bare copper wire—electrocution.

An oversize fuse may not melt wires where you can see them, but it may have damaged wire insulation in a place where you can't. Have an electrician inspect the electrical system. Installing type-S fuse socket inserts can prevent overfusing.

"Pennying" a fuse is another unsafe way to deal with an overloaded circuit that keeps blowing fuses. In this case, someone unscrews a fuse, inserts a penny or a blank metal slug into the bottom of the socket—a dangerous act in itself—and then reinstalls the fuse. The penny allows current to bypass the fuse and the protection it offers. Here,

again, have an electrician examine the circuits for damage to the wire insulation.

Panel covers that don't fit, have gaps, or are missing are unsafe. So if you see covers that have been cut to fit a breaker, housing knockouts that are missing, bus bars that are visible when the panel cover is on, or mismatched components, hire a licensed electrician to assess and correct those problems. Some older brands of panels and breakers, such as Federal Pacific® and Zinsco®, have a host of well-documented failures and so should be carefully checked and, where necessary, replaced **B**.

Missing cable connectors or unfilled knockouts enable mice and vermin to enter the panel and nest in it, which can be a fire hazard. Missing connectors also allow cables to be yanked, stressing electrical connections inside the panel **C**. A missing cable clamp may also allow the sharp edge of the panel to slice through thermoplastic cable sheathing, which could energize the panel (if the grounding of the system is not correct) and electrocute anyone who touches it **D**.

A properly grounded panel will have a large grounding wire running from the panel

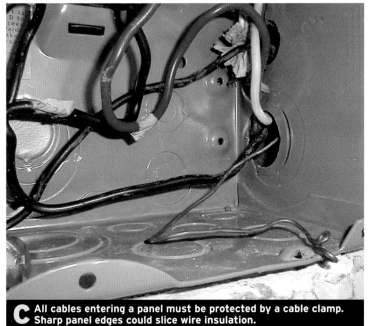

C All cables entering a panel must be protected by a cable clamp. Sharp panel edges could slice wire insulation.

D Service entrance cable enters a panel through a defective bushing. The sharp edge has nearly cut through the cable sheathing.

UNSAFE!

These fuses are too large (30 amps) for the load rating of the circuit wires, which could melt and start a fire.

The scorch marks on this receptacle indicate arcing inside the outlet—electrical leaps between connections that have worked loose.

Stay out of panels!

Only a licensed electrician should work in a service panel or sub-panel—or even remove the cover. Even with the main fuse or breaker turned off, some parts inside a panel are always *hot* (p. 264) and could electrocute you. The panel may not be correctly grounded. Or the inside of a panel may be so crowded (see "Play it safe," on p. 11) that it will be difficult to get a cover back on without pinching (and possibly damaging) wires.

to a grounding electrode (which could be a metal underground water pipe, a ground rod driven into the earth, or a Ufer electrode). For the entire electrical system to be grounded, there must be a continuous ground wire or other effective grounding path running from each device or fixture to the service panel and, by extension, to the grounding electrode. Cold water and gas pipes must also be connected (bonded) to the grounding bus in the panel.

➔ **For more on grounding, see p. 12.**

ASSESSING THE CONDITION OF WIRING

Cables may be visible as they near the service panel and as they run through attics and basements. If there are covered junction boxes, carefully remove the covers and examine the wire splices inside—without touching them. You can also turn off power and pull a few receptacles out to better examine the wires.

Deteriorated sheathing is a potential shock hazard, so note brittle fiber insulation and bare wire, but avoid touching it. If cable sheathing has been chewed on by mice, rats, or squirrels, it should be replaced.

NM cable (cable protected by nonmetallic sheathing) must be stapled within 8 in. of single-gang boxes that don't have cable clamps, and within 12 in. of other boxes, and supported by stapling or another method at least every 4½ ft. (54 in.). A cable running through a drilled hole is considered supported. Sagging wire is hazardous because it can get inadvertently strained, jeopardizing electrical connections. Likewise, all boxes must be securely mounted. All NM cable entering metal boxes must be gripped by cable clamps. Single-gang plastic boxes do not require the strain relief of cable clamps, but double-gang (and larger) plastic boxes have integral plastic tension clamps that afford some strain relief on cable.

Small-gauge aluminum wiring (10 or 12 gauge) is a fire hazard unless it is correctly spliced to a copper wire with a COPALUM® connector, or terminated to CO/ALR-rated outlets and switches. If it is incorrectly terminated in a copper-rated-only device, the two metals will expand and contract at different rates each time the circuit is under load. This can lead to loose connections, arcing, overheating, and house fires. Aluminum-to-aluminum splices require special splicing techniques, either COPALUM connectors or another listed and approved method.

Wire splices (whether copper to copper, copper to aluminum, or aluminum to aluminum) must be housed within a covered junc-

Unstapled cable and unsecured boxes can be inadvertently yanked and stress electrical connections. Work this sloppy suggests substandard wiring throughout the house.

tion box or outlet box. Wires that are spliced outside a box or inside an uncovered box can be a fire hazard because of the dangers of arcing. Loose connections not contained in a cover box can easily ignite combustibles nearby because arcs can reach several thousand degrees Celsius.

Knob-and-tube wiring, although outdated, is usually safe unless individual wire insulation is deteriorated, splices are incorrectly made, the wiring is overloaded, or the wiring is buried in thermal insulation. Typically, splices that were part of the original installation will not be in a junction box but must be wrapped with electrical (friction) tape and supported by porcelain knobs on both sides of each splice. Nonoriginal splices must be housed in covered boxes. Have knob-and-tube wiring assessed or modified by an electrician familiar with it; it's quirky stuff. The NEC does not allow knob-and-tube wiring to be buried in insulation.

Knob-and-tube wiring lacks an equipment ground (a separate grounding wire), so it offers no protection should a faulty appliance get plugged into a receptacle. On the other hand, a knob-and-tube system is run completely on insulators, a plus. The conductors of knob-and-tube wiring were copper, coated with a thin layer of tin (to protect the copper from sulfur in the rubber wire insulation). Uninformed inspectors often mistake the tinned copper wire for aluminum wire.

A 30-YEAR PRO'S TAKE ON REWIRING

If the wiring in an older home appears to be sound and in good repair (see the warning signs below), it's probably OK to continue using it, even though it may not meet code requirements for a new installation. If you are planning to gut the house completely, it makes sense to rip out all the old wiring and completely rewire the house. If you're remodeling only part of the house, leave most of the old wiring in place if it is sound and spend your money rewiring the kitchen, baths, and laundry circuits. That will give you more bang for your buck.

However, you should replace old wiring that's unsafe. If you observe any of these conditions, the wiring should be replaced:

- Circuits that have been extended improperly, as evidenced by loose connections, unprotected splices, or insufficient support.
- Circuits that contain mismatched wire types or sizes, such as NM cable spliced to knob-and-tube wiring outside of a junction box.
- Knob-and-tube wiring whose insulation has deteriorated or that has been damaged. Also, if knob-and-tube wiring in the attic has been covered with loose-fill insulation or insulation batts, that is a serious code violation that could lead to overheating and fire danger.
- Circuits wired with unsheathed wires (other than properly done knob-and-tube) rather than with sheathed cable or conduit.

IS THE SYSTEM ADEQUATELY SIZED?

If receptacles in your house teem with multiplugs and extension cords, you probably need to add outlets. But there are more subtle clues: If you blow fuses or trip breakers regularly, or if the lights brown out when you plug in a toaster or an electric hair dryer, you may need to add new circuits to relieve the overload on existing circuits. This section will help you figure out whether your system has the capacity to do so.

> **For more on how electrical service works, see p. 8.**

These days, 3-wire service feeding a 100-amp service panel is the minimum required by the NEC, and many electricians install 150-amp or 200-amp panels if the homeowners plan to enlarge the house at some point or acquire a lot of heavy-energy–using appliances, such as electric ranges and hot tubs. If there are only two large wires running from the utility pole to the house, they deliver only 120v service.

A house with 2-wire service probably has a 30-amp or 60-amp main fuse or breaker, which is inadequate for modern usage.

Rules of thumb

The only sure way to know if you've got enough capacity to add an outlet or a circuit is to calculate electrical loads (p. 180). But for the benefit of those who wish that an electrician would just offer an offhand opinion of what works most of the time, here are a few rules of thumb.

Fuse-box service. If you've got a fuse box with a 30-amp or 60-amp main fuse, the best advice we can give is to upgrade your service. Don't add outlets or circuits until you replace the fuse box with a breaker panel. Fused mains are often abused by people trying to bypass their protection, so insurance companies often charge higher premiums on houses with fuse boxes.

Adding outlets. If you have a breaker panel with space to add an additional breaker, you can most likely add a circuit to feed a new outlet or two or more lights. If, for example, you have 3-wire service and a

>> >> >>

(p. 180)

ASSESSING A CIRCUIT'S CAPACITY

To recap briefly, electricity, impelled by *voltage*, flows from the power source. (*Amperes* are the rate of electron flow.) Along the way (at outlets), it encounters resistance and does work. (*Watts* are a measure of power consumed.) It then returns to the power source, its voltage reduced or spent.

Or, expressed as mathematical formulas,

watts = voltage $\times$ amperes

amperes = watts $\div$ voltage

To determine the capacity of a circuit you want to extend, identify the circuit breaker controlling the circuit and note the rating of the breaker. If it's a general-purpose circuit, the breaker will probably be 15 amp or 20 amp. A circuit controlled by a 15-amp breaker has a capacity of 1,800w (15 amp $\times$ 120v); one controlled by a 20-amp breaker has 2,400w.

The total wattage of all loads on the circuit (including the extension) must not exceed these capacities; otherwise, you risk overheating wires. To avoid overloading, it's a good idea to reduce the capacity by 20 percent. For example, 80% of 1,800w is 1,440w for a 15-amp circuit; 80% of 2,400w equals 1,920w for a 20-amp circuit.

CIRCUIT CAPACITIES

Amperes × Volts*	Total capacity (watts)	Safe capacity** (watts)
15 × 120	1,800	1,440
20 × 120	2,400	1,920
30 × 120	3,600	2,990

*Amperes multiplied by volts equals watts. **Safe capacity = 80% of total capacity

3-wire service, made up of two large, insulated hot conductors wrapped around a stranded bare wire messenger cable (neutral), supplies enough power for modern needs.

IS THE SYSTEM ADEQUATELY SIZED? (CONTINUED)

100-amp main, you may have excess capacity.

Adding a circuit for general use. If there is an unused space in the panel, have an electrician determine whether the panel can handle another circuit.

Adding a kitchen or bath circuit. If you want to add a bath fan or some new light fixtures, and there's space in the panel, have an electrician see if you can add a circuit. Adding a 20-amp, small-appliance circuit to reduce the load on an existing circuit is smart.

Remodeling a kitchen. Kitchens are complicated and often full of big energy users. Use the chart at right to help you add up the loads. If there aren't many open spaces for breakers, you may need to upgrade to a larger panel.

Adding dedicated circuits. If you need to add dedicated circuits for heavy-use items such as an electric range (50 amps) or a hot tub (60 amps), get out the calculator and do the math.

EXAMPLE OF LOAD CALCULATION FOR SINGLE-FAMILY DWELLING

CALCULATING GENERAL LIGHTING LOAD

Type of Load	NEC Reference	Calculation	Total VA
Lighting Load	Table 220.12	2,000 sq. ft. × 3 VA	6,000 VA
Small Appliance Load	Section 220.52	2 circuits × 1,500 VA	3,000 VA
Laundry Load	Section 220.52	1 circuit × 1,500 VA	1,500 VA
Total General Lighting			**10,500 VA***

Ⓐ CALCULATING DEMAND FOR GENERAL LIGHTING LOAD

Type of Load	Calculation	Demand Factor (DF)	Total VA
General Lighting	First 3,000 VA × DF	100%	3,000 VA
General Lighting	7,500‡ × DF	35%	2,625 VA
Total Lighting, Small Appliances & Laundry		Ⓐ	**5,625 VA**

Ⓑ CALCULATING DEMAND FOR LARGE-LOAD APPLIANCES

Type of Load	Nameplate Rating	Demand Factor (DF)	Total VA
Electric Range	Not Over 12KVA	Use 8KVA	8,000 VA
Clothes Dryer	6,600 VA × DF	100%	6,600 VA
Water Heater	6,600 VA × DF	100%	6,600 VA
Other Fixed Appliances	0 VA × DF	100%	0 VA
Total Load for Large Appliances		Ⓑ	**21,200 VA**

Minimum Service Size	Total VA (Ⓐ+Ⓑ)	26,825 VA
	Total VA /240V	111.77 VA

The minimum service size is the next standard size above the total VA calculated. Based upon these calculations, the minimum service size is 125 amps.

*Use this to calculate Ⓐ
‡Total General Lighting Load 10,500 VA − First 3,000 VA = 7,500 VA

USING THIS TABLE

1. Square ft. for general lighting load is for the entire dwelling, including habitable basements or attics.
2. NEC requires a minimum of two small appliance loads, but it is important to add small fixed kitchen appliances such as microwaves, disposals, dishwashers, large range hood, computers, etc.
3. Minimum of one laundry load is required for a single-family dwelling.
4. The demand factor calculation is designed to take actual use into account (e.g., it is unlikely all lights and small appliances will be running at one time).
5. All large load appliances (high wattage) are added at 100%.
6. The final load calculation is the minimum. Often increasing capacity has little cost impact and is a good practice.

GENERAL WIRING GUIDELINES

GROUNDING REQUIREMENTS!

In a service panel, connect ground and neutral wires to a neutral/ground bus.

Large copper ground wire is clamped to a grounding electrode (rod).

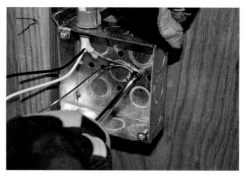

All metal boxes and metal appliance housings require grounding.

The main water pipe must be properly bonded.

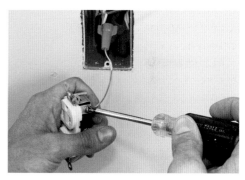

Attach ground pigtails to green ground screws on devices such as receptacles and switches.

Electricians follow the NEC, as adopted (or amended) by local jurisdictions, which was compiled to promote safe practices and prevent house fires. Consider these requirements before you start drawing plans, but be sure to consult local electrical code—it is the final authority in your area.

The guidelines given here apply to all circuits in the house, whether general lighting or heavy-use appliance circuits. Local codes rarely require you to change existing circuits—as long as they are safe—but new electrical work should reflect current electrical code.

Circuit wiring

Wire gauge must be large enough to carry the circuit load and be protected by a comparably sized breaker or fuse at the panel. General-use and lighting circuits are typically 14AWG wire, protected by 15-amp breakers; kitchen, bath, and workshop circuits usually have 12AWG wire, protected by 20-amp breakers.

See the facing page for more on calculating circuit loads.

Acceptable cable

Most circuits are wired with NM cable because the cable is protected behind a finish surface such as drywall or plaster. When circuit wiring is to be left unprotected and exposed, it must be armored cable or in conduit.

➤ For more on cable and conduit, see p. 28.

Grounding

All receptacles, appliances, and electrical equipment must be connected (bonded) to the service panel via an equipment grounding conductor (ground wire). NM cable contains a separate ground wire, whereas armored cable sheathing and metal conduit provide the path to ground if properly installed.

Boxes

All electrical connections must take place in covered boxes. Boxes where connections are made must be accessible, that is, not buried in a wall or ceiling. Based on local code requirements, boxes may be plastic or metal. If metal, the box must also be connected to the equipment grounding conductor (bonded). If NM cable is used, the ground wire must be connected to a metal box with either a ground screw or a ground clip. If AC cable or metal conduit is used, it must be properly attached to the box to ensure effective bonding. If the box is plastic, it does not need to be (and cannot be) grounded; run a ground wire to the device or fixture only.

GENERAL-USE CIRCUIT REQUIREMENTS

General-use circuits are intended primarily for lighting, but small loads that are connected via a cord and plug, such as televisions, fans, and vacuums, are allowed—as long as the power they draw doesn't exceed the capacity of the circuit.

Lighting and small loads

Though 14AWG wire is sufficient for lighting, electricians often run 12AWG wire on general-use circuits to accommodate additional capacity. Calculate lighting loads at 3w per square foot, or roughly one 15-amp circuit for every 500 sq. ft. of floor space. When laying out the lighting circuits, do not put all the lights on a floor on one circuit. Otherwise, should a breaker trip, the entire floor would be without lights.

Receptacles

There must be a receptacle within 6 ft. of each doorway, and spaced at least every 12 ft. along a wall. (This is also stated as, "No space on a wall should be more than 6 ft. from a receptacle.") Any wall at least 2 ft. wide must have a receptacle; and a receptacle is required in hallway walls 10 ft. or longer. Finally, any foyer of more than 60 sq. ft. must have a receptacle on any wall 3 ft. or longer.

Outlets

The NEC does not specify a maximum number of lighting or receptacle outlets on a residential lighting or appliance circuit, though local jurisdictions may. Figure roughly 9 outlets per 15-amp circuit and 10 outlets per 20-amp circuit.

Light switches

There must be at least one wall switch that controls lighting in each habitable room, in the garage (if wired for electricity), and in storage areas (including attics and basements). There must be a switch controlling an outside light near each outdoor entrance. Three-way switches are required at each end of corridors and at the top and bottom of stairs with six steps or more. When possible, put switches near the lights they control. It should be noted that the light switch may control a receptacle (considered "lighting") in habitable rooms except in kitchens and bathrooms.

GFCI protection

The NEC requires GFCI protection on all bathroom receptacles; all receptacles serving kitchen counters; dishwasher outlets; receptacles within 6 ft. of any sink, tub, or shower stall; laundry-area receptacles; all outdoor receptacles; all unfinished basement receptacles; receptacles in garages and accessory buildings; receptacles in crawlspaces or below grade level; and all receptacles near pools, hot tubs, whirlpools, and the like.

AFCI protection

Since 2014, the NEC requires arc-fault-circuit-interrupter (AFCI) protection on all 15-amp and 20-amp receptacles in kitchens and laundry rooms, bedrooms, living rooms, rec rooms, parlors, libraries, dens, sunrooms, and hallways, and on switches serving any of those areas. For more, see pp. 40 and 281.

see pp. 40 and 281.

KITCHEN LIGHTING BASICS

Kitchen lighting should be designed to utilize natural light during the day and achieve a balance of general lighting and task lighting at night. Do not be afraid of energy-efficient lighting such as fluorescent. Today's energy-efficient lighting is instant, dimmable, and available in colors that match incandescent light. Kitchen lighting is often highly regulated for energy efficiency. Check with local building officials before you begin your design.

GENERAL LIGHTING

General lighting is meant to illuminate the space generally and can come from recessed cans, surface-mounted fixtures, track lighting, or cove uplighting. Consider cabinetry and appliances when laying out new light fixtures. A general rule is 2w incandescent or 1w fluorescent per square foot of kitchen area, but even illumination is the goal.

TASK LIGHTING

Task lighting is meant to provide a higher level of illumination at work areas (sinks, countertops, and islands) and can be achieved with recessed cans, pendants, or undercabinet fixtures. If cabinets are over countertops, undercabinet fixtures (T5 fluorescent or LED strips) are by far the best choice and should be spaced for even illumination of the counter surface. For islands and sinks choose a recessed can with a slightly higher wattage and narrower lamp beam spread, or install pendants with similar attributes.

Arc-fault breakers are designed to detect arcing patterns of current for very short time intervals.

REQUIREMENTS ROOM BY ROOM

Kitchen and bath appliances are heavy power users, so their circuits must be sized accordingly.

Bathroom circuits

Bathroom receptacles must be supplied by a 20-amp circuit. The NEC allows the 20-amp circuit to supply the receptacles of more than one bathroom or to supply the receptacles, lights, and fans (excluding heating fans) in one bathroom. Receptacles in bathrooms must be GFCI-protected, either by a GFCI receptacle or a GFCI breaker. Bathroom ventilation fans are required in new and remodeled bathrooms in many jurisdictions regardless of whether there are operable windows, so always check local codes.

Small-appliance circuits

There must be at least two 20-amp small-appliance circuits in the kitchen serving the kitchen countertops. No point along a kitchen countertop should be more than 2 ft. from an outlet—in other words, space countertop receptacles at least every 4 ft. Every counter at least 12 in. wide must have a receptacle.

Kitchen lighting

Adequate lighting is particularly important in kitchens so people can work safely and efficiently. Lay out a good balance of general and task lighting. Be aware that many jurisdictions have energy-efficiency requirements for lighting in kitchens, so check with your local building authority first.

Bathroom lighting

It is important to illuminate the face evenly in mirrors. Common practice is to place good-quality light sources either above the vanity mirror or on either side of it. Be careful when using recessed cans over the vanity because they can leave shadows across the face. Many jurisdictions also have energy-efficiency requirements for lighting in bathrooms, including the use of high-efficacy lighting and vacancy sensors.

Dedicated circuits

All critical-use and fixed appliances should and in some cases (depending on the demand of the appliances and size of the circuit) must have their own dedicated (separate) circuits. These fixed appliances may include the water pump, freezer, refrigerator, oven, cooktop, microwave, furnace and/or whole-house air-conditioning unit, window air conditioner, and electric water heater. A bathroom heater requires a dedicated circuit, whether it is a separate unit or part of a light/fan. Laundry room receptacles must be on a dedicated circuit; so must an electric clothes dryer.

PRO TIP

Map your electrical system and place a copy near the panel so that you can quickly identify an outlet later if a circuit breaker trips or a fuse blows. Be specific when labeling each breaker.

DEVELOPING A FLOOR PLAN

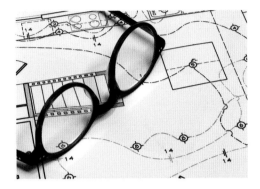

Drawing a set of project plans can help you anticipate problems, find optimal routes for running cable, minimize mess and disruption, and make the most of your time and money. A carefully drawn set of plans is also an important part of the code compliance and inspection process.

If you're replacing only a receptacle, switch, or light fixture, you usually don't need to involve the local building department. But if you run cable to extend a circuit, add a new circuit, or plan extensive upgrades, visit the building department to learn local code requirements and take out a permit. Your wiring plans should be approved by a local building inspector before you start the project.

Phone first

Call the building department and ask if local codes allow homeowners to do electrical work or if it must be done by a licensed electrician. You may be required to take a test to prove basic competency. This is also a good time to ask if the municipality has pamphlets that give an overview of local electrical code requirements.

Read up

Make a rough sketch of the work you propose, develop a rudimentary materials list, and then apply for a permit. At the time you apply, the building department clerk may be able to answer questions generated by the legwork you've done thus far. This feedback often proves invaluable.

MATERIALS LIST: LIGHTING AND SWITCHES	
This materials list was derived from "Electrical Plan: Lighting and Switches Layer," on p. 187.	
ROUGH	
Fixture housings	Type 4, 5, and 6
4 ea.	3/0 or 4/0 metal boxes with bar hangers (verify fixture requirements)
3 ea.	4/0 NM boxes with bar hangers (wall fixtures only)
4 ea.	One-gang NM adjustable boxes
2 ea.	Two-gang NM adjustable boxes
4 ea.	Three-gang NM boxes
17 ea.	Romex connectors
500 ft.	14/2 NM Romex: 24 fixtures × 15 ft. ave. = 360 ft. (use excess for home runs, 3 × 50 = 150 ft.)
105 ft.	12/3 NM Romex (use remaining from power rough)

NOTE:
Staples, screws, and nail plates from power rough materials list (facing page).

Recommendations:
Verify all surface-mounted fixtures before rough. Some have very small canopies and must have a 3/0 or even a one-gang box.

For undercabinet lights, do not install a box. Stub cable out of wall approximately 6 in. higher than the bottom of the upper cabinet. This way the drywall can be notched and the cable brought down to the perfect height by the cabinet installer. If undercabinet fixtures are to be installed at the front of the cabinet, some trim piece or metal sheath must be put over the NM cable to protect it from the wall to the fixture.

For recessed and other ceiling lighting, lay out fixtures on the floor and use a plumb bob or laser to set fixtures on the ceiling.

To align straight rows of ceiling fixtures, use a taut line.

TRIM	
Trims and lamps	Type 4, 6, 5
Fixtures and lamps	Type 1, 2, 3, 5, 8, 9, 10
6 ea.	Single-pole Decora switches
5 ea.	Three-way Decora switches
2 ea.	Single-pole Decora dimmers
1 ea.	Four-way Decora dimmer
1 ea.	Decora timer
3 ea.	Three-gang plastic Decora plates
1 ea.	Two-gang Decora plate
4 ea.	One-gang plastic plates
4 ea.	Romex connectors

Inspectors inspect

Inspectors are not on staff to tell you how to plan or execute a job, so make your questions as specific as possible. Present your rough sketch, discuss the materials you intend to use, and ask if there are specific requirements for the room(s) you'll be rewiring. For example, must bedroom receptacles have AFCI protection? Must kitchen wall receptacles be GFCIs if they are not over a counter? Be specific.

Draw up plans

Based on the feedback you've gotten, draw detailed plans. They should include each switch, receptacle, and fixture as well as the paths between switches and the device(s) they control. From this drawing, you can develop your materials list. Number each circuit or, better yet, assign a different color to each circuit. When you feel the plans are complete, schedule an appointment with an inspector to review them.

Listen well and take notes

Be low-key and respectful when you meet with the inspector to review your plans. First, you're more likely to get your questions answered. Second, you'll begin to develop a personal rapport. Because one inspector will often track a project from start to finish, this is a person who can ease your way or make it much more difficult. So play it straight, ask questions, listen well, take notes, and–above all–don't argue or come in with an attitude.

On-site inspections

Once the building department approves your plans, you can start working. In most cases, the inspector will visit your site when the wiring is roughed in and again when the wiring is finished. Don't call for an inspection until each stage is complete.

MATERIALS LIST: POWER	
This materials list was determined from "Electrical Plan: The Power Layer," on p. 187.	
ROUGH	
18 ea.	One-gang NM adjustable boxes
1 ea.	One-gang metal cut-in box
1 ea.	Two-gang NM adjustable box (oven)
3 ea	Boxes NM (Romex) connectors
1 ea.	Box (500) $3/4$-in. staples (to be used in rough lighting also)
1 ea.	Box (100) nail plates (to be used in rough lighting also)
500 ft.	12/2 NM Romex (2 × 250 ft. rolls): 20 units @ 15 ft. ave. = 300 ft. (4 home runs @ 50 ft. ave. = 200 ft.)
250 ft.	12/3 NM Romex (1 × 250 ft. roll): 2 home runs @ 50 ft. ave. = 100 ft. (use remainder in rough lighting)
50 ft.	10/3 NM (purchase cut to length): 1 home run @ 50 ft.
1	Bag (250) red wire connectors (to be used in rough lighting also)
1	Container (500) wafer-head #10 × $3/4$-in. screws
TRIM	
16 ea.	Duplex receptacles 15-amp or 20-amp rated
3 ea.	GFCI receptacles (15 amp with 20-amp feed through)
1 ea.	30-amp/220v receptacle (verify with range manufacturer)
16 ea.	One-gang plastic duplex plates
1 ea.	30-amp/220v plate

NOTE:
GFCIs are packaged with their plates.

PRO TIP

If you're remodeling, keep in mind that every finish surface you drill or cut into is a surface that you'll have to patch later. So minimize cutting and drilling.

ELECTRICAL NOTATION

Start by making an accurate floor plan of the room or rooms to be rewired on graph paper using a scale of 1/4 in. = 1 ft. Indicate walls and permanent fixtures such as countertops, kitchen islands, cabinets, and any large appliances. By photocopying this floor plan, you can quickly generate to-scale sketches of various wiring schemes.

Use the appropriate electrical symbols to indicate the locations of receptacles, switches, light fixtures, and appliances.

→ **For a key of electrical symbols, see "Common Electrical Symbols," at right.**

Especially when drawing kitchens, which can be incredibly complex, use colored pencils to indicate different circuits. You can also number circuits, but colored circuits are distinguishable at a glance. Use solid lines to indicate cable runs between receptacles and switches and dotted lines to indicate the cables that run between switches and the light fixtures or receptacles they control.

The beauty of photocopies is that you can experiment with different options quickly. As you refine the drawings, refer back to the list of requirements given earlier to be sure that you have an adequate number of receptacles, that you have GFCI receptacles over kitchen counters, that there are switches near doorways, and so on. Ultimately, you'll need a final master drawing with everything on it. But you may also find it helpful to make individual drawings—say, one for lighting and one for receptacles—if the master drawing gets too busy to read.

If you have questions or want to highlight a fixture type, use callouts on the floor plan. As you decide which fixtures and devices you want to install, develop a separate materials list and use numbered keys to indicate where each piece goes on the master drawing. Finally, develop a list of all materials, so you'll also have enough boxes, cable connectors, wire connectors, staples, and so on. In short, list all you need to do the job.

COMMON ELECTRICAL SYMBOLS

Symbol	Name
Duplex receptacle	
GFCI duplex receptacle	GFCI
Fourplex receptacle	
240v receptacle	
Weatherproof duplex receptacle	WP
Duplex receptacle, split-wired	
Single-pole switch	S
Three-way switch	S_3
Switch leg	
Home run (to service panel)	
Recessed light fixture	R
Wall-mounted fixture	
Ceiling outlet	
Ceiling pull switch	S
Junction box	J
Vent fan	VF
Ceiling fan	CF
Telephone outlet	▶
2-wire cable	
3-wire cable	

Pendant lights in the **dining area** are noted by a dotted green switch leg running from the two ceiling boxes to the single-pole switch on the wall.

All circuits for recessed, drop, and undercabinet lighting are noted in different colors. Be certain to track each circuit back to the appropriate wall switch.

Whether for 120v wall outlets or 240v appliance outlets, each circuit should end with a home run back to the service panel.

Any receptacle that serves the countertop must be GFCI-protected. Refrigerators, however, should be run on a non-GFCI receptacle.

ELECTRICAL PLAN: LIGHTING AND SWITCHES LAYER

A professional's electrical floor plan may be daunting at first, but it will start to make sense as you become familiar with the symbols used. To make the plans easier to read, they have been divided into two layers: (1) lighting and switches and (2) power, which consists of receptacles and dedicated circuits. (There's some overlap.) The circled letters are callouts that indicate areas warranting special attention. The circled numbers correspond to a master list of lighting fixtures that the electrician developed with the architect. Drawing switch legs and circuits in different colors makes a plan much easier to read.

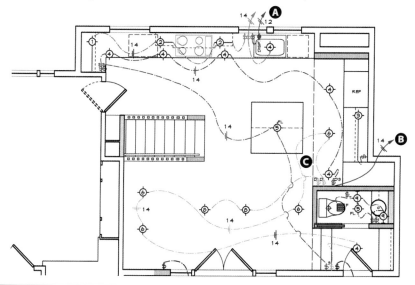

A Running 12/2 cable will accommodate the disposal circuit.

B Use 14/2 cable for all general lighting home runs (cable runs back to the service panel).

C Verify the dimmer load; dimmers must be de-rated when ganged together.

ELECTRICAL PLAN: THE POWER LAYER

This kitchen remodel is typical in that it has many dedicated circuits (also called designated circuits) and, per code, at least two 20-amp small-appliance circuits wired with #12 cable. Circled letters are callouts that correspond to the lettered notes.

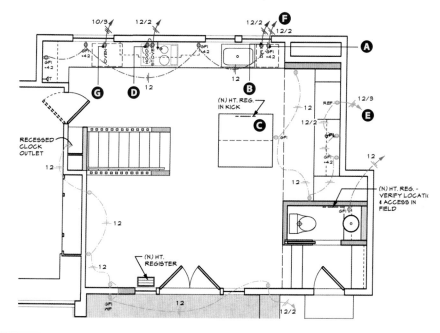

A Wire the GFCI receptacle at the beginning of the run so it affords protection to receptacles downstream.

B Dishwasher circuit. Install under the sink in the cabinet.

C Single-location GFCI protection.

D Stove is gas, so the receptacle is only for the igniter and clock and is OK to run with the hood. Leave NM cable stubbed at the ceiling, and leave 3 ft. to 4 ft. of slack for termination in the hood/trim. (*Note:* Never run a stove igniter off a GFCI-protected circuit because it will trip the GFCI every time the stove is turned on.)

E Use 12/3 cable for the home run, so a single cable takes care of the dedicated refrigerator circuit and the countertop receptacle (small-appliance) circuit.

F Home run for counter (small-appliance) circuit 2.

G Oven outlet. Refer to unit specifications to verify receptacle or hard-wired connection.

WIRING SCHEMATICS

RECEPTACLE IN MID-CIRCUIT

By splicing like wire groups and running *pigtails* (short wires) to the receptacle in this conventional method, you ensure continuous current downstream.

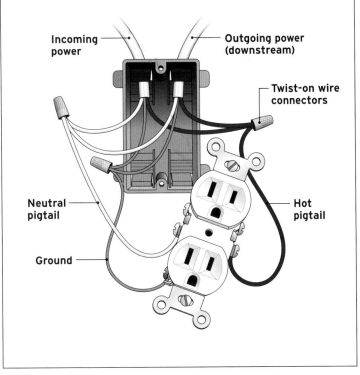

Incoming power

Outgoing power (downstream)

Twist-on wire connectors

Neutral pigtail

Hot pigtail

Ground

RECEPTACLE AT END OF CIRCUIT

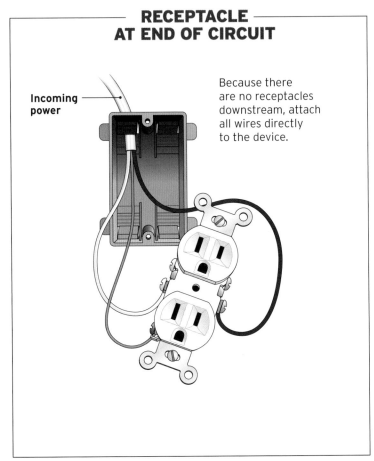

Incoming power

Because there are no receptacles downstream, attach all wires directly to the device.

The diagrams in this section show most of the circuit wiring variations that you're likely to need when wiring receptacles, fixtures, and switches. Unless otherwise noted, assume that incoming cable (from the power source) and all others are 2-wire cable with ground, such as 14/2 w/grd or 12/2 w/grd (#14 wire should be protected by 15-amp breakers; #12 wire should be protected by 20-amp breakers).

➜ **See "Appliances," on p. 228, for more wiring schematics.**

All metal boxes must be grounded. Assume that nongrounded boxes in the wiring diagrams are nonmetallic (plastic) unless otherwise specified. In sheathed cables, ground wires are bare copper. Black and red wires indicate hot conductors. White wires indicate neutral conductors, unless taped black to indicate that the wire is being used as a hot conductor in a switch loop (p. 54).

GANGED RECEPTACLES IN METAL BOX

A two-gang metal box with fourplex (*double duplex*) receptacles uses a ground screw or ground clip to connect a ground pigtail to the box.

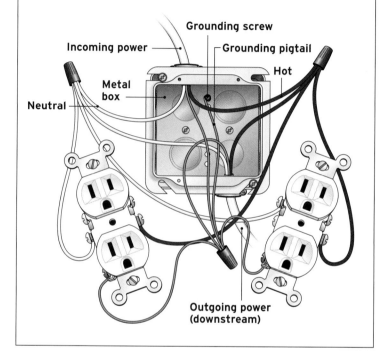

Grounding screw

Incoming power

Grounding pigtail

Hot

Metal box

Neutral

Outgoing power (downstream)

GFCI RECEPTACLE, MULTIPLE-LOCATION PROTECTION

A GFCI receptacle can protect devices* downstream if wired as shown. Attach wires from the power source to terminals marked "line." Attach wires continuing downstream to terminals marked "load." As with any receptacle, attach hot wires to brass screws, white wires to silver screws, and a grounding pigtail to the ground screw. *Note:* Here, only ground wires are spliced; hot and neutral wires attach directly to screw terminals.

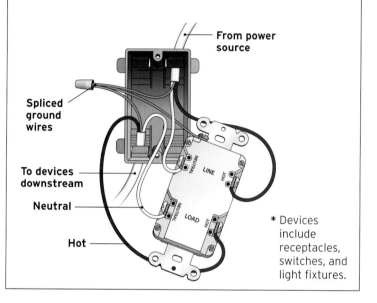

From power source

Spliced ground wires

To devices downstream

Neutral

Hot

LINE

LOAD

* Devices include receptacles, switches, and light fixtures.

GFCI RECEPTACLE, SINGLE-LOCATION PROTECTION

This configuration provides GFCI protection only at the GFCI receptacle. All devices downstream remain unprotected. Here, splice hot and neutral wires so the power downstream is continuous and attach pigtails to the GFCI's "line" screw terminals. With this setup, receptacle use downstream won't cause nuisance tripping of the GFCI receptacle.

Incoming power

To devices downstream

Neutral wires spliced

Hot wires spliced

Line brass

Ground wires spliced

Line silver

Ground screw

WIRING SCHEMATICS (CONTINUED)

LIGHT FIXTURE AT END OF CABLE RUN

Switch wiring at its simplest: Incoming and outgoing hot wires attach to the terminals of a single-pole switch. Neutrals and grounds are spliced through.

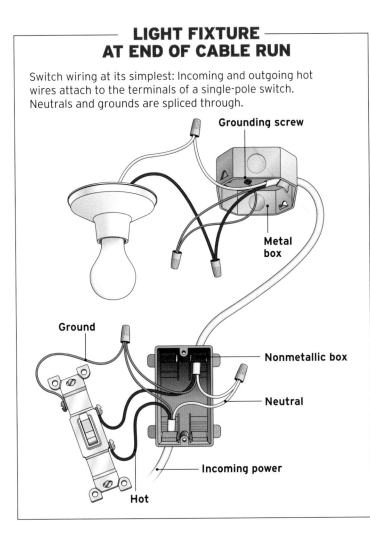

Grounding screw

Metal box

Ground

Nonmetallic box

Neutral

Incoming power

Hot

A SIMPLE SWITCH WITH A "SWITCH LOOP": THE MODERN METHOD

The 2017 NEC requires that there be a neutral in every switch box because some electronic timer switches and other energy-saving controls need a neutral. Thus, if you want to use a switch-loop approach, you must use 3-wire cable, connect the neutral at the power source, and then cap off the neutral in the switch box.

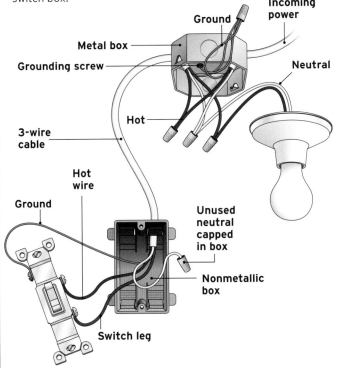

Ground

Incoming power

Metal box

Neutral

Grounding screw

Hot

3-wire cable

Hot wire

Ground

Unused neutral capped in box

Nonmetallic box

Switch leg

GANGED SWITCHES, TWO FIXTURES

This is a typical setup for switches by exterior doors. For example, one single-pole switch controls an exterior light fixture, while the second switch controls an interior fixture.

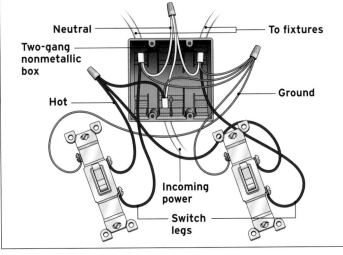

Neutral

To fixtures

Two-gang nonmetallic box

Hot

Ground

Incoming power

Switch legs

CLOSEUP: THREE-WAY SWITCH

Three-way switches control a fixture from two locations. Each switch has two brass screws and a black screw (common terminal). The hot wire from the source attaches to the common terminal of the first switch. Traveler wires between the switches attach to the brass screws. Finally, a wire runs from the common terminal of the second switch to the hot lead of the fixture.

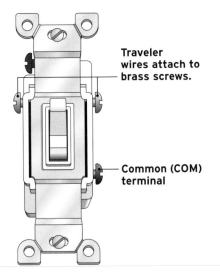

Traveler wires attach to brass screws.

Common (COM) terminal

THREE-WAY SWITCHES, LIGHT FIXTURE BETWEEN

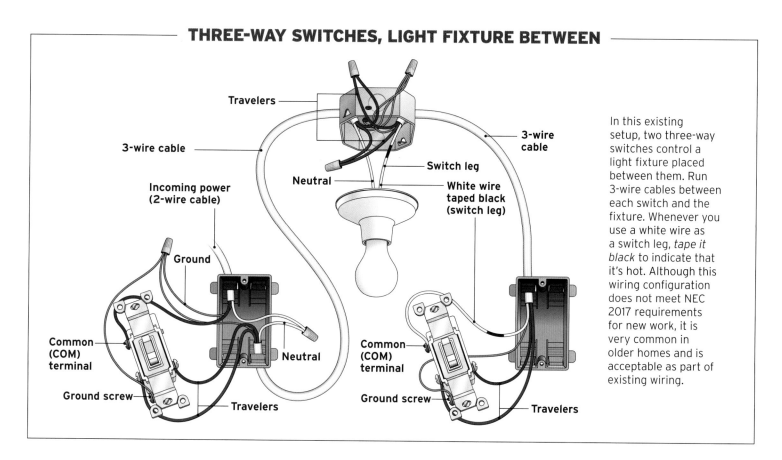

Travelers

3-wire cable

3-wire cable

Incoming power (2-wire cable)

Switch leg

Neutral

White wire taped black (switch leg)

Ground

Common (COM) terminal

Neutral

Common (COM) terminal

Ground screw

Ground screw

Travelers

Travelers

In this existing setup, two three-way switches control a light fixture placed between them. Run 3-wire cables between each switch and the fixture. Whenever you use a white wire as a switch leg, *tape it black* to indicate that it's hot. Although this wiring configuration does not meet NEC 2017 requirements for new work, it is very common in older homes and is acceptable as part of existing wiring.

THREE-WAY SWITCHES, LIGHT FIXTURE AT START OF CABLE RUN

Here, incoming power enters through the fixture box. Acceptable in existing wiring but does not meet NEC 2017 requirements for new work.

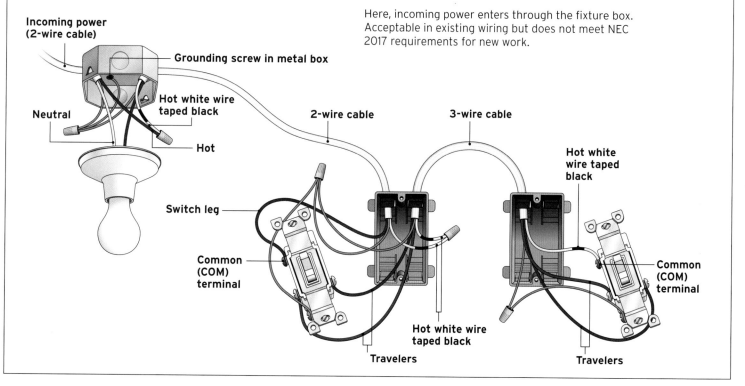

Incoming power (2-wire cable)

Grounding screw in metal box

Hot white wire taped black

Neutral

Hot

2-wire cable

3-wire cable

Hot white wire taped black

Switch leg

Common (COM) terminal

Common (COM) terminal

Hot white wire taped black

Travelers

Travelers

WIRING SCHEMATICS (CONTINUED)

THREE-WAY SWITCHES, LIGHT FIXTURE AT END OF CABLE RUN

Two three-way switches precede the fixture on the circuit.
Meets NEC requirements for new work.

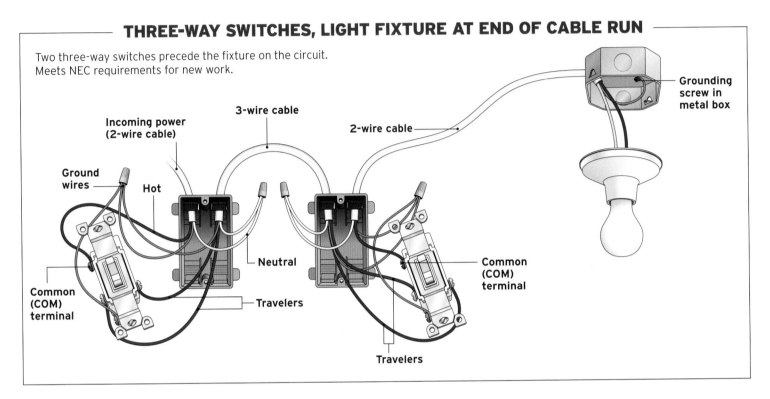

- Grounding screw in metal box
- 3-wire cable
- Incoming power (2-wire cable)
- 2-wire cable
- Ground wires
- Hot
- Neutral
- Common (COM) terminal
- Travelers
- Common (COM) terminal
- Travelers

SPLIT-TAB RECEPTACLE CONTROLLED BY SWITCH, SWITCH UPSTREAM, REGULAR RECEPTACLE DOWNSTREAM

This setup is commonly used to meet NEC requirements if there is no switch-controlled ceiling fixture. As shown, the switch controls only the bottom half of the split-tab receptacle. The top half of the split-tab receptacle and all receptacles downstream are always hot. Removing the tab is shown in photo 1 on p. 49.

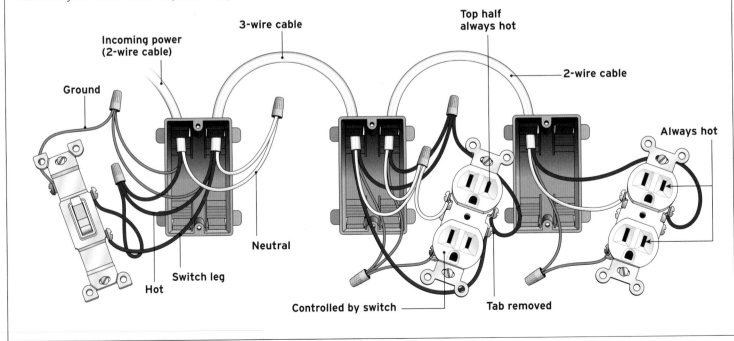

- 3-wire cable
- Top half always hot
- Incoming power (2-wire cable)
- 2-wire cable
- Ground
- Always hot
- Neutral
- Switch leg
- Hot
- Controlled by switch
- Tab removed

SPLIT-TAB RECEPTACLE CONTROLLED BY SWITCH, SWITCH AT END OF CABLE RUN

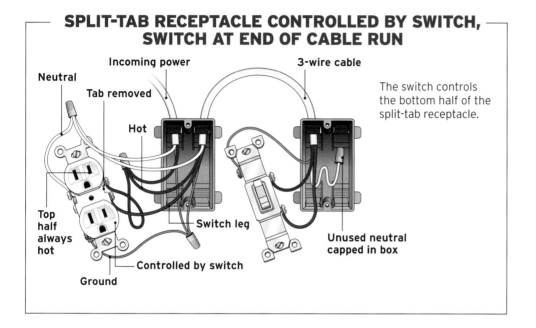

Neutral

Tab removed

Incoming power

3-wire cable

Hot

Top half always hot

Switch leg

Controlled by switch

Ground

Unused neutral capped in box

The switch controls the bottom half of the split-tab receptacle.

120/240V DRYER RECEPTACLE

This dedicated circuit requires a 10/3 cable with ground and a two-pole 30-amp breaker. Two 120v hot wires terminate to "hot" setscrews on the receptacle and the breaker poles; the neutral wire terminates to the "neut" setscrew on the receptacle and the neutral/ground bus bar in the service panel.

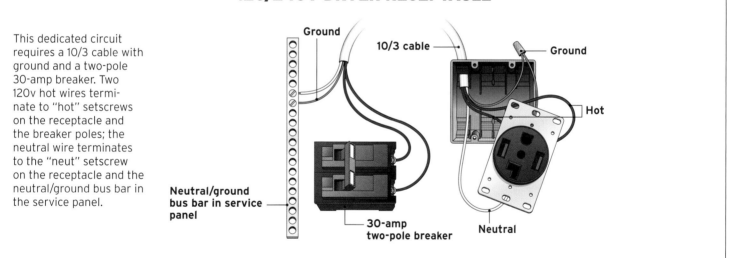

Ground

10/3 cable

Ground

Hot

Neutral/ground bus bar in service panel

30-amp two-pole breaker

Neutral

ROUGH-IN WIRING

ROUGH-IN WIRING REFERS TO THE first phase of a wiring installation. It is the stage at which you set outlet boxes and run electrical cable to them—as opposed to finish wiring, or connecting wires to devices and fixtures.

Rough-in wiring is pretty straightforward when studs and joists are exposed. Whether a house is new or old, running wires through exposed framing is called *new work,* or new construction. If the framing is covered with finish surfaces such as plaster and drywall, however, the job is referred to as *remodel wiring* or *old work.* Remodel wiring is almost always more complicated and costly because first you must drill through or cut into finish surfaces to install boxes and run cable, and later you need to patch the holes you made.

GETTING STARTED

Rough-in basics, p. 196

Tools for rough-in, p. 198

Materials for rough-in, p. 200

Laying out the job, p. 202

OUTLET BOXES

Installing new work boxes, p. 204

Installing ceiling boxes, p. 205

RUNNING CABLE

Drilling for cable, p. 206

Pulling cable, p. 207

Feeding cable through corners, p. 208

Fishing cable behind finish walls, p. 209

Fishing cable to a ceiling fixture, p. 210

RETROFIT WORK

Cutting a wall box into plaster, p. 212

Cutting a wall box into drywall, p. 212

Retrofitting a ceiling box, p. 213

Creating a wiring trench, p. 214

Pulling cable to retrofit boxes, p. 215

MAKING UP BOXES

Making up an outlet box, p. 216

Making up a can light, p. 217

Making up a single-gang switch box, p. 218

Making up a multigang switch box, p. 219

METAL CABLE & CONDUIT

Flexible metal cable, p. 220

Installing AC cable, p. 221

Installing MC cable, p. 222

Working with EMT steel conduit (interior), p. 223

Making bends with metal conduit (interior), p. 224

Fishing wire through conduit, p. 225

Prepping receptacles for surface metal boxes, p. 226

Wiring outlets, p. 227

ROUGH-IN BASICS

Wait until rough carpentry is complete before you begin rough-in wiring. Part of an electrician's job is setting boxes so they'll be flush to finished surfaces. Before an electrician starts working, modifications to the framing—such as furring out or planing down irregular studs and ceiling joists—must be complete.

Where to start

Wait until the plumbers are gone. Waste pipes are large and often difficult to locate, which usually means a lot of drilling and cutting into studs and joists. Once the plumbing pipes are in place, you'll clearly see what obstacles you face and will have more room to move around.

Check your plans often. If there's not a table on-site where you can roll out your electrical plans, staple them to a stud—preferably at eye level so you can read them easily. Checking and rechecking the plans is particularly important if you're not a professional electrician.

Be flexible. As you lay out devices, you'll realize that not everything specified on the plans is possible; most plans are developed without knowing exactly what the framing looks like or where obstructions are. Do all the rough-in wiring with the power off.

Organize your work

Perform one task at a time. Each task—such as setting boxes or drilling—requires a different set of tools. So once you have the tools out to do a given task, go around the room and complete all similar tasks. You'll become more proficient as you go: You waste less time changing tools, and the job goes much faster. In general, the sequence of rough-in tasks looks like this:

1. Walk the room with plans, marking outlet locations on walls and floor.
2. Snap chalklines or shoot laser lines to pinpoint box elevations.
3. Attach boxes to studs and ceiling joists.
4. Drill holes for cable runs.
5. Pull cable through holes and into boxes.
6. Make up boxes—strip wire ends, splice grounds, splice current-carrying conductors, attach mud rings, and push wires into boxes.
7. Rough-in inspection.

After the inspection, finish surfaces are installed. Then, at the trim-out or finish stage, wires are attached to the devices and fixtures.

The rough-in inspection

At the rough-in stage, inspectors look for a few key signs of a job well done: cables properly sized for the loads they'll carry; the requisite number and type of outlets specified by code; cables protected by nail plates as needed; neat, consistent work throughout the system; and, above all, ground wires spliced and, in metal boxes, secured to a ground screw. If grounds aren't complete, you won't pass the rough-in inspection.

When running cable around doors and windows, **find the easiest path. Consider drilling through top or bottom plates and running cable in the space above or below.**

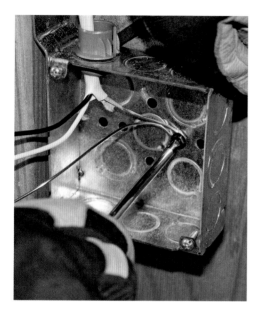

During the rough-in inspection, **inspectors demand solid ground-wire splices and, in metal boxes, a ground screw or clip that secures the ground wire.**

At this inspection, only grounds need to be spliced. But since you've got the tools out, it makes sense to splice neutrals and continuous hot wires (those not attached to switches).

➤ **For more on grounding, see p. 12.**

When all splices are complete, carefully fold the wire groups into the box. When you come back to do the trim-out stage, simply pull the wires out of the box, connect wires to devices, and install devices and cover plates.

Connecting circuit wires to a main panel or subpanel is the very last step of an installation. As noted throughout this book, you should **avoid handling energized cables or devices**.

REMODEL WIRING SAFETY ESSENTIALS

Before removing box covers or handling wires, turn off the power to the area and use a voltage tester to be sure it's off.

First remove the fuse or flip off the circuit breaker controlling the circuit and post a sign on the main panel warning people of work in progress. Better yet, if you've got circuit breakers, do as the pros do and install a breaker lockout so it will be impossible for anyone to turn it on. Breaker lockouts are available at electrical supply houses and most home centers.

➤ **For more on lockouts, see p. 264.**

Testing for power is particularly important in remodel wiring, because walls and ceilings often contain old cables that are energized. Always test the tester first—on an outlet you know is energized—to be sure the tester is working correctly. A noncontact tester is especially useful in remodel situations. Touch the tester tip to cable sheathing or wire insulation: If a cable, wire, or electrical device is energized, the tip will glow. Whenever possible, do a follow-up test with a probe tester (p. 16).

Whatever tester you use, test it first on an outlet that you know is live to make sure the tester is working properly.

Always use a voltage tester to test for power before touching cables, devices, or fixtures. Then follow up with a probe tester. Here, a noncontact tester detects voltage through cable insulation.

 SAFETY ALERT

Make an emergency plan. It may be as simple as carrying a cell phone or having a friend close by—never do electrical work alone. Calling 911 is an obvious first step if an emergency occurs. On the job site, you should also post directions to the nearest hospital and a list of phone numbers of people to contact.

TOOLS FOR ROUGH-IN

Most of the tools you'll need for rough-in wiring are discussed in "Tools & Materials" (p. 18), so here we'll focus on tools that make rough-in easier and more productive. All hand tools should have cushioned handles and fit your hand.

Safety tools include voltage testers (a noncontact tester and a probe tester), eye protection, work gloves, hard-soled shoes, kneepads, a dust mask, and a hard hat. Hard hats are clunky but essential when you're working in attics, basements, or any other location with limited headroom. Every job site should also have a fire extinguisher and a first aid kit visibly stored in a central location.

Adequate lighting, whether drop lights or light stands, is essential to both job safety and accuracy. If a site is too dark to see what color wires you're working with, your chances of wrong connections increase.

Sturdy stepladders are a must. In the electrical industry, only fiberglass stepladders are OSHA compliant because they're nonconductive. Wood ladders are usually nonconductive when dry, but if they get rained on or absorb ambient moisture, wood ladders can conduct electricity.

Shop vacuums, push brooms, dust pans, and garbage cans help keep the workplace clean. And a clean site is a safe site. Clean up whenever debris makes footing unsafe, especially if you're cutting into walls or ceilings. Plaster lath is especially dangerous because it's loaded with sharp little nails that can pierce the soles of your shoes.

Layout tools include tape measures, spirit levels, chalklines, and lasers. *Rough-in* is a misleading term because there's nothing rough or crude about locating fixtures or receptacles—layout is very exacting. For that reason, levels and plumb lasers are indispensable when laying out outlets **A**.

The most-used hand tools are the same pliers, cutters, strippers, levels, and screwdrivers mentioned throughout this book. It's also handy to have a wire-nut driver **B** if you've got dozens of splices to make up.

A Lasers make for quick work when setting boxes.

B A wire-nut driver speeds up wire splices.

D An 18-in. auger bit bores easily through several studs.

E A wire reel prevents kinking cable as you pull it.

There's also a nut-driver bit that fits into a screw gun **C**, but it tends to overtighten wire connectors if you're not experienced in using it. If you'll be cutting into and patching plaster or drywall, get a jab saw (drywall saw), a utility knife, and a taping knife. A flat bar (for prying) and an old, beat-up wood chisel are always busy in remodels, too.

Power tools help speed many tasks. Always wear eye protection when using them. A screw gun is preferable to nailing most of the time because you can easily remove a screw if you want to reposition, say, an outlet box.

A right-angle drill with a 1/2-in. chuck is the workhorse of rough-in wiring because it has the muscle to drill through hard old lumber. If you will be drilling through nail-infested wood, get a "nail-eater bit"; a number of companies make them. If you use a standard 6-in.-long auger bit, the drill head and bit will fit between studs and joists spaced 16-in. on-center. It enables you to drill perpendicular to the framing to make wire pulling easier. Longer bits also have their merits: An 18-in. self-feeding auger bit **D** bores easily through several studs or doubled wall plates; it is also long enough that you probably

C A nut-driver bit speeds up splicing, but be careful not to overtwist wires.

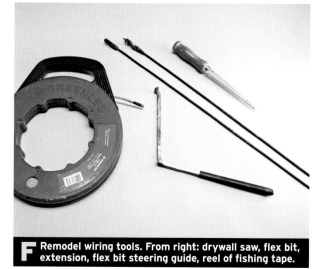

F Remodel wiring tools. From right: drywall saw, flex bit, extension, flex bit steering guide, reel of fishing tape.

A well-organized tool belt prevents you from looking for tools all day long.

won't need a ladder to drill through top plates.

To cut larger holes in plaster or drywall–say, to retrofit pancake boxes or recessed light cans–use a fine-toothed hole saw.

Use a jab saw or an oscillating multi-tool to cut individual box openings into finish surfaces. Use a Universal E-cut multi-tool blade to cut through finish surfaces. When cutting through plaster lath, alternate cuts on each side of the opening rather than cutting one side completely. This will keep the lath from fluttering and cracking the plaster. Use a reciprocating saw to cut through framing or through plaster lath to create a wiring trench.

➤ **For more on creating a wiring trench, see p. 214.**

Use a demolition sawblade to cut through wood that contains nails or screws. It'll hold up to such heavy work.

There are a number of specialty tools designed to ease rough-in. A wire reel, a rotating dispenser that enables you to pull cable easily to distant points, is worth having. Reels hold 250 ft. of cable **E**. A 25-ft. fishing tape–a flexible steel, fiberglass, or nylon tape–enables you to pull cable behind finish surfaces **F**. In most cases, however, it's simpler to use a flex bit to drill through framing in one direction.

➤ **For more on pulling cable, see pp. 209–211.**

A 48-in. drill extension will increase the effective drilling length of a flex bit. Use a flex bit steering guide to keep the flex bit from bowing excessively.

MATERIALS FOR ROUGH-IN

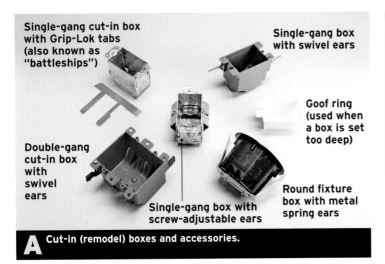

Single-gang cut-in box with Grip-Lok tabs (also known as "battleships")

Single-gang box with swivel ears

Goof ring (used when a box is set too deep)

Double-gang cut-in box with swivel ears

Single-gang box with screw-adjustable ears

Round fixture box with metal spring ears

A Cut-in (remodel) boxes and accessories.

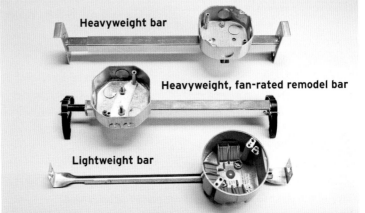

Heavyweight bar

Heavyweight, fan-rated remodel bar

Lightweight bar

B Adjustable bar hangers.

C A recessed light fixture with adjustable bar hangers.

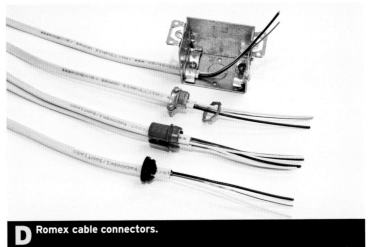

D Romex cable connectors.

As with tools, most of the materials installed during the rough-in phase are discussed in "Tools & Materials" and can be installed either in new construction or remodel wiring. All materials must be UL- or NRTL-listed, which indicates that they meet the safety standards of the electrical industry. There are, however, a number of specialized boxes, hanger bars, and other elements intended for remodel wiring that can be installed with minimal disruptions to existing finish surfaces.

Remodel (cut-in) boxes mount to existing finish surfaces—unlike new-work boxes, which attach to framing. Most cut-in boxes have lips (flanges) that rest on the plaster or drywall surface to keep boxes from falling

into the wall or ceiling cavity. Spring clamps, folding tabs, or screw-adjustable wings on the box are then expanded to hold the box snug to the backside of the wall or ceiling. The devices that anchor boxes vary greatly **A**.

Code requires that ceiling boxes be mounted to framing. Expandable remodel bar hangers accommodate this requirement **B**. Adjustable hangers also allow you to locate recessed light fixtures exactly **C**.

Cable connectors (also called clamps) solidly connect cable to the box to prevent strain on electrical connections inside the box **D**. Cable clamps also prevent sheathing from being scraped or punctured by sharp box edges. Plastic boxes come with integral

plastic spring clamps inside. If you use metal boxes, insert plastic push-in connectors into the box knockouts; no other cable connector is as quick or easy to install in tight spaces.

PRO TIP
Don't forget to leave 8 in. to 10 in. of cable sticking out of each box for connecting devices later.

Ordering materials

In general, order 10 percent extra of all boxes and cover plates (they crack easily) and the exact number of switches, receptacles, light fixtures, and other devices specified on the plans. It's okay to order one or two extra switches and receptacles, but because they're costly, pros try not to order too many extras.

Cable is another matter altogether. Calculating the amount of cable can be tricky because there are infinite ways to route cable between two points. Electricians typically measure the running distances between several pairs of boxes to come up with an average length. They then use that average to calculate a total for each room. In new work, for example, boxes spaced 12 ft. apart (per code) take 15 ft. to 20 ft. of cable to run about 2 ft. above the boxes and drop it down to each box. After you've calculated cable for the whole job, add 10 percent.

Cable for remodel jobs is tougher to calculate because it's impossible to know what obstructions hide behind finish surfaces. You may have to fish cable up to the top of wall plates, across an attic, and then down to each box. Do some exploring, measure that imaginary route, and again create an average cable length to multiply. If it takes, say, 25 ft. for each pair of wall boxes and you have eight outlets to wire, then 8 outlets × 25 ft. = 200 ft. Add 10 percent, and your total is 220 ft. Because the average roll of wire sold at home centers contains 250 ft., one roll should do it.

Have materials on hand when it's time to start installing boxes. Electricians often walk from room to room, dropping a box wherever floor plans indicate. Double-check to be sure placement meets code requirements.

Rough-in recap: Electrical code

- **Circuit breakers, wiring, and devices must be correctly sized for the loads they carry. For example, 20-amp circuits require 12AWG wire and receptacles rated for no greater than 20 amps. Mismatching circuit elements can lead to house fires.**

- **All wire connections must be good mechanical connections. There must be good pressure between the connectors you are joining, whether wires are spliced together or connected to a device. For that reason, buy devices with screw terminals rather than cheap back-wired (stab-in) devices whose internal clamps can deform (see p. 42). Deformed clamps can lead to loose wires, arcing, and house fires.** (see p. 42)

- **All wire connections must be housed in a covered box.**

- **Boxes must be securely attached to framing so that normal use will not loosen them.**

- **Box edges must be flush to finish surfaces. In noncombustible surfaces (drywall, plaster) there may be a 1/4-in. gap between the box edge and the surface. But in combustible surfaces, such as wood paneling, there must be no gap.**

- **All newly installed devices must be grounded. Code allows you to replace an existing two-prong receptacle or to replace a nongrounded box that has become damaged. However, if you install a new three-prong receptacle, it must be grounded. The only exception: You can install a three-prong receptacle into an ungrounded box if that new device is a GFCI receptacle. If you extend a circuit, the entire circuit must be upgraded to current code.**

- **In new rough-in work, cable must be supported within 12 in. of any box and every 4 1/2 ft. thereafter.**

LAYING OUT THE JOB

With electrical plans in hand, walk each room and mark box locations for receptacles, switches, and light fixtures. Each device must be mounted to a box that houses its wiring connections. The only exceptions are devices that come with an integral box, such as bath fans, recessed light cans, and undercabinet light fixtures ❶.

Mark receptacles and switches on the walls first. Then mark ceiling fixtures. If studs and joists are exposed, use a vividly colored crayon that will show up on the wood. If there are finish surfaces, use a pencil to mark walls at a height where you can see the notations easily—these marks will be painted over later. Near each switch box, draw a letter or number to indicate which fixture the switch controls.

Once you've roughly located boxes on the walls, use a laser level ❷ to set exact box heights for each type of box.

➡ **For more on box heights, see "Rough-in recap: Box locations," on the facing page.**

You can also use a hammer to establish the bottom lines of the boxes ❸. Many electricians prefer to determine level with the laser, then snap a permanent chalkline at that height so they can move the laser to other rooms ❹.

To locate ceiling fixtures, mark them on the floor ❺ and use a plumb laser ❻ to transfer that mark up to the ceiling ❼. This may seem counterintuitive, but it will save you a lot of time. Floors are flat, almost always the same size and shape as the ceilings above, and—perhaps most important—accessible and easy to mark. In complex rooms, such as kitchens, draw cabinet and island outlines onto the floor as well. Those outlines will help you fine-tune ceiling light positions to optimally illuminate work areas.

1 Begin the layout by walking the room and marking box locations.

2 Use a laser level to set box heights above counters.

3 A hammer handle quickly establishes box heights at roughly 12 in.

4 You can snap a level chalkline to indicate box tops or bottoms.

Avoiding hot wires In remodels, there may be live wires behind finish surfaces. Use a noncontact tester to initially test receptacles, switches, fixtures, and any visible wires. Then follow up with a probe tester, if possible. The cables feeding those devices will be nearby. Wall receptacles are usually fed by cables running 1 ft. to 3 ft. above. Switches often have cable runs up to a top plate; each ceiling fixture has cable running to the switch(es) controlling it. Avoid drilling or cutting into those areas, and you'll minimize the risk of shock.

5 Many electricians prefer to mark ceiling fixture centers on the floor.

6 They then use a plumb laser to transfer marks to the ceiling.

7 Center your hole saw on each ceiling mark.

PRO TIP

When marking box locations on finish surfaces, use a pencil—never a crayon, grease pencil, or felt-tipped marker. Pencil marks won't show through new paint. Also, grease pencils and crayons can prevent paint from sticking.

Rough-in recap: Box locations

- Whatever heights you choose to set outlets and switches, be consistent.
- Code requires that no point along a wall be more than 6 ft. from an outlet. Set the bottom of wall outlets 12 in. to 15 in. above the finished floor surface, or 18 in. above the finished floor surface to satisfy Americans with Disabilities Act (ADA) requirements.
- Place the top of switch boxes at 48 in. and they will line up with drywall seams (if sheets run horizontally), thus reducing the drywall cuts you must make.
- In kitchens and bathrooms, place the bottom of countertop receptacles 42 in. above the finished floor surface. This height ensures that each receptacle will clear the combined height of a standard countertop (36 in.) and the height of a backsplash (4 in.), with 2 in. extra to accommodate cover plates.

INSTALLING NEW WORK BOXES

1 To install an adjustable box, press its bracket flush against the stud edge and screw the bracket to the edge or side of the stud.

2 Nail-on boxes cannot be adjusted, so use the depth gauge on the side to ensure that box edges will be flush to finish surfaces.

3 Boxes with integral brackets have small points at top and bottom that sink into the stud. A mud ring brings the box flush to the wall.

4 To provide solid support for multigang boxes, first install an adjustable box bracket that spans the studs.

In this section we'll assume that framing members are exposed and that boxes will be attached directly to them. Once you've used your plans to locate receptacle, switch, and light-fixture boxes on walls and ceilings, installing them is pretty straightforward. Electrical codes dictate box capacity and composition.

> **For more on box capacity and composition requirements, see p. 24.**

In residences, 18-cu.-in. single-gang PVC plastic boxes are by far the most commonly used. This size is large enough for a single outlet or a single switch and two cables. Otherwise, use a 22.5-cu.-in. single-gang box or a four-square box with a plaster ring.

Set each box to the correct height, then set its depth so that the box edge will be flush to the finish surface. If you use adjustable boxes, simply screw them to a stud **1**. To raise or lower the box depth, turn the

adjusting screw. Side-nailing boxes typically have scales (gradated depth gauges) on the side **2**. If not, use a scrap of finish material (such as ½-in. drywall) as a depth gauge. Metal boxes frequently have brackets that mount the box flush to a stud edge **3**; after the box is wired, add a mud ring (plaster ring) to bring the box flush to the finish surface.

Multiple-gang boxes mount to studs in the same way. But if plans locate the box away

from studs or a multigang box is particularly wide, nail blocking between the studs or install an adjustable box bracket and screw the box to it **4**. (The bracket is also called a *screw gun bracket*, because a screw gun is typically used to mount it and to attach boxes to it.)

About knockouts Once you've mounted boxes, remove the appropriate number of box knockouts and install cable clamps. Single-gang, new-construction plastic boxes don't need clamps: Simply strike a screwdriver handle with the heel of your hand to drive out the knockout. To remove a metal-box knockout, jab it with the nose of needle-nose pliers to loosen it, then use the pliers' jaws to twist it free. Page 26 shows how.

INSTALLING CEILING BOXES

INSTALLING A RECESSED CAN

1 When the can height is where you want it, fasten its hanger bars to the joists.

2 Slide the can to fine-tune its position. Tighten the screws to lock it in place.

INSTALLING A BOX TO THE JOIST

3 If a box position needs to be offset slightly from a joist, nail it to blocking.

INSTALLING A BOX BETWEEN JOISTS

4 For boxes that occur midway between joists, use an adjustable bar hanger.

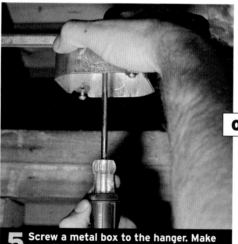

5 Screw a metal box to the hanger. Make sure the box edge is flush to the surface.

or

6 Alternately, you can nail 2×4 blocking between the joists.

Boxes for ceiling lights are most often 4-in. octagonal or round boxes or recessed light fixtures with integrated junction boxes. Setting ceiling boxes in new work is similar to setting wall boxes, with the added concern that the ceiling box be strong enough to support the fixture. Many electricians prefer to use metal boxes for ceiling fixtures. Ceiling fans require fan-rated boxes.

➜ For more on laying out the job, see p. 202.

In many cases, you'll need to reposition the box to avoid obstacles or line it up to other fixtures, but it's quick work if the box has an adjustable bar hanger. To install a recessed can, for example, extend its two bar hangers to adjacent ceiling joists. Then screw or nail the hangers to the joists **❶**. Slide the can along the hangers until its opening (the light well) is where you want it and then tighten the setscrews on the side **❷**.

To install a 4-in. box, simply nail or screw it to the side of a joist. If you need to install it slightly away from a joist, first nail 2× blocking to the joist, then attach the box to the blocking **❸**. The box edge must be flush to finish surfaces.

To install a 4-in. box between joists, first screw an adjustable hanger bar to the joists **❹**, then attach the box to it **❺**. Alternately, you can insert 2× blocking between the joists and screw the box to it **❻**.

➜ For a detailed look at installing hanger bars, see p. 81.

DRILLING FOR CABLE

Once boxes are in place, you're ready to run cable to each of them. It's rather like connecting dots with a pencil line. To prevent screws or nails from puncturing cables, drill in the middle of studs or joists whenever possible. If the edges of any holes you drill are less than 1¼ in. from the edge of a framing member, you must install steel nail-protection plates. Always wear eye protection when drilling.

Drill for cables running horizontally (through studs) first. It doesn't matter whether you start drilling at the outlet box closest to the panel or at the last outlet on the circuit. Just be methodical: Drill holes in one direction as you go from box to box. However, if you're drilling for an appliance that has a dedicated circuit—and thus only one outlet—it's usually less work to drill a hole through a top or bottom plate and then run cable through the attic or basement instead of drilling through numerous studs to reach the outlet.

If possible, drill holes thigh high **①**. Partially rest the drill on your thigh so your arms won't get as tired. This method also helps you drill holes that are roughly the same height—making cable-pulling much easier. Moreover, when you drill about 1 ft. above a box, you have enough room to bend the cable and staple it near the box without crimping the cable and damaging its insulation.

For most drilling, use a 6-in., ¾-in.-diameter bit. Use an 18-in. bit to drill lumber nailed together around windows, and doorways **②**. Using an 18-in. bit is also safer because it enables you to drill through top plates without standing on a ladder. Standing on the floor is a big advantage, as the reaction torque from a heavy-duty drill can throw you off a ladder if a bit binds up **③**.

PRO TIP

Drilled holes don't need to be perfectly aligned, but the closer they line up, the easier it is to pull cable through them.

1 When drilling for cable runs, rest the drill on your thigh. This method eases drilling and places holes at a convenient height.

2 Use an 18-in. ship bit to drill through multiple studs.

3 The 18-in. ship bit also allows you to drill through top wall plates while standing on the floor.

PULLING CABLE

For greatest efficiency, install cable in two steps: (1) Pull cable between outlets, leaving roughly 1 ft. extra beyond each box for future splices, and (2) retrace your steps, stapling cable to framing and installing nail-protection plates. As with drilling, it doesn't matter whether you start pulling cable from the first box of a circuit or from the last box. If there are several circuits in a room, start at one end and proceed along each circuit, pulling cable until all the boxes are wired. Don't jump around: You may become confused and miss a box.

In new construction, electricians usually place several wire reels by the panel and pull cables from there toward the first box of each circuit ❶. These circuit segments are called "home runs." Once electricians have run cable to all the home-run boxes, they move a reel next to each box and continue to pull cable outward until they reach the last box ❷. When doing remodel wiring in a house with a crawlspace, however, electricians often start at the last box and pull cables toward the panel. When they reach the first boxes of several circuits, they will move the wire reels to those locations. From there, they feed, say, three cables down to a helper in the crawlspace. The helper can pull all the cables toward the panel at the same time. This method is much faster than pulling single cables three different times.

Staple cable along stud centers to prevent nail or screw punctures. It's acceptable to stack two cables under one staple ❸, but use standoffs ❹ to fasten three or more cables traveling along the same path. (Multi-gang boxes are fed by multiple cables, for example.) Standoffs and ties bundle cables loosely to prevent heat buildup. As you secure cable, install nail plates where needed ❺.

1 Place a wire reel near the beginning or end of each circuit.

2 Avoid crimping cable as you pull it through narrow spaces.

3 Drive staples just snug to the cable.

4 When bundling two or more cables, use standoffs.

5 For cable within 1¼ in. of a stud edge, install a steel plate.

PRO TIP

Put a piece of red tape on the first box in each circuit to ensure that you run cable from it to the panel. On a complex job with many circuits, you might run cable *between* all the outlets in a circuit but forget to install the home-run cable that will energize the circuit. Not something you want to discover after the drywall is up.

FEEDING CABLE THROUGH CORNERS

1 To feed cable through a corner, drill a level hole on one side of the built-up studs.

2 Drill a second hole, at the same height, so the holes intersect.

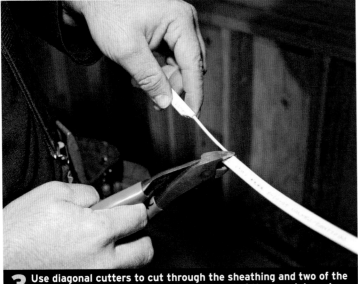

3 Use diagonal cutters to cut through the sheathing and two of the three wires in the cable, then loop the end of the remaining wire.

4 Wrap the end of the cable so it slides through the hole easier, then work the looped wire through the holes.

Corners are usually built by nailing three or four studs together, so feeding cable through them can be tricky. Drill intersecting holes at the same height, as shown in photos **1** and **2**. Use diagonal cutters to cut through the sheathing and two of the wires, thus leaving a single wire protruding from the cable **3**.

Use pliers to loop the end of the wire. Then wrap tape around the end of the cable and onto the wire to create a tapering point that will slide easier through the hole. Push the wire through the corner holes until it emerges from the other side **4**. If the wire gets hung up midway through, insert a finger from the other side to fish for its end.

FISHING CABLE BEHIND FINISH WALLS

Most electricians hate fishing wire behind existing walls. It can be tricky to find the cable and time-consuming to patch the holes in plaster or drywall. If you're adding a box or two, try fishing cable behind the wall. But if you're rewiring an entire room, it's probably faster to cut a "wiring trench" in the wall. Before cutting into or drilling through a wall, however, turn off power to the area. If you'd like to avoid fishing altogether, see "Installing a Wireless Switch," on p. 60.

> **For more on cutting a wiring trench, see p. 214.**

If you're adding an outlet over an unfinished basement, fishing cable can be straightforward. Outline and cut out an opening for the new box, insert a flex bit into the opening, and then drill down through the wall's bottom plate ❶ (wear gloves to protect hands). When the bit emerges into the basement, a helper can insert one wire of the new cable into the small "fish hole" near the bit's point. As you slowly back the bit out of the box opening, you pull new cable into it ❷. No fish tape required! The only downside is that the reversing drill can twist the cable. This problem is easily avoided by sliding a swivel kellum over the cable end instead of inserting a cable wire into the flex bit hole ❸ (see p. 210). Because the kellum turns, the cable doesn't.

Alternatively, you can start by removing a wall box. The closest power source is often an existing outlet. Cut power to that outlet and test to make sure it's off. The easiest way to access the cable is to disconnect the wires to the receptacle ❹ (see p. 210) and remove it. Then remove the box ❺ (see p. 210), which may require using a metal-cutting reciprocating-saw blade to cut through the nails holding the box to the stud. Fish a new cable leg to the location and insert the new and old cables into a new cut-in box. Secure the cut-in box to the finish surface, splice the cables inside the box, and connect pigtails from the splices to the new receptacle. >> >> >>

RUNNING CABLE TO A NEW OUTLET

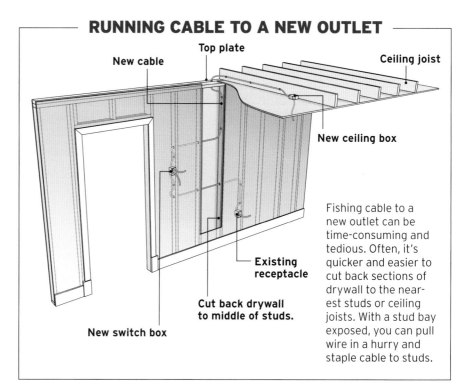

New cable — Top plate — Ceiling joist

New ceiling box

Existing receptacle

Cut back drywall to middle of studs.

New switch box

Fishing cable to a new outlet can be time-consuming and tedious. Often, it's quicker and easier to cut back sections of drywall to the nearest studs or ceiling joists. With a stud bay exposed, you can pull wire in a hurry and staple cable to studs.

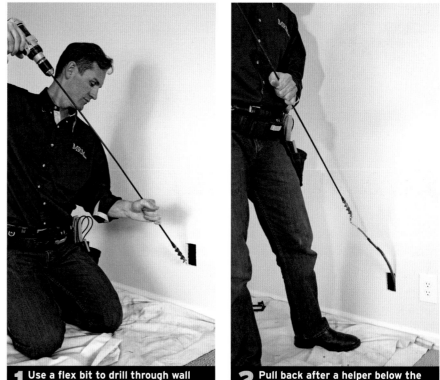

1 Use a flex bit to drill through wall plates.

2 Pull back after a helper below the floor attaches the cable.

FISHING CABLE BEHIND FINISH WALLS (CONTINUED)

3 A swivel kellum grip slides over the end of the cable being fished so the cable doesn't twist.

or

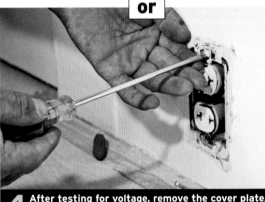

4 After testing for voltage, remove the cover plate, unscrew the receptacle from the box, and pull it out.

5 Remove the old outlet box, drill, fish new cable, and splice the old cable to the new.

FISHING CABLE TO A CEILING FIXTURE

1 To run cable to a ceiling fixture, start by drilling an exploratory hole with a small-diameter bit.

Fishing cable to ceiling fixtures or wall switches is usually a bit complicated. If there is an unfinished attic above or a basement below, run the cable across it, then route the cable through a stud bay to the new box in the ceiling. To run cable to a ceiling light, for example, drill up through the fixture location using a 3/16-in. by 12-in. bit to minimize patching later **1**. Use a bit at least 6 in. long so a helper in the attic can see it—use a longer one if the floor of the attic is covered with insulation. Measure the distance from the bit to the wall; a helper in the attic can use that measurement to locate the nearest stud bay to drill an access hole into. If you're working alone, loop the end of a stiff piece of wire about 1 ft. long **2** and insert it in the drilled hole; friction will keep the wire upright in the hole until you can locate it in the attic.

If there's no access above the ceiling and/or cable must cross several ceiling joists to get from a switch to a light fixture, you'll have to cut into finish surfaces at several points **3**. To access cable in a stud bay, you'll need a cutout to expose the top plate. Using a flex bit may minimize the number of holes you must cut to drill across ceiling joists. But as noted earlier, it may ultimately take less time to cut and repair a single slot running across several joists than to patch a number of isolated holes. Whatever method you choose, make cuts cleanly to facilitate repairs. First outline all cuts using a utility knife.

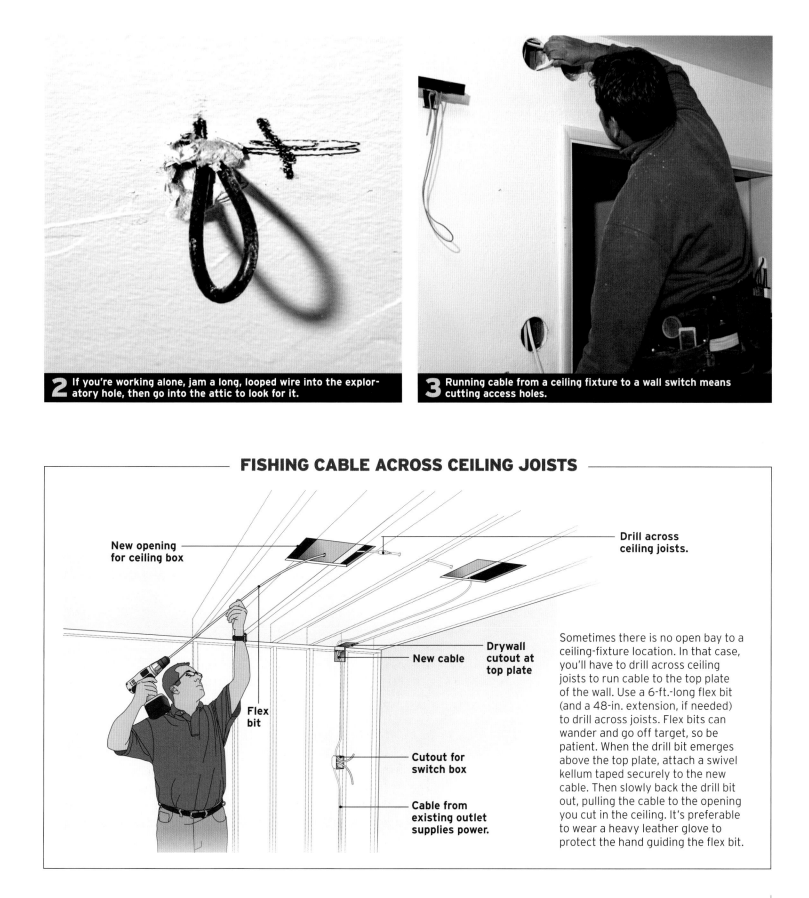

2 If you're working alone, jam a long, looped wire into the exploratory hole, then go into the attic to look for it.

3 Running cable from a ceiling fixture to a wall switch means cutting access holes.

FISHING CABLE ACROSS CEILING JOISTS

New opening for ceiling box

Drill across ceiling joists.

Flex bit

Drywall cutout at top plate

New cable

Cutout for switch box

Cable from existing outlet supplies power.

Sometimes there is no open bay to a ceiling-fixture location. In that case, you'll have to drill across ceiling joists to run cable to the top plate of the wall. Use a 6-ft.-long flex bit (and a 48-in. extension, if needed) to drill across joists. Flex bits can wander and go off target, so be patient. When the drill bit emerges above the top plate, attach a swivel kellum taped securely to the new cable. Then slowly back the drill bit out, pulling the cable to the opening you cut in the ceiling. It's preferable to wear a heavy leather glove to protect the hand guiding the flex bit.

CUTTING A WALL BOX INTO PLASTER

If existing house wiring is in good condition and an existing circuit has the capacity for an additional outlet, turn off the power, cut a hole in the wall, fish cable to the location, and secure a remodel box (cut-in box) to the finish surface. This process is called cutting-in or retrofitting a box, and, of course, it requires boxes with special mounting mechanisms.

Hold the new box at the same height as other outlet or switch boxes and trace its outline onto the wall. Use a stud finder or drill a small exploratory hole to locate studs or wood lath behind. Look for water pipes or other wires. If you hit a stud, move the box. If you hit lath, keep drilling small holes within the opening to find the edges of the lath. If you position the box correctly, you'll need to remove only one or two lath sections ❶.

Use a utility knife to score along the outline to minimize plaster fractures. Remove the plaster within the outline using a chisel. Then cut out the lath, using a cordless jigsaw, sabersaw, or, even better, an oscillating multi-tool (p. 21) with a Universal E-Cut blade ❷. As you cut through the lath strip, alternate partial cuts from one side to the other to avoid cracking the plaster. Then carefully remove the plaster beneath the box ears, so they can rest on lath. Before inserting cut-in boxes, remove box knockouts, insert cable clamps, strip sheathing off the ends of incoming cable, and feed cable into the cable clamps. If more than one cable enters the box, write the destination of each on the sheathing. Secure the box by screwing its ears to the lath ❸.

1 Position the box and then trace the box outline onto the wall.

2 After you chisel out the plaster within the outline, use a sabersaw to cut lath.

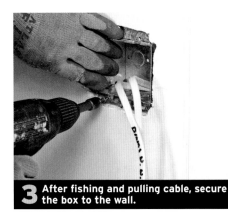

3 After fishing and pulling cable, secure the box to the wall.

CUTTING A WALL BOX INTO DRYWALL

Adding a cut-in box to drywall is essentially the same as adding one to plaster. Start by drilling a small exploratory hole near the proposed box location to make sure there's no stud in the way.

There are a number of cut-in boxes to choose from. The most common have side-mounted ears that swing out or expand as you turn their screws. Hold the box against the drywall, plumb it ❶, then trace the outline of the box onto the wall ❷. Align the blade of a jab saw (drywall saw) to the line you want to cut and hit the handle of the saw with the heel of your hand ❸.

There is no one right way to cut out a box opening; just take it slow. If the box outline is intricate or the jab saw produces a ragged line, switch to a utility knife. If you secure the cutout with a piece of painter's tape ❹ as you finish the cut, the drywall's paper face will be less likely to tear and the cutout won't fall into the wall cavity—useful, should you need to patch the hole.

1 Locate the new outlet between studs, then plumb it.

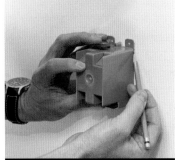

2 Carefully trace the box outline onto the drywall.

3 Use a jab saw to cut the opening in drywall.

4 Attach a piece of painter's tape to the cutout.

Run cable(s) to the new outlet, remove knockout(s) in the box, and slide the box onto the cable and into the opening **❺**. Code does not require that you add cable clamps for a single-gang plastic box–integral plastic clamps in the box will secure the cable.

Tighten the box mounting screws **❻**, which will expand side-mounted ears to extend and draw the box tight to the drywall **❼**.

5 Feed cable into the box, and insert the box into the hole.

6 Tighten the mounting screws, which will . . .

7 . . . extend side-mounted ears on the cut-in box.

RETROFITTING A CEILING BOX

As with all retrofits, turn off power to the area and explore first. Follow the mounting recommendations for your fixture. Attach the fixture box to framing.

If there's insulation in an attic above, remove it from the affected area. Be sure to wear eye protection and a dust mask when drilling through any ceiling–it's a dusty job.

Mark the box location and use a fine-tooth hole saw to cut through plaster or drywall **❶**. Place the centering bit of the hole saw on the exact center of the box opening. Drill slowly so you don't damage adjoining surfaces–or fall off the ladder.

If the ceiling is drywall, you're ready to run cable through the hole in the ceiling. If the ceiling is plaster, cut through the lath or leave the lath intact and screw a pancake box through the lath and into the framing. Before attaching a pancake box, remove a knockout, test-fit the box in the hole, and trace the knockout hole onto the lath. Set the box aside and drill through the lath, creating a hole through which you can run cable **❷**.

Feed cable to the location and fit a cable connector into the box. Insert the cable into the connector, slide the box up to the ceiling **❸**, and secure it **❹**. Strip the cable sheathing and attach the ground wire to a ground screw in the box. Strip insulation from the wire ends and you're ready to connect the light fixture.

1 Use a fine-tooth hole saw to cut the box hole.

2 Drill through the lath.

3 Fish cable through the lath and feed it through the box.

4 Screw the pancake box to framing or blocking.

CREATING A WIRING TRENCH

1 Use a chalkline to mark the top and bottom lines of the wiring trench.

2 To ensure a clean cut line and make patching easier, use a utility knife to first score along the chalklines.

3 Cut along the chalklines, holding the reciprocating saw at a low angle. Do not cut the lath.

4 If walls are drywall, simply pull out the isolated strips. If plaster, use a hammer to remove the plaster and expose the lath.

5 Use a hammer and a flat bar to pry the lath free from the studs. Work slowly to minimize damage.

6 Pull out any nails still stuck in the studs; this will make later repairs easier.

When adding multiple outlets or rewiring an entire room, cutting a wiring trench in finish surfaces instead of fishing cable behind them is much faster. Before cutting or drilling, however, turn off the power to the areas affected. Be sure to wear eye protection and a dust mask.

If there are no windows in the walls to be rewired, cut the trench about 3 ft. above the floor so you won't have to kneel while working. If there are windows, cut the trench under the windows, leaving at least 1 in. of wall material under the windowsill to facilitate repairs. If there's plaster, make the trench as wide as two strips of lath. Snap parallel chalklines to indicate the width of the trench **1**. Then use a utility knife to score along each line **2**. Scoring lines first produces a cleaner cut and easier repairs.

Next use a reciprocating saw with a demolition blade to cut through the plaster or drywall. Hold the saw at a low angle: You'll be less likely to break blades or cut into studs **3**. Using a hammer, gently crush the plaster between the lines **4**. Use a utility bar (flat bar) to pry out the lath strips or drywall section. If you expose any cables in the walls, use a noncontact tester to make sure they're not hot **5**. Next, drill through the studs so you can run cable in the trench. Wherever there's an outlet indicated, expand the trench width to accommodate the boxes.

Finally, pull any lath or drywall nails from stud edges **6**. They're easy to overlook because they're small; if you pull them now, patching the trench will go smoothly.

PULLING CABLE TO RETROFIT BOXES

Once you've cut a wiring trench and drilled the holes, installing the boxes and pulling cable are straightforward and much like the basic sequences shown in "Tools & Materials."

➤ **For more on installing boxes, see p. 26.**

If you're installing metal boxes, remove knockouts and insert cable connectors into their openings ❶. Then screw boxes to studs; screwing is less likely to damage nearby finish surfaces ❷. Be sure that the box will be flush to finish surfaces or, if you'll install plaster rings later, flush to the stud edge. Whenever you install boxes side by side—as with the outlet and low-voltage boxes shown here—install them plumb and at the same height ❸.

Installing cable in remodels can be tricky because space is tight and you must avoid bending cable sharply, which can damage wire insulation ❹. Install nail plates wherever the edge of the hole is less than 1¼ in. from the stud edges. Feed cable through the cable connectors into the boxes ❺. Finally, staple the cable to the framing within 8 in. of a single-gang box without clamps, or within 12 in. of other boxes. If there's not room to loop the cable and staple it to a stud, it's acceptable to staple it to other solid framing, such as the underside of a sill ❻.

1 For metal boxes, start by removing knockouts and then insert a connector.

2 Screw the box to the side of a stud.

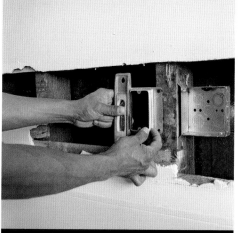

3 For the best appearance, install outlets that are side by side at the same height.

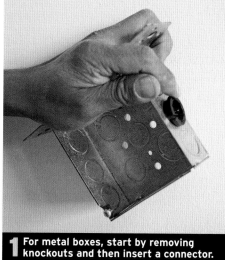

4 Run cable to each box.

5 Feed the cable through cable connectors.

6 Staple the cable within 12 in. of each box.

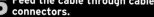

MAKING UP AN OUTLET BOX

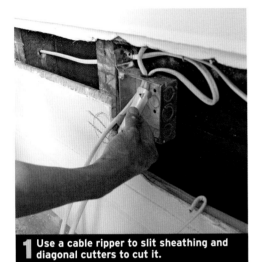

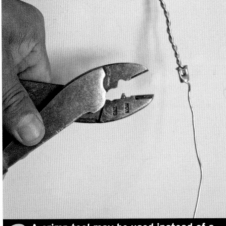

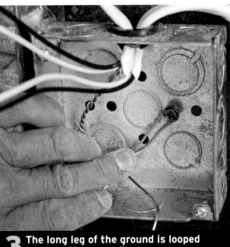

1 Use a cable ripper to slit sheathing and diagonal cutters to cut it.

2 A crimp tool may be used instead of a wire nut for the ground.

3 The long leg of the ground is looped beneath the grounding screw.

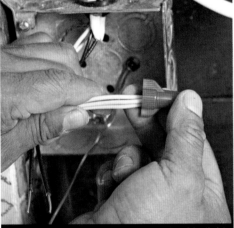

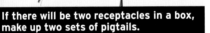

4 Strip insulation from the ends of individual wires and splice like wires together.

5 If there will be two receptacles in a box, make up two sets of pigtails.

6 Fold the wires into the box and install a plaster ring.

Electricians call the last stage of rough wiring *making up a box*. After removing sheathing from cables, rough-cut individual wires about 8 in. long, group like wires, and, to save time later, splice all wire groups.

Use a cable ripper **1** to remove the plastic cable sheathing. (Most professional electricians favor utility knives for removing sheathing, but DIYers should use a cable ripper to avoid nicking wire insulation.) Once you've slit the sheathing with the cable ripper, pull back the sheathing and the kraft paper inside and snip off both, using diagonal cutters. Because cable clamps grip sheathing—not individual wires—there must be at least 1/4 in. of sheathing still peeking under cable clamps when you're done.

Typically, electricians start by splicing the ground wires, which are usually bare copper. (If they're green insulated wires, first strip approximately 3/4 in. of insulation off their ends.) If you use standard wire connectors (Wire-Nut is one brand), trim the ground wires and butt their ends together, along with a 6-in. pigtail, which you'll connect later to the green ground screw of a receptacle. However, many pros prefer to twist the ground wires together, leave one ground long, and thread it through the hole in a special wire connector—or crimp the wires **2**. If the box is metal, first bond the ground wire to the box, using a grounding clip (p. 227) or a grounding screw **3**.

Splicing hot and neutral wire groups is essentially the same **4**. Trim hot wires to the same length. Strip 3/4 in. of insulation off the cable wires and the pigtail, and use lineman's pliers to twist the wires. Then screw on a wire connector. If the box will contain two receptacles, create two groups of pigtails **5**.

Once wire groups are spliced, gently accordion-fold the wires back into the box until you're ready to wire switches and receptacles **6**.

➜ **Attaching wires to receptacles and switches is covered at length in "Receptacles & Switches."**

MAKING UP A CAN LIGHT

Wiring a recessed can light or a ceiling box is essentially the same as making up an outlet box, although can lights frequently have stranded wire leads. Always follow the installation instructions supplied with your lighting unit.

Run cable to the can light, stapling it at least every 4½ ft. to the side of the ceiling joist and within 12 in. of the box. Also, make sure that the cable is at least 1¼ in. from the joist edge, so drywall screws or nails can't puncture it. Because you'll be working over your head and junction boxes are cramped, you may want to remove the sheathing before feeding cable into the box ❶. Here again, cable clamps grip sheathing—not individual wires—so there must be at least ¼ in. of sheathing still peeking under cable clamps when you're done. Then strip insulation from individual wires ❷.

Group ground wires, neutral wires, and hot wires. Then splice each group using wire connectors. Electricians typically start by splicing ground wires. Typically, a ground screw and a grounding pigtail are factory-installed in the can ❸. They then splice the neutral wires and, finally, the hot wires. When all wire groups are spliced, fold them carefully into the junction box and attach the cover.

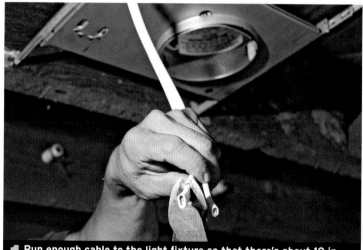

1 Run enough cable to the light fixture so that there's about 10 in. sticking out of its junction box.

2 Feed the cable into the junction box, remove the sheathing, and strip the insulation from the ends of individual wires.

3 Use wire connectors to splice paired wire groups, starting with the ground wire group. Fold the spliced wires into the box.

PRO TIP

The ground screw must compress the ground wire evenly. Never cross the ground wire (or any other wire) over itself, because the screw would touch only that high spot.

MAKING UP A SINGLE-GANG SWITCH BOX

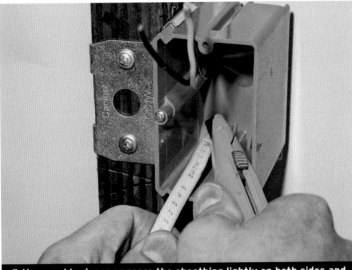

1 Use a cable ripper or score the sheathing lightly on both sides and give it a quick tug to slide it off the wires.

2 Use lineman's pliers to twist the grounds together. Leave one ground longer to be attached to the device.

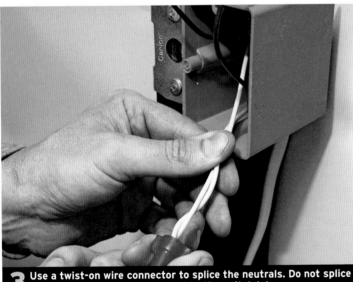

3 Use a twist-on wire connector to splice the neutrals. Do not splice the hot wires; they are attached to the switch later.

4 Fold the wires in an accordion pattern and tuck them into the box.

Single-gang switch boxes are most commonly plastic, so begin by using a screwdriver or needle-nose pliers to remove its knockout(s). Feed cable (or cables) into the knockout(s) and staple it within 8 in. of the box. There's no need to insert cable clamps: Two-gang and larger as well as some single-gang plastic boxes have an integral spring clamp inside the knockout to prevent cable from being yanked out. Leave about 8 in. to 10 in. of wire sticking out of the box.

If a single cable enters the switch box, you're looking at a "switch loop" (p. 54), in which an outlet or light fixture is closer to the power source. Code requires that new switch loops be served by 3-wire cable, because some electronic switches require a neutral wire. Historically, though, switch loops were also served by 2-wire cable and the white wire was used as a hot wire: See pp. 54-55 for the full story. In either case, remove the cable sheathing and tuck the wires into the box.

If there are two cables entering the switch box, one is incoming power and the other is a switch leg. Remove the cable sheathing **❶**, then twist the grounds together and add a grounding pigtail before splicing them with a wire connector **❷**. Strip insulation from the ends of the neutral wires and splice them **❸**. Fold the wires into the box **❹**.

MAKING UP A MULTIGANG SWITCH BOX

The tricky part of making up a multigang switch box is keeping track of the wires. As you feed each cable into the box, use a felt-tipped marker to identify each cable's origin or destination. Write directly on the cable sheathing. Start by feeding the incoming cable into the box and marking it *hot*. This incoming cable will supply 120v from a panel or from an outlet upstream when the cable is connected later.

Next, nail a standoff to the side of the stud so you can secure each cable as you feed it into the switch box ❶. Before inserting a cable into a knockout, however, note which fixture or device the switch leg controls ❷. Be specific and use labels such as *sconce*, *can ctr* (center can), and *perim* (perimeter fixture).

As you pull each cable into the box, strip the sheathing and slide off the small section that has writing on it ❸. When all the cables have been stripped, separate and twist the bare ground wires clockwise. Leave one ground about 6 in. longer than the others for each device in the box, then feed it through the hole in the end of a special ground wire connector ❹. This longer ground wire will run to a ground screw on each switch.

Strip the insulation from the ends of the neutral wires; then use a wire connector to splice them together ❺. Fold both ground- and neutral-wire groups into the box.

Cut a hot-wire pigtail 8 in. to 9 in. long for each switch and splice all pigtails to the hot wire of the incoming cable—the one that was earlier marked *120v* ❻. Finally, pair a hot pigtail with each switch leg ❼. Fold the wire pairs into the box. When it's time to wire the switches later, you'll connect a hot pigtail to one screw terminal and a switch-leg wire to the other screw terminal.

If a cable serves a three-way or four-way switch, indicate whether a wire is a "traveler" or "common."

➡ **For more on three- and four-way switches, see "Receptacles and Switches," pp. 61-64.**

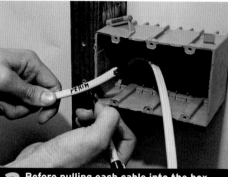

1 Nail a standoff to secure three or more cables.

2 Before pulling each cable into the box, indicate which fixture it controls.

3 Score and remove the sheathing. Slide the label back on.

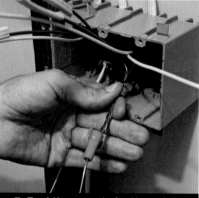

4 Feed the ground wire through the hole in the connector, and twist on the connector.

5 Twist on a wire connector to splice the neutral wire group.

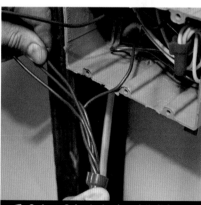

6 Cut an 8-in. hot-wire pigtail for each switch in the box. Cap each pigtail.

7 When boxes contain multiple switches, indicate which fixture each switch leg controls.

⚠ SAFETY ALERT

If a box has more than one circuit in it, all the grounds must be spliced together, but the neutrals of the different circuits must be kept separate.

FLEXIBLE METAL CABLE

1 Flexible metal cable must be at least 1¼ in. from stud edges.

2 Staple AC or MC cable within 12 in. of the box and 4½ ft. between boxes.

3 To cut AC or MC cable, bend the cable till the jacket splits, then snip.

or

When using a Roto-Split, follow manufacturer's instructions.

CABLE CONNECTORS

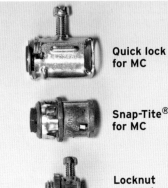

Quick lock for MC

Snap-Tite® for MC

Locknut connector for AC

In residences, MC and AC cable is most often used in short exposed runs—typically between a wall box and the junction box of an appliance. The cable's metal jacket protects the wiring inside, but you should still take pains to avoid puncturing MC or AC cable with a nail or a screw. For this reason, when flexible metal cable is run through stud walls, it's a good practice to run it through the center of the stud **1**. If several cables run through a stud, align holes vertically to avoid compromising the strength of the stud. Use nail-protection plates if a cable is closer than 1¼ in. to a stud edge.

➔ **For more on nail-protection plates, see p. 207.**

Secure or support flexible metal cable within 12 in. of boxes **2** and at least every 4½ ft. along the span of the run—electricians typically staple it every 3 ft.

Flexible metal cable should also be secured to the underside of every joist it crosses or run through holes drilled through joists. Again, use nail-protection plates if the cable is less than 1¼ in. from a joist edge.

AC and MC cable require specialized connectors to secure them to boxes. You can use a hacksaw with a metal-cutting blade or diagonal cutters to cut through cable's metal jacket **3**, but a Roto-Split is the tool of choice. Whatever tool you use, cut through only one coil of the metal jacket to sever it. To prevent damaging the wire insulation within, cut no deeper than the thickness of the metal jacket. After cutting through the metal jacket, insert plastic anti-short bushings to protect the wire insulation from the sharp edges of the metal jacket.

CABLE, CONDUIT & MOISTURE

Moisture can short out electrical connections or, over time, degrade conductors and connectors. Thus it's important to use materials in appropriate locations.

- Nonmetallic (NM) sheathed cable (one brand is Romex): Dry locations only.

- Metal-clad (MC), MCAP cable, or armored cable (AC): Dry locations; can be used in wet locations only if specifically listed for that use.

- Underground-feeder (UF) cable: Can be buried; when used in interiors, same rules as for NM cable.

- Electrical metallic tubing (EMT): Wet or dry locations; okay in wet locations if fittings (couplings and connectors) are listed for use in wet locations; may be in direct contact with earth, if suitable and approved by local code.

- Rigid metal conduit (RMC): Same rules as for EMT; may be buried in earth or embedded in concrete.

- PVC plastic conduit (schedule-40 PVC): Can be exposed if listed for direct sunlight or buried underground; fittings are inherently rain-tight, so can be installed outdoors and in damp crawlspaces.

INSTALLING AC CABLE

To install AC cable, start by marking the box heights onto the studs and installing the metal boxes flush to finish surfaces or flush to the stud edges. Remove a box knockout for each cable. Then drill the studs and run the AC cable through each hole. Staple it every 4½ ft. along the run and within 12 in. of each box.

Use a Roto-Split to cut through a single coil of the cable's metal jacket, then slide off the severed jacket section to expose the wires inside. Use diagonal cutters to snip off the kraft paper covering the wires ❶. Slide a plastic antishort bushing between the wires and the metal jacket ❷. Next, wrap the silver bonding wire around the outside of the jacket ❸. Wrapping this wire bonds the jacket and creates a continuous ground path.

Slide a setscrew connector over the end of the AC cable and tighten the setscrew to the metal jacket ❹. The screw compresses the cable jacket and the bonding wire, holding them fast and ensuring a continuous ground. Insert the threaded end of the connector into a box knockout. Then tighten the locknut that secures the connector ❺.

Attach a mud ring to the box to bring it flush to finish surfaces, which will be installed later, and fold the wires into the box ❻.

1 Pull and snip the kraft paper to expose the insulated wires and bare bonding tracer.

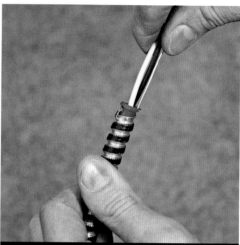

2 Insert an antishort bushing between the wires and the jacket to prevent shorts.

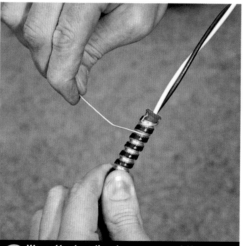

3 Wrap the bonding tracer around the outside of the metal jacket.

4 To ensure a solid ground path, tighten a setscrew connector over the cable end.

5 To secure the AC cable to the box, tighten a locknut onto the connector.

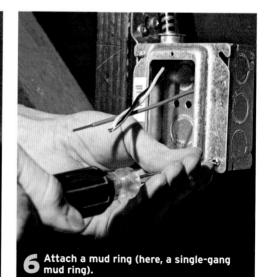

6 Attach a mud ring (here, a single-gang mud ring).

INSTALLING MC CABLE

MC cable is similar to AC cable, except that MC cable contains an insulated ground wire. Unlike AC cable, MC cable does not rely on its metal jacket to create a continuous ground for the circuit.

After using a hacksaw, diagonal cutters, or a Roto-Split to cut through the metal jacket of MC cable, slide on an antishort bushing to protect the wires inside from the sharp edges of the jacket. Remove the plastic wrapping ❶. Slide a quick-lock clamp over the end of the cable and snap the clamp into a box knockout. Then tighten the clamp screw to secure the MC cable to the box ❷.

To create a continuous ground, use wire strippers to strip the ends of the incoming ground wire ❸. Use a wire connector to splice the incoming ground, the ground-screw pigtail, and a grounding pigtail that attaches to the device ❹. Then fold the wires into the box and screw on a mud ring to bring the box flush to finish surfaces, which are installed later.

Terminating MCAP (or MCI) cable (p. 28) is slightly different than terminating MC cable. You don't have to bring the cable ground wire into the panel box to terminate it. Instead, pull back the bare ground wire around the aluminum jacket and snap on the quick-connectors. Insert the connector into a panel knockout and you're done. Quick-connectors have spring-loaded clips that connect snugly to the panel, so there are no screws to tighten as there are with lock-nut clamps.

PRO TIP

If you're pulling conduit wires in a residence, you probably don't need to use pulling lubricant. Use lubricant when:

■ Pulling long distances—more than 100 ft.

■ Pulling wires through multiple 90-degree bends.

■ Pulling "fat" wires, such as 10AWG or larger.

■ Pulling the maximum number of wires a conduit can hold.

1 MC cable contains an insulated ground wire instead of a bonding wire (as AC cable does).

2 MC cable does not rely on its metallic jacket to create a ground path. Thus you can use a quick-lock clamp to attach MC cable.

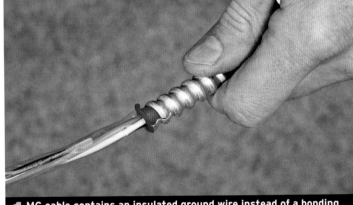

3 Strip the end of the incoming ground wire.

4 Use a wire connector to splice all three ground wires.

WORKING WITH EMT STEEL CONDUIT (INTERIOR)

1 To steady the pipe as you cut it, brace it with your legs.

2 Use a reaming tool to remove burrs, which could nick insulation.

3 Use a setscrew coupling to join lengths of conduit. Tighten the screws snugly.

4 To secure pipe to a box, install a set-screw connector into a box knockout.

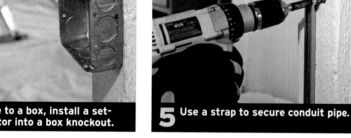

5 Use a strap to secure conduit pipe.

PRO TIP

Use a hacksaw to cut metal conduit. Do not use the tubing cutters often used to cut plumbing pipe because they create a razor-sharp burr inside the conduit that is almost impossible to remove with a reaming tool.

Because EMT conduit is easy to work with, it's the rigid conduit type most commonly used. The main difference between conduit and flexible metal cable is that conduit comes without wire inside. Fortunately, pulling wire into conduit is a straightforward operation.

Assembling conduit is also straightforward. After cutting conduit pipe to length and deburring it, insert pipe ends into setscrew couplings and tighten the screws to secure the pipes. Threaded male fittings connect the pipe to boxes and condulets–covered fittings that facilitate wire-pulling or enable changes in pipe direction. You can buy prebent fittings such as capped-elbows (two-piece elbows that you can access to

pull wires) and sweeps (single-piece elbows with a wide turning radius). Or you can rent a conduit bender to change pipe direction.

By code, EMT conduit must be strapped within 3 ft. of every junction box and at least every 10 ft. along runs. In actual practice, electricians strap pipe runs every 6 ft. to 8 ft. to prevent sagging.

Work from a layout sketch that indicates the power source, structural members, obstructions, existing outlets, and the locations of new outlets. Mount all the outlet boxes at the same height, and plumb a side of each one. Plumbed boxes look better and align better with conduit pipes.

Use a hacksaw with a metal-cutting blade to cut EMT pipe. EMT pipe typically comes in

10-ft. lengths **1**. After cutting the pipe, use a reaming tool to remove the burrs inside and out **2**.

To join EMT pipe, insert pipe ends into setscrew couplings **3**. To secure pipe to a box, use a setscrew connector on the box knockout **4**. In general, plumb vertical conduit sections before strapping them into place **5**. On the other hand, you may want pipe to follow an angled architectural element such as a brace, as shown in Photo 3 on the following page.

MAKING BENDS WITH METAL CONDUIT (INTERIOR)

To change directions in a metal conduit system, you can either bend the pipe or install directional fittings such as offset adaptors, elbows, or condulets. EMT pipe is rigid, but its walls are thin enough to bend easily with a conduit bender.

Pros bend conduit whenever possible. Bending pipe reduces the number of specialty fittings to buy and enables pipe to follow the contours of surfaces and structural elements. It's not necessary or desirable for conduit to follow every last jog or bulge in a wall; the simpler you can make an installation, the better it will look and the faster it will progress.

To bend pipe, use a felt-tipped marker to mark the beginning of the bend on the pipe. Slide the pipe into the bender **1**. Gently step on one side of the bender and simultaneously pull on the lever bar **2**. The raised marks on the outer curve of the bender indicate the angle you're creating in the pipe—typically, 15, 22½, 30, 45, or 60 degrees.

After bending the conduit—but before cutting it to final length—test-fit the piece to see if it lines up with the connector on the box **3** or to a coupling that joins two pipe sections. With practice, you can also offset pipe **4**. Offsetting creates two bends in opposite directions so a length of conduit can move from one plane to another.

There are a couple of rules to keep in mind as you bend conduit. First, there's a minimum requirement bend-radius for conduit: 10× the diameter. For ½-in.-diameter conduit, for example, the minimum bend radius is 5 in.

Second, each turn makes it harder to pull wire. So between each pair of boxes, you can have no more than 360 degrees of bends. Splice wires only in a junction or outlet box.

1 Mark the start of the bend on the pipe; then position it in the bender.

2 Pull and simultaneously step on one side of the bender.

3 Test-fit the piece to see if it lines up with the pipe connector.

4 Conduit benders can also create multiple offset angles.

USING DIRECTIONAL FITTINGS

You can also use directional fittings to make turns. A T-condulet enables you to run wires in different directions and doubles as a pulling point when fishing wire. To attach pipe to a condulet, first screw a locknut onto the threaded shaft of a male adaptor. Turn the adaptor most of the way into the condulet hub and turn the locknut clockwise until it seats against the hub. Back-tightening the locknut in this manner ensures grounding continuity.

Use a T-condulet as a pulling point when fishing wires. Here, wires from the source diverge in two directions.

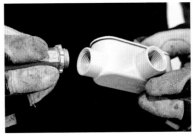

To attach pipe to a condulet, use an adapter and back-tighten the locknut until it lodges against the hub.

FISHING WIRE THROUGH CONDUIT

You can start fishing wire from either end of the circuit. If you're tapping into an existing outlet, it makes sense to fish from that outlet—after first turning off the power to the outlet and testing to make sure it's off.

In the installation shown here, a four-square extension box was mounted over an existing (recessed) box. Thus new wires can be pulled into the extension box and spliced to an existing cable to provide power for the circuit extension being added.

The fish tape can be fed easily into the conduit pipe ❶. At the other end of the conduit, tape wires to the fish tape ❷. To make wire pulling easier, leave the wire ends straight—do not bend them over the tape, but stagger them slightly so the bundled wires taper slightly. Wrap electrical tape tightly around the wire bundle so that wires stay together and won't snag as they're pulled. The pulling will also go easier if you pull stranded wire rather than solid wire, which is stiffer and less flexible.

Finally, use a wire caddy ❸, even if you have to build one out of scrap pipe and lumber. Using wire spools on a caddy helps minimize tangles.

TAPPING INTO AN EXISTING OUTLET

Tapping into an existing outlet is often a convenient way to supply power to a conduit extension. Remove the cover plate from the outlet, detach wires from the old receptacle, then use lineman's pliers to straighten the old wires so they'll be easier to splice to wires running to the new outlets.

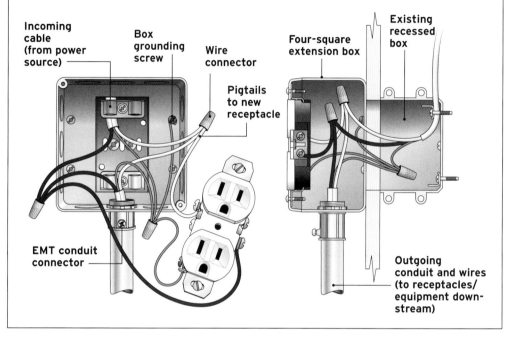

Incoming cable (from power source)

Box grounding screw

Wire connector

Pigtails to new receptacle

Four-square extension box

Existing recessed box

EMT conduit connector

Outgoing conduit and wires (to receptacles/equipment downstream)

1 Push the fish tape down into the conduit.

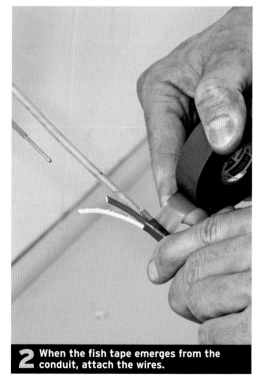

2 When the fish tape emerges from the conduit, attach the wires.

3 As you pull wires through the conduit, the spools on the wire caddy turn.

PREPPING RECEPTACLES FOR SURFACE METAL BOXES

1 Use diagonal cutters to snip the "plaster ears" off the receptacles so they'll fit into the industrial raised covers.

2 Attach solid pigtails to screw terminals.

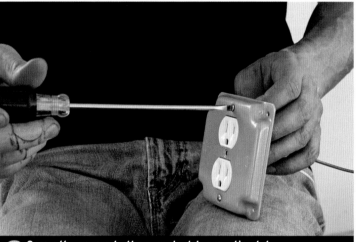

3 Screw the covers to the receptacle's mounting tabs.

4 Screw the ground pigtail to the box.

To save time, professionals often divide receptacle wiring of a conduit system into several smaller tasks, each of which can be done with a single tool. Your conduit system may have slightly different materials, but these prep techniques should save you time.

Standard duplex receptacles come with plaster ears intended to seat against plaster or drywall surfaces. Consequently, the ears may not fit into metal boxes or behind the industrial raised covers often installed in conduit systems. Use diagonal cutters to snip off the ears **1** so they fit inside such covers.

To speed the assembly, precut all the pigtails that you'll attach to receptacles. To loop pigtail ends, strip 1/2 in. of insulation, insert the stripped ends into the little hole on the stripper jaw, and twist your wrist.

Use a screw gun to attach the looped ends to the receptacle screw terminals **2**. Remember to loop the pigtail ends clockwise so that when the screw tightens (clockwise), the loop stays on the screw.

Next, attach the prewired receptacles to the covers. Typically, there is a pair of

machine screws (and nuts) that screw into the mounting tabs at top and bottom, and a single short screw for the center hole in the front of the receptacle **3**.

Finally, screw a ground pigtail to the box **4**. The threaded hole for the ground screw is raised slightly to facilitate surface mounting. If you surface-mounted a box on a concrete wall and the box didn't have this detail, the ground screw would hit concrete before it tightened all the way down—thus jeopardizing grounding continuity.

WIRING OUTLETS

1 Strip ½ in. of insulation from the ends of the stranded wire.

2 Splice the ground wires first, then neutral wires, then hot wires.

3 After splicing like-colored wire groups, fold them into place.

4 Then screw the receptacle cover to the box.

If you've already attached pigtails to the receptacle screw terminals, the connections at outlet boxes on a conduit system will go quickly. *Note:* In the project shown here, the red wire is the hot conductor, the white wire is neutral, and green is the ground conductor. Code requires that green or bare wires are always the designated ground.

Use wire strippers to strip ½ in. of insulation from the wires pulled through the conduit **1**. Splice the receptacle pigtails to like-colored circuit wires pulled through the conduit. Typically, electricians splice the ground wires first, which means splicing three wires: the receptacle pigtail, the grounding pigtail to the box, and the circuit ground **2**. If the metal conduit serves as the ground, there will be no circuit ground wire.

When splicing stranded wire to solid wire, strip the stranded wire slightly longer than the solid wire, so the stranded-wire end sticks out beyond the solid wire. By doing this, you force the stranded-wire end into the wire connector first, ensuring a solid connection. Use lineman's pliers to twist wires slightly before screwing on the connector.

Once you've spliced all wire groups, fold the wires into the box **3** and attach the cover. Hold the cover tight against the box and attach it with the cover screws **4**.

GROUNDING CABLE & CONDUIT SYSTEMS

Every newly installed circuit must have continuous grounding. Steel conduit acts as its own ground path. MC cable contains an insulated ground because its metal jacket does *not* serve as a ground path; it exists solely to protect the wires inside. AC cable's metal jacket, on the other hand, *does* serve as a ground path. To ensure a continuous ground in AC cable runs, wrap and secure the cable's thin silver bonding wire.

If code requires steel conduit, AC, MC, or MCAP cable, you must use steel boxes. Steel boxes must be grounded as well. In addition to tightening the cable or conduit couplings to the box knockouts, screw a grounding pigtail into the threaded hole in the box. The box pigtail is then spliced to circuit grounds and pigtails that run to the device.

Alternatively, if you're using solid wire, you can use a grounding clip to ground a metal box. (Code prohibits using a grounding clip with stranded wire.) If the incoming ground wire is insulated, strip approximately 6 in. of the insulation and slide the grounding clip onto a section of bare wire. This will allow enough wire beyond the clip so you can splice the bare wire end to other grounds or attach it directly to the grounding screw on a device.

Premade grounding pigtails come with one end looped around a green ground screw. If your job is large, using premade grounds can save a lot of time.

Using a ground clip to ground a metal box is suitable for solid conductors only.

APPLIANCES

WIRING APPLIANCES, LIKE WIRING general-use circuits, is primarily a matter of solidly connecting conductors and following the requirements of the NEC and the manufacturer. Many appliances are big energy users, so it's particularly important to size circuit wires and breakers based on appliance loads. When your new appliances arrive, read—and save—the owner's manuals that come with them. Owner's manuals contain essential information on how to install the appliance, how to register the appliance and comply with its warranty, how to identify and order replacement parts, and other useful information. Increasingly, manufacturers offer owner's manuals online, so if your appliance lacks a manual, download a copy. Always turn off power—and test to be sure it's off—before wiring appliances.

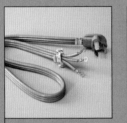

BASICS

A quick look at kitchen appliances, p. 230

Preparing an unfinished appliance cord, p. 231

GARBAGE DISPOSERS

Installing a garbage disposer, p. 232

OVENS

Roughing in an oven outlet, p. 234

Wiring a drop-in oven, p. 235

HOUSEHOLD APPLIANCES

Wiring laundry setups, p. 236

Installing baseboard heaters, p. 238

Electric water heaters, p. 239

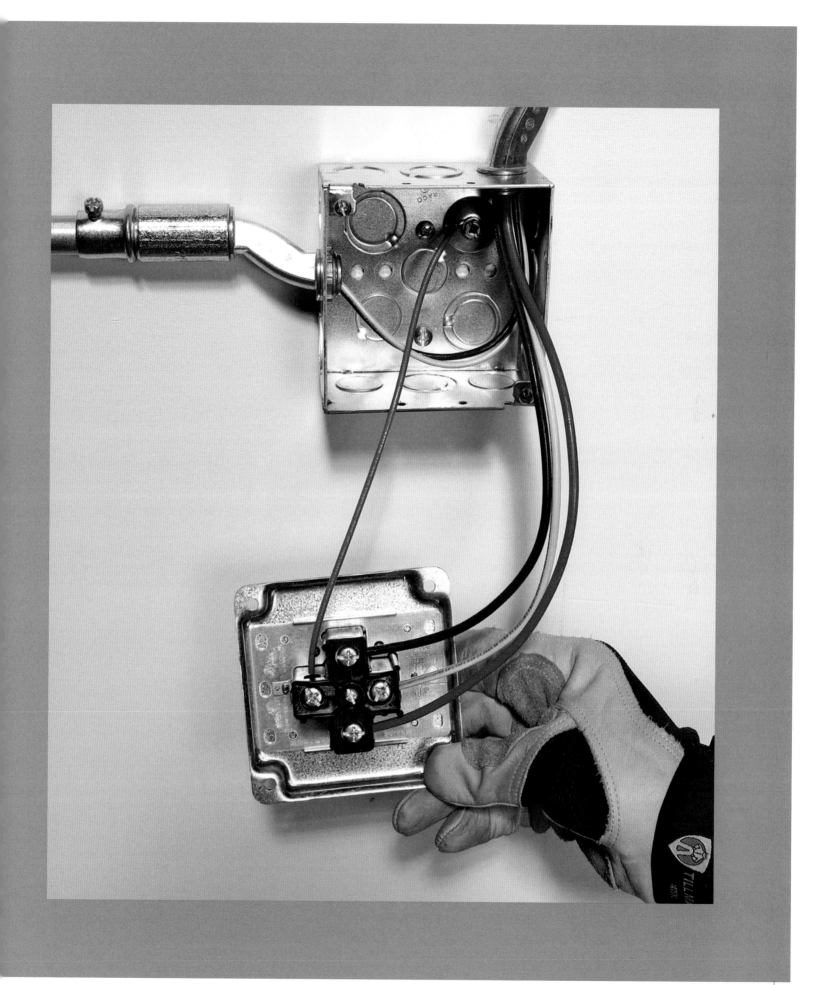

A QUICK LOOK AT KITCHEN APPLIANCES

There's a lot going on in a modern kitchen. Typically it contains a refrigerator, a dishwasher, a garbage disposer, a range hood, a slew of small countertop appliances, and, in many cases, an electric range, cooktop, or oven.

➡ For more on wiring range hoods, see p. 173.

Appliances have different wiring requirements. Smaller ones such as disposers, dishwashers, and range fans require 120v; other appliances require 240v; and others—such as electric ranges—require both 120v and 240v. Range burners and ovens use 240v, but a range's timer and clock use 120v.

Let's start with a handful of important concepts.

Covered junction boxes

All electrical connections must take place in a covered junction box—either an integral box inside the appliance or in a covered junction box secured to a framing member, such as a wall stud.

Equipment grounding

All appliances must have an equipment-grounding conductor that connects to both the appliance frame (or housing) and to the metal outlet box for the safe discharge of fault currents.

Accessible disconnect means

Appliances typically have an accessible "disconnect means" so you can cut the power.

(This is in addition to the fuse or breaker controlling the circuit.) For appliances that slide out—such as a dishwasher or a refrigerator—the disconnect means is typically a cord and a receptacle plug. Appliances that are *hard wired*, such as drop-in cooktops and wall ovens, must have an access panel near the junction box where incoming circuit wires connect to *appliance whips* made of flexible conduit.

Dedicated circuits

Code requires that every fixed appliance must be served by a separate, *dedicated* circuit—a circuit that serves only that appliance. This includes large energy users such as electric ranges, electric water heaters, and clothes dryers that require heavier wire and higher-rated breaker (or fuse) protection.

➡ For more on dedicated circuits, see p. 183.

COMMON ELECTRICAL APPLIANCE REQUIREMENTS

User	Typical Wire Size*	Fuse or Breaker
Small-appliance circuit	12AWG	20 amps
Refrigerator (120v)[†,‡]	12AWG	20 amps
Stand-alone freezer (120v)[†,‡]	12AWG	20 amps
Dishwasher (120v)[†,‡]	12AWG	20 amps
Disposer (120v)[†,‡]	12AWG	20 amps
Microwave (120v)[†,§]	12AWG	20 amps
Range (120/240v)[†,‡]	10AWG	30 amps
Range (120/240v)[†,‡]	8AWG	40 amps
Range (120/240v)[†,‡]	6AWG	50 amps
General utility/workshop	12AWG	20 amps
Laundry circuit (washer)[Đ]	12AWG	20 amps
Clothes dryer (120/240v)[†,‡]	10AWG	30 amps
Water heater (240v)[†,‡]	10AWG	30 amps
Baseboard heater (120v)[†,‡]	12AWG	20 amps (max. 1,500w on circuit)
Baseboard heater (240v)[†,‡]	10AWG	30 amps (max. 5,760w on circuit)
Whole-house fan[†]	12AWG	20 amps
Window air-conditioner (240v)[†,‡]	10AWG	20 amps

*Ratings given for copper (CU) wiring.
[†]Requirements vary; check rating on appliance nameplate and follow manufacturer's specifications.
[‡]Requires dedicated circuit.
[§]Microwaves are typically rated 15 amps but are installed on 20-amp kitchen circuits.
[Đ]Requires designated circuit.

PRO TIP
Don't use ground-fault-circuit-interrupter (GFCI) protection for a gas cooktop or a range with an electric igniter. When the igniter fires, it will cause the GFCI to trip unnecessarily.

PREPARING AN UNFINISHED APPLIANCE CORD

There are many different types of appliance cords. Some cords come with a molded plug and precrimped connectors that attach to terminals on the appliance. Other cords have a molded plug but an unfinished end that you must strip and splice to the lead wires of an appliance. In most cases, the splice is housed in an integral junction box inside an appliance.

The cord seen here is a typical 120v cord that you might attach to a smaller fixed appliance, such as a garbage disposer. It contains a hot wire, a neutral wire and—in the center—a sheathed ground wire. Look closely at the cord and you'll see that its sheathing has a ribbed side and a smooth side. The ribbed side contains a neutral wire that must be spliced to the neutral wire of the appliance; the smooth side contains a hot wire ❶.

Start by snipping and separating the three stranded wires within the cord ❷. Using a utility knife, carefully slice and peel back the cord's outer (gray) insulation from the middle wire. As you do so, you'll expose the ground wire's green insulation. Only the ground wire has this additional layer of insulation ❸. Next use a wire stripper to remove 1/2 in. of insulation from the ends of all three cord wires ❹. Now you're ready to splice those wires to the lead wires on the appliance.

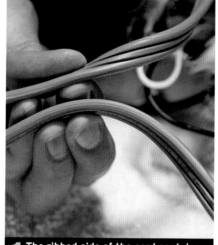

1 The ribbed side of the cord contains the neutral wire.

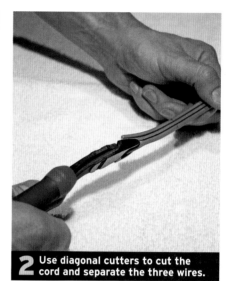

2 Use diagonal cutters to cut the cord and separate the three wires.

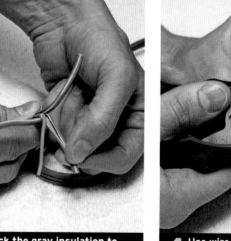

3 Peel back the gray insulation to expose the ground wire.

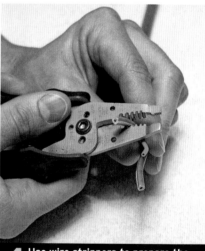

4 Use wire strippers to prepare the ends of all three cord wires.

PIGTAIL

For eons, how-to books had sections about replacing appliance plugs. Forget that. Today, you can easily find replacement cords—also called appliance pigtails—with molded plugs and precrimped connectors, which are far easier and safer to install. By the way, always grab the plug—not the cord—when unplugging an appliance.

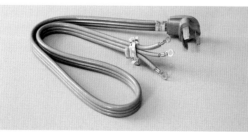

Replacing the entire cord is often easier than replacing a broken plug.

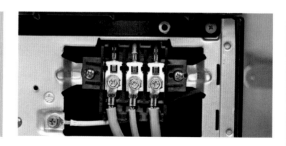

The connectors on the appliance pigtail attach to terminals on the appliance.

INSTALLING A GARBAGE DISPOSER

1 The bundled yellow cables will supply the garbage disposer and dishwasher.

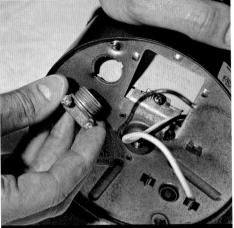

2 Remove the cover plate from the junction box and screw on a connector.

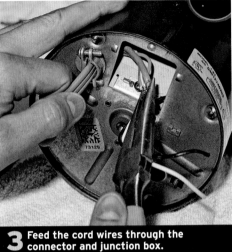

3 Feed the cord wires through the connector and junction box.

4 Tighten the cable connector to prevent stress on the wire connections.

5 Connect the appropriate wires with wire connectors.

6 Raise the disposer into place and turn it until the mounting rings lock into place.

Though installation of a disposer is largely the same from brand to brand, be sure to follow the instructions that come with your unit. Typically, plumbing supply and waste pipes are stubbed out, and 12AWG cable is roughed in before the finish walls and cabinets are installed **1**. After the base cabinet is in place, install a 20-amp duplex receptacle to supply power to the disposer and dishwasher. The receptacle for the disposer should be a switched receptacle.

➜ **For more on wiring a split-tab receptacle, see p. 49.**

Install the sink and attach the disposer mounting assembly in the sink outlet. Then route the dishwasher overflow pipe into the cabinet under the sink.

With these prep steps done, you're ready to attach the appliance cord. Remove the cover plate from the bottom of the unit and pull its wire leads. Then screw a cable connector into the knockout in the bottom of the unit **2**. Separate and strip cord wires and feed them through the cable connector. Use needle-nose pliers to pull the wires through the junction box **3**, and then tighten the cable connector **4**.

Attach the green ground wire to the ground screw in the junction box. Then use wire connectors to splice like wires—neutral to neutral, hot to hot **5**. Fold all wires into the junction box and replace the cover plate. Lift the disposer until its mounting ring engages the mounting ring on the bottom of the sink. Turn the unit until the rings lock **6**.

Slide the tube from the dishwasher onto the dishwasher inlet stub and tighten its clamp **7**. Attach the P-trap to the discharge outlet on the disposer **8**. Plug the disposer plug into the switched half of the undersink receptacle. The second plug runs to the dishwasher.

7 Slide the dishwasher drain onto the inlet stub and tighten its clamp.

8 Attach the P-trap to the discharge outlet on the disposer.

DISPOSERS & DISHWASHERS

Disposers and dishwashers are often 120v, 15-amp appliances, so both are supplied by 12AWG cable. Most garbage disposers have a covered junction box on the bottom, to which a plugged cord attaches. You can also hard wire a disposer, but having a receptacle in the cabinet under the sink enables a homeowner to quickly unplug the unit should he or she need to repair or replace it. Typically, an undersink outlet is controlled by a switch above the counter, as shown in "Wiring a Garbage Disposer," at left.

A dishwasher and a disposer often plug into a split-tab receptacle located in the sink cabinet. A split-tab receptacle is a standard duplex receptacle whose middle tab has been removed to create a duplex receptacle fed by two circuits—that is, by two hot wires.

Because they slide out for installation and maintenance, dishwashers are also installed with a cord and plug. Most of the time, the dishwasher junction box is located in the front of the unit, just behind the kick panel. After attaching cord wires to wire leads in the junction box, run the cord in the channel behind the dishwasher to reach to an outlet.

WIRING A GARBAGE DISPOSER

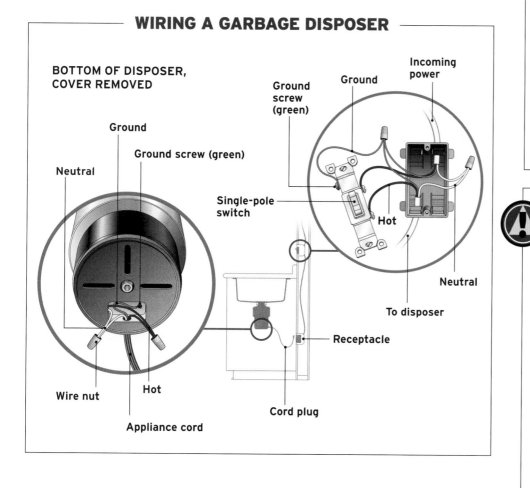

BOTTOM OF DISPOSER, COVER REMOVED

Neutral

Ground

Ground screw (green)

Wire nut

Hot

Appliance cord

Cord plug

Ground screw (green)

Ground

Incoming power

Single-pole switch

Hot

Neutral

To disposer

Receptacle

⚠ SAFETY ALERT

The NEC specifies that you connect the two hot wires of a split-tab receptacle to a double-pole breaker. When you flip off the toggle for a double-pole breaker, you shut off both hot wires. If you instead connect the hot wires of a split-tab receptacle to separate, single-pole breakers and then flip off only one breaker, you might test the top half of the split-tab receptacle and conclude—mistakenly—that the bottom half was off, too. Attaching both hot wires to a double-pole breaker prevents such a potentially lethal mistake.

ROUGHING IN AN OVEN OUTLET

Roughing in an oven outlet is not that different from roughing in any other outlet. Remove the knockout from a four-square box, insert a plastic cable connector, and then feed in the 10/3 NM cable that will power the range. Staple the cable within 12 in. of the box; drive the staple just snug **1**.

Although an experienced electrician can use a utility knife to strip sheathing from any cable, using a cable ripper that can accommodate large-gauge wire makes sense for nonprofessionals **2**. Hold the ripper channel snug to the cable and pull it down the length of the cable to score the sheathing **3**.

Pull back the sheathing to expose wires inside. Then use diagonal cutters to cut the sheathing free. Leave $1/2$ in. to 1 in. of sheathing inside the box **4**. Attach the ground wire to the box using a green ground screw in a threaded hole. Wrap the wire clockwise around the screw so it will stay in place as the screw tightens down on it **5**.

Fold the wires neatly into the box so they can be easily pulled out during the trim-out phase, when they'll be attached to a 30-amp receptacle or hard wired directly to a metal-clad appliance whip. Finally, attach a two-gang mud ring to the outlet box so it will be flush to the finish surface **6**.

PRO TIP

Be sure to verify the ampacity of your range or cooktop. Many require 40A or 50A circuits, which will require larger-gauge cable.

1 10/3 NM cable is run to a four-square box.

2 Use a cable ripper that can accommodate larger-gauge wire.

3 Pull the ripper to score the sheathing.

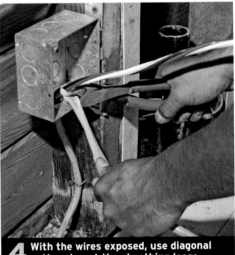

4 With the wires exposed, use diagonal cutters to cut the sheathing loose.

5 Leave the ground wire long to be spliced to the ground in the appliance whip.

6 Attach a mud ring to bring the box flush.

WIRING A DROP-IN OVEN

Drop-in ovens and other stationary appliances must be hard wired. For the project shown here, an electric oven has been installed in a base cabinet, and the wires in its MC cable are ready to be connected to 10AWG wires, roughed into a four-square box. The edge of the box must be flush to the cabinet back, because plywood is flammable. If the box or its mud ring is below the cabinet back, add a four-square box extension to bring it flush **1**.

Install a two-piece, right-angle cable connector (a flex-90) to the end of the cable whip. Slide the bottom of the connector onto the end of the whip and screw on the top of the cable connector **2**. Remove the stamped knockout on the four-square cover; then feed the whip wires and the connector end through the knockout **3**. Tighten a locknut onto the threaded connector end to lock the cable connector to the cover.

To ground the outlet box, loop the incoming ground wire under a green ground screw **4**. Splice that ground wire to the appliance ground. Use wire strippers to remove 1/2 in. of insulation from the neutral and hot wires on the incoming cable **5**; then use wire connectors to splice like-colored wires together **6**: black to black, red to red, and white to white. To ensure that wire connectors grip the wires securely, use lineman's pliers. (There are two hot wires—red and black—because the oven requires 240v.)

Tuck them into the box. Then attach the cover to protect the connections within **7**.

1 A four-square box extension brings the outlet flush.

2 A right-angle cable connector is attached.

3 Remove a knockout and feed the wires through.

4 Wrap the incoming cable ground under a ground screw.

5 Remove 1/2 in. of insulation from the wires.

6 Fold the wires into the box.

7 Attach the cover to the box.

PRO TIP

Appliances are usually the same depth as base cabinets (24 in.) so appliance faces will be even with cabinet faces. Because most appliances are installed against a wall, manufacturers often build a recessed area in the back of the appliance to accommodate electrical connections. Refer to the user's manual prior to rough-in.

ELECTRIC RANGES, OVENS, AND COOKTOPS

When discussing cooking appliances, you'll need to keep several terms straight: The enclosed cooking area in which you roast a turkey is an *oven*; you place pots and frying pans on *cooktop* burners. A *range* has both an oven and a cooktop.

In any case, the heating elements of ranges, ovens, and cooktops generally require 240v, but today's smart appliances come with a plethora of timers, clocks, sensors, buzzers, and other gizmos that use 120v. For this reason, many units require 120/240v wiring, with two hot wires, an insulated neutral, and an equipment ground wire.

As noted elsewhere, if the unit slides in and out for maintenance, it is usually installed with a plug inserted into a matched receptacle. The outlet box that contains that receptacle may be surface mounted or recessed (so that the receptacle can be flush mounted). If the unit drops in and stays put, it is typically hard wired to a junction box via an appliance whip.

WIRING LAUNDRY SETUPS

In the photo sequence shown on the facing page, the metal conduit is the equipment ground. To bond each receptacle to the system, there is a green grounding pigtail that runs from each box's grounding screw to a receptacle ground screw. In this installation, wires are not yet attached to a power source, so they are safe to handle.

➤ **For more on installing metal conduit, see pp. 223–227.**

Start by fishing wire to the box nearest to the power source. Here, five insulated wires had to be fished: three 10AWG wires (hot-hot-neutral) to feed the 120/240v dryer receptacle; and two 12AWG wires (hot-neutral) to feed the 120v washer receptacle. Untape the fished-wire bundle and trim each set of wires to rough length so that at least 6 in. to 8 in. of wire sticks out of each box ❶.

Attach a green grounding pigtail to each box and strip 1/2 in. of insulation off the ends of the incoming wires. If the point of a grounding screw hits the masonry wall, you may need to shorten the grounding screw so that it doesn't run into the masonry. The green pigtail grounds the device to the box; attach the pigtails first to the ground terminal on each receptacle ❷. Next attach the neutral wires to each receptacle, then the hot wire(s) ❸. Tighten each screw terminal, then gently tug each wire to be sure it's well attached.

The receptacle for the washer is a standard 20-amp receptacle. Use a wire stripper to create loops that you can attach to the screw terminals on the receptacle ❹. Once both receptacles are wired, fold the wires into their respective boxes and attach the cover plates ❺. If you install an industrial raised cover, secure the receptacle to the cover, then screw the cover to the box. Once you've installed the covers, attach circuit wires to breakers in the panel.

>> >> >>

MEASURING PIPE LENGTH

To determine the length of conduit pipe running between two outlet boxes, measure from the centerline of each box (A).

Subtract 2 in. from the centerline of each box (B).

Subtract the distance each adaptor sticks out of the box (C).

Add the distance that pipe ends fit into adaptor sockets (D).

Pipe length = A − 2B − 2C + 2D

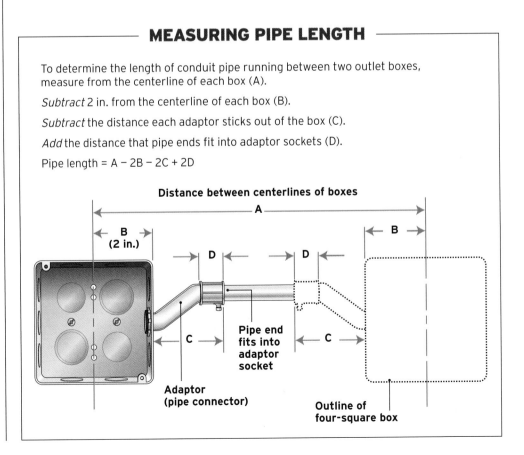

Distance between centerlines of boxes

A

B (2 in.)

B

D D

C C

Pipe end fits into adaptor socket

Adaptor (pipe connector)

Outline of four-square box

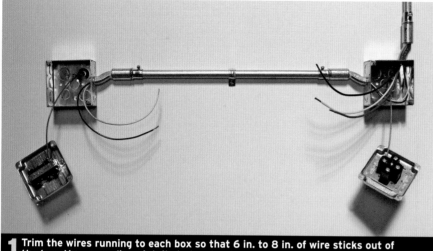

1 Trim the wires running to each box so that 6 in. to 8 in. of wire sticks out of the box. Use grounding pigtails to bond receptacles to metal conduit.

WIRING REQUIREMENTS FOR LAUNDRY SETUPS

Clothes washers and dryers are often wired with two surface-mounted receptacles.

As with electric ranges, electric dryers typically require 120/240v wiring because, in addition to their 240v heating elements, dryers are equipped with several elements that use 120v—such as drum motors, timers, and buzzers. So dryer circuits include two hot wires, a neutral wire, and an equipment ground wire.

Equipment grounds on washers and dryers connect to appliance housings to provide a safe route for fault current should a short circuit occur. Washer circuits are usually wired with 12AWG wire and protected by a 20-amp breaker or fuse; dryer circuits are wired with 10AWG wire and protected by a 30-amp breaker or fuse. But, as always, note the nameplate ratings on your appliances and wire them accordingly.

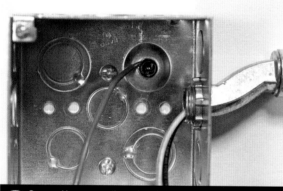

2 Screw the grounding pigtail into a specially machined screw hole in the outlet box. Such holes are typically located in a raised portion so the screw head can fully compress the wire.

3 The 120/240v dryer receptacle has screw terminals for two hot wires (red and black), a neutral wire (white), and a ground wire or pigtail (green).

4 The 120v washer receptacle is a standard 20-amp receptacle; strip and loop wire ends before attaching them to screw terminals.

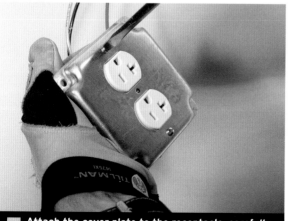

5 Attach the cover plate to the receptacle, carefully fold the wires into the outlet box, and mount the cover to the box.

THE IMPORTANCE OF 4-POLE, 4-WIRE DRYER RECEPTACLES

In many older homes, 120/240v, 3-pole, 3-wire, nongrounded receptacles for appliances such as dryers and ranges are common. Older dryers were configured so that the neutral also served as the equipment ground; thus the circuit serving such a dryer had two hots and one neutral conductor.

The shift from nongrounding-type receptacles to grounded receptacles and appliances was made to improve safety and was required by the NEC in the early 1970s. Newer dryers had cords and plugs with 4 wires: hot, hot, neutral, ground.

Code allows a nongrounded receptacle to be replaced with another nongrounding receptacle, but code requires a grounded receptacle (120/240v, 4-pole 4-wire) if there is some way to bring an equipment-grounding conductor in the outlet box. Code also requires a grounded 4-pole, 4-wire receptacle for all new installations.

INSTALLING BASEBOARD HEATERS

Baseboard heaters are increasingly popular as a backup to a central heating system. Installing units with in-heater thermostats is a better choice than installing a central wall thermostat that controls all units. Baseboard units with in-heater thermostats are easier to install and more cost-effective to operate because they deliver heat to areas where it's needed most. Because most baseboard units are installed under windows, units with in-heater thermostats can respond faster to cold air as it enters.

Baseboard heaters are available in 120v and 240v models, but 240v models are generally more efficient. As a rule of thumb, you can connect several small heaters to one cable running from the main panel, as long as their combined continuous load doesn't exceed 80 percent of the cable's rating. In other words, if you run 12AWG cable with 20-amp protection, the continuous current should not exceed 16 amps. But because wattage varies from model to model, follow the installation instructions that come with your model.

Wiring an in-heater thermostat is pretty straightforward. Rough in wiring to each heater location, remove a cover plate on one end of each unit, feed the incoming cable through a cable connector, and splice the incoming circuit wires to the thermostat wires. Make sure to attach a grounding pigtail to the metal housing of the unit. Thermostats will be single-pole or double-pole switches. Double-pole thermostats are required by the NEC for 240v heaters, so that the thermostat, when off, cuts power to both legs of the unit, which is required for safety.

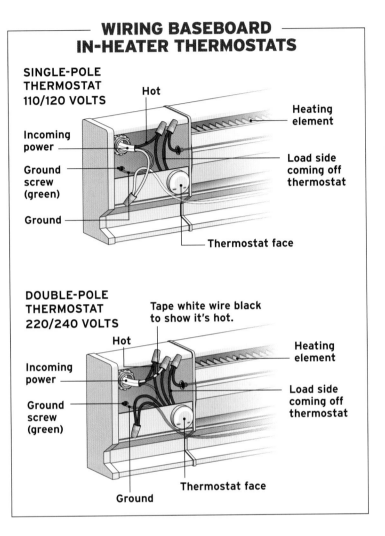

WIRING BASEBOARD IN-HEATER THERMOSTATS

SINGLE-POLE THERMOSTAT 110/120 VOLTS
- Hot
- Incoming power
- Ground screw (green)
- Ground
- Heating element
- Load side coming off thermostat
- Thermostat face

DOUBLE-POLE THERMOSTAT 220/240 VOLTS
- Tape white wire black to show it's hot.
- Hot
- Incoming power
- Ground screw (green)
- Ground
- Heating element
- Load side coming off thermostat
- Thermostat face

ELECTRIC WATER HEATERS

Replacing an electric water heater generally requires a permit, even if you attach the replacement to existing pipes. The reason is safety: Inspectors want to ensure that gas- and oil-fired units are properly vented and that electric heaters are correctly wired. Inspectors are particularly concerned that temperature and pressure relief (TPR) valves are correctly installed, because TPR valves keep water heaters from exploding in the event of a malfunction. For these reasons and for warranty issues, have a professional install your water heater. The drawing below is offered for information only.

WIRING A 240V WATER HEATER

Here's a look at a typical water heater installation. Three things to note: (1) The cutoff "switch" can be a circuit breaker or a fused switch rated for the load of the water heater, typically 30 amps. Place the disconnect (cutoff) switch close to the unit. You may use the circuit breaker in the service panel as the disconnect if it is within sight of the water heater and it is capable of being locked in the "OFF" position. (2) If you use 2-wire cable to wire the water heater, tape the white wire with red or black tape on both ends to indicate that it is being used as a hot conductor. (3) Use flexible metallic cable (rather than rigid conduit) between the cutoff switch and the water heater for extra safety in earthquake regions.

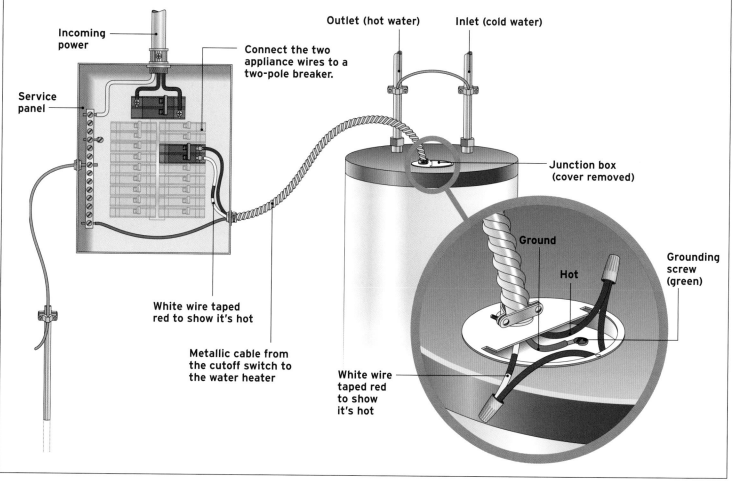

Incoming power

Connect the two appliance wires to a two-pole breaker.

Outlet (hot water)

Inlet (cold water)

Service panel

Junction box (cover removed)

Ground

Grounding screw (green)

Hot

White wire taped red to show it's hot

Metallic cable from the cutoff switch to the water heater

White wire taped red to show it's hot

OUTDOOR WIRING

ADDING AN OUTDOOR RECEPTACLE, a motion-sensor light, a video camera, or low-voltage path lights can increase your security and safety and enable you to enjoy your property more fully. As smartphone apps help you set up many types of motion-sensor lights and video cams, they are increasingly easy to install. But before you start any project, review local building code requirements for outdoor installations. The same goes for adding electrical vehicle (EV) chargers, often installed in open-air carports or garages. We recommend that a licensed electrician install your charger.

Above all, be safe: Before working on an existing outlet or fixture, turn off the power at the service panel or fuse box and test to be sure the power is off. Also, never operate power tools in damp or rainy conditions.

BEFORE YOU BEGIN

OUTDOOR OUTLETS

OUTBUILDINGS

OUTDOOR PATH LIGHTS

MOTION-SENSOR LIGHTS

ELECTRIC VEHICLE (EV) CHARGERS

PLANNING YOUR OUTDOOR SYSTEM

Start by walking the property and noting where you'd like additional outlets, lights, and so on. Make a list. As you go, imagine activities that take place in different locations at night and day. Is there enough light along the path when you come home at night? Are there enough outlets to entertain or to do chores on the weekend? At this stage, think big and anticipate future uses, especially if you must dig up the lawn to install your present project. With a little advance planning, you can avoid digging up the lawn a second time, later.

If your wish list is extensive, next make a scale drawing of the house and yard on graph paper. Note sidewalks, paths, and important landscape elements such as trees and large bushes. Note electrical devices that you'd like to add and existing ones that need upgrading. The drawing will be especially useful when it's time to calculate the number of fixtures and amount of cable you'll need. If you intend to take power from an existing outlet, note where the nearest outlet is, even if it's inside the house.

Getting power

Once you know roughly where you want to add exterior outlets or light fixtures, figure out how to get power to them. This will depend, in part, on how many devices you're adding.

If you're adding just one exterior receptacle, for example, find the exterior or interior receptacle closest to the one you want to add outside. If you position the new receptacle in the same stud bay as an interior receptacle, you'll simplify the task immensely because you won't have to drill through any studs.

Before cutting holes in anything, however, calculate the load on the circuit. Add up the wattage of all the lights and appliances presently in use and the wattage of the new outlet or light you want to add. If the total load on a 15-amp circuit exceeds 1,440w, run

a new grounded circuit from the panel to the exterior device instead. Likewise, if you are running power to an outbuilding, run a new grounded circuit from the panel.

Install a 20-amp circuit if your plans call for electrical usage that exceeds the load limits of an existing circuit, includes a large number of receptacles, or contains three or more large flood lamps or other large lighting fixtures rated more than 300w each. If you will be using large, stationary tools in a workshop or heating the area with electricity, you may need to add several 120v and 240v circuits. Again, calculate the loads involved.

Two important points: First, the NEC allows you to tap into a general-use or lighting circuit only. You may not tap into

circuits feeding kitchen-countertop receptacles or bathroom receptacles or into any dedicated circuits that supply power to air-conditioners, clothes washers or dryers, or other power-hungry appliances. Second, if you discover that the circuit you'd like to tap into is wired with nongrounded NM cable, BX armored cable, or knob-and-tube—don't tap into that circuit. The new extension may not be properly protected. Instead, run a new grounded circuit from the panel. In addition, don't forget weatherproof housings or covers and GFCI protection.

Finally, take your plans for new circuits or extensions to existing line-voltage circuits to the local building department and have them sign off before you start.

Outdoor safety: Checking codes and utilities
Outdoor outlets and fixtures are exposed to weather; because moisture greatly increases the chance of electrical shocks, local codes are strict about what materials you can use and how they must be installed. In general, you don't need a permit to install low-voltage lights because the chance of shock is low, but if you want to add an outdoor receptacle or a light fixture that uses line voltage (120v or 240v), you'll need a permit.

If you'll be running cable underground, check with local utilities before you dig. Call 811 (or visit www.call811.com). There may be water pipes, gas lines, telephone or cable lines, or electrical cables buried in the yard. Often, utilities will send out a technician to show you where such lines are located. If your lawn has a sprinkler system, note where sprinkler heads are and try to avoid the water pipes that feed them. Remember that only a licensed electrician should install hot tubs and swimming pools and the like because such installations require special grounding methods.

CHOOSING OUTDOOR LIGHTS

There is a wide variety of light fixtures to choose from. For starters, choose line-voltage lights (120v) if you want to deter intruders, accent an architectural feature, or illuminate a work area such as an outdoor grill. To light up a walkway or add accent lights to the landscaping, however, low-voltage lights (12v or 24v) are usually a more economical choice and are generally easier to install. There are also lo-vo solar units (no wiring needed) that charge during the day and glow softly all night.

In general, don't install more light than you need to serve the function for a given area. Outdoor lights that are too bright waste energy and will be too glaring for intimate dining or entertaining at night. Your neighbors will also thank you for not spot-lighting their house when they're trying to relax or sleep.

In addition to overhead lights, side-mounted lights, step-riser lights, in-ground fixtures, post-mounted lights, and stake-mounted lights, there are many switching options. You can control lights with smartphones, standard on–off switches, timers, motion detectors, and photocells that turn lights on when the sun goes down.

Outdoor lights are available in an array of styles. Here, Mission-style lights brighten a stone stairway.

PRO TIP

Put security lights high on a porch or under the eaves. Lights that can be reached without a ladder can be easily unscrewed.

A WIRELESS SECURITY CAMERA

Given the many devices that smartphones control inside our homes, it's not surprising that there is now a Wi-Fi security camera you can install outside. The Stick Up Cam is the outdoor cousin of the Ring Video Doorbell (p. 108). It communicates using the same app and employs many of the same technologies, including motion-detector sensors, HD video with night vision (infrared LEDs), Cloud video recording, and two-way audio.

When someone approaches your home, their movement activates the video camera and sends an alert to your smartphone so that you can monitor and interact with—watch and talk to—your "visitor." This unexpected conversation is usually enough to scare off intruders. For roughly $30 a year, you also can store video clips for up to six months, to view, download, and share as you like.

Weather-resistant and wireless, the cam can be easily installed high on a wall or under an eave, its motion zones and sensitivity can be adjusted, and its rechargeable batteries last six to twelve months with regular usage. If someone steals the unit, Ring will replace it free. To monitor the perimeter of your house you might need several Stick Up Cams, but at $199 each that shouldn't break the bank.

TOOLS & MATERIALS

A Use a square-nosed shovel to create shallow slots so you can tuck lo-vo cable into the ground.

B Rent a ditch-digging machine, also known as a trencher, to save time and avoid a sore back.

The tools you need to install outdoor wiring are pretty much the same ones needed to wire a house interior. The big exceptions, obviously, are digging and earth-moving tools. A *square-nosed shovel* or *spade* is the most useful tool when you're making a shallow slot for low-voltage cable **A**. If you're actually digging a trench, use a trenching shovel with a pointed nose and a reinforced shoulder that you can stamp on with a boot to drive it deep.

Digging trenches is hard work, however; so when the pros have to dig a long or deep one, they rent a gas-powered ditch-digging machine, also known as a *trencher* **B**. A trencher looks like a cross between a pow-ered garden tiller and a chainsaw and typi-cally cuts a trench 4 in. to 6 in. wide and as

deep as 24 in. Spread sheet plastic on either side of the trench so you can place the dirt from the trench nearby—which makes refill-ing the trench easier. Wear heavy boots, heavy gloves, safety glasses, and ear plugs when operating a trencher.

Materials

The NEC requires that all exterior outlets and circuits have GFCI protection. This pro-tection includes the following:

- A GFCI receptacle installed in a weather-proof box.
- A standard receptacle installed in a weatherproof box protected by a GFCI receptacle installed *upstream* (toward the power source).
- A circuit protected by a GFCI breaker.

Exterior light fixtures do not need GFCI protection. If the box is surface mounted, it needs to be raintight. If the box is recessed in the wall, it does not. The fixture must be listed for *damp locations* if under eaves and listed for *wet locations* if directly exposed to weather.

There are two common types of weather-proof covers (also called raintight covers) (see top photo on the facing page). A *weather-proof while-in-use cover* has a plastic cover that shuts over an electrical cord, such as that used for holiday lights. A *weathertight cover* is a gasketed cover that shuts tight over the receptacles when not in use. For any receptacle exposed to rain or splash, the NEC requires covers to be the "weather-proof in-use" type, per NEC 406.9(B)(1). For receptacles in damp locations but not subject to beating rain or water runoff, a simple weathertight cover is required, but an in-use cover is not required, per 406.9(B). Also, all exterior receptacles are required to be of the "weather-resistant" type.

Aboveground, electrical cable must be housed in conduit with raintight fittings (see bottom photo at right). You can use polyvinyl chloride (PVC), thin-walled electrical metallic tubing (EMT) conduit, threaded intermediate metal conduit (IMC), or rigid steel conduit (RSC). PVC fittings are glued together to achieve a raintight fit; EMT conduit uses compression fittings; and IMC and RSC use threaded fittings or compression fittings. *Note:* Common EMT conduit fittings (both setscrew and compression type) are intended for interior use, are not raintight, and therefore are not suitable for exterior use. Look for compression fittings that are identified as raintight.

Belowground, you can run flexible underground feeder (UF) cable at a depth acceptable to local codes—typically, 18 in. deep. Some codes allow you to dig a shallower trench if the cable runs in steel conduit, but because threading steel conduit requires special equipment and advanced skills, it's not a reasonable option for most nonprofessionals.

SAFETY ALERT

Avoid plugging or unplugging devices into exterior receptacles—or using corded power tools outside—when it's raining or snowing.

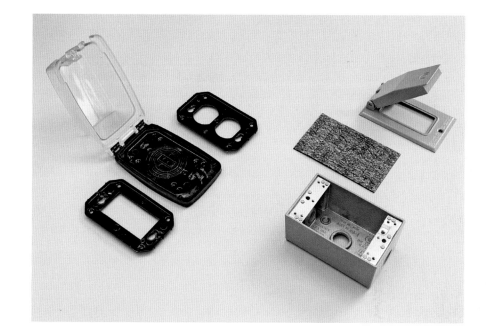

Raintight (weatherproof) covers **include a weatherproof while-in-use receptacle cover with adapter plates (left) and a weatherproof box with gasketed cover (right). Plastic adapter plates enable you to use the cover with a duplex or GFCI receptacle. The weatherproof box gasket is precut, so it accepts either a duplex or GFCI receptacle.**

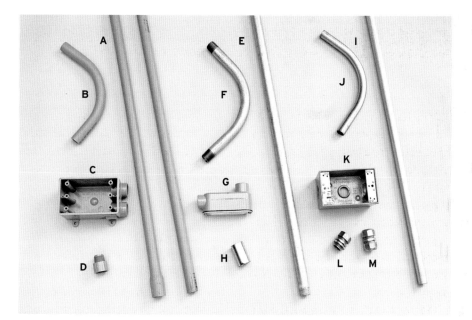

Overview of exterior conduit types, fittings, and boxes: A, 1/2-in. PVC pipe; B, PVC elbow; C, PVC box with unthreaded openings (for slip-in fittings); D, male adapter (MA) PVC fitting, which can be used with a threaded box or conduit; E, RSC pipe; F, RSC elbow; G, LB condulet; H, RSC coupling; I, EMT pipe; J, EMT elbow; K, bell box with three threaded holes; L, threaded EMT compression fitting; M, EMT compression coupling. *Note:* The LB conduit and bell box accept any 1/2-in. (trade size) threaded fitting— whether PVC adapter, EMT, or RSC.

TAPPING INTO AN EXISTING OUTLET

1 Turn off the power, remove the cover plate, and unscrew the receptacle.

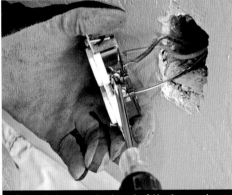

2 Pull the receptacle out of the box and remove the wires attached to its terminals.

3 Use a screwdriver to pry out a knockout.

7 Pull the new cable through and attach a cable clamp.

8 Leaving one ground wire long, use a green grounding nut to splice.

When adding a single outdoor receptacle, it's usually easiest to tap into an interior outlet within the same stud bay. In the installation shown here, the electrician solved the box-capacity problem by replacing the old receptacle with a commercial-grade duplex receptacle. Instead of splicing new and old wires and using pigtails—which would have required twist-on wire connectors and thus a larger box—he joined incoming and outgoing wires by inserting them into terminal holes in the back of the receptacle and then tightened down the terminal screws. *Note:* Wiring a commercial-grade receptacle in this manner is not the same as backwiring a standard receptacle because standard receptacles have inferior spring clamps that are unreliable.

➡ **For information about backwiring, see p. 42.**

Start by turning off the power to the receptacle at the panel or fuse box; then use a voltage tester to make sure the power is off. Remove the cover plate and unscrew the mounting screws securing the receptacle to the outlet box **❶**.

Pull the receptacle out of the box, being careful not to touch the screw terminals; then test them again with a probe tester (see p. 16) to make sure they're not energized **❷**.

Detach the wires from the terminals, fold them out of the way, and look for a knockout in the box to remove. Typically, a pair of knockouts will be hidden beneath an integral cable connector—unscrew it. Then remove a knockout from the outlet box **❸**. Drill through the exterior wall and into the same stud bay as the interior receptacle **❹**. Then, inside the house, push fish tape through the knockout hole and into the stud bay **❺**. Outside, a helper can catch the tape, pull it out of the hole you just drilled, and attach the new cable to it **❻**.

Inside, pull the fish tape and the attached cable into the box. Pull about 1 ft. of new cable out of the box and then replace the integral cable clamp **❼** to secure the cable. Strip the cable sheathing and splice like wires together, starting with the ground

wires. Use a special green grounding nut to splice the grounds **❽**. Use wire strippers to remove $1/2$ in. of the insulation from the ends of the hot and neutral wires **❾**.

To save space in the old box, insert the stripped wire ends into terminal holes in the back of the spec-grade (commercial-grade) receptacle **❿**. Because spec-grade receptacles solidly clamp wire ends, this connection is as solid as any splice. Fold the wires into the box as you push the receptacle into place until it is fully seated in the box—do not use mounting screws to pull the receptacle into the box because this could strip the screw threads. Then replace the cover and screw it into place.

➡ **See "Mounting & Wiring an Exterior Outlet," on p. 248.**

4 Outside, have a helper drill through the siding.

5 Push the fish tape through the knockout hole, into the stud bay.

6 Outside, retrieve the fish tape and attach the new cable.

9 Use wire strippers to remove ½ in. of insulation off the wire ends.

10 Connect all wires; gently push the receptacle into the box.

PRO TIP

To power holiday lights safely, plug them into a GFCI receptacle housed in a waterproof while-in-use box cover. But before installing the lights, calculate the total wattage of all the bulbs so you don't overload the circuit.

ADDING AN OUTDOOR RECEPTACLE

If you tap into an existing receptacle at the end of a circuit, there should be enough room inside the box to bring a cable to feed the new outdoor receptacle. However, if there are already two cables in the box—incoming and outgoing—you may need to replace the existing box with a larger one.

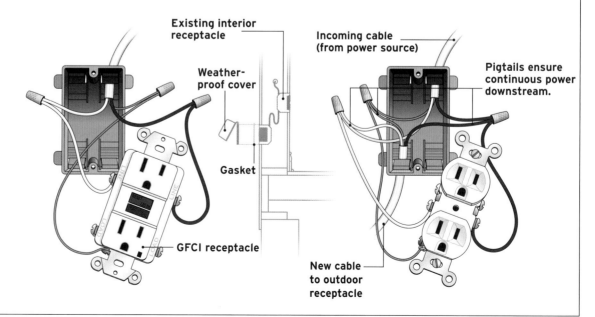

Existing interior receptacle

Incoming cable (from power source)

Pigtails ensure continuous power downstream.

Weather-proof cover

Gasket

GFCI receptacle

New cable to outdoor receptacle

MOUNTING & WIRING AN EXTERIOR OUTLET

1 Feed the cable through the connector in the box and secure it to the building.

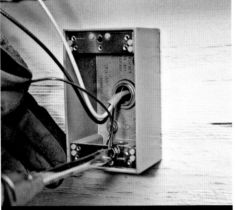

2 Loop the bare ground wire around the green grounding screw.

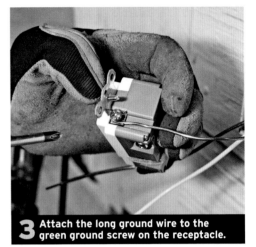

3 Attach the long ground wire to the green ground screw on the receptacle.

4 Insert wires into terminals: brass screw for hot wire; silver screw for neutral wire.

5 Fold and tuck the wires into the box. Then secure the receptacle to the box.

6 Fit the gasket around the receptacle and screw on the weatherproof cover.

Once the new cable is spliced to the cable in an existing receptacle, feed the cable through the cable connector in the back of the exterior box and mount the box. (The hole drilled in the exterior wall must be wide enough for the cable connector or the box won't sit flat to the wall.) To mount the box, use mounting ears or the small holes in the back. Apply siliconized caulking to the hole before attaching the box. Plumb the box and screw it to the outside of the building **❶**.

Strip sheathing from the cable and ground the box by looping the bare ground wire around the green grounding screw. Leave this ground wire long **❷**. Use a wire stripper to remove ½ in. of the insulation from the ends of the neutral and hot wires. Next, loop and attach the long ground wire to the green ground screw on the GFCI receptacle **❸**. Then connect the hot and neutral wires in their respective screw-terminal holes **❹**.

If the GFCI receptacle has plaster ears, use diagonal cutters to remove them; otherwise, the receptacle may not fit into the box. Fold the wires and push the receptacle into the box; then screw down the mounting screws that secure the receptacle to the box **❺**. A weatherproof gasket is used to keep water away from the wires—set it in place around the receptacle before you attach the cover **❻**.

PRO TIP

GFCI receptacles are larger than standard duplex receptacles, so there will not be enough room in a single-gang box if you also need to splice an outgoing cable to feed another outdoor outlet downstream. In that case, install a deep box or install an extension to the single-gang box.

RUNNING POWER TO AN OUTBUILDING

The first step to wiring an outbuilding is to figure out how many lights and outlets you need. If your needs are modest, you may be able to tap into an existing outlet in the main house and extend the circuit from it. Calculate the total loads for the existing circuit and the extension to see if the circuit has enough capacity. Otherwise, run a new circuit from the panel to the outbuilding.

If the outbuilding isn't more than 50 ft. from the house and has a few lights and outlets, it usually can be supplied by a 120v, 20-amp circuit and 12/2 w/grd UF cable. But check with local building authorities before you start. Get the necessary permit, code requirements, and inspection schedules.

The hardest part of the job is usually digging the trench, because local codes typically require it to be 18 in. deep. Fortunately, you can rent a gas-powered trencher to do the digging for you. After removing the dirt from the trench, pick out any rocks or debris that could damage the cable. Then lay the UF cable in the trench, flattening it as you go ❶.

>> >> >>

1 As you walk along the trench, unwind the cable. Ideally, it should lie flat in the bottom of the trench.

RUNNING POWER TO AN OUTBUILDING

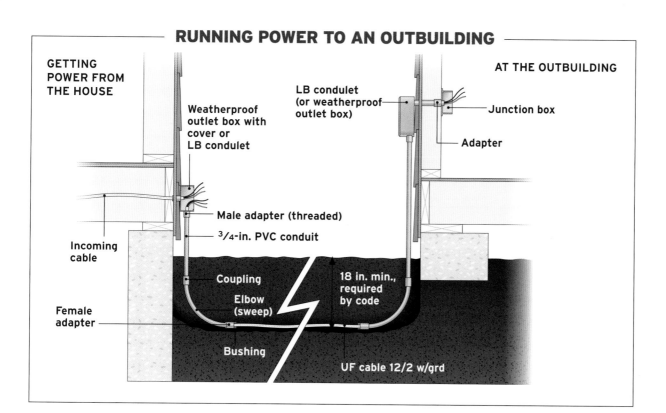

GETTING POWER FROM THE HOUSE

AT THE OUTBUILDING

Weatherproof outlet box with cover or LB condulet

LB condulet (or weatherproof outlet box)

Junction box

Adapter

Male adapter (threaded)

³/₄-in. PVC conduit

Incoming cable

Coupling

Elbow (sweep)

18 in. min., required by code

Female adapter

Bushing

UF cable 12/2 w/grd

RUNNING POWER TO AN OUTBUILDING (CONTINUED)

Use electrical-grade PVC conduit, couplings, and adapters to protect the UF cable between the bottom of the trench and the outdoor boxes in which connections will be made. At the house, UF cable is typically spliced to an interior wire in a covered single-gang, weathertight box ❷. On the other end, the cable typically passes through an LB condulet and a short length of PVC pipe before terminating in a junction box inside the outbuilding ❸.

2 A PVC stub protects UF cable as it emerges from the ground.

3 Strap rigid PVC pipe (with LB condulet) to the outbuilding.

WORKING WITH PVC CONDUIT

PVC conduit can be heated and bent, allowing you to change pipe direction with far less cutting and fewer fittings than you would need for rigid pipe. PVC conduit is intended to be used outside: It is flexible, durable, and waterproof; but its assemblies are not as protective as metal pipe or cable. Be sure to use only the gray PVC conduit rated for electrical work (also called schedule-40 PVC conduit). White PVC plumbing pipe is unsuitable as electrical conduit; moreover, heating it can release noxious fumes. Wear work gloves to avoid burns when heating gray PVC pipe.

It's best to use a hacksaw with a metal-cutting blade to cut PVC pipe, though any fine-tooth saw will work. Make the cut as square as possible. Use a pocket knife or curved file to remove burrs from the pipe end, then wipe it with a rag. Apply an even coat of PVC cement to the outside of the pipe and the inside of the fitting. If you're bending pipe, screw the threaded adaptor into the outdoor box or conduit first, then glue the bent pipe to the adapter.

To bend PVC pipe, heat it with a MAP-gas torch; one common brand is the Bernz-Omatic®. You can also use a hot box or a

PVC heating blanket (Greenlee®). Keep the torch point moving constantly, rotate the pipe periodically, and tape the pipe ends to contain the heat and speed up the process. When the pipe droops, it's ready to shape. Place it against an irregular wall or foundation and it will conform to that contour. Strap the pipe close to the outdoor box and the foundation. To secure straps to the foundation, first predrill with a masonry bit. Then insert expandable plastic anchors into the holes and drive strap screws into the anchors.

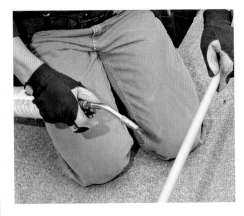

To bend PVC pipe, heat it with a handheld MAP-gas torch. Rotate the pipe and keep the torch moving to heat the pipe evenly.

When the heated PVC pipe begins to droop, you know it's ready to bend. Shape it to fit the side of the building or foundation.

Use straps to secure the pipe to exterior walls and foundations.

INSTALLING LOW-VOLTAGE PATH LIGHTS

Low-voltage lights make nighttime paths and walkways safer, are easy to install, and pose almost no shock threat. However, turn power off to the circuit you'll be working on to be doubly sure. Always follow the installation instructions that come with your low-voltage kit. Kits usually include light assemblies, lo-vo cable, posts, ground stakes, and a timer-transformer power pack whose transformer reduces house current from 120v to 12v.

In the installation shown here, the power pack was mounted inside the garage, so PVC conduit was installed to protect the lo-vo cable as it traveled up the exterior wall into the garage. If you install the power pack outside, you probably won't need conduit. If you do install conduit, start by inserting a fish tape down the conduit ❶. Separate the two wires in the lo-vo cable, snip one, loop and tape the remaining wire to the fish tape, and pull the lo-vo cable through the conduit.

Place the lights where they'll best illuminate a walkway or highlight a landscape feature, then run the lo-vo cable to them ❷. Run cable along the ground and cover it with a few inches of mulch, or use a square-nosed shovel to create a shallow slot for the cable. Stomp on the shovel so it goes down 4 in., then rock the shovel from side to side to create a V-shaped slot ❸. Press the cable into the slot ❹; then stamp your feet to close the soil over the cable.

>> >> >>

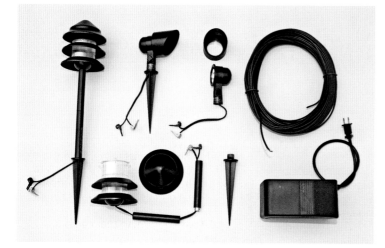

Lo-vo light kits typically contain **screw-together parts: lamps, shades, riser posts, and ground stakes.** At right: a coil of lo-vo cable and a power pack—a combination timer and transformer to step down voltage to 12v.

1 After installing PVC conduit, insert a fish tape down the conduit and pull the wires through.

2 Place the lights and run the cable to each of them.

3 Use a square-nosed shovel to create a small slot to bury the cable.

4 Press the lo-vo cable into the slot, making sure that it's fully covered.

INSTALLING LOW-VOLTAGE PATH LIGHTS (CONTINUED)

Each light fixture has two wire leads that terminate in sharp-pointed cable connectors. When snapped together, the connectors pierce the insulation of the lo-vo wires and supply each light with 12v current **5**. To power the system, attach lo-vo cable wires to the terminals on the power pack **6**. Mount the power pack securely to the wall and plug it into the outlet. Power packs are equipped with timers so that the lights come on and turn off whenever you like—whether you're home or away **7**.

5 Connectors are used to join the cable in the ground to each light.

6 Attach the wires of the lo-vo cable to transformer terminals. (Power is off.)

7 Once hung, plug the power pack into a nearby outlet and set the timer.

LOW-VOLTAGE LIGHT PARTS

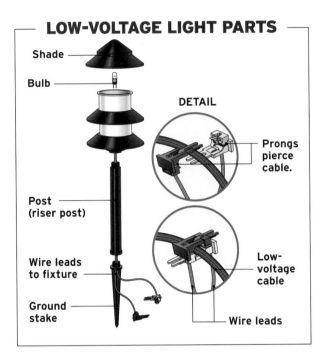

Shade

Bulb

DETAIL

Prongs pierce cable.

Post (riser post)

Low-voltage cable

Wire leads to fixture

Ground stake

Wire leads

RUNNING LO-VO CABLE UNDER A SIDEWALK

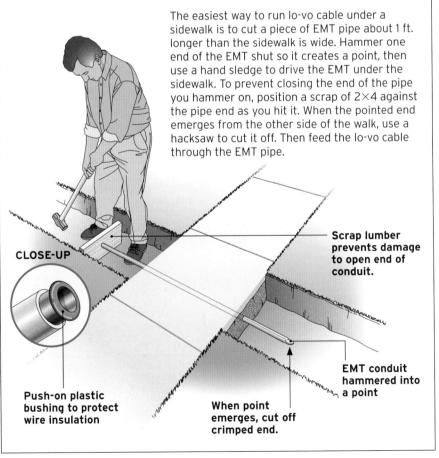

The easiest way to run lo-vo cable under a sidewalk is to cut a piece of EMT pipe about 1 ft. longer than the sidewalk is wide. Hammer one end of the EMT shut so it creates a point, then use a hand sledge to drive the EMT under the sidewalk. To prevent closing the end of the pipe you hammer on, position a scrap of 2×4 against the pipe end as you hit it. When the pointed end emerges from the other side of the walk, use a hacksaw to cut it off. Then feed the lo-vo cable through the EMT pipe.

Scrap lumber prevents damage to open end of conduit.

CLOSE-UP

Push-on plastic bushing to protect wire insulation

When point emerges, cut off crimped end.

EMT conduit hammered into a point

INSTALLING A MOTION-SENSOR LIGHT

Motion-sensor lights require 120v and must be mounted on boxes rated for outdoor use. The fixture must be listed for damp locations if installed under eaves, or listed for wet locations if directly exposed to weather. Exterior boxes should have flexible gaskets between the box and the fixture base and threaded openings with closure plugs. If the box has only standard knockouts, it is not raintight.

In the sequence shown here, we installed a Defiant® motion security light. Closely follow the installation instructions that came with your light.

If there is an existing fixture, cut power to it and test with a noncontact tester to be sure it is off. Unscrew the mounting screws and gently pull the old fixture away from the box ❶. Be careful not to touch exposed wires. Then, using a probe tester, test the wire splices. When you are certain the wires are not energized, disconnect the splices. If the existing junction box is damaged or inappropriate, replace it.

Screw the new light's mounting bracket to the box ❷. Feed the supply wires through the hole in the wiring plate. Screw the plate to the threaded hole in the middle of the bracket ❸. Connect the ground wire from the junction box to the ground screw on the wiring plate ❹. Insert the neutral wire and the hot wire into the appropriate terminals ❺ and tighten the terminal-block screws to secure the wires. (If the wire ends are not straight, you may want to cut and re-strip them first.)

To secure the light fixture to the wiring plate, align the posts on the plate to the corresponding holes in the fixture ❻. Then bolt the fixture securely. At this point you may want to adjust the lamp heads and the motion sensor below ❼. Now you can download the Defiant app onto a smartphone and follow the prompts to pair the light to the app, adjust the light settings, and test the sensor.

1 Unscrew the mounting screws and gently pull the existing fixture away from the box.

2 Screw the new light's mounting bracket to the junction box.

3 Feed incoming wires through the wiring plate and screw it to the bracket.

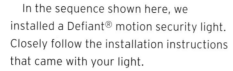

4 Attach the ground wire to the ground screw on the wiring plate.

5 Insert and tighten the neutral and hot wires to the terminals on the wiring plate.

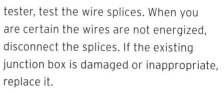

6 Align the posts on the plate to the holes on the back of the fixture, then bolt the fixture securely.

7 Adjust the lamp heads and the motion sensor below.

EV HOME CHARGING DOCKS

As electric vehicles (EVs) have become increasingly widespread, so has a misconception about the wall-mounted boxes used to charge them. Almost everyone calls the boxes "EV chargers," but the charger is actually inside the car, where it converts AC power to the DC needed to charge the car's battery pack. Technically, the box is "Electric Vehicle Service Equipment (EVSE)"–which we'll call an EV charging dock.

Once you get beyond the jargon and competing claims of companies that make EVSEs, you soon realize that EV charging docks are the safest way to send power to an EV's onboard charger. The EVSE communicates with the EV and, when it is safe, starts the flow of electrical current to the car. Once you know which features are essential, choosing a charging dock is not that difficult. However, you should hire a licensed electrician to install your EVSE.

The J1772 standard

The J1772 connector is an industry-standard connector that fits all electric vehicles except for Tesla® models, whose proprietary connector enables Tesla owners to use its network of superchargers. However, Tesla does provide an adaptor that enables car owners to use standard J1772 connectors.

In addition to a five-pin configuration isolated within the connector, the J1772 standard also includes several levels of shock protection and the ability to communicate with the vehicle. In other words, no electricity flows until the vehicle (EV) tells the EVSE to do so via the J1772 connector.

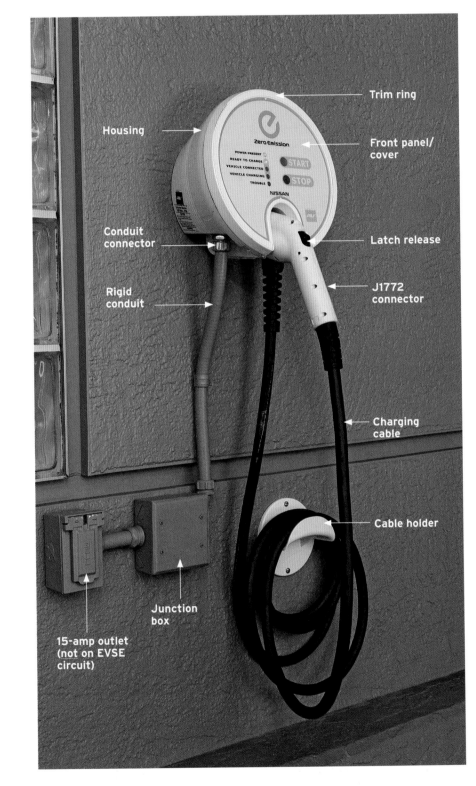

Housing

Trim ring

Front panel/ cover

Conduit connector

Latch release

Rigid conduit

J1772 connector

Charging cable

Cable holder

Junction box

15-amp outlet (not on EVSE circuit)

CHOOSING AN EV CHARGING DOCK

Check the auto manufacturer's charging specifications for your EV, which you'll find in the owner's instruction booklet or on the metal nameplate of your car. If you have not yet decided which electric vehicle to buy or are thinking of getting an EV with greater capacity, things can get a bit more complicated.

Several factors determine how quickly you can charge your electric vehicle:

■ *The type of EV you have:* a plug-in hybrid electric vehicle (PHEV) such as a Toyota Prius® or a Chevrolet Volt®, which still have gasoline engines, or an all-electric car (BEV), which relies wholly on its batteries, such as the Nissan Leaf®.

■ *The capacity of your EV's battery pack,* expressed in kilowatt-hours (kWh). The capacity of the battery pack determines how far you can drive solely on electricity –also referred to as your car's "electrical autonomy" or driving range. The bigger the battery pack, the greater the range and the longer it can take to charge your EV.

■ *The power of your EV's on-board charger,* expressed in kilowatts (kW). Basically, the onboard charger determines the speed of electrical flow into your battery pack. This factor is also called the "vehicle acceptance rate."

■ *Whether you use a Level I or Level II charging dock.* Level I docks run at 120v and charge slowly, typically delivering 1.4 to 1.8 kW, whereas Level II charging docks installed in the home typically run 240v and deliver 3.8 to 7.2 kW. Level II charging docks in commercial areas typically run at 208v, delivering 6.0 to 6.2 kW (although depending upon the installation they may deliver higher kW).

The chart below gives an idea of the interplay of these factors.

Keeping it simple

No matter what level of charging dock you install, your car will only charge as fast as the capacity of its onboard charger. For example, the Nissan Leaf comes standard with a 3.3 kW charger (upgradeable to 6.6 kW) and the Ford Focus® comes standard with a 6.6 kW charger. For optimal use, make sure that whatever charging dock solution you use has at least the capacity to deliver kW at the level your car can handle. For most EVs, that is a Level II dock. That said, your driving habits may be a determining factor. Here are two scenarios:

Scenario one. Most plug-in EVs come with a portable Level I charging set supplied by the auto maker. The set consists of a compact control box with two cords running out of it: a short cord with a standard three-prong household plug, and a longer cord (15 ft. to 20 ft.) that terminates in a J1772 connector that fits most electrical vehicles. >> >> >>

HOW LONG DOES IT TAKE TO CHARGE AN ELECTRIC VEHICLE?

Charging Level	Power Supply	Charger Power	Miles of Range for 1 Hour of Charge	Charging Times from Empty to Full*	
				BEV	PHEV
Level 1	120VAC Single Phase	1.4 kW @ 12 amp (onboard charger)	3-4 miles	17 hours	7 Hours
Level 2	240VAC Single Phase up to 19.2 kW (up to 80 amps)	3.3 kW (onboard)	8-10 miles	7 hours	3 Hours
		6.6+ kW (onboard)	17-20 miles	3.5 hours	1.4 Hours
DC Fast Charge Level 2	200-450 VDC up to 90 kW (approximately 200 amps)	45 kW (offboard)	50-60 miles (80% per 0.5 hr charge)	30-45 Minutes (to 80%)	10 Minutes (to 80%)

Source: California PEV Collaborative (CG303).
*SAE "Charging Configurations and Rating Terminology," Society of Automotive Engineers Hybrid Committee version 031611, 2011.
SAE Assumptions: BEV = 25 kWh usable battery; PHEV = 8 kWh usable battery; calculations reviewed and edited by EPRI.

Battery Electric Vehicle (BEV) assumes a 25 kWh usable battery pack size; for purposes of this table, SAE data reflect a charging scenario of "empty to full" where charging starts at 20% State of Charge (SOC) and will stop at 100% SOC.

Plug-in Hybrid Electric Vehicle (PHEV) assumes an 8 kWh usable battery pack size; charging starts from 0% SOC since the hybrid mode is available.

CHOOSING AN EV CHARGING DOCK (CONTINUED)

If you drive only 30 to 40 miles per day—and have a PHEV—an overnight charge from a Level I charging kit should meet your needs. Or if you have a BEV with a driving range of 100 miles and usually drive only half that distance, your batteries will be only half depleted, so, here again, an overnight charge from a Level I home dock should charge you fully.

According to one study, roughly a third of EV owners rely on Level I home docks.

Scenario two. For optimal use, we recommend installing a Level II, 30-amp home charging dock if you can afford to do so. (See "Costs and Incentives" on the facing page.) As you can see in the chart on p. 255, 30-amp service can enable you to add roughly 20 miles of driving range in about an hour. So, even if you drive greater distances during the day, a faster charge could enable you to enjoy a night out instead of sitting home waiting for your EV to recharge.

A 30-amp Level II dock should also give you the future capacity you'll need if you upgrade to an EV with a greater range. Moreover, EV battery packs and driving ranges are almost certain to increase. Nissan, for example, recently upped the driving range of a Leaf model (30 kWh) to 155 miles, after years of hovering near the 100-mile mark.

Plug-and-play or hard-wired?

If your home charging dock is a Level I plug-in and will be located outside, say, under a carport that is open to the weather, local building codes will require that the dock be served by a GFCI-protected, dedicated circuit, and the receptacle will need a weather-tight-in-use cover. Otherwise, it will need to be hard-wired by means and methods suitable for exposure to weather.

Level II plug-and-play chargers (portable cordsets) are recommended only for indoor (garage-type) applications. Exterior Level II applications should be hard wired with means and methods suitable for exposure to weather. Level II plug-and-play charging units usually come with a pigtail (pre-attached cord and plug) that you can plug directly into a NEMA 6-50R receptacle. Later on, if you move to a new home, you can easily take a plug-and-play dock with you. Hard-wired charging docks, by contrast, tend to be better looking—neater and more compact. At the end of this chapter, we show

INSTALLING A LEVEL II, 240VAC HOME CHARGING DOCK

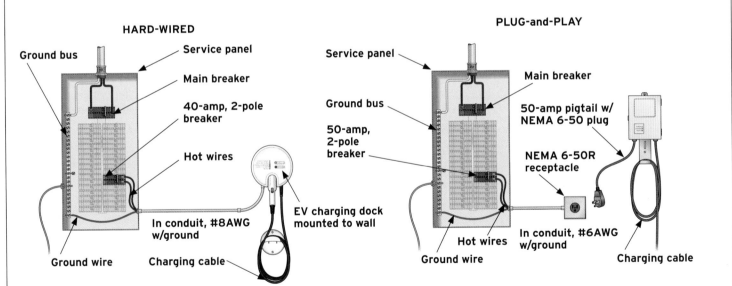

Hard-wired charging dock. Most Level II EV charging docks are 30 amp (240VAC). They should be protected by a 40-amp, two-pole breaker, with a minimum wire size of #8AWG—often run in conduit from the electrical panel to the home charging dock. Inside the dock, the two hot wires terminate to a hot-terminal block; the ground wire terminates to a grounding strip or terminal. Follow the installation instructions of your home charging dock.

Plug-and-play charging dock. 240VAC, Level II EV charging docks often come with a 50-amp pigtail that plugs into a NEMA 6-50R receptacle. Although plug-and-play docks also run at 30-amps (depending on the EV), many manufacturers upsize the pigtail to 50 amps as a safety margin. So if your plug-and-play dock has a 50-amp pigtail, it makes sense to upsize the breaker to 50 amps and to run #6AWG wire from the panel to the receptacle. *Note:* If your portable cordset is a Level I charging dock, it will plug into a GFCI-protected 120-volt receptacle—typically, a NEMA 6-20R.

installing a hard-wired AeroVironment®
home charging dock, in which conductors
attach directly to terminals inside the unit.

Costs and incentives

Level II, 30-amp EVSEs (hard-wired or
plug-and-play) from reputable makers such
as GE®, Leviton, Bosch®, Clipper Creek™,
Schneider Electric®, or AeroVironment cost
$600 to $1,000. Because of competition
from Internet vendors, prices are coming
down, but slowly. First-time EV buyers are
understandably cautious, so they often buy
the EVSE recommended by the car dealer,
along with an installation package, but they
pay a premium for this service.

It's tough to estimate the cost of an installation. For starters, the location of a dock
greatly impacts the cost of installing it. If
you install your EVSE in a garage with a service panel or subpanel nearby, it should be
relatively inexpensive to run electrical cable
or conduit from the panel to the device.

However, if your home has an older
60-amp to 100-amp electrical service and
you want to install a Level II charging dock,
you may need to upgrade the service to
200-amps, which could cost $2,000 or more.
You might want to have an electrician inspect
your home's electrical system and calculate
loads (p. 180) before you buy an electrical
vehicle. Some installers can perform a load
calculation if you send them a photo of your
panel and answer a few questions.

In addition, there may be municipal fees
for an EVSE installation permit and utility
charges to install a second meter to monitor
your EV's energy usage. In some states,

**Charging docks come largely prewired to ease
installation and enhance safety.**

that second meter will allow you to charge
your EV at discounted rates during off-
peak hours.

At this writing (2017), there are many
incentives that benefit EV owners. Under
the Federal Tax Credit for Alternative Fuel
Infrastructure, homeowners who install an
EVSE are eligible for a tax credit of 30% of
the cost, not to exceed $30,000. In Califor-
nia, Property-Assessed Clean Energy (PACE)
financing allows property owners to bor-
row funds to pay for energy improvements,
including purchasing and installing an EVSE.
The borrower repays over a defined period
of time through a special assessment on the
property.

Local utility companies often offer incentives to reduce energy use during peak
hours. Go online to learn more, and be
sure to include business incentives in your
search: Farmers Insurance®, for example,
offers a 10% discount on major coverages
for people who drive hybrids and other
alternative fuel vehicles. Two good places to
start looking: www.pevcollaborative.org and
www.driveclean.ca.gov.

Wi-Fi EVSEs? No thanks.

Although gener-
ally bullish about
smartphone
control, we'll pass
on Wi-Fi-enabled
charging docks.
Their timers,
meters, and touch
screens generally
duplicate moni-
toring functions
already available on
your car.

Meeting code requirements

Most municipalities require homeowners to
apply for a permit before installing an EVSE.
In many cases you can apply online, typically
through the city building department. Permit
applications vary widely but most require
these four pieces of documentation:

- *A plot plan* that shows the proposed location of the EVSE parking space in relation
  to existing buildings, structures, and other
  parking spaces.
- *Electrical load calculations* showing that
  the home's electrical system can handle
  the additional load of the proposed EV
  charging dock.
- *Electrical diagrams* showing the service
  panel, where the EVSE connects to the
  power, and the location of the home charging dock.
- *EVSE charging specifications*, as spelled
  out in the manufacturer's installation
  instructions.

Once the permit has been issued and
the EVSE has been installed, you'll need
to schedule an inspection by the building

department. *Note:* Your municipality may insist that the EVSE installation be done by a licensed electrician. Although local building codes vary, electrical inspections are generally based upon the most recent National Electrical Code (NEC).

Here are a few NEC requirements relevant to EVSEs (see NEC Article 625 for more):

- All EVSE equipment must be listed and labeled according to NEC specifications.
- Level I EVSE: A 15-amp or 20-amp standard residential outlet is acceptable for 120-volt charging; the circuit to be protected by a 15-amp or 20-amp single-pole circuit breaker.
- Level II EVSE: A dedicated circuit is required for any 240-volt EV charging dock; the circuit to be protected by a 30-amp to 50-amp, two-pole circuit breaker. (*Note:* Some fast-charging vehicles will require larger circuit breakers; follow manufacturer's specifications.)

- EVSE connectors must comply with Society of Automotive Engineers standard J1772.
- EVSE equipment must have the capability to detect and interrupt current flow when unsafe conditions exist, the vehicle or batteries are damaged, charging cords become excessively strained, or the vehicle becomes disconnected from the charging dock.

PRO TIP
If you'll be plugging your Level I dock into a 15-amp or 20-amp receptacle, upgrade it to a heavy-duty (spec-grade) receptacle. Cheap, residential-grade receptacles won't stand up to repeated insertions.

Sizing EVSE breakers *Always follow the EVSE manufacturer's recommended circuit breaker size.* As a rule of thumb, the breaker controlling an EVSE circuit must be rated 25 percent higher than the rating of the charging dock's output. Thus a 30-amp Level II charging dock requires a circuit protected by at least a 40-amp breaker. A 40-amp Level II charging dock (which many fast-charging EV models require) should be protected by a 50-amp circuit breaker.

INSTALLING A HARD-WIRED CHARGING DOCK

In this sequence, we show the installation of a hard-wired Level II, 240VAC charging dock made by AeroVironment. We chose this model because the company has a history of making such devices stretching back to its collaboration with GM on the first viable electric vehicle, the EV1. AeroVironment's ability to understand the safety features consumers need and the quality automakers expect have made it the brand of choice for eight major auto companies.

Note: Always follow the installation instructions that come with your charging dock. To ensure a safe and successful installation, we recommend that you hire a licensed electrician familiar with home charging docks to install yours. (Accordingly, when we say "you" in the following sections, we are referring to the installer/

electrician.) Lastly, all work must be done on *unenergized wiring—with the power not yet connected.* Installing the circuit breaker and powering the circuit is the last step of the installation.

First steps

Begin by assessing the capacity of your electrical system to support the additional full load of a Level II charging dock without any demand factor (see "Is the System Adequately Sized?," p. 180). If your electrical service is 100A or smaller, you will probably need to upgrade your service. Also make sure you have space in your service panel to add a two-pole circuit breaker.

When the assessment is complete, apply for a permit to begin the installation, as described in "Meeting code requirements"

on p. 257. If you live in a region where electric utilities encourage the use of EVs by offering special rates for overnight charging, contact your utility about installing a second meter to monitor your dock's energy use.

Locating the charging dock

The location for your charging dock should satisfy two criteria. First, it should be close to your EV's parking space. Docks come with charging cords up to 25 ft. long, but the closer your car is to the charger, the less likely that you will trip over or damage the cord. If you have two EVs, roughly center the dock between the vehicles' parking spaces.

The second criterion is that the dock be as close as possible to the power source, to minimize the expense of running armored cable or conduit from the service panel to the charging dock. As panels are frequently installed inside a garage, locating the dock is often easy.

Although most charging docks are designed to be weatherproof, installing yours indoors or otherwise protecting it from the weather will optimize your convenience. Many manufacturers also recommend that charging docks not be installed near external heat sources, such as water heaters or furnaces, or in direct sunlight.

Charging docks must be securely mounted to a wall stud, to a masonry wall, or to a firmly anchored post. In the shipping carton that contains the EVSE, manufacturers typically provide several kinds of fasteners, including anchors for bolting devices to masonry walls. Installation instructions will also specify which tools you will need.

Running wire, mounting the device

Run conductors (wires) from the service panel to the charging dock location, using armored cable (p. 220) or THHN/THWN wires pulled through rigid conduit (p. 223). But do not install a circuit breaker yet. Allow enough extra wire so that you can pull it easily and terminate it inside the EVSE housing. Your EVSE installation guide will specify the size and number of conductors you need to run. Most 240VAC charging docks require three conductors —two hot wires and a ground—but a few devices, such as Tesla's, also require a neutral and thus, four conductors.

Pull wire. If you are pulling #12 or #10 wire, $1/2$-in. conduit can accommodate three conductors; if pulling #8 or #6 wire, use $3/4$-in. conduit. At our site, there was already $3/4$-in. conduit running to a nearby junction box, so after disconnecting power to the box we removed a knockout, added a length of conduit, and pulled three conductors up to the dock location: two #8 conductors and one #10.   >> >> >>

EV CIRCUIT PROTECTION

Size of EV Charger Circuit Breaker	Required Minimum Size of Conductors (THNN wire)
20 amp	#12
30 amp	#10
40 amp	#8
50 amp	#8
60 amp	#6
70 amp	#6

Note: If a run is long, the wire may need to be upsized to compensate for voltage drop.

Carefully open the box that contains your EVSE, noting any damaged or missing parts. (Check parts against the enclosed parts list.) If you find damage, photograph it with your cell phone. Save the box and shipping materials in case you need to return the EVSE or file a claim for shipping damage.

When you open your charging dock's box, check parts against the invoice and use your cell phone to photograph any damage.

Because there was a junction box near the proposed EVSE location, the electrician disconnected power to the box, removed a knockout, added a length of conduit, and pulled three conductors up to the dock location. A nearby receptacle was on a separate circuit.

INSTALLING A HARD-WIRED CHARGING DOCK (CONTINUED)

Remove knockouts. Next, determine how conductors will enter the dock, which usually has several entry points (knockouts). If your wiring will run inside wood-framed walls, it will most likely emerge behind the charging dock: Remove the knockout on the back of the dock. If your wiring will run inside conduit surface-mounted to the wall—as ours was—remove a knockout on the underside of the dock. Important: Per code, remove only one knockout or seal unused but removed knockouts.

Mount the EVSE. Mounting details vary. Some EVSEs have a metal mounting plate that bolts to the wall, to which the dock attaches. Others are bolted to the wall through holes in the back of the dock housing. In either case, plumb the dock, insert a pencil, and trace the mounting holes onto the wall. If it's a stud wall, you'll know that holes are over a stud; if a masonry wall, drill in the center of the traced holes and insert bolt anchors. Use the washered bolts provided to secure the mounting plate or the dock housing to the wall.

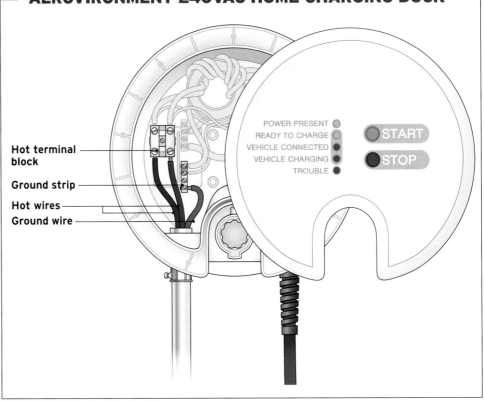

AEROVIRONMENT 240VAC HOME CHARGING DOCK

Hot terminal block

Ground strip

Hot wires

Ground wire

POWER PRESENT
READY TO CHARGE
VEHICLE CONNECTED
VEHICLE CHARGING
TROUBLE

START
STOP

Because the conduit made several tight turns within a short distance, the electrician used a woven fiberglass pulling tape to pull wires into the body of the charging dock.

Again, closely follow the mounting instructions for your charging dock. The AeroVironment Level II dock we installed gives installers the option of disconnecting a pilot wire inside the housing to better access a mounting hole.

Wiring the EVSE

If wires (conductors from the service panel) enter a knockout in the back of the charging dock, remove the dock cover and pull them into the dock housing before mounting the dock. Pull in enough wire so that you don't have to make sharp bends to reach the terminal blocks; sharp bends can constrict wire and stress connections.

If wires run through conduit and enter a knockout on the underside of the dock, as shown in the photo at left, secure the conduit connector to the knockout, then pull wires into the dock housing. A metal fish tape is often used to pull conductors

through conduit (p. 225), but here we used a woven fiberglass pulling tape (Muletape® is one brand) because we had several tight turns within a short distance and didn't want to get hung up. (*Note:* In some cases the installer may need to make a hole at the back of the bottom of the housing, depending on the conduit location entrance.)

Terminate wires. Trim wire ends evenly and strip about 3/8 in. of insulation from the ends. Connect the ground wire to the ground strip inside the charging dock; then connect the two hot wires to the hot-terminal block. Use a calibrated torque screwdriver (torque wrench) to tighten terminal screws to manufacturer's specs; in our case 20 in./lb.

Before you secure the cover of the charging dock, make sure that all wires are safely within the housing so they won't get pinched by the cover. Tighten the cover screws by hand so the screws don't strip the plastic

Using a torque screwdriver or wrench, **connect the green ground wire(s) to the ground strip inside the dock,** and then **connect the two hot wires to the hot-terminal block.**

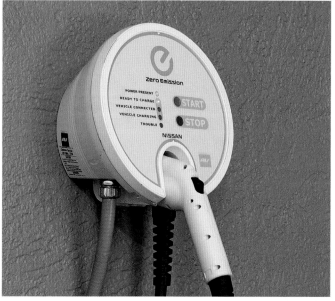

When all connections are complete and the cover is secured, install the circuit breaker and power the circuit. Green lights should indicate that the EVSE is ready to charge.

The J1772 connector is an industry-standard connector that fits all electric vehicles except for Teslas. Tesla provides an adaptor that allows car owners to use a J1772 connector.

components of the charging dock. Install trim rings and the like.

Mount the cable hanger to the wall, roughly 1 ft. below the charging dock. For the best appearance, vertically align the center of the cable hanger with the center of the dock.

Powering up

When connections inside the charging dock are complete and the cover is secure, install the 40-amp two-pole circuit breaker in the service panel; this breaker controls the dedicated circuit that powers the 240VAC, Level II charging dock. Once panel connections are complete, turn the breaker switch on to power the circuit.

At this point, two green lights on the cover of the EVSE should indicate "Power Present" and "Ready to Charge." The installation guide will then walk you through a self-test to make sure that the EVSE is correctly wired and functioning properly. That done, you're ready to schedule an inspection.

The Code, EVSEs, and GFCI protection

If you are plugging a Level I charging dock into a 15-amp or 20-amp receptacle in your garage, by Code that outlet must be GFCI protected (pp. 14 and 40). However, if you are installing a 240v, Level II charging dock, Code does not require GFCI protection for its circuit. Properly installed, a Level II EVSE is safe because inherent GFCI protection is part of the J1772 protocol for EV charging stations. In other words, GFCI protection is wired into the device.

PANELS & SUBPANELS

THIS CHAPTER RECAPS THE BASICS of electrical service; then shows how to create a neat, well-organized panel; install a one-pole breaker (for general-use, lighting, and small-appliance circuits); install a two-pole breaker (for large-appliance circuits); install AFCI and GFCI breakers; and set up a subpanel.

Caution: Only a licensed electrician should work inside an electrical panel. There are several reasons for this caution:

- In service panels, there is an area above the main breaker that stays energized even after that breaker is set to an OFF position (p. 264).
- There is no easy way for a nonprofessional to be sure that an existing system is correctly grounded. In some cases, just removing a panel cover is risky.
- Local building codes may specify that any upgrade requiring a permit be done by a licensed electrician.
- Work not done by a licensed electrician may nullify appliance or equipment warranties or even void your homeowner's insurance should a mishap occur.

UNDERSTANDING PANELS

ADDING A CIRCUIT

INSTALLING A SUBPANEL

UNDERSTANDING SERVICE PANELS & SUBPANELS

PERSONAL PROTECTION EQUIPMENT

A qualified person testing or working in a potentially energized electrical panel must wear personal protection equipment (PPE) as specified in NFPA 70E® PPE Hazard Level 1, Table 130.7 (C) (16). "The PPE requirements of 130.7 are intended to protect a person from arc flash and shock hazards." This protective equipment includes the following:

- Hard hat
- Arc-rated long-sleeve shirt and pants or arc-rated coverall
- Arc-rated face shield or arc flash suit hood
- Safety glasses or safety goggles
- Hearing protection (ear canal inserts)
- Heavy-duty leather gloves (over) rubber insulating gloves
- Leather work shoes

Reproduced with permission from NFPA70E-2012, *Electrical Safety in the Workplace*, Copyright© 2011, National Fire Protection Association. This reprinted material is not the complete and official position of the NFPA on the referenced subject, which is represented only by the standard in its entirety.

SAFETY WARNING

In service panels, a small area around the main breaker stays hot even after the breaker is set to the off position. The only way to cut *all* power in a service panel is to pull the meter—which we don't recommend and which is illegal in many jurisdictions. Typically, only the utility company can cut a meter seal or pull a meter.

Avoid touching the service conductors that attach to the main breaker—they stay hot even when the main breaker is turned off.

LOCK 'EM OUT!

Once you've shut off power in a service panel, tape the panel shut and post a warning sign of work in progress. Pros prefer to use a *panel lockout*, however, which limits panel access to the person holding the key; electrical suppliers and home centers sell them.

P ower from the utility company is typically delivered through three large conductors, which may enter the house overhead or underground. Overhead service wires are called a *service drop*. The drop runs to a *weatherhead* atop a length of rigid conduit. When fed underground, service conductors are installed in buried conduit or run as underground service-entrance (USE) cable.

Whether it arrives overhead or underground, 3-wire service consists of a service neutral and two energized (hot) service conductors—which are also called *Service Phase A and Service Phase B*—two phases of alternating current (AC). Three-wire service delivers 120v relative to ground, and 240v between the energized conductors.

>> >> >>

⚠ SAFETY ALERT
If you are at all uncertain whether a panel is energized, do not remove its cover. Call a licensed electrician. Many jurisdictions forbid panel work by nonlicensed electricians.

TESTING: THE KEY TO WORKING SAFELY

Always turn off the power **before working on an electrical system. If you are working in a subpanel, turn off the subpanel disconnect in the service panel.**

First test the noncontact tester on a receptacle or device that you know is hot. Here, the tester indicates that subpanel breakers are energized.

Test breakers after power to the subpanel has been shut off.

Carefully remove the subpanel cover **and touch the tester to the insulated portion of a hot feed or to a main lug.**

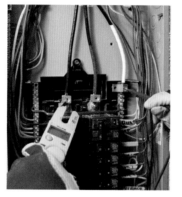

Use a multimeter, a more sensitive tester, to verify earlier readings. First touch tester probes to Phase A lug (hot) and to the neutral bus.

Test Phase B lug (hot) and the neutral bus.

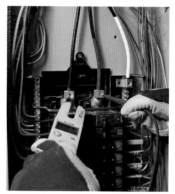

Test Phase A lug and Phase B lug. If the tester shows no voltage on any of these tests, the subpanel is de-energized and safe to work in.

Cut power inside a service panel by switching off the main breaker, or by removing the main fuse in a fuse box. This de-energizes the hot buses. *Note:* Incoming hot service conductors—and the lugs where they terminate—will still be energized—as shown on the facing page. Unscrew the panel cover and set it aside.

To cut power to a subpanel, flip off the subpanel breaker in the service panel—and lock the service panel so no one can turn the subpanel breaker back on. That should de-energize the subpanel so it can be safely opened and worked in.

But *always test, never guess.* As shown above, we recommend using two testers.

TESTING WITH A NONCONTACT TESTER

Start with a noncontact tester, which can detect voltage through wire insulation. First test the tester to make sure it is working correctly.

Before removing the subpanel cover, touch the tester to several breakers in the ON position. If the tester tip doesn't glow, the panel is probably dead. But keep testing to be sure: Remove the cover and test again inside the panel. Touch the tester to insulated portions of the two main feeds, and to the main lugs.

TESTING WITH A MULTIMETER

Test lugs with a multimeter. Be careful not to touch the bare-metal probes of this tool. Set your multimeter on AC VOLTAGE and touch its probes to hot and neutral *bus lugs* in this sequence:

■ Phase A lug (hot) to neutral lug
■ Phase B lug (hot) to neutral lug
■ Phase A (hot) to Phase B (hot)

If all of these tests do not detect voltage, you can work safely in the subpanel.

UNDERSTANDING SERVICE PANELS & SUBPANELS (CONTINUED)

THREE-WIRE SERVICE DROP

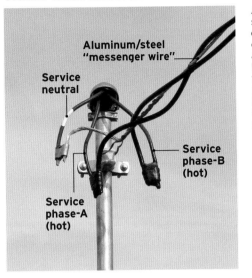

Aluminum/steel "messenger wire"

Service neutral

Service phase-A (hot)

Service phase-B (hot)

A typical 3-wire service drop **consists of two insulated hot conductors wrapped around a stranded bare aluminum wire with an internal steel messenger cable—the bare aluminum wire also serves as a neutral.**

SERVICE ENTRANCES

Older homes may have overhead service, but underground service is increasingly common. The utility's responsibility ends where the service-drop cables are spliced to the service conductors running to the meter. In some areas, Code requires that underground conductors be housed in conduit.

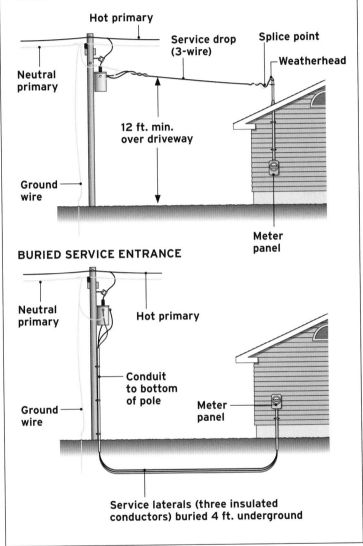

AERIAL SERVICE ENTRANCE

Hot primary

Service drop (3-wire)

Splice point

Weatherhead

Neutral primary

12 ft. min. over driveway

Ground wire

Meter panel

BURIED SERVICE ENTRANCE

Neutral primary

Hot primary

Ground wire

Conduit to bottom of pole

Meter panel

Service laterals (three insulated conductors) buried 4 ft. underground

SERVICE ENTRANCE TO THE EAVES SIDE

When the service drop approaches over eaves, the service riser is sent up through the eaves and the point at which the riser emerges from the roof jack is caulked.

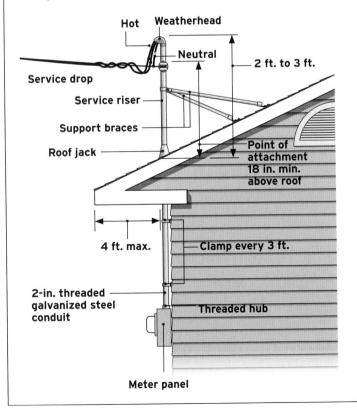

Hot Weatherhead

Neutral

2 ft. to 3 ft.

Service drop

Service riser

Support braces

Roof jack

Point of attachment 18 in. min. above roof

4 ft. max.

Clamp every 3 ft.

2-in. threaded galvanized steel conduit

Threaded hub

Meter panel

POWER TO THE PANEL

PANELS, SUBPANELS & CONDUCTORS

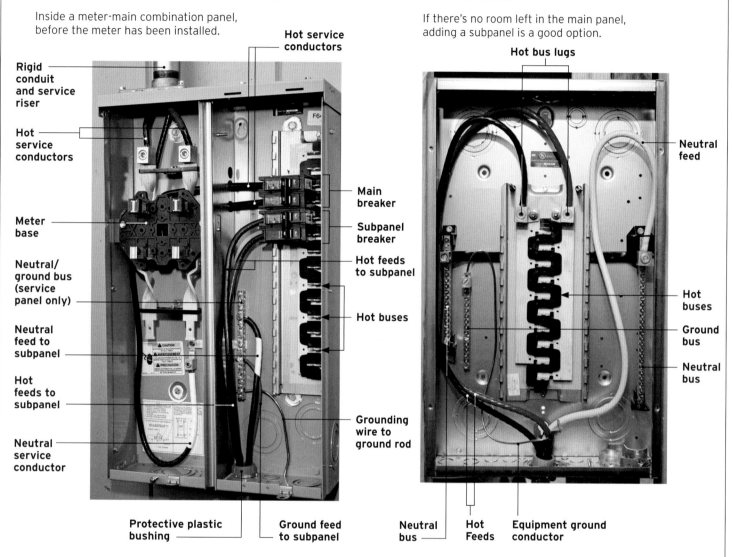

Inside a meter-main combination panel, before the meter has been installed.

If there's no room left in the main panel, adding a subpanel is a good option.

Rigid conduit and service riser

Hot service conductors

Hot service conductors

Main breaker

Subpanel breaker

Meter base

Hot feeds to subpanel

Neutral/ ground bus (service panel only)

Hot buses

Neutral feed to subpanel

Hot feeds to subpanel

Neutral service conductor

Grounding wire to ground rod

Hot bus lugs

Neutral feed

Hot buses

Ground bus

Neutral bus

Protective plastic bushing

Ground feed to subpanel

Neutral bus

Hot Feeds

Equipment ground conductor

Service conductors run to a meter base, where they attach to lug-screws (lugs) on the *line side* of the meter. When a meter is inserted into the base, power flows to the *load-side* meter lugs, and then on to a main disconnect (main breaker) in the *service panel*. As it straddles the two sets of terminals on its base, the meter measures the wattage of electricity as it is consumed.

At the service panel, the two hot service conductors from the meter base attach to lugs on the main breaker. The service neutral attaches to the main lug of a neutral/ ground bus. *Important*: In service panels, neutral and ground wires terminate at a shared neutral/ground bus (or buses). However, *in subpanels and all other outlets downstream from the service panel*, ground and neutral components must be electrically isolated from each other. Thus, in a subpanel, neutral wires attach to a neutral bus and ground wires attach to a ground bus— that is, the buses are separate and electrically isolated.

The two hot feeds (Phase A and Phase B) to a panel energize the *hot buses* that run down the middle and distribute power to various branch circuits when breakers are snapped on to the buses and circuit wires are attached to the breakers. The two hot buses, electrically separated by a plastic insulator running between them, are named for the hot feeds that energize them: hence, Phase A bus and a Phase B bus. (We will say more about A and B phases in "Installing a Two-Pole Breaker," p. 276.)

GROUNDING THE SYSTEM

A GROUNDING BUSHING

A grounding bushing can be a very important detail. Usually the teeth of a conduit locknut bite into the metal panel enclosure and establish an effective ground. However, where there are concentric or eccentric knockouts (metal punch-outs held by small welds, as seen in this photo), a good ground often cannot be established. A grounding bushing is used to ensure a good mechanical ground between the conduit and the enclosure. The ground wire that loops through the grounding bushing terminates at the panel's ground bus.

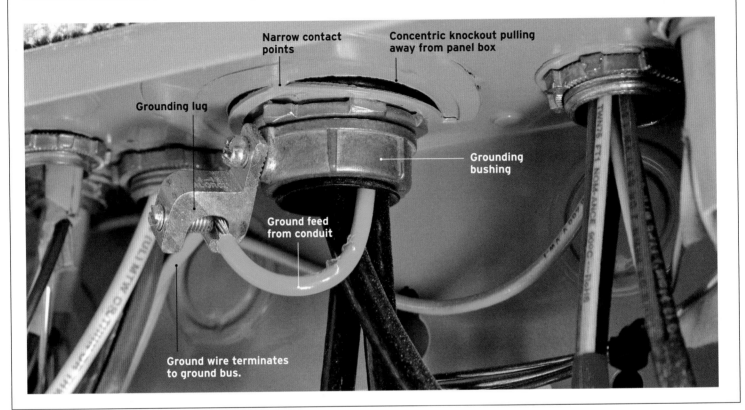

Narrow contact points

Concentric knockout pulling away from panel box

Grounding lug

Grounding bushing

Ground feed from conduit

Ground wire terminates to ground bus.

As explained at length in "Working with Electricity" (p. 4), electricity moves in a circuit, eventually returning to its source unless its path is interrupted. The return path is through the white neutral wires that bring current back to the main panel. Ground wires provide the current with an alternative low-resistance path.

Ground wires (more accurately called *equipment grounding conductors*) connect to every part of the electrical system that could possibly become energized—metal boxes, receptacles, switches, fixtures—and, through three-pronged plugs, the metallic covers and frames of tools and appliances. Ground conductors, usually bare copper or green insulated wire, create an effec-tive path back to the service panel in case the equipment becomes energized. When a breaker detects the excessive flow of a fault current, the breaker trips and shuts off all power to the circuit.

The neutral/ground bus

In the service panel, the ground wires attach to a neutral/ground bus bar, which is bonded to the metal panel housing via a *main bond-ing jumper*. If there's a ground fault in the house, the main bonding jumper ensures the current can be safely directed to the ground—away from the house and the people inside. It is probably the single most important connection in the entire electrical system.

Some grounding protects buildings

Attached to the neutral/ground bus in the service panel is a large, usually bare, copper ground wire—the grounding electrode conductor (GEC)—that clamps to either a *ground rod* driven into the earth or an *Ufer grounding electrode* in the footing of a concrete foundation. The primary function of the grounding electrode system (GES) is to divert lightning and other outside high voltages to earth before they can damage the building's electrical system. The GES has almost nothing to do with reducing hazards from wiring problems *inside* the house. That's the role of the equipment grounding conductors.

SIZING FOR THE LOAD

Sizing a service panel is covered in "Planning" (p. 174). Typically, electricians calculate total household loads (ampacity), then add 20 percent to 25 percent for future needs. For a family in a 2,000-sq.-ft. house, a 125-amp service panel is probably adequate, but a 200-amp panel is often recommended for an "average" household in a 3,000-sq.-ft. house that is not heated with electricity. The NEC allows a maximum of 42 breaker spaces in a single panel. If your system still has capacity but you've used up the available panel spaces, add a subpanel. If your needs exceed system capacity, upgrade the service.

> **For more on calculating household needs, see p. 179.**

Similarly, all conductors—whether they feed a service panel or energize wall outlets—must be sized according to the loads they carry. A home with a 200-amp service panel, for example, should be fed by three 2/0 copper THHN/THWN conductors, whereas a 15-amp general-use household circuit must be fed with at least a #14AWG cable. If you'd like more information on sizing conductors, get the most recent National Electrical Code or a copy of *Code Check: Electrical* (Taunton Press), which does a good job of summarizing NEC tables. For a thorough discussion of electrical safety, visit the OSHA/NIOSH website on electrical safety: www.cdc.gov/niosh/docs/2009-113.

ORGANIZING A PANEL BOX

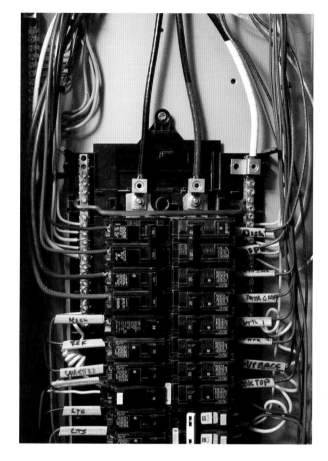

A neat, well-organized subpanel bundles wires to conserve space and improve access. Ideally, wire groups are installed in layers and wires are bent at right angles to buses or breakers. Label short sheathing sections (slugs) to indicate which circuits wires serve.

A neat, well-organized service panel or subpanel is easier and safer to work in; it will also be an easier panel in which to add circuits later on. To create an orderly panel, plan where everything will go and then methodically execute that plan.

Label circuits

In "Rough-in Wiring" (p. 194), we emphasize labeling cables at outlets so that when it comes time to attach wires to devices, you'll always know which switch controls which circuit. Labeling is equally important—perhaps more important—to identify the many cables converging on a panel box. Before you run each cable to the panel, use a permanent marker to write—right on the end of the Romex sheathing—which circuit the cable feeds: "Kitch A," "Bath B," "2d Flr Lights," and so on.

Remove knockouts, insert connectors

Typically, most cables will approach and enter the panel from one direction—from above, if the panel is in the basement. Remove knockouts for the cables, starting with the largest cables, which take up more room and, being stiffer, are more difficult to muscle into place. Insert a cable connector (clamp) into each knockout you remove. Large feeder cables (#4AWG or larger) require insulated fittings (bushings) to protect wire insulation from sharp conduit edges. Most Romex cable,

>> >> >>

ORGANIZING A PANEL BOX (CONTINUED)

however, doesn't require bushings—just appropriately sized cable connectors. Larger circuit cable (#10AWG and #8AWG) fits one per connector, but most household circuit cable (#12AWG or #14AWG) can fit two to a connector—but never more than two. (Cable connectors' capacity is marked on the box or the instruction sheet.)

Strip sheathing, identify hots

Once you have pulled cables into the box and tightened cable connectors, strip Romex cable sheathing, leaving at least ¼ in. of sheathing extending into the panel box. *Note:* As you remove each cable's sheathing, cut off the labeled end and slip that short piece of sheathing (called a "slug") over the end of the cable's hot wire. Bend the wire to keep the slug on. If cable feeds a 240v circuit, slip the slug over both of the cable's hot wires. If a cable hot wire attaches to an AFCI or a GFCI breaker, slide the slug over its neutral, too; the neutral must attach to the AFCI or GFCI breaker, as explained below.

As you strip sheathing, the panel quickly fills up with the "spaghetti" of individual wires; many electricians drive a nail to one side of the box and loosely drape wires over the nail as they strip them, to get them out of the way. Once all the cable sheathing has been stripped, you can loosely group like-wire groups—grounds, neutrals, and hots—in advance of terminating them (attaching wires to lugs) inside the panel. As is customary in all phases of house wiring, terminate the ground wires first.

Snap breakers onto buses

There is no one right sequence for installing panel elements, but many pros prefer to snap in all the breakers to the busing at this point—before terminating any wires. Placing breakers onto the buses gives you an overview of where everything will go and ensures that larger two-pole breakers will be located where they can be wired most easily—and positioned correctly in relation to hot-bus phasing. (More about that in a second.)

Electricians typically put two-pole breakers near the main lugs—in most panels, at the top of the hot buses. Here's why:

1. Two-pole breakers serving 120v/240v or 240v circuits must be correctly *phased*. That is, the top jaws of a two-pole breaker must clip

ACCORDING TO CODE

By definition, a 120v/240v receptacle will have two hots, one neutral, and a ground. Large appliances such as dryers require 120v/240v wiring because they need 120v to operate their electronic switches or timers. A 240v circuit will have only two hots and a ground—no neutral—because there is no need to derive 120v from a 240v circuit.

PRO TIP

Adding a circuit is easy in a well-organized panel because like-wire groups tend to be installed in layers. Ground wires, installed first, are the bottom layer; then neutrals. Hot wires attach to breakers last, so they are typically the top layer. An electrician in a de-energized panel can carefully slide his hand under the hot-wire layer and lift it *en masse* to gain access to buses or wires underneath, then fold the hots down flat when he's done.

THE IMPORTANCE OF CORRECT PHASING

The two large hot conductors in a service panel or subpanel connect to the two hot buses that distribute power to house circuits. Those two hot wires (and their buses) are called Phase A and Phase B because they are two phases of the alternating current (AC) that are 180° of rotation apart. These phases feed into the house from utility lines. (See the photo on p. 266.)

To balance electrical loads between phases in the panel, bus *blades* (the parts that stick up and breakers snap on to) alternate between Phase A and Phase B as you move up or down a panel. It must be noted, however, that the two buses are electrically isolated from each other by a plastic insulator weaving between them. (The photo at right shows this clearly.)

Wiring a panel can be a straightforward matter if you have an understanding of alternating current and phases; this is another reason why only a licensed electrician should work in a panel. There are certain instances where if you get phasing wrong, you can create hazardous conditions.

A HAZARDOUS EXAMPLE!

Let's say that an amateur electrician runs a 12/3 cable to feed two different 120v circuits. In other words, each of the cable's two hot wires will feed a different circuit, while the circuits share the cable neutral (or "common neutral"). This setup is appropriate only if the two hot wires are connected to different phases (e.g., one hot wire on Phase A and one on Phase B). If the circuit(s) is built correctly, the common neutral will carry the unbalanced return load back to the panel.

If the circuit is built incorrectly and the two hot wires are connected to the same phase, the common neutral will carry the sum of the return loads back to the panel. For example, in a proper installation, if one hot wire in a 12/3 cable is connected to Phase A and carries 15 amps and the other hot wire connected to Phase B carries 18 amps, the common neutral will carry 3 amps (or the unbalanced return load) back to the panel.

However, if both hot wires are connected to Phase A, then the neutral in the same example will carry 33 amps back to the panel (or the sum of the return loads). In this instance, since #12 wire is rated for 20 amps, the neutral would be carrying 165% of its rated capacity—a very hazardous condition.

Moreover, the breakers that the hot wires are attached to *won't* snap off because standard breakers monitor only outgoing current in the hot wires. The 33 amps of combined return current would look normal to the breakers. So current will continue to flow.

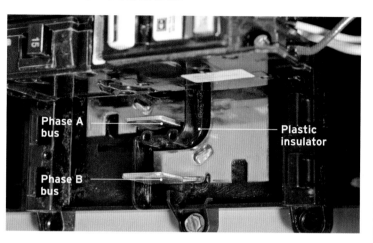

Hot buses are electrically isolated from each other by a plastic insulator between them.

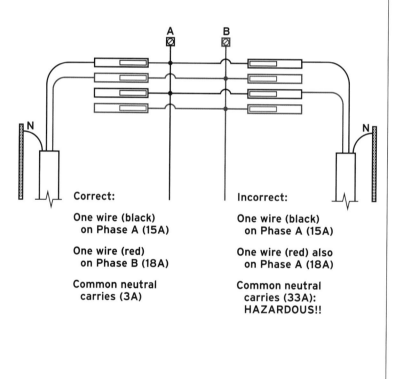

Correct:

One wire (black) on Phase A (15A)

One wire (red) on Phase B (18A)

Common neutral carries (3A)

Incorrect:

One wire (black) on Phase A (15A)

One wire (red) also on Phase A (18A)

Common neutral carries (33A): HAZARDOUS!!

onto an Phase A bus and the bottom jaws onto a Phase B bus. If you install a bunch of one-pole breakers at the top, two-pole breakers lower down may not land on correct phase-positions on the buses. (The perils of ignoring phasing is discussed above.)

2. If you put larger breakers at the top, you will need shorter runs of large-gauge wire to reach those breakers. No. 10AWG and No. 8AWG wire, for example, are stiff, hard to work with, and take up

space. If you wire large breakers first—when the panel is relatively empty—you will have more room to wrestle stiff wire into place.

3. Snap AFCI and GFCI breakers to buses next, after 120v/240v and 240v breakers are in place. Here, the issue is not the size of wires but the number of them. As you'll see on p. 277, you must attach neutral wires directly to AFCI and GFCI breakers rather than to neutral buses—which means running neutrals slightly longer distances.

>> >> >>

ORGANIZING A PANEL BOX (CONTINUED)

Various breakers. From upper left, clockwise: one-pole 15A, one-pole 20A, one-pole 20A GFCI, one-pole 20A AFCI, two-pole 30A (for 240v loads).

Terminate wires

Your panel layout will determine in part where you attach the wires. In other words, terminate wires on the side they come in, if possible. That's just common sense. Wires making long loops to get to a bus on the other side take up space. Thus, if you have wires coming down from both sides, it makes most sense to divide wire groups. To facilitate this, panels typically have neutral and ground bus bars on both sides.

Attach grounds first. As noted earlier, it's customary to first separate out ground wires and terminate them to a ground bus. So if most of your cables enter at the top of a panel, it's most logical to start at the top of a ground bus bar and work down as you terminate individual wires. In this manner, subsequent wires can come in right over the top of those installed earlier, creating a relatively flat layer.

Bundle wire groups loosely to conserve space but stop strapping bundles just above a bus so you have room to turn wires toward the bus. Take a pair of pliers and turn the first wire toward the bus, noting how long its "leg" must be to reach the bus. Maintain that same length as you terminate subsequent wires, so that all turns are consistent. (Snip excess wire as you go.) That's just a personal preference: The important detail is tightening down bus screws so that each wire is tightly held.

Attach neutrals to buses, except for neutrals that feed AFCI or GFCI breakers. *In a service panel,* attach neutrals to a common ground/neutral bus; *in a subpanel,* attach neutrals to a separate neutral bus. As with grounds, if panel cables come in from the top, start at the top of the neutral bus and work down methodically so subsequent wires will lie flat.

AFCI and GFCI breakers, on the other hand, have factory-attached neutral coils. Attach those coils to a neutral bus, as shown in photo 1 on p. 277. Then terminate circuit-cable neutrals to designated lugs on AFCI or GFCI breakers, as shown in photo 2 on p. 277.

Terminate hots to breakers. As with grounds and neutral wires, move in one direction as you attach hot wires to breakers–typically from top to bottom, if panel feeds enter at the top of the panel. (This will create a flat layer of hot wires with a neat, workmanlike look.) As you did with grounds and neutrals, loosely bundle hot wires till you are ready to start bending them towards breaker lugs. A sweeping bend looks best, so try to maintain that angle for all hot wires as you attach them to breakers on both sides of the panel. Strip $3/8$ in. to $1/2$ in. of insulation from the ends of hot wires before inserting them into breaker lugs. This will ensure that breaker screws will tighten down on bare wire.

If you placed larger two-pole breakers at the top of the hot buses, you will attach larger-gauge wires first. The labeled slugs you slipped on the hot wires will tell you which hot wire attaches to which breaker. Correctly matching wire gauge to breaker amps is essential because both will be rated for the loads that circuit will carry. When attaching the two hot wires served by two-pole breakers, electricians typically maintain the A-B phasing established earlier, to match the Phase A (black) and Phase B (red) feeds.

As with all electrical connections, screw breaker lugs tightly on hot wires so there is a solid mechanical connection. This will ensure a good electrical connection.

ADDING A CIRCUIT

1 Remove a knockout from the existing panel.

2 Insert the threaded shaft of the cable connector (clamp) into the knockout.

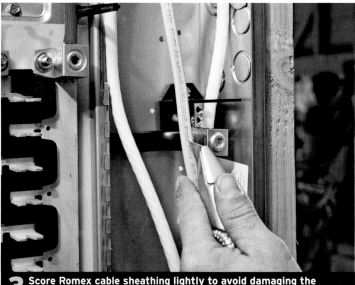

3 Score Romex cable sheathing lightly to avoid damaging the wire insulation inside.

O*nly a licensed electrician should work inside a panel.*
When adding a circuit to an existing panel, first cut the power to the panel and test to be sure it's off. If working in a subpanel, turn off the subpanel breaker in the service panel, where feeds to the subpanel originate. If working in a service panel, the area about the main lugs will always be hot—even when the main breaker is off—so take care to avoid that area and wear appropriate safety equipment (p. 264).

(*Note:* The sequences that follow differ slightly from "Organizing a Panel Box," on pp. 269-272, because they show circuits being added to a subpanel that is already wired.)

After disconnecting power to the panel, remove its cover, determine where the new circuit cable will enter the panel, and use a sturdy pair of needle-nose pliers or a screwdriver to jab out a knockout **1**. Into the knockout, install the appropriate cable con-

nector (clamp) for the cable you're using—in our sequence, NM cable (Romex). Pull the cable through the connector, and tighten the connector to prevent strain on electrical connections **2**. To avoid stressing connections, staple incoming cable within 12 in. of the panel.

Score the cable sheathing by making two diagonal passes and sliding the sheathing off. Or score the sheathing lightly down the middle **3**, peel back the sheathing, and use diagonal cutters to snip it off. Leave at least $1/4$ in. of sheathing sticking into the panel. Snap the breaker onto an open space on the bus bar, then rough-cut cable wires so they will be long enough to reach that breaker—you can trim off excess later. Separate the ground, neutral, and hot wires and strip about $3/8$ in. to $1/2$ in. of insulation off the ends of insulated wires. Torque all bus and breaker lug connections as specified by manufacturer.

WIRING A STANDARD ONE-POLE BREAKER

Typically, 15-amp or 20-amp one-pole breakers control general-use, lighting, or small-appliance circuits; they might also run a furnace, a pool pump, or a garbage disposer. In the photo sequence shown here, a single-pole breaker is being installed in a subpanel whose power has been turned off.

Terminate the ground wire first ❶. In a subpanel, the ground will attach to a separate ground bus bonded to the metal panel. Insert only one ground wire beneath a lug screw. Note the consistent angle of all grounds in which they bend toward the bus. Look closely and you will also see that both ground and neutral wires are bundled with plastic ties to keep the box orderly.

Next strip insulation from the neutral wire and connect it to the neutral bus ❷. Because this is a subpanel, the neutral bus sits atop a black plastic bracket that electrically isolates the neutral bus from the metal panel box.

Snap the one-pole breaker onto a hot bus ❸. The heel of the breaker seats on a plastic cleat and then pivots so that its jaws engage a metal bus sticking up. Press down to seat the breaker securely. Strip 3/8 in. to 1/2 in. of insulation from the end of the hot wire, then connect it to the lug screw on the end of the breaker ❹. *Note:* Before attaching the hot wire, slip on the labeled slug of sheathing that identifies the circuit it feeds. Tighten the breaker lug to secure the hot wire.

Before flipping on the breaker, use a multimeter to test the new circuit for dead shorts, as described in "Trade Secret" on the facing page. Once you are certain that the circuit has no shorts, remove a breaker-knockout from the sub-panel cover, replace the cover, energize the subpanel, and flip on the new breaker.

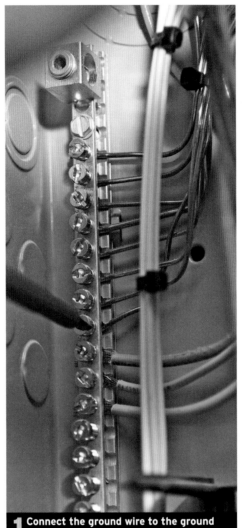

1 Connect the ground wire to the ground bus of the subpanel.

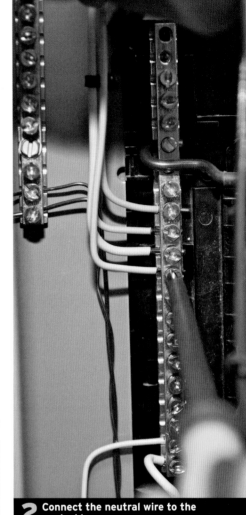

2 Connect the neutral wire to the neutral bus.

3 Snap the breaker to a hot bus.

4 Insert the hot wire into the breaker lug and tighten it down.

TESTING A NEW CIRCUIT FOR SHORTS

After terminating (attaching) all circuit wires–but before re-energizing the panel or plugging devices into the circuit–use a multimeter to test the circuit for dead shorts. Set the meter to the resistance setting (ohms).

Touch multimeter probes to the breaker lug (where hot wires terminate) and to the ground bus. Next touch tester probes to the breaker lug and the neutral bus. In other words, hot to ground, then hot to neutral. If the multimeter indicates no dead shorts, the circuit is correctly wired. Remove breaker knockout(s) from the panel dead-front, replace the cover on the panel, and energize the panel. Then flip the breaker on.

Amateur electricians mistakenly think you can use the breaker to test for dead shorts: Don't do it. That's not what a breaker is designed to do. Use a multimeter to test, with the power off. It's the right tool and a safer procedure.

120v twin breaker If your electrical system has unused capacity but you've run out of breaker spaces, you may be able to replace a standard 12-amp one-pole breaker with a 20-amp twin *(pancake)* breaker. A twin is two slim, one-pole breakers that fit into a standard one-pole breaker space. *Note:* The panel must be designed and listed for the use of such breakers. The number of twin breakers allowed varies–some panels allow none, some allow use of twin breakers in some spaces, some allow their use in every space. It is important to know which spaces in a panel can take twin breakers, because putting in too many circuits can lead to overheating of the panel and the breakers.

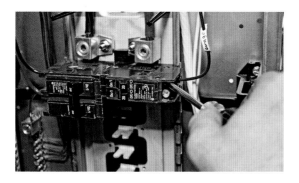

After installing a circuit breaker–but before re-energizing the panel and flipping on the breaker–use a multimeter set to test resistance (ohms). First make sure there are no loads on the circuit (e.g., light fixtures or appliances turned on). Touch the tool's probes to (1) breaker lug and ground bus, then (2) breaker lug and neutral bus. You are looking for *dead shorts*–a reading of no resistance (0 ohms). If you get a 0 ohms reading DO NOT turn on the new breaker until you correct the problem. Dead shorts are commonly caused by drywall screws or nails driven through a cable, improperly wired devices, or connections in an outlet box that have come apart.

Before re-energizing the panel, **test the circuit for shorts. Touch the tester probes to the breaker lug and ground bus, then touch the probes to the breaker lug and neutral bus.**

INSTALLING A TWO-POLE BREAKER

In residences, two-pole breakers typically control ovens, dryers, ranges, AC condensers, and other big energy users. The photo sequence at right shows a 30-amp, two-pole breaker being installed in a subpanel. As 120v/240v wiring tends to be appliance-specific, this circuit feeds a dryer receptacle. As the dryer's electronic components need 120v, this 30-amp circuit was wired with 10/3 w/grd Romex cable. In addition to two hot wires, the cable contains a neutral wire and a ground.

After calculating that the electrical system had sufficient capacity to add a 30-amp circuit and that there was room in the subpanel for a double breaker ❶, the electrician turned off the subpanel breaker in the service panel and then tested the subpanel to be sure the power was off. That done, he removed the panel cover, removed a knockout in the panel box, installed a cable connector and fed 10/3 w/grd cable through it, tightened the cable connector, and removed the cable's protective sheathing.

He terminated the cable's bare ground wire at the subpanel's ground bus, stripped insulation from the end of the neutral wire, and terminated it at the neutral bus. Before snapping a two-pole breaker onto hot buses ❷, he made sure that it would land on a correct A-B bus position, that is, that the top jaws of the two-pole breaker would connect to a Phase A bus and the bottom jaws to a Phase B bus.

After slipping a labeled slug onto the cable's black hot wire, the electrician terminated it to the breaker's upper lug, then terminated the red hot wire to the breaker's lower lug ❸. He tightened both screws to ensure solid connections, then used a multimeter to test the circuit for *dead shorts*, as described on p. 275. Finding no dead shorts, he removed two breaker knockouts (two-pole breaker) from the subpanel cover, replaced the cover, energized the subpanel, and flipped on the new breaker.

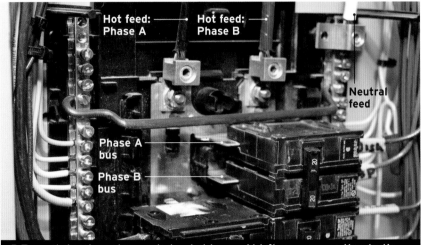

1 Two-pole breakers clamp onto two hot buses. At left, you can see the plastic cleats that receive the heel of the breaker; at right, two hot-bus blades.

2 Place the heel side of the breaker on the plastic cleats, then pivot the breaker so its jaws snap onto hot-bus blades.

3 Attach the circuit ground wire to the ground bus, neutral wire to neutral bus, then two hot wires to two-pole breaker lugs.

INSTALLING AN AFCI BREAKER

Installing a one-pole, 15-amp AFCI (arc-fault-circuit-interrupter) breaker is exactly the same as installing a one-pole GFCI (ground-fault-circuit-interrupter) breaker. But before we see how to install one, here is a quick refresher about how each of these code-required devices protects you.

AFCI breakers are designed to detect arcing patterns of current in very short time intervals—such as when there is a loose connection on a receptacle and electricity arcs (jumps) between conductors. Drywall nails or screws puncturing a cable are other common causes of arc faults. When an AFCI breaker detects such patterns, it shuts off power to protect you from house fires.

GFCI breakers are designed to sense an imbalance between the amount of current flowing from the hot wire and returning on the neutral wire, which suggests a ground-fault current is leaking to ground somewhere. GFCIs can detect minuscule (5 milliamp) current leaks and shut off power almost instantaneously—typically within $\frac{1}{40}$ second—to protect people from potentially fatal shocks.

Always turn off power to a panel and test to be sure it's off. After pulling the new circuit cable into the subpanel, the electrician secured it with a cable connector and stripped its sheathing, as described above. As is customary, he first terminated the cable's bare ground wire to the ground bus.

Every AFCI (and every GFCI) breaker has a coiled neutral conductor that is molded into the breaker at the factory. After snapping the AFCI breaker onto a hot bus, the electrician attached that coiled neutral to the neutral bus ❶. The electrician then stripped $\frac{3}{8}$ in. to $\frac{1}{2}$ in. of insulation from the end of the circuit-cable neutral and terminated it to the AFCI breaker lug, designated by a small white dot next to it ❷. *Note:* Most circuit neutral wires terminate to a neutral bus. But here the circuit neutral attaches to the *breaker* so it can sense fluctuations in current throughout the circuit.

Finally, the electrician stripped insulation from the end of the circuit hot wire and attached it to the remaining breaker lug ❸. He used a multimeter to test for a dead short in the circuit. Finding nothing out of the ordinary, he removed a breaker knockout from the subpanel cover, replaced the cover, and energized the subpanel. Then he flipped the AFCI breaker on and pressed the white TEST button on the face of the breaker. The TEST button should snap off immediately; if it doesn't, the breaker is probably defective and should be replaced immediately. Inspectors are very serious about AFCI protection, so always test AFCI breakers after installing them—even if they are right out of the box.

» » »

INSTALLING AN AFCI BREAKER

1 Terminate the circuit ground wire. Then terminate the coiled, factory-attached white wire of the AFCI breaker to the neutral bus.

2 Next, terminate the circuit neutral to the neutral lug on the AFCI breaker. A small white dot on the breaker indicates the neutral lug.

3 Terminate the circuit hot wire to the hot lug on the AFCI breaker.

INSTALLING AN AFCI BREAKER (CONTINUED)

TWO-POLE AFCI BREAKERS

Since the 2008 NEC, AFCI protection is required for branch circuits in all areas inside the house except bathrooms, kitchen, garage, and unfinished basements and attics.

AFCI breakers are wired somewhat differently from conventional breakers, with an integral coiled neutral attaching to the neutral bus and the circuit neutral attaching to an AFCI breaker neutral lug. The circuit hot then attaches to the AFCI breaker hot lug.

This configuration allows an AFCI breaker to monitor current flow throughout the circuit, but it sometimes leads to problems when inexpert installers use 3-wire cable to serve two circuits—one of which must be AFCI-protected and the other is not. Their mistaken solution is to attach one hot wire of the 3-wire cable to an AFCI breaker and the other hot to a regular (non-AFCI) breaker. They then find that the AFCI breaker doesn't work—it keeps flipping off.

The solution: If you want to use 3-wire cable to provide AFCI protection to at least one of the circuits, you must install a two-pole AFCI breaker and attach both hot wires to it. The cable's neutral attaches to the breaker's neutral lug, as described above. In this manner, the AFCI can monitor current flow in both circuits.

If you run 3-wire cable to serve two circuits and at least one of the new circuits must be AFCI-protected, you must terminate *both* cable hot wires to a two-pole AFCI breaker.

PRO TIP

GFCI *breakers* are relatively uncommon because GFCI receptacles are a cheaper way to get protection and easier to access and reset when they trip. A 30-amp GFCI breaker, however, is standard protection for hot tubs.

INSTALLING A SUBPANEL

There are many reasons to install a subpanel:

- Increasingly, main service panels are installed outside so firefighters can disconnect power before going into the house—in this case, a subpanel inside contains all the branch circuits.
- When a system has unused capacity but the service panel has no available slots for more circuit breakers, a subpanel allows for expansion.
- A subpanel distributes power to a separate building.
- A subpanel can offset voltage drops on circuits that are too distant (70 ft. or 80 ft.) from the service panel. In this case, the larger-gauge wires that feed subpanels suffer less voltage drop than the smaller-gauge wires of branch circuits.

Size subpanels based on anticipated loads. If you're adding a subpanel in the same building as the main panel so you can add lighting and general-use circuits, install a 60-amp subpanel with at least 12 breaker slots. If the subpanel is distributing power to a distant building, install a 100-amp or 150-amp subpanel.

People frequently add subpanels when planning a major kitchen remodel, because kitchens have a lot of appliances. Locate the subpanel as close as possible to the kitchen.

When adding a subpanel to an existing system, an electrician first shuts off power at the service panel and tests to be sure the power is off.

If studs are spaced 16 in. on-center, install a standard, 14½-in.-wide panel. Use at least four 1¼-in. by 10 screws to mount the panel ❶; screws should embed at least 1 in. into studs. Install the panel at a comfortable height, so it will be easy to wire and access—and make sure that there is room for mandatory clearances around it (see "Locating a Subpanel," on the facing page). Remove a concentric knockout in the panel and install a connector appropriate to the cable or conduit that feeds the panel. Also install a protective cable bushing. Here, the feed is a #2 Romex cable. Pull 3 ft. of cable into the panel, tighten the connector, and strip the cable sheathing ❷. (Note the cross-brace between the studs, just below the panel.)

Code requires that you secure the cable within 12 in. of the panel, but 2/0 cable is stiff. Strapping cable to a stud would force it to enter the panel at a sharp angle, which could stress the knockout. It is far easier to strap the cable to a brace in the middle of the stud bay and run the cable straight into the panel.

Secure the ground wire to the main lug of the subpanel ground bus ❸. Cut the three insulated feed wires, allowing enough extra to loop them gently. Avoid sharp bends, which can damage wire. Strip 1 in. of insulation from the feed ends. Use an Allen wrench or torque wrench to connect the feed wires to their respective lugs ❹. Loop the hot feeds around the perimeter of the panel, distancing them from the neutral feed so there will be an open area through which to run smaller circuit wires ❺. Looping the wire generously also ensures that there will be enough extra cable in case you need to strip and reconnect feed ends later ❻.

1 Use at least four screws when installing a subpanel between 16-in. o.c. studs.

2 Pull the feeder cable into the sub-panel; strap the cable to a cross-brace.

3 First connect the ground wire from the feeder cable to the ground-bus lug.

4 Connect the neutral wire to the neutral-bus lug.

5 Strip the hot feed ends and attach them to hot-bus lugs.

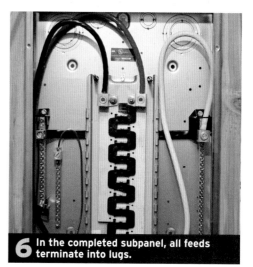

6 In the completed subpanel, all feeds terminate into lugs.

LOCATING A SUBPANEL

Any panel—whether a main or a subpanel—must have sufficient clearance around it. NEC minimums require 78 in. of headroom, 36 in. free space in front of the panel, and 30 in. across the face of the panel. The panel should be installed at a comfortable height, meaning that no breaker handle may be higher than 72 in.

The area must be dry and easily accessed. Do not install a subpanel in a bathroom, kitchen, or clothes closet. If you install a panel in a fire wall (typically the wall between an attached garage and the living area), you will need to check your local codes for measures required to maintain the wall's fire rating. If you place the panel in an interior wall, a typical subpanel will fit between studs that are 16 in. on-center.

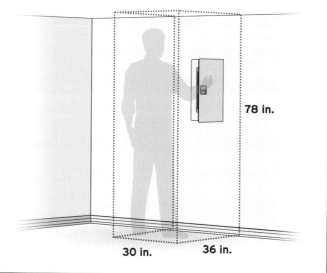

78 in.

30 in.   36 in.

GLOSSARY

ACCESSIBLE Not permanently concealed by the structure or finishes. Able to be accessed without damaging the building.

AMPACITY (AMPS) The amount of current a circuit or conductor can safely carry (conduct). Measured in amperes (amps).

AMPS The measure of the number of electrons flowing through a system (current).

ARC FAULT CIRCUIT INTERRUPTER (AFCI) A circuit breaker designed to de-energize a circuit within a period of time if it senses arcing. An arc is a spark between conductors or connections.

BONDING JUMPER (MAIN) Conductor connecting the neutral conductor to the grounding electrode conductor in a service panel.

CABLE An assembly of several conductors. Most often refers to plastic- or metal-sheathed cable that contains several individual wires.

CFL Compact fluorescent lightbulb

CIRCUIT (BRANCH) Circuit originating at a circuit breaker or fuse in an electrical panel and feeding utilization equipment (lights, switches, receptacles, appliances).

CIRCUIT BREAKER A device intended to de-energize a circuit if current exceeds specified parameters.

CONDUCTOR Technically, anything that conducts electricity. Most often, it denotes a wire.

CONDULET A conduit body with a cover designed to act as a pulling point in a conduit run, to change conduit direction, or as an intersecting point of multiple conduit runs.

CURRENT The flow of electrons in a system. Current is measured in amperes (amps). There are two types of current: DC (direct current) and AC (alternating current). Typically, AC is found in homes and buildings.

ENERGIZED Live. The presence of voltage in a circuit or conductor.

FEEDERS Large conductors that supply a service panel, subpanel, or other high-current piece of equipment.

FIXTURE A light fixture (table lamp, sconce, chandelier, recessed can, etc.).

FUSE BOX A metal box designed to house fuses installed for circuit protection.

GROUND A connection to earth (the ground). To make such a connection.

GROUND BUS A piece of metal designed to connect multiple wires to a grounding electrode conductor.

GROUND FAULT A fault situation in which an energized conductor or piece of equipment comes in contact with grounded metal parts.

GROUND FAULT CIRCUIT INTERRUPTER (GFCI) A special receptacle or circuit breaker intended to protect people by de-energizing a circuit within a specific period of time if current to ground exceeds specified parameters.

GROUNDING CONDUCTOR A wire in an electrical system designed to bond metal parts of the electrical system to the earth (ground).

GROUNDING ELECTRODE CONDUCTOR A wire of a gauge determined by the ampacity of a service panel that connects the service panel (and ground bus) to a grounding electrode (ground rod or equivalent).

GROUND SCREW A green-colored screw used to connect ground conductors to boxes and devices.

LED Light-emitting diode.

LINE SIDE The direction from which power enters; also referred to as "upstream." The direction from the device toward the circuit breaker or fuse.

LISTED Equipment and materials included on a list published by an organization, acceptable to the authority having jurisdiction, that states that the equipment or materials meet specific design criteria or are suitable for the use intended. Most commonly UL (Underwriter's Laboratory) listed.

LOAD SIDE The direction toward which power is consumed; also referred to as "downstream." The direction from the device away from the circuit breaker or fuse.

LOCATION, DAMP Protected from weather and not subject to saturation (under eves, canopies, etc.).

LOCATION, DRY Not subject to moisture (interior, protected from weather).

LOCATION, WET Underground; exposed to weather; subject to saturation.

LUG A screw-terminal used to clamp down a bare-wire end. Lugs come in a range of sizes. Main lugs secure incoming feeders; breaker lugs secure circuit wires that terminate in circuit breakers.

MAIN CIRCUIT BREAKER A large-ampacity circuit breaker that protects and acts as a means to de-energize a service panel or subpanel.

MC Metal clad cable

NEMA National Electrical Manufacturers Association.

NEUTRAL The neutral or grounded conductor (not ground conductor) is the return path for current in an electrical system; designated by a white or light (or natural) gray color. The neutral is bonded to ground at the service panel.

NEUTRAL BUS A piece of metal designed to connect multiple wires to the neutral conductor.

OHMS The measure of resistance to the flow of electrons (current).

OVERLOAD A situation in which the current flowing through a circuit or circuit conductor exceeds the safe operating ampacity of the conductor.

PLUG The device at the end of an appliance or light fixture cord (cord cap) that is designed to connect the appliance or fixture to a receptacle. (The plug on your lamp fits into the receptacle in the wall.)

RECEPTACLE Device designed for the connection of a plug.

ROMEX Type of NM cable, sheathed with nonmetallic material.

SCREW SHELL The metal conductive interior body of a light socket or fuse holder with large threads (or ridges) that allow a bulb or fuse to be screwed in.

SERVICE DROP Conductors from the utility pole to the point of connection (weather head).

SERVICE-ENTRANCE CONDUCTORS (OVERHEAD) Conductors between the point of connection (meter lugs) and a point outside (weather head) connected to the service drop.

SERVICE-ENTRANCE CONDUCTORS (UNDERGROUND) The conductors between the point of connection (meter socket) and the utility transformer or secondary pull box (service lateral).

SERVICE PANEL (MAIN PANEL) The primary electrical panel located immediately after the meter socket and housing the main circuit breaker or main fuses and/or other devices designed to de-energize and protect circuits.

SPLICE The point at which two wires or conductors are joined or connected together. For branch circuits, splices are commonly made with pressure connectors (wire nuts).

SUBPANEL An electrical panel that is supplied from a service panel and is installed either to provide additional circuit breakers or to distribute branch circuits at a distance from the service panel.

SWITCH A device that opens and closes a circuit, controlling the operation of a light fixture, fan, other equipment, or appliances.

VOLTAGE, NOMINAL (VOLTS) A value assigned to a circuit or system to designate its class. Modern single-family residences in the U.S. typically have 120/240v systems.

VOLTAGE TO GROUND (VOLTS) The difference in potential (voltage) between a single energized conductor and ground (neutral or equipment ground).

WATERTIGHT Enclosures built to prevent the intrusion of moisture.

WATTAGE (WATTS) A measure of power consumed.

WEATHERPROOF Equipment or enclosures built so that weather will not interfere with their operation.

WIRE A generic term for an individual conductor, most often used when specifying its size, such as # 12 AWG (Average Wire Gauge).

RECENT ELECTRICAL CODE UPDATES

The National Electrical Code (NEC) is the basis for most local electrical codes. The NEC's governing authority, the National Fire Prevention Association, revises and publishes the Code every three years, so the information in *Wiring Complete*, Third Edition includes updates from the NEC 2017-2020 Code cycle.

Local building authorities often take several years to adopt changes made on the national level, so your local codes may not yet include some of the requirements found here. Yet local codes always have the final say. That said, the Code updates summarized here are based upon extensive research by NFPA study groups of senior electricians and should serve you well now and in the future.

Here are four code changes worth noting:

1. Use a torque tool—a torque screwdriver or torque wrench—to terminate conductors at electrical equipment. Safe electrical connections depend upon tightly securing wires, whether to setscrews on receptacles, switches, or other devices, or to panelboard lugs. Insufficiently tightened connections can lead to arcing and the increased likelihood of house fires. Yet a 2010 field study published in *IAEI* magazine found that "installers incorrectly tighten electrical terminations at least 75 percent of the time when not using a torque wrench." Correct torque values (the pressure required to adequately tighten conductors) can be found on the electrical equipment itself, and are contained in torque tables from UL Standard 486A-B and in section 110.14(D) of the NEC.

2. AFCI protection is now required for the whole house. Arc-fault-circuit-interrupter (AFCI) protection has expanded with each update of the NEC. In the 2017-2020 NEC, AFCI protection is now required for "all 120-volt, single-phase, 15-amp and 20-amp branch circuits supplying outlets or devices installed in dwelling units." As Michael McAlister, this book's co-author puts it, "For years I advised my clients that installing AFCIs is the least expensive additional fire insurance that you can buy."

3. More locations require tamper-resistant receptacles. As explained on p. 40, the shutters of tamper-resistant receptacles require simultaneous pressure on all plug prongs before they slide open—thus preventing an inquisitive child from getting an electrical shock. The new Code extends this protection to "nonlocking-type 15A and 20A, 125V and 250V receptacles" in numerous locations. The extension to 250V receptacles—say, an outlet in a garage or a workshop—is a welcome addition to protecting kids wherever they go exploring.

4. Energy storage systems come of age. An energy storage system is a device or several devices capable of storing energy for future use. These days, battery storage is the most developed technology. The new code's Article 706 is not likely to impact present wiring projects, but it is a clear indication the NEC is beginning to both recognize, prepare for, and draft codes for the future of energy storage devices.

PHOTO CREDITS

INDEX